# Frommer's® 97

# Chicago

## by Julie L. Belcove

Macmillan • USA

## ABOUT THE AUTHOR

**Julie L. Belcove** grew up in Chicago and lived there until 1993. Now a resident of New York, she is Beauty News Editor of *Women's Wear Daily* and a regular contributor to *W* magazine. She is also the author of *Travel & Leisure New York*.

## MACMILLAN TRAVEL

A Simon & Schuster Macmillan Company
1633 Broadway
New York, NY 10019

Find us online at **http://www.mgr.com/travel** or
on America Online at Keyword: **Frommer's.**

Copyright © 1997 by Simon & Schuster, Inc.

MACMILLAN is a registered trademark of Macmillan, Inc.
FROMMER'S is a registered trademark of Arthur Frommer. Used under license.

ISBN 0-02-861151-9
ISSN 1040-936X

Editor: Alice Fellows
Production Editor: Michael Thomas
Map Editor: Douglas Stallings
Design by Michele Laseau
Page Creation by Lissa Auciello, Jerry Cole, Toi Davis, Sean Decker, Stephanie Hammet, Pete Lippincott, and Tom Missler
Maps copyright © by Simon & Schuster, Inc.

## SPECIAL SALES

Bulk purchases (10+ copies) of Frommer's and selected Macmillan travel guides are available to corporations, organizations, mail-order catalogs, institutions, and charities at special discounts, and can be customized to suit individual needs. For more information write to: Special Sales, Macmillan General Reference, 1633 Broadway, New York, NY 10019.

Manufactured in the United States of America

# Contents

## 6   Dining  72

## 7   What to See & Do in Chicago  119

## 8   Chicago Strolls  155

# List of Maps

## AN INVITATION TO THE READER

In researching this book, we discovered many wonderful places—hotels, restaurants, shops, and more. We're sure you'll find others. Please tell us about them, so we can share the information with your fellow travelers in upcoming editions. If you were disappointed with a recommendation, we'd love to know that, too. Please write to:

*Frommer's Chicago 97*
Macmillan Travel
1633 Broadway
New York, NY 10019

## AN ADDITIONAL NOTE

Please be advised that travel information is subject to change at any time—and this is especially true of prices. We therefore suggest that you write or call ahead for confirmation when making your travel plans. The authors, editors, and publisher cannot be held responsible for the experiences of readers while traveling. Your safety is important to us, however, so we encourage you to stay alert and be aware of your surroundings. Keep a close eye on cameras, purses, and wallets, all favorite targets of thieves and pickpockets.

## WHAT THE SYMBOLS MEAN

### ✪ Frommer's Favorites

Hotels, restaurants, attractions, and entertainment you should not miss.

### ⑤ Super-Special Values

Hotels and restaurants that offer great value for your money.

The following abbreviations are used for credit cards:

| | | | |
|---|---|---|---|
| AE | American Express | EC | EuroCard |
| CB | Carte Blanche | JCB | Japan Credit Bank |
| DC | Diners Club | MC | MasterCard |
| DISC | Discover | V | Visa |
| ER | enRoute | | |

# Chicago Past & Present

**A** person or a place has only one chance to make a first impression. In the case of Chicago, that first impression may be its brilliant, varied skyline—towers trying to poke holes through the clouds—or the water of Lake Michigan shimmering in the sunlight, or a rollerblader whooshing down the sidewalk, about to run you down. Not until your arrival, of course, will you know what's going to strike you most about the city, but here's a briefing of what you'll find: a diverse, sophisticated city with a bounty of cultural institutions, fine restaurants, and first-class shopping.

## 1 Frommer's Favorite Chicago Experiences

- **Going to a Cubs Day Game:** There may be no better place to spend an afternoon than at Wrigley Field watching the Cubbies try to hit 'em onto Waveland. (See Chapter 7 for details.)
- **Listening to Music Under the Stars:** Pack a picnic and take the train (or drive) out to Highland Park's Ravinia, summer home of the Chicago Symphony. The music festival also books a wide range of other performers, from jazz to gospel. (See Chapter 10 for details.)
- **Eating BBQ Ribs:** Okay, they're not exactly health food, but you're on vacation. Get yourself over to Carson's and order a full, succulent slab. (See Chapter 6 for details.)
- **Taking an Architectural Tour:** By foot, bus, or boat, an architectural tour will set the scene for you and will give you a solid basis for appreciating that magnificent skyline. (See Chapter 7 for details.)
- **Seeing a Play at Steppenwolf:** The theater that gave Gary Sinise and John Malkovich their start puts on a full season of plays, many of them new and innovative. (See Chapter 10 for details.)
- **Looking at the Impressionist Paintings at the Art Institute:** Monet, Manet, Degas, Renoir, and Cézanne, the Art Institute has them all in an impressive collection—the largest outside the Louvre. (See Chapter 7 for details.)
- **Strolling Through Lincoln Park Zoo:** It's the nation's oldest public zoo, and it's still free. And while you're at it, take a jaunt east to the lake, and just admire its splendor. (See Chapter 7 for details.)
- **Buying Knits on Sale at Henri Bendel:** Bendel's puts its rainbow of women's knit tops (in wool, silk, or cotton) on sale around the

# Chicago & Vicinity

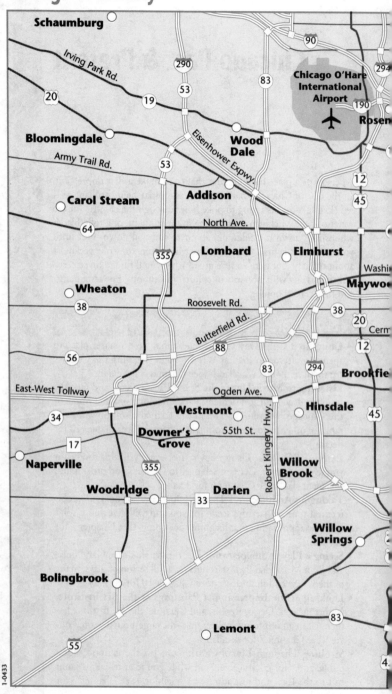

*Hog Butcher for the World, Tool Maker, Stacker of Wheat, Player with Railroads and the Nation's Freight Handler; Stormy, husky, brawling, City of the Big Shoulders.*
　　　　　　　　—Carl Sandburg, "Chicago," from *Chicago Poems* (1916)

midpoint of every season. If you buy then, as a gift or for yourself, you can save 30%, 40%, or even 50%. (See Chapter 9 for details.)

- **Watching the Penguins at Shedd Aquarium:** From underground windows, you can see the adorable waddlers swimming in their pool. (See Chapter 7 for details.)
- **Gallery-Hopping:** If you're in the market for something to hang over the sofa, or if you just like marveling at what's out there, try exploring the art galleries of either River North (west of the Magnificent Mile) or Bucktown/Wicker Park, which is centered at North, Damen, and Milwaukee Avenues. Both neighborhoods have many good places to eat, too.

## 2　The City Today

No, it's no longer the "hog butcher to the world." Nor is it a city of gangsters emptying their tommy guns on the streets (though 1990s versions of gangs certainly exist). Today, the typical visitor will discover that Chicago is more glittery than gritty, more Paris than prairie, an exciting and cosmopolitan city.

One way Chicago has been able to remain vital while other cities decayed is that, unlike Detroit and many other American cities, middle- and upper-class residents have not fled to the suburbs, and, unlike Manhattan, you can take full advantage of what the city has to offer without being really wealthy. Chicago has managed to keep itself attractive to the monied, to the artistic community, and to young professionals, which in turn has helped save marginal areas—although gentrification has its flip side, and can play havoc with working-class or ethnic neighborhoods. Although some of Chicago's ethnic areas have disappeared, new ones have grown up, and the visitor will find that Chicago is still a fascinating city of great diversity.

But, of course, the biggest excitement of the summer of 1996 was the second coming of Michael Jordan and the fourth NBA championship in six years.

## 3　A Look at the Past

### Dateline

- **1673** French explorers Marquette and Jolliet discover portage at Chicago linking the Great Lakes region with the Mississippi River valley.
- **1779** Afro-French-Canadian trapper Jean Baptiste DuSable establishes a trading post on the north bank of the Chicago River. A settlement follows two years later.
- **1794** Gen. "Mad" Anthony Wayne defeats the British in

*continues*

By virtue of its location, Chicago became the great engine of America's westward expansion. The particular patch of land where Chicago now stands straddles a key point along an inland water route linking Canada, via Lake Erie, to New Orleans and the Gulf of Mexico by way of the Mississippi River.

The French, busy expanding their own territory in North America throughout the 17th and 18th centuries, were the first Europeans to survey the topography of the future Chicago. The French policy in North America was simple—to gradually settle the Mississippi Valley and the Northwest Territory (modern Michigan, Illinois, Wisconsin, and Minnesota). The policy relied on an alliance between religion and commerce: The French sought a monopoly over the fur trade with the Native American tribes, whose pacification and loyalty they attempted to ensure by converting them to Catholicism.

The team of Jacques Marquette, a Jesuit missionary, and Louis Jolliet, an explorer, personified this policy to perfection. In 1673 the pair found a very short portage between two critically placed rivers, the Illinois and the Des Plaines. One was connected to the Mississippi, and the other, via the Chicago River, to Lake Michigan and then onward to Montréal and Québec.

Chicago owes its existence to this strategic 1$^1$/$_2$-mile portage trail that the Native Americans had blazed in their own water travels over centuries of moving throughout this territory. Marquette himself was on the most familiar terms with the Native Americans, who helped him make his way over the well-established paths of their ancestral lands. The Native Americans, of course, did not anticipate the European settlers' hunger for such prime real estate.

**FIRST SETTLEMENT**   Over the next 100 years, the French used this waterway to spread their American empire from Canada to Mobile, Alabama. Yet the first recorded settlement in Chicago, a trading post built by a Frenchman, Jean Baptiste Point DuSable, did not appear until 1781. By this time the British already had conquered the territory, part of the spoils of 70 years of intermittent warfare that cost the French most of their North American holdings. After the American War of Independence, the Illinois Territory was wrested from British/Native American control in a campaign led by the revolutionary war hero Gen. "Mad" Anthony Wayne, which ended with a treaty in 1795 ceding the land around the mouth of the Chicago River to the United States.

Between DuSable's day and 1833, when Chicago was officially founded, the land by the mouth of the Chicago River served as a military outpost that guarded the strategic passage and provided security for a few trappers and a trading post. The military base, Fort Dearborn, which stood on the south side of what is now the Michigan Avenue Bridge, was first garrisoned in 1803 under the command of Capt. John Whistler, grandfather of the famous painter. At first the settlement grew slowly, impeded by continued Native American efforts to drive the new Americans from the Illinois Territory. During the War of 1812, its inhabitants abandoned Fort Dearborn, and many were slain during the

the Battle of Fallen Timbers; disputed Illinois Territory is finally ceded to the young American Republic by treaty a year later.

- **1803** Garrison of Fort Dearborn is established in Chicago, commanded by the grandfather of artist James McNeill Whistler.
- **1812** Residents of Fort Dearborn are slain by Native Americans trying to reclaim their lost territory.
- **1816** Fort Dearborn man-ned anew.
- **1818** Illinois Territory admitted to statehood.
- **1833** Town of Chicago officially incorporated, with little more than 300 residents.
- **1850** Chicago's population roughly 30,000.
- **1856** Chicago is chief railroad center in the U.S.
- **1860** Republican National Convention in Chicago nominates Abraham Lincoln for the presidency.
- **1865** Chicago stockyards are founded.
- **1870** City's population numbers almost 300,000, making it perhaps the fastest-growing metropolis in history.
- **1871** Great Chicago Fire burns large sections of the city; rebuilding begins while the ashes are still warm.
- **1885** The nine-story Home Insurance Building, the world's first skyscraper, is erected.
- **1886** Dynamite bomb explodes during political rally near Haymarket Square, causing a riot in which eight policemen are killed.
- **1892** The first elevated train goes into operation.
- **1893** Chicago, completely recovered from the Great

*continues*

Fire, hosts the World Columbian Exposition.

- 1894 Workers of the Pullman Car Company plant join the American Railway Union in a general strike; President Cleveland sends federal troops to Chicago.
- 1896 William Jennings Bryan delivers "Cross of Gold" speech before delegates of the Democratic National Convention.
- 1903 Theodore Roosevelt nominated for presidency by the Republican National Convention.
- 1905 Wobblies, or Industrial Workers of the World (IWW), founded in Chicago.
- 1909 Daniel Burnham's Chicago Plan, the first comprehensive municipal plan ever offered to an American city, is published.
- 1919 "Black Sox" bribery scandal stuns baseball.
- 1919–33 During Prohibition, Chicago becomes a "wide-open town"; rival mobs battle violently throughout the city for control of distribution and sale of illegal alcohol.
- 1932 Franklin Delano Roosevelt is nominated for presidency by the Democratic National Convention.
- 1956 Richard J. Daley begins term as mayor; he is widely regarded as the "last of the big-city bosses."
- 1968 Anti–Vietnam War protests in conjunction with Democratic National Convention end in police riot.
- 1983 Harold Washington becomes the first African-American mayor of Chicago.
- 1992 A retaining wall collapses; the Loop is flooded underground by water from Chicago River.

evacuation. But before long the trappers drifted back, and by 1816 the military, too, had returned.

Conflict diminished after that, but even as a civil engineer surveyed the building lots of the early town, as late as 1830 periodic raids continued, ceasing only with the defeat of Chief Black Hawk in 1832. A year later, the settlement of 300-plus inhabitants was officially incorporated under the name *Chicago,* said to derive from a Native American word referring to the powerful odors of the abundant wild vegetation in the marshlands surrounding the riverbanks.

**COMMERCE & INDUSTRY**   Land speculation began immediately, as Chicago was carved piecemeal and sold off to finance the Illinois and Michigan Canal that would eliminate the narrow land portage and fulfill the long-standing vision of connecting the two great waterways. Thus the domesticated East would be linked to the pioneer West, with Chicago at midpoint, directing the flow of commerce in both directions. Commercial activity was quick to follow: Within two to three years, local farmers in the outlying areas were producing a surplus. Chicago grew in size and wealth, shipping grain and livestock to the eastern markets and lumber to the treeless prairies of the West. Ironically, by the time the Illinois and Michigan Canal was completed in 1848, the railroad had arrived, and the water route that gave Chicago its raison d'être was rapidly becoming obsolete. Boxcars, not boats, grabbed the title of principal mode of transportation throughout the region. The combination of the railroad with the emergence of local manufacturing, and later, the Civil War, caused Chicago to grow wildly.

The most revolutionary product of the era sprang from the mind of a Chicago inventor Cyrus McCormick, whose reaper filled in for the farmhands who now labored on the nation's battlefields. Local merchants not only thrived on the contraband trade in cotton, but they also secured lucrative contracts from the federal government to provide the army with tents, uniforms, saddles, harnesses, lumber, bread, and meat. By 1870 Chicago's population had grown to 300,000, a thousand times greater than its original population, in the brief interval of 37 years since the city's incorporation.

**THE GREAT FIRE**   A year later the city lay in ashes. The Great Chicago Fire of 1871 began somewhere on the southwest side of the city on October 8 (legend places its exact origin in the O'Leary shed), jumped the river, and continued northward through

## Impressions

*I have struck a city—a real city—and they call it Chicago. The other places don't count. Having seen it, I urgently desire never to see it again. It is inhabited by savages.*
—Rudyard Kipling, *From Sea to Sea* (1889)

*It rained and fogged in Chicago and muddy-flowing people oozed thick in the canyon-beds of the streets. Yet it seemed to me more alive and more real than New York.*
—D. H. Lawrence, letter to Mrs. Bessie Freeman (August 1923)

the night of the following day, when it was checked by the use of gunpowder on the south side and rainfall to the north and west, just before spreading to the prairie. In its wake, the fire destroyed 18,000 buildings and left 90,000 homeless, miraculously taking a toll of only 300 lives.

One thing the fire could not destroy was Chicago's strategic location, and on that solid geographic footing the city began to rebuild as soon as the rubble was cleared. By chance, Chicago's railroad infrastructure—factories, grain warehouses, and lumberyards—was also spared, being located beyond the circle of fire on the southern periphery of the city. By 1873 the city's downtown business and financial district was up and running again, and two decades later Chicago had sufficiently recovered to host the 1893 World Columbian Exposition commemorating the 400th anniversary of the discovery of America.

**AN AMERICAN ATHENS**   The Great Fire gave an unprecedented boost to the professional and artistic development of the nation's architects—drawn by the unlimited opportunities to build, they gravitated to the city in droves. And the city raised its own homegrown crop of architects. Chicago's deserved reputation as an American Athens, packed with monumental and decorative buildings, is a direct by-product of the disastrous fire that nearly brought the city to ruin. In the meantime, Chicago's population continued to grow as many immigrants forsook the uncultivated farmland of the prairie to join the city's labor pool. Chicago still shipped meat and agricultural commodities around the nation and the world, but the city itself was rapidly becoming a mighty industrial center in its own right, creating finished goods, particularly for the markets of the ever-expanding western settlements.

**THE CRADLE OF TRADE UNIONISM**   Chicago never seemed to outgrow its frontier rawness. Greed, profiteering, exploitation, and corruption were as critical to its growth as hard work, ingenuity, and civic pride. The spirit of reform arose most powerfully from the ranks of the working classes, whose lives, despite the city's prosperity, were plagued by poverty and disease. When the sleeping giant of labor finally awakened in Chicago, it did so with a militancy and commitment that was to inspire the union movement throughout the nation.

By the 1890s many of Chicago's workers were already organized into the American Federation of Labor. The Pullman Strike of 1894 united black and white railway workers for the first time in common struggle for higher wages and workplace rights. The Industrial Workers of the World, the Wobblies, which embraced for a time so many great voices of American labor—Eugene V. Debs, Big Bill Haywood, Helen Gurley Flynn—was founded in Chicago in 1905.

**AN AFRICAN-AMERICAN CAPITAL**   The major change in Chicago in the 20th century, however, stems from the enormous growth of the city's African-American population. Coincident with the beginning of World War I, Chicago became the destination for thousands of blacks leaving Mississippi and other parts of the Deep

South. Most settled on the South Side. With the exception of Hyde Park, which absorbed the black population into a successfully integrated, middle-class neighborhood, Chicago over the decades gained a reputation as the most segregated city in the United States. Today, though increased black representation in local politics and other institutions has eased some racial tensions, the city remains far more geographically segregated than most of its urban peers.

**THE CHICAGO MACHINE**   While Chicago was becoming a center of industry, transportation, and finance, and a beacon of labor reform, it was also—again by virtue of its location—becoming a powerhouse in national politics. Between 1860 and 1968 Chicago was the site of 14 Republican and 10 Democratic presidential nominating conventions. (Some even point to the conventions as the source of Chicago's "Windy City" nickname, laying the blame on a politician who was full of hot air.) The first of the conventions gave the country one of its most admired leaders, Abraham Lincoln, while the 1968 convention was witness to the so-called Days of Rage, a police riot against demonstrators who had camped out in Grant Park to protest the Vietnam War. As TV cameras rolled, the demonstrators chanted, "The whole world is watching." And it was; many politicos blame Mayor Richard J. Daley for Hubert Humphrey's defeat in the general election. (Maybe it was a wash; some also say Daley stole the 1960 election for Kennedy.)

A few words about (the original) Mayor Daley: He did not invent the political machine, but he certainly perfected it. As Theodore White writes in *America in Search of Itself,* "Daley ran the machine with a tribal justice akin to the forest Gauls." Daley understood that as long as the leaders of every ethnic and special-interest group had their share of the spoils—the blacks controlled the South Side, for example, and the Polish-Americans kept their neighborhoods segregated—he could retain ultimate power. His reach extended well beyond Chicago's borders; he controlled members of Congress in Washington, and every four years he delivered a solid Democratic vote in the November elections. Since his death in 1976, the machine has never been the same. One election produced the city's first female mayor, Jane Byrne, and another, the city's first black mayor, Harold Washington. Neither was a novice at politics, but neither could hold the delicate balance of (often conflicting) groups that kept Daley in power for 20 years. Today, Daley's son Richard M. may have inherited his father's former office, but the estate did not include the Cook County machine. Mayor Richard M. Daley has abandoned his late father's power base of solid white working-class Bridgeport for the newly developed (some would say yuppie) Burnham Park just south of the Loop. The middle-aged baby boomer appears to be finding himself, but many in the city still enjoy calling him—with more than a hint of condescension—Richie. He remains locked in a struggle with the downstate Republicans, led by Governor Jim Edgar.

The city has ongoing problems. With roughly 2.8 million people total, Chicago's black and white populations are almost equal in size—a rarity among today's urban areas—but the city's residential districts continue to be some of the most segregated in the country. Families are also trying to cope with the school system, which has been undergoing a major restructuring, but whose outlook is still dismal. In 1995 federal government seized control of the city's public housing, pledging to replace the disastrous high-rises with smaller complexes in mixed-income neighborhoods. It is a long-term goal, but authorities have begun the gradual process of tearing down the notorious Cabrini Green, where then-Mayor Jayne Byrne moved briefly to show her support for the crime-victimized residents.

The city had the chance in 1996 to redeem itself from the 1968 debacle that was the Democratic Convention. From August 26 to 29, at the United Center, Chicago gave the Dems—or maybe it's the other way around—one more try.

## 4 Famous Chicagoans

**Jane Addams** (1860–1935)   Founder of Hull House and the leading spirit behind the American Settlement House Movement.

**Nelson Algren** (1909–81)   The novelist who penned *The Man with the Golden Arm* and *Chicago: City on the Make.*

**L. Frank Baum** (1856–1919)   He wrote *The Wizard of Oz* while living in Chicago.

**Al Capone** (1899–1947)   The most famous mobster of them all, he will be forever linked with Chicago and the dark days of Prohibition.

**Nat "King" Cole** (1919–65)   The crooner with such hits as "Unforgettable," "Mona Lisa," and "Straighten Up and Fly Right."

**Richard J. Daley** (1902–76)   The father of the current mayor, he was one of the most powerful political bosses in the United States during his own reign as Chicago's mayor.

**Clarence Darrow** (1857–1938)   The brilliant defense attorney best known for squaring off against perennial presidential candidate William Jennings Bryan during the famous Scopes Monkey Trial.

**Walt Disney** (1901–66)   The film producer learned to draw cartoons in Chicago.

**Ernest Hemingway** (1899–1961)   The great American novelist and Nobel laureate grew up in the Chicago suburb of Oak Park.

**Mahalia Jackson** (1911–72)   A household name even among those who don't think of themselves as great fans of American gospel music.

**Michael Jordan** (b. 1963)   He grew up in North Carolina, and he lives in the suburbs, but Air Jordan will forever be associated with the city he gave three NBA championships in a row.

**Cyrus McCormick** (1809–84)   The inventor of the reaper, his dying words were "Work! Work!"

---

### Chicago Inventions

Here are a few cracker-jack inventions that were the brainchildren of Chicagoans:

- Roller skates, 1884
- Steel-frame skyscraper, 1885
- Elevated railway, 1892
- Cracker Jack, 1893
- Zipper, 1896
- Window envelope, 1902
- Hostess Twinkie, 1930
- Pinball game, 1930
- Spray paint, late 1940s
- McDonald's restaurant, 1955

**Potter Palmer** (1826–1902)  The famous department store magnate also built the Palmer House Hotel.

**Hyman Rickover** (1900–86)  The father of the nuclear submarine.

**Carl Sandburg** (1878–1967)  Leading American poet and Lincoln's biographer.

**Theodore Thomas** (1835–1905)  Founder of the Chicago Symphony.

**Scott Turow** (b. 1949)  Author of the novel *Presumed Innocent,* he still toils as a lawyer by day.

**Muddy Waters** (1915–83)  The king of Chicago blues.

**Johnny Weissmuller** (1904–84)  He overcame childhood polio to become a champion Olympic swimmer and Hollywood's most famous Tarzan.

**Oprah Winfrey** (b. 1954)  She has built an empire out of a TV talk show.

**Florenz Ziegfeld** (1869–1932)  Theatrical producer and founder of the Ziegfeld Follies.

## 5 Rising Like the Phoenix: Chicago's Public Architecture & Art

**ARCHITECTURE**  The Great Fire of 1871 couldn't have come at a better time. As the city began to rebuild from its ashes, gathering to its skirts the best and brightest young architects, it had technology on its side. The construction industry was beginning to experiment with new materials, one of which, steel, helped make skyscrapers possible. The other invention that enabled architects to build skyward was the elevator, and the world's first skyscraper, the Home Insurance Building, was erected in Chicago in 1885. Coupled with these engineering innovations was an open-mindedness on the part of the civilians that could come only in a frontier town where, less than 60 years earlier, had stood only fort and trading post. Chicago was not a Paris or a London; without tradition and history to limit them, the architects of the day were inspired to create the world's first truly modern city.

In the first years after the fire, Daniel Burnham, Louis Sullivan, and Dankmar Adler were among the leading architects to reconstruct the city. It was Burnham, from his offices in the Railway Exchange Building he had designed at 224 S. Michigan Ave. (now the Santa Fe Building), who devised the Plan for Chicago in 1909. Nicknamed "Paris on the Prairie," the plan outlined Burnham's vision for the great midwestern city, complete with grand boulevards, parks, and a sacred lakefront. The city today owes the fact that it is so livable to this early urban planning.

Having created its own tradition of nontradition, Chicago fostered the development of Frank Lloyd Wright's "Prairie School," and, still later, of Ludwig Mies van der Rohe's Bauhaus modernism.

I do not mean to suggest that every building, regardless of its wackiness, goes up without criticism. But Chicago seems to love the controversy. Take Helmut Jahn's blue and orange James R. Thompson Center (formerly the State of Illinois Center)—some would say "please!"—at 100 W. Randolph (at LaSalle Street)—a decade or so after it opened, Chicagoans still pick fights over it.

As Chicago has become a virtual open-air museum of architecture, so has it made a commitment to public art, adorning its streets and parks with monumental sculpture by some of the 20th century's biggest names—Picasso, Calder, Oldenburg, Moore, Chagall, and Miró among them.

**THE ARTS**   I have noticed that some visitors arrive in Chicago still expecting little more than a provincial town. That attitude amazes Chicagoans, and it amazes me. The flowering of its performing arts gives evidence that Chicago is a cosmopolitan city. The renowned Chicago Symphony holds a position as a world leader, and the Lyric Opera is highly esteemed. Theater is thriving in Chicago, perhaps more so even than New York. Both the Steppenwolf and Goodman theater companies have brought home Tony Awards in recent years. Beyond the Broadway-style mega-productions—which are certainly not alien to this city—Chicago possesses more than 100 innovative theaters that are energized by the neighborhoods where they reside.

## 6  Recommended Books & Films

**BOOKS**   So many great American writers either have come from Chicago, lived here during their productive years, or set their work within the city's confines that it is impossible to recommend a single book that says all there is to say about Chicago. I'll suggest a few that will get you started. Upton Sinclair's *The Jungle* tells the tale of a young immigrant encountering the filthy, brutal city. Its 1906 publication caused an uproar that led to the passage of the Pure Food and Drug Act. Theodore Dreiser's *Sister Carrie* is in the same vein of social consciousness at the turn of the century. James T. Farrell's trilogy *Studs Lonigan*, published in the thirties, explores the power of ethnic and neighborhood identity in Chicago.

Other books set (in full or in part) within the city are Clancy Sigal's *Going Away*, John Dos Passos's *USA*, Philip Roth's *Letting Go*, and Saul Bellow's *The Adventures of Augie March* and *Humboldt's Gift*. Richard Wright spent time in Chicago and wrote about it in *Native Son* and *Cooley High*. Hemingway was a native son (Oak Park), though he didn't write much about the city. Chicago has had several fabled poets, including Carl Sandburg and Vachel Lindsay, and the brilliant troubadour and popular novelist Nelson Algren wrote *Chicago: City on the Make*. Even Bertolt Brecht set a play, *Saint Joan of the Stockyards*, in Chicago.

And, of course, no one has given a voice to the people of Chicago as has Studs Terkel—in *Division Street America, Hard Times,* and *Working.* These books as well as his own paean to the city, *Chicago*, reveal much about the place he adopted as his own.

**FILMS**   Boosted by a few hit films and the beachhead established here by filmmaker John Hughes *(Home Alone, The Breakfast Club),* Chicago has been building its profile in the movie industry. As with books, the movies that take place in Chicago are far too numerous to mention, so I'll stick to the options that in my subjective, but highly astute, estimation give the best flavor of the city. Right up there at the top of my list is *Hoop Dreams,* a heartbreaking documentary about two inner-city teens who see basketball as their only way out. A couple of good ones to rent are *The Blues Brothers,* the John Belushi and Dan Aykroyd comedy about a couple of musicians on a mission from God, and Hughes's *Ferris Bueller's Day Off,* starring Matthew Broderick as a high school senior playing hooky to visit many of the same sights you'll probably see on your trip. Among the several action and suspense movies that capture the feel of Chicago are *The Fugitive,* with Harrison Ford and Tommy Lee Jones; *Backdraft,* with William Baldwin, Kurt Russell, and Robert DeNiro as firefighters; and, for a period gangster flick, *The Untouchables,* with Kevin Costner, Sean Connery, and DeNiro.

# 2 Planning a Trip to Chicago

**A**fter choosing a destination, most prospective travelers have two fundamental questions: What will it cost? and How do I get there? This chapter will answer both of these questions and also will resolve other important issues—such as when to go and where to obtain more information about Chicago.

The calendar of events will help you plan for (or avoid) festivals, shows, and parades, and the temperature and precipitation chart will help you decide which jacket to bring. If you are single, traveling with children, a person with a disability, a senior citizen, or a student, you will find some special tips and names of organizations that cater to your needs in this chapter, as well.

## 1 Visitor Information

### SOURCES OF INFORMATION

The **Chicago Office of Tourism,** Chicago Cultural Center, 78 E. Washington St., Chicago, IL 60602 (☎ 312/744-2400, 800/2CONNECT, or TDD 312/744-2947, or on the World Wide Web at http://www.ci.chi.il.us.), will mail you a packet of material, including up-to-date calendars that survey special events at four-month intervals.

Chicago has several independent neighborhood associations, and each can provide visitors with additional information on specific areas of town. Such resources are listed where these neighborhoods are highlighted in the text.

Another excellent source of free information is your local travel agent, who can give you up-to-date information on bargain airline fares and package land arrangements that often mean additional savings for you.

### MONEY

While most people today depend upon their credit or charge cards, U.S. dollar **traveler's checks** are a safe, negotiable way to carry currency. Most downtown restaurants, hotels, and shops accept traveler's checks, and banks generally exchange them for cash. Once you get away from downtown and the more affluent neighborhoods, however, smaller restaurants and shops may be reluctant to accept traveler's checks. American Express offices are open Monday through

| What Things Cost in Chicago | U.S. $ |
| --- | --- |
| Taxi from O'Hare Airport to city center | 25.00–30.00 |
| Bus fare to any destination within the city | 1.25 |
| Double room at the Drake hotel (very expensive) | 205.00–265.00 |
| Double room at the Raphael hotel (moderate) | 150.00–185.00 |
| Double room at the City Suites Hotel (inexpensive) | 85.00 |
| Lunch for one at the Frontera Grill (moderate) | 15.00 |
| Lunch for one at Ed Debevic's (budget) | 7.00 |
| Dinner for one, without wine, at the Everest Room (very expensive) | 75.00 |
| Dinner for one, without wine, at Zum Deutschen Eck (moderate) | 25.00 |
| Dinner for one at Mity Nice (budget) | 15.00 |
| Glass of beer | 2.00 |
| Coca-Cola | 1.25 |
| Cup of coffee | 1.00 |
| Adult admission to top of Sears Tower | 6.50 |
| Movie ticket | 7.50 |
| Theater ticket | 10.00–40.00 |

Friday from 9am to 5pm, and one office is also open on Saturday from 10am to 3pm. See "Fast Facts: Chicago" in Chapter 4 for office locations.

**Automated Teller Machines (ATMs)** everywhere accept cards connected to their particular networks, so before your trip, ask your bank for a directory of the banks connected to its network to find out which Chicago ATMs you can use to access your account.

Foreign visitors should also see Chapter 3 for monetary descriptions and currency-exchange information.

## 2  When to Go

### THE CLIMATE

Although not entirely deserved, Chicago has a reputation for being *really* cold in the winter. In truth, it's about as cold as any other northern city. Still, the February weather does not exactly inspire a leisurely stroll through Lincoln Park Zoo. So most visitors prefer planning trips to Chicago for late spring through early fall.

If you like moderate temperatures, the ideal time to visit is early autumn, when the days are most likely to be consistently pleasant.

Chicago's weather seems to be strongly influenced by the proximity of Lake Michigan. At its most humane, the lake cools the city with gentle breezes, particularly welcome during those hours of sweltering humidity that often accompany the dog days of summer, but that same offshore breeze can strengthen to a biting wind throughout the long winter. If you dress properly, however, you certainly can consider Chicago a four-season destination. After all, the city does not curl up and hibernate just because the mercury drops below zero or goes up to 90°. As an added incentive to "off-season" travelers, keep in mind that during the winter, hotel rates are rock-bottom.

**Chicago's Average Temperatures and Precipitation**

|            | Jan  | Feb  | Mar  | Apr  | May  | June | July | Aug  | Sept | Oct  | Nov  | Dec  |
|------------|------|------|------|------|------|------|------|------|------|------|------|------|
| High °F    | 20.2 | 33.9 | 44.3 | 58.8 | 70.0 | 79.4 | 85.3 | 82.1 | 75.5 | 64.1 | 48.2 | 35.0 |
| Low °F     | 13.6 | 18.1 | 27.6 | 38.8 | 48.1 | 57.7 | 62.7 | 61.7 | 53.9 | 42.0 | 31.4 | 20.3 |
| Rain (in.) | 1.60 | 1.31 | 2.59 | 3.66 | 3.15 | 4.08 | 3.63 | 3.53 | 3.35 | 2.28 | 2.06 | 2.10 |

# CHICAGO CALENDAR OF EVENTS

The best way to stay on top of the city's current crop of special events is to ask the Chicago Office of Tourism (☎ 312/744-2400 or 800/2CONNECT) to mail you a copy of its quarterly publication, the **Chicago Illinois Calendar,** plus the latest materials produced by the Mayor's Office of Special Events (☎ 312/744-3315, or the **Events Hotline,** ☎ 312/744-3370) with information on Chicago neighborhood festivals. Or you can opt for spontaneity and simply take potluck when you arrive. The one thing you can count on, whether or not you research the topic in advance, is that you'll be able to choose from a slew of events, regardless of what month you visit Chicago.

Of the annual events, the most lively and unpredictable tend to revolve around the national parades and the street celebrations staged by many of Chicago's numerous ethnic groups. In addition, food, music, art, and flower fairs have their special niches in the city's yearly schedule.

Remember that new events may be added to this list every year, and that occasionally special events are discontinued or rescheduled. So to avoid disappointment, be sure to telephone in advance to either the sponsoring organization, the Chicago Office of Tourism, or the Mayor's Office of Special Events to verify dates, times, and locations. Some events charge an admission fee or request a donation.

January

- **New Year's Day 5K Run/Walk,** Lincoln Park (☎ 312/868-3010). One way to usher in the new year.
- **Chicago Boat, Sport, and RV Show,** McCormick Place, 2300 S. Lake Shore Dr. (☎ 312/836-4740). This extravaganza with big-time entertainment is scheduled for January 22–26.
- **Sports Fishing, Travel, and Outdoor Show,** O'Hare Expo Center, 9291 W. Bryn Mawr Ave. (☎ 312/692-2220). Generally held toward the end of the month, it attracts lots of folks in plaid flannel.

February

- **Chicago Cubs Fan Convention** (☎ 312/951-CUBS). This annual confab for Cubbies fans offers a chance to talk baseball with players and coaches.
- **Azalea Flower Show,** Lincoln Park Conservatory, 2400 N. Stockton Dr. (☎ 312/294-4770), and the Camellia Flower Show at the Garfield Park Conservatory (☎ 773/533-1281). Both are held all month long at a time when you won't see many other (uncut) flowers in the city.
- **Chinese New Year Parade,** on Wentworth and Cermak Streets (☎ 312/326-5320). Join in as the sacred dragon whirls down the boulevard and restaurateurs pass out small envelopes of money to their regular customers. Call to verify the date, which varies from year to year.
- **Chicago Auto Show,** McCormick Place, 2300 S. Lake Shore Dr. (☎ 708/954-0600). Hundreds of cars and trucks, domestic and foreign, current and futuristic, on display.

- **University of Chicago Folk Festival,** on campus at Mandel Hall, 57th and University Avenues. Call 773/702-9793 for more information.
- **Black History Month.** It's celebrated with special events at the Chicago Cultural Center, the Museum of Science and Industry, and the DuSable Museum.
- ✪ **The Medinah Shrine Circus.** The Shriners' annual big-top event to benefit charity.
    **Where:** Medinah Temple, 600 N. Wabash (☎ 312/266-5050). **When:** Spread over three weeks between late February and early March. **How:** Tickets may be purchased through Ticketron or ordered directly from the Shriners through the telephone number listed above.

## March

✪ **St. Patrick's Day Parade.** Expect the usual enthusiasm and an occasional donnybrook. The Chicago River is dyed kelly green for the occasion.
    **Where:** Along Dearborn Street from Wacker Drive to Van Buren. **When:** March 17. **How:** The best place to view the parade is around Wacker and Dearborn.

- **International Kennel Dog Show,** McCormick Place, 2300 S. Lake Shore Dr. (☎ 773/237-5100). Come see all the breeds, common and downright peculiar, scheduled for March 28–30.

## April

- **Opening Day.** For the Cubs, call 773/404-CUBS; for the White Sox, call 773/924-1000. The calendar may say spring, but be warned, Opening Day is usually freezing in Chi-town.
- **Spring and Easter Flower Show,** Lincoln Park Conservatory, 2400 N. Stockton Dr. Call 312/294-4700 for more information.
- **Hyde Park House,** University of Chicago, 969 E. 60th St. (☎ 773/667-3932). Featuring the latest in restoration and renovation concepts and materials. Generally held the second weekend in April.

## May

- **Buckingham Fountain Color Light Show,** in Grant Park, at Congress and Lake Shore Drive. The water and the lights are turned on in the landmark fountain daily from May 1 to October 1, from 9 to 11pm.
- **Polish Constitution Day Parade,** along Clark Street from Wacker Drive to Congress (☎ 312/744-3315). Early May. The Polish-Americans are still a tight-knit community in Chicago.
- **Annual Art & Crafts Exposition,** American Indian Center. Call 773/275-5871 for more information.
- **Chicago International Art Exposition,** Navy Pier, 600 E. Grand Ave. (☎ 312/787-6858 or 312/595-PIER). This five-day event involves the participation of 160 Chicago art galleries and exhibits the work of more than 1,500 artists.
- **Greek-American Parade,** south on Michigan Avenue from Wacker Drive to Congress (☎ 312/744-3315). May 14.
- **Armed Forces Day Parade,** south on LaSalle Street from Wacker Drive to Congress (☎ 773/926-2258). May 20.
- **Wright Plus Tour.** An annual tour of Frank Lloyd Wright's home and studio in Oak Park (☎ 708/848-1500). The second or third week in May.
- **Beverly Housewalk.** An organized tour of this South Side neighborhood (☎ 773/233-3100) starts at 2153 W. 111th St. in late May.
- **International Theater Festival of Chicago.** Various theaters participate; call 312/664-3370 for more information. Held biennially in even-numbered years.

- **Printer's Row Book Fair,** on Dearborn Street from Harrison to Polk (☎ 312/987-1980). An outdoor book fair in the neighborhood named for its association with the printed word. May 31–June 1.

## June

❂ **Ravinia Festival.** Ravinia is the summer home of the Chicago Symphony and venue of many first-rate visiting orchestras, chamber ensembles, pop artists, and so forth.

> **Where:** Ravinia Park, Highland Park. **When:** June through September. **How:** Call 773/728-4642 for ticket reservations.

- **Neighborhood Festivals.** Many begin this month at various city locations. Call 312/744-3315 for more information.

❂ **Chicago Blues Festival.** A much-awaited and heavily attended event with dozens of acts.

> **Where:** Petrillo Music Shell, at Jackson and Columbus Drives in Grant Park (☎ 312/744-3315). **When:** Usually staged the second weekend of June. **How:** Free; get there in the afternoon to get a good spot on the lawn for the evening show.

- **Asparagus Fest,** on Lincoln, Lawrence, and Western Avenues. This local food festival near Lincoln Square occurs in early June. Call 773/878-7331 for more information.

❂ **Gospel Festival.** This festival features the flip side of the blues and is another huge draw.

> **Where:** Petrillo Music Shell, at Jackson and Columbus Drives in Grant Park (☎ 312/744-3315). **When:** Second or third weekend in June. **How:** Free; just show up.

- **Puerto Rican Day Parade,** along Clark Street from Wacker Drive to Congress (☎ 312/744-3315). One of Chicago's animated Latino street celebrations. First Saturday in June.

- **Wells Street Art Fair,** 1900 N. Lincoln Ave. This Chicago tradition is always held in Old Town the second weekend in June (☎ 312/337-1938).

- **Filipino American Council Parade,** along Clark Street from Wacker Drive to Congress. June 12.

- **Celebrate State Street,** along State Street from Jackson to Lake Street (☎ 312/782-9160). Outdoor festivities are geared to the commercial resuscitation of "that great street."

- **Andersonville Midsommerfest,** along Clark Street from Foster to Catalpa (☎ 773/728-2995). This event recalls the heyday of this neighborhood as Chicago's principal Swedish community. Third weekend in June.

- **Grant Park Concerts,** Petrillo Music Shell, at Jackson and Columbus Drives in Grant Park (☎ 312/294-2920). The free outdoor musical concerts in the park begin the last week in June.

❂ **Gay and Lesbian Pride Week Parade.** The parade is the colorful culmination of a week of activities by Chicago's gay and lesbian community.

> **Where:** Halsted Street, from Belmont Avenue to Broadway, south to Diversey Parkway, and east to Sheridan Road. **When:** June 29. **How:** Take up a spot on Broadway for the best view. Call 773/348-8243 for information.

## July

❂ **Taste of Chicago.** Scores of Chicago's restaurants cart their fare to food stands set up throughout the park.

**Where:** In Grant Park. **When:** Eight days of street feasting, in late June and the first week of July. **How:** Free admittance; you pay for the sampling, of course. Call 312/744-3315 for information.

- **Fourth of July.** The holiday is celebrated in Chicago on the third of July: Concerts, fireworks, and a parade are the highlights of the celebration in Grant Park.
- **Annual Old-Fashioned Fourth of July Celebration,** Chicago Historical Society grounds, Clark Street and North Avenue (☎ 312/642-4600).
- **Gallery 37.** The outdoor art show (☎ 312/744-8925) of the Chicago Cultural Center, along State Street between Washington and Randolph. Early July.
- **Annual American Spanish Dance Festival,** put on by the Ensemble Español Spanish Dance Theater at Northeastern Illinois University, 5500 N. St. Louis (☎ 773/583-4050, ext. 3015). This free event is held over a two-week period in mid-July.
- **Chicago-Mackinac Island Boat Race,** with the starting line at the Monroe Street Harbor (☎ 312/861-7777). The grandest of the inland water races is scheduled toward the end of July.

## August

- **Taste of River North,** on Superior between Franklin and Wells. Call 312/645-1047 for more information on this neighborhood festival.
- **Medieval Faire,** in Lincoln Park (☎ 773/880-5200). This event features troubadours, jugglers, acrobats, and other market-day entertainments inspired by the Middle Ages. First weekend of August.
- **Illinois State Fair,** in Springfield (☎ 217/782-6661). Livestock, homemade pies, carnival rides, the whole bit. Middle of the month.
- **Venetian Night,** from Monroe Harbor to the planetarium (☎ 312/744-3315). The boat carnival on the lake is complete with fireworks.
- **Bud Billiken Parade and Picnic.** An African-American celebration (☎ 312/225-2400). The parade route follows 39th Street and King Drive to 55th Street and Washington Park. Second Saturday in August, beginning at 10am.
- ✪ **Air & Water Show.** A popular perennial aquatic and aerial spectacular. **Where:** North Avenue Beach. **When:** Scheduled each summer toward the end of August. **How:** Free. Since the crowds are intense, an alternative viewing spot is Oak Street Beach, along the Gold Coast. Call 708/498-5071 for details.

## September

- ✪ **Jazz Festival.** The Jazz Festival is Chicago style, and plenty steamy. **Where:** Petrillo Music Shell, Jackson and Columbus Drives in Grant Park. **When:** First week of September; almost always over Labor Day weekend. **How:** Free; come early and stay late. Call 312/744-3370 for information.
- **"Viva! Chicago" Latin Music Festival.** The Latin beat in all its dynamic and sultry variations from mariachi to mambo, at the Petrillo Music Shell, Grant Park, Jackson and Columbus Drives. Second weekend in September (☎ 312/744-3340).
- **Berghoff Octoberfest,** Adams Street between Dearborn and State Streets (☎ 312/427-3170). A popular three-day beerfest at one of Chicago's oldest and best-loved restaurants, right down in the Loop. Usually held in mid-September.
- **Mexican Independence Day Parade,** along Michigan Avenue between Wacker Drive and Congress. Call 312/744-3315 for more information.
- **Chicago Federation of Labor Parade,** along Dearborn between Wacker Drive and Van Buren Street. Call 312/744-3315 for information; early in the month.

October

- **Columbus Day Parade,** Dearborn Street from Wacker Drive to Congress (☎ 312/828-0010). Italian-American Day by any other name. The closest Monday to October 12.
- **Chicago International Antique Show,** Navy Pier (☎ 312/787-6858). The show takes place at mid-month over a four-day period; it's not a flea market.
- **Chicago International Film Festival** (☎ 312/644-3400). It's held the last week of October or the first week of November at various theaters.
- **The Big Top.** This is the month that Ringling Brothers, Barnum & Bailey comes to Chicago.

November

- **Christmas Around the World,** at the Museum of Science and Industry, 57th Street and Lake Shore Drive (☎ 773/684-1414). The traditional Christmas exhibit opens in late November and stays open until New Year's.
- **Chrysanthemum Show,** Garfield Park Conservatory, 300 N. Central Park Ave. (☎ 773/826-3175), and Lincoln Park Conservatory, at Fullerton and Stockton (☎ 312/294-2493). The show lasts for two weeks in mid-November.
- **Veterans' Day Parade,** in the Loop (☎ 312/744-3515).
- **Christmas Tree Lighting,** Daley Center Plaza, in the Loop (☎ 312/744-3315). Toward the end of the month.
- ✪ **Michigan Avenue Holiday Lights Festival.** Beginning at dusk, a procession of horse-drawn carriages works its way south along Michigan Avenue, with lights being illuminated block by block as the procession passes. Carolers, elves, and minstrels appear with Santa along the avenue throughout the day and into the evening.

    **Where:** Michigan Avenue from Oak Street to the Chicago River. **When:** Toward the end of November; call 312/642-3570 for the exact date and scheduling.

December

- *A Christmas Carol,* performed at the Goodman Theatre, 200 S. Columbus Dr. Call 312/443-3800 for information and tickets.
- *Nutcracker* **ballet,** at the Arie Crown Theater, McCormick Place, 23rd Street and Lake Shore Drive (☎ 312/791-6000). This charity event is sponsored every year for two weeks during mid-December by the *Chicago Tribune.*
- **Caroling to the Animals,** Lincoln Park Zoo, 2200 N. Cannon Dr. (☎ 773/935-6700). Call for the precise date of this mid-month event, which is of special interest to preschoolers.
- **Christmas Flower Show,** at the Lincoln Park Conservatory, at Fullerton and Stockton (☎ 312/742-7736), and at Garfield Park Conservatory, 300 N. Central Park Ave. (☎ 312/746-5100). The show begins the last week of December and continues through the holidays into January.

## 3  Health & Insurance

Before you leave on your trip, be sure you are protected with adequate health insurance coverage.

**INSURANCE**    Most travel agents sell low-cost health, loss, and trip-cancellation insurance to their vacationing clients. Rates for these short-term policies are generally reasonable, and these policies allow you to supplement existing coverage with a minimum of complications. Other forms of travel-related insurance are also available, including coverage for lost or damaged baggage. Often a single policy provided by your travel agent will protect you in all of these areas and will also provide supplementary medical coverage.

## 4  Tips for Special Travelers

**FOR TRAVELERS WITH DISABILITIES**   Most of Chicago's sidewalks, as well as major museums and tourist attractions, are fitted with wheelchair ramps. More and more hotels are also providing special accommodations and services for wheelchair-bound visitors, such as large bathrooms, ramps, and, for the hearing impaired, telecommunications devices.

For specific information on facilities for people with disabilities who are traveling in Chicago, call or write the **Mayor's Office for People with Disabilities,** located at 510 N. Peshtigo Court, Room 405B, Chicago, IL 60611 (☎ 312/744-6673 for voice; 312/744-4964 for TT/TDD), and staffed from 8:30am to 4:30pm Monday through Friday.

Also, the **Society for the Advancement of Travel for the Handicapped,** 347 Fifth Ave., Suite 610, New York, NY 10016 (☎ 212/447-SATH), can offer some support.

**FOR SENIORS**   In Chicago, the term "seniors" usually refers to men and women age 65 and older. Seniors regularly receive discounts at museums and attractions, as well as for various forms of entertainment, such as movie or theater tickets. Seniors may also seek discounts at hotels and restaurants, many of which are willing to offer reduced prices, though they may not advertise the fact. Airlines also offer senior discounts, but first compare these fares with any available promotional tickets.

One excellent source of travel information for seniors is the **American Association of Retired Persons (AARP),** 601 E St. NW, Washington, DC 20049 (☎ 202/434-2277). Members are offered discounts on car rentals, hotels, airfares, and even sightseeing. AARP travel arrangements are handled by American Express. **Grand Circle Travel,** 347 Congress St., Boston, MA 02210 (☎ 617/350-7500 or 800/221-2610) offers escorted tours and cruises for retired persons, including singles.

Seniors have many resources available to them in Chicago, including discounted fares for public transportation, discounted admission for museums and other attractions, and citywide programs; call the Chicago Park District at 312/294-2309 for specific information.

**FOR SINGLES**   **Jens Jurgen, Travel Companion,** P.O. Box P-833, Amityville, NY 11701 (☎ 516/454-0880), attempts to match single travelers with likeminded companions, and it is now the largest such company in the United States. For $99 for an eight-month membership, a new applicant fills out a form stating his or her preferences and needs and then receives a list of potential partners in reply.

**FOR WOMEN**   The **Women and Children First Bookstore,** 5233 N. Clark (☎ 773/769-9299), is an excellent source of information for women, as is the **Community Information and Referral Service** (☎ 312/876-0010).

**FOR GAY MEN & LESBIANS**   A good resource for access to various gay and lesbian networks is the **Gay and Lesbian Pride Week Planning Committee** (☎ 773/348-8243), which functions year-round. **Horizon Community Services** (☎ 312/879-CARE) provides referrals daily from 7am to 10pm. **Gay and Lesbian Pride Week** is a major event on the Chicago calendar each June, highlighted by a lively parade on the North Side.

**FOR FAMILIES**    Traveling with infants and small children requires some additional planning. Airlines will provide special children's meals with 24 hours' notice, but not baby food, which you must supply. Most hotels maintain an active list of babysitters.

For special tips on how to travel successfully with children, you might consider a subscription to *Family Travel Times,* a newsletter put out by the organization TWYCH (Travel with Your Children), 80 Eighth Ave., New York, NY 10011 (☎ 212/206-0688). Subscribers may also call with questions between 10am and noon, eastern standard time.

**FOR STUDENTS**    Students will find that their valid high school or college IDs can mean discounts on travel, theater, and museum tickets, and at some nightspots.

Chicago has many fine colleges and universities, all of which are centers of student life and study. The University of Chicago (☎ 773/702-1234) is in Hyde Park; the University of Illinois at Chicago (☎ 312/996-3000) is near the Loop on the Near West Side; Loyola of Chicago (☎ 773/274-3000) is on Sheridan Road in Rogers Park; and Northwestern University (☎ 312/491-7271) is in the northern suburb of Evanston.

# 5  Getting There

## BY PLANE

**THE MAJOR AIRLINES**    Domestic carriers that fly regularly to Chicago include **American** (☎ 800/433-7300), **Continental** (☎ 800/525-0280), **Delta** (☎ 800/241-4141), **Kiwi** (☎ 800/538-5494), **Northwest** (☎ 800/225-2525), **Southwest** (☎ 800/435-9792), **TWA** (☎ 800/221-2000), **United** (☎ 800/241-6522), and **USAir** (☎ 800/428-4322). Commuter service is also provided by several regional airlines. International service to Chicago is also extensive via such operators as **Aer Lingus** (☎ 800/223-6537), **Air Canada** (☎ 800/426-7000), **Air France** (☎ 800/237-2747), **Alitalia** (☎ 800/223-5730), **British Airways** (☎ 800/247-9297), **Japan Air Lines** (☎ 800/565-7000), **KLM** (☎ 800/777-5553), **Lufthansa** (☎ 800/645-3880), **Swissair** (☎ 800/221-6644), and **Mexicana** (☎ 800/531-7921). The toll-free numbers listed are for use in the United States only.

**FINDING THE BEST AIRFARE**    The easiest, but not necessarily the cheapest, way to purchase an airline ticket is through your local travel agent. A travel agent is a convenience that doesn't cost you anything, but don't expect your travel agent to spend an inordinate amount of time trying to find you the cheapest ticket available—doing so not only will take up his or her time, but will also lead to a smaller commission from the airline.

To get the lowest possible fare, you will probably have to do some digging yourself. Call several carriers that fly to Chicago and ask them to quote you the lowest fare available. Airlines have sales, special promotions, and fare wars all the time, so shop around, but remember, in general, the lower the fare, the more restrictions and penalties apply to changing dates and itineraries.

The lowest regular fare is referred to as economy class, and it often requires that you travel during the week and stay over Saturday night. The next lowest fares are called coach. Keep in mind that airfares fluctuate wildly from class to class and often from airline to airline, depending on the competition within your market, and whether the city is a hub.

Many travelers in recent years have opted to act as their own travel agents, seeking out the lowest possible airfares offered by consolidators, charters, and even courier services.

## Impressions

*At a literary conference at Notre Dame, I ... ran into a poet who is noted for his verse celebrating the ecology, née Nature. He lives in a dramatic house nailed together completely from uncut pieces of hickory driftwood, perched on a bluff overlooking the crashing ocean. ... I remarked that this must be the ideal setting in which to write about the ecological wonders. "I wouldn't know," he said. "I do all my writing in O'Hare."*

—Tom Wolfe, "The Intelligent Coed's Guide to America," in
*Mauve Gloves and Madmen, Clutter and Vine,* 1976

**Consolidators** (also called bucket shops) buy blocks of tickets directly from the airlines. In a sense, they speculate in air-passage futures, and they can sell their "buckets" at prices that are often far below official rates. There are many well-known and legitimate bucket shops, and a number of fly-by-night operations as well. If you have any doubts about a particular company, consult your local branch of the Better Business Bureau.

**Charter** companies generally offer one-time flights to specific destinations. Charter flights can be an inexpensive means of traveling to a faraway destination, but generally they do not operate in the Chicago market. The same tends to be true for **courier** flights; you are more likely to arrange a courier flight to Hong Kong, or perhaps from coast to coast in the United States, than to Chicago. Newspaper travel supplements and the Yellow Pages are good sources for information on the offerings or whereabouts of consolidators, charter companies, and courier services.

**CHICAGO'S AIRPORTS**    Chicago's **O'Hare International Airport** has been—and to my knowledge still is—the world's busiest airport. It's located northwest of the city proper, about a 25- to 30-minute drive from downtown, depending, of course, on the severity of traffic. A cab ride into the city will cost you about $25. But for $1.50, you can take the El (vernacular for the elevated train), which will efficiently get you downtown in about a half hour, regardless of traffic. O'Hare also has outposts for every major car-rental company (see Chapter 4 for details).

For foreign visitors, O'Hare has five information booths with multilingual staffs who speak languages ranging from French, Spanish, and German to Italian, Russian, Japanese, Cantonese, and Tagalog. The booths are open daily from 8am to 8pm.

On the opposite side of the city, the Southwest Side, is Chicago's other major airport, **Midway.** Although it's smaller than O'Hare, and fewer airlines have routes here, Midway is closer to the Loop. Chicago recently extended the El there, so now you can make it downtown for $1.50. Most major car-rental companies have counters at Midway, as well.

**Meigs Field** is an in-town airstrip for private planes. It's just south of the Loop on a little hunk of land that juts out into Lake Michigan.

**Continental Air Transport** (☎ 312/454-7800) services most first-class hotels in Chicago; check with your bell captain. The cost is $14.75 one-way ($25.50 round-trip) to O'Hare, and $10.75 one-way ($19 round-trip) to Midway.

For limo service from either O'Hare or Midway, call **Carey of Chicago** (☎ 312/663-1220), or **Chicago Limousine Services** (☎ 312/726-1035). Cost, with tip and tax, comes to about $75.

## BY TRAIN

Rail passenger service, while it may never approach the grandeur of its heyday, has made enormous advances in service, comfort, and efficiency since the creation of

Amtrak in 1971. As in the past, but on a reduced scale, Chicago remains the hub of the national passenger rail system. Traveling great distances by train is certainly not the quickest way to go, nor always the most convenient. But many travelers still prefer it to flying or driving.

When you arrive in Chicago, the train will pull into **Union Station** at Adams and Canal Streets (☎ 312/558-1075 or 800/872-7245). Bus nos. 1, 60, 151, and 156 all stop at the station, which is just west across the river from the Loop. The nearest El stop is at Congress and Clinton (on the O'Hare–Congress–Douglas line), which is a fair walk away, especially when carrying luggage.

Consult your travel agent or call **Amtrak** (☎ 800/USA-RAIL). Ask the reservations agent to send you Amtrak's useful travel planner with information on train accommodations and package tours. For Amtrak information in Chicago, call 312/558-1075.

## BY BUS

The **Greyhound Bus Station** in Chicago is at 630 W. Harrison (☎ 800/231-2222), not far from Union Station. Call your local Greyhound terminal for information nationwide on routes, schedules, and fares. Bus No. 61 passes in front of the terminal building, and the nearest El stop is at Clinton and Congress on the O'Hare–Douglas line.

## BY CAR

Chicago is serviced by interstate highways from all major points on the compass. I-80 and I-90 approach from the east, crossing the northern sector of Illinois, with I-90 splitting off and emptying into Chicago via the Skyway and the Dan Ryan Expressway. From here I-90 runs through Wisconsin following a northern route to Seattle. I-55 snakes up the Mississippi Valley from the vicinity of New Orleans and enters Chicago from the west along the Stevenson Expressway, and in the opposite direction provides an outlet to the Southwest. I-57 originates in southern Illinois and forms part of the interstate linkage to Florida and the South, connecting within Chicago on the west leg of the Dan Ryan. I-94 links Detroit with Chicago, arriving on the Calumet Expressway and leaving the city via the Kennedy Expressway en route to the Northwest.

Here are a few approximate driving distances in miles to Chicago: from Milwaukee, 90; from St. Louis, 290; from Detroit, 279; from Albuquerque, 1,293; from Phoenix, 1,729; from Washington, D.C., 695; from New York City, 840; and from Los Angeles, 2,112.

# For Foreign Visitors

Although American fads and fashions have spread across Europe and other parts of the world so that America may seem like familiar territory before your arrival, there are still many peculiarities and uniquely American situations that any foreign visitor will encounter.

## 1 Preparing for Your Trip

### ENTRY REQUIREMENTS

**DOCUMENT REGULATIONS**   Canadian citizens may enter the United States without visas; they need only proof of residence.

Citizens of the United Kingdom, New Zealand, Japan, and most western European countries traveling on valid passports may not need a visa for fewer than 90 days of holiday or business travel to the United States, providing that they hold a round-trip or return ticket and enter the United States on an airline or cruise line participating in the visa waiver program.

Note that citizens of these visa-exempt countries who enter the United States first may then visit Mexico, Canada, Bermuda, and/or the Caribbean islands and reenter the United States by any mode of transportation without needing a visa. Further information is available from any United States embassy or consulate.

Citizens of countries other than those stipulated above, including citizens of Australia, must have two documents: a valid passport, with an expiration date at least six months later than the scheduled end of the visit to the United States, and a tourist visa, available without charge from the nearest United States consulate.

To obtain a visa, the traveler must submit a completed application form (either in person or by mail) with a $1^{1}/_{2}$-inch square photo and demonstrate binding ties to a residence abroad. Usually you can obtain a visa at once or within 24 hours, but it may take longer during the summer rush from June to August. If you cannot go in person, contact the nearest U.S. embassy or consulate for directions on applying by mail. Your travel agent or airline office may also be able to provide you with visa applications and instructions. The U.S. consulate or embassy that issues your visa will determine whether you will be issued a multiple- or single-entry visa and any restrictions regarding the length of your stay.

## Impressions

*Chicago ... perhaps the most typically American place in America.*
—James Bryce, *The American Commonwealth,* 1888

**MEDICAL REQUIREMENTS**   No inoculations are needed to enter the United States unless you are coming from, or have stopped over in, areas known to be suffering from epidemics, particularly cholera or yellow fever.

If you have a disease requiring treatment with medications containing narcotics or with drugs requiring a syringe, carry a valid signed prescription from your physician to allay any suspicions that you are smuggling drugs.

**CUSTOMS REQUIREMENTS**   Every adult visitor may bring in, free of duty: 1 liter of wine or hard liquor; 200 cigarettes or 100 cigars (but no cigars from Cuba) or 3 pounds of smoking tobacco; and $100 worth of gifts. These exemptions are offered to travelers who spend at least 72 hours in the United States and who have not claimed them within the preceding six months. It is altogether forbidden to bring into the country foodstuffs (particularly cheese, fruit, and meats) and plants (vegetables, seeds, tropical plants, and so on). Foreign tourists may bring in or take out up to $10,000 in U.S. or foreign currency with no formalities; larger sums must be declared to Customs upon entering or leaving.

## INSURANCE

Unlike most other countries, there is no national health system in the United States. Because the cost of medical care is extremely high, we strongly advise every traveler to secure health coverage before setting out.

You may want to take out a comprehensive travel policy that covers (for a relatively low premium) sickness or injury costs (medical, surgical, and hospital); loss or theft of your baggage; trip-cancellation costs; guarantee of bail in case you are arrested; and costs of accident, repatriation, or death. Such packages (for example, "Europe Assistance" in Europe) are sold by automobile clubs at attractive rates, as well as by insurance companies and travel agencies.

## MONEY

**CURRENCY & EXCHANGE**   The U.S. monetary system has a decimal base: one American dollar ($1) = 100 cents (100¢).

Dollar bills commonly come in $1 ("a buck"), $5, $10, $20, $50, and $100 denominations (the last two are not welcome when paying for small purchases and are not accepted in taxis or at subway ticket booths). There are also $2 bills (seldom encountered).

There are six denominations of coins: 1¢ (one cent or a penny), 5¢ (five cents or a nickel), 10¢ (ten cents or a dime), 25¢ (twenty-five cents or a quarter), 50¢ (fifty cents or a half dollar, seldom encountered), and the rare $1 piece.

The foreign-exchange bureaus so common in Europe are rare even at airports in the United States and nonexistent outside major cities. Try to avoid having to change foreign money, or traveler's checks denominated other than in U.S. dollars, at a small-town bank, or even a branch in a big city. In fact, leave any currency other than U.S. dollars at home—it may prove more nuisance to you than it's worth.

**TRAVELER'S CHECKS**   Traveler's checks denominated in U.S. dollars are readily accepted at most hotels, motels, restaurants, and large stores. But the best place to change traveler's checks is at a bank. Do not bring traveler's checks denominated in other currencies.

**CREDIT CARDS**   The method of payment most widely used is the credit card: Visa (BarclayCard in Britain), MasterCard (EuroCard in Europe, Access in Britain, Chargex in Canada), American Express, Diners Club, Discover, and Carte Blanche. You can save yourself trouble by using "plastic money" rather than cash or traveler's checks in most hotels, motels, restaurants, and retail stores (a growing number of food and liquor stores now accept credit cards). You must have a credit card to rent a car. It can also be used as proof of identity (often carrying more weight than a passport), or as a "cash card," enabling you to draw money from banks that accept them.

## SAFETY

**GENERAL**   While tourist areas are generally safe, crime is on the increase everywhere, and U.S. urban areas tend to be less safe than those in Europe or Japan. This is particularly true of large U.S. cities. Visitors should always stay alert. It is wise to ask the city's or area's tourist office if you're in doubt about which neighborhoods are safe. Avoid deserted areas, especially at night. Don't go into any city park at night unless there is an event that attracts crowds—a concert in the park or the like. Generally speaking, you can feel safe in areas where there are many people and many open establishments.

Avoid carrying valuables with you on the street, and don't display expensive cameras or electronic equipment. Hold on to your pocketbook, and place your billfold in an inside pocket. In theaters, restaurants, and other public places, keep your possessions in sight.

Remember also that hotels are open to the public, and in a large hotel, security may not be able to screen everyone entering. Always lock your room door—don't assume that once inside your hotel you are automatically safe and no longer need to be aware of your surroundings.

**DRIVING**   Safety while driving is particularly important. Question your rental agency about personal safety, or ask for a brochure of traveler's safety tips when you pick up your car. It's a good idea to ask the agency to show you on a map how to get to your destination.

Recently more and more crime has involved cars and drivers. If you drive off a highway into a doubtful neighborhood, leave the area as quickly as possible. If you have an accident, even on the highway, stay in your car with the doors locked until you assess the situation or until the police arrive. If you are bumped from behind on the street or are involved in a minor accident with no injuries and the situation appears to be suspicious, do not get out of your car. Go directly to the nearest police precinct, or to a well-lighted service station or all-night store to call the police (dial 911).

If you see someone on the road who indicates a need for help, do *not* stop. Take note of the location, drive on to a well-lighted area, and telephone the police by dialing 911.

Park in well-lighted, well-traveled areas if possible. Always keep your car doors locked, whether attended or unattended. Look around you before you get out of your car, and never leave any packages or valuables in sight. If someone attempts to rob you or steal your car, do *not* try to resist the thief/carjacker—report the incident to the police department immediately.

## 2 Getting to the U.S.

Travelers from overseas can take advantage of the APEX (Advance Purchase Excursion) fare offers by all the major U.S. and European carriers.

**British Airways** (☎ 800/247-9297 in the U.S. or 081/897-4000 in the U.K.) offers direct flights from London's Heathrow Airport to Chicago. Its fares range from U.S. $734 round-trip during the summer high season to U.S. $519 during the low-traffic winter months. **Virgin Atlantic** (☎ 800/862-8621 in the U.S. or 02/937-4774 in the U.K.) offers competitive (and frequently lower) fares from London's Gatwick Airport to Chicago.

Some of the other major international carriers that service Chicago are **Aer Lingus** (☎ 800/223-6537 in the U.S.), **Air Canada** (☎ 800/426-7000 in the U.S.), **Air France** (☎ 800/237-2747 in the U.S.), **Japan Air Lines** (☎ 800/565-7000 in the U.S.), **KLM** (☎ 800/777-5553 in the U.S.), **Lufthansa** (☎ 800/645-3880 in the U.S.), **Swissair** (☎ 800/221-6644 in the U.S.), and **Mexicana** (☎ 800/531-7921 in the U.S.).

Some large American airlines (for example, TWA, American, Northwest, United, and Delta) offer travelers on their transatlantic or transpacific flights special discount tickets under the name **Visit USA,** allowing travel between any U.S. destinations at minimum rates. They are not for sale in the United States, and must, therefore, be purchased before you leave your foreign point of departure. This system is the best, easiest, and fastest way to see the United States at low cost. You should obtain information well in advance from your travel agent or the office of the airline concerned, since the conditions attached to these discount tickets can be changed without advance notice.

The visitor arriving by air, no matter what the port of entry, should cultivate patience and resignation before setting foot on U.S. soil. Getting through immigration control may take as long as two hours on some days, especially summer weekends. Add the time it takes to clear Customs and you will see that you should make very generous allowances for delay in planning connections between international and domestic flights—an average of two to three hours at least.

In contrast, for the traveler arriving by car or by rail from Canada, the border-crossing formalities have been streamlined to the vanishing point. And for the traveler by air from Canada, Bermuda, and some places in the Caribbean, you can sometimes go through Customs and Immigration at the point of departure, which is much quicker and less painful.

For further information about travel to and arriving in Chicago, see "Getting There" in Chapter 2.

## 3 Getting Around the U.S.

Flying is the fastest, and most expensive, mode of domestic travel in the U.S. For a list of the major carriers that service Chicago from within the U.S., see "Getting There" in Chapter 2.

Travel **by car** is perhaps the best way to see the U.S. if you have the time to really wander. After all, the U.S. is an automobile culture, so the roads here are excellent. But the real adventure is off the interstates, and onto the "blue" highways, the secondary roads, along which the small towns of America are strung like beads on a wire.

International visitors can also buy a **USA Railpass,** good for 15 or 30 days of unlimited travel on Amtrak. The pass is available through many foreign travel agents.

Prices for a 15-day pass are $208 off-peak, $308 peak; a 30-day pass costs $309 off-peak, $389 peak. (With a foreign passport, you can also buy passes at some Amtrak offices in the U.S., including locations in San Francisco, Los Angeles, Chicago, New York, Miami, Boston, and Washington, D.C.) Reservations are generally required and should be made for each part of your trip as early as possible.

Visitors should also be aware of the limitations of long-distance rail travel in the U.S. With a few notable exceptions (for instance, the Northeast Corridor line between Boston and Washington, D.C.), service is rarely up to European standards: delays are common, routes are limited and often infrequently served, and fares are rarely significantly lower than discount airfares. Thus, cross-country train travel should be approached with caution.

The cheapest way to travel the U.S. is **by bus.** Greyhound, the nationwide bus line, offers an Ameripass for unlimited travel for 7 days (for $250), 15 days (for $350), and 30 days (for $450). However, bus travel in the U.S. can be both slow and uncomfortable, so this option is not for everyone.

While Chicago has an excellent public transportation system (see Chapter 4, "Getting Around"), local public transportation is sketchy or nonexistent except in a few of the larger U.S. cities.

## FAST FACTS: For the Foreign Traveler

**Automobile Organizations**    Auto clubs will supply maps, suggested routes, guidebooks, accident and bail-bond insurance, and emergency road service. The major auto club in the United States, with 955 offices nationwide, is the American Automobile Association (AAA). Members of some foreign auto clubs have reciprocal arrangements with AAA and enjoy its services at no charge. If you belong to an auto club, inquire about this before you leave. AAA can provide you with an International Driving Permit validating your foreign license. You may be able to join AAA even if you are not a member of a reciprocal club. To inquire, call 800/336-4357. In addition, some car-rental agencies now provide these services, so you should inquire about their availability when you rent your car.

**Automobile Rentals**    To rent a car you need a major credit card. A valid driver's license is required, and you usually need to be at least 25 years old. Some companies do rent to younger people but add a daily surcharge. Be sure to return your car with the same amount of gas you started out with; rental companies charge excessive prices for gasoline.

**Business Hours**    Banks are open weekdays from 9am to 3 or 4pm, although there's 24-hour access to the automatic tellers (ATMs) at most banks and other outlets. Generally, offices are open weekdays from 9am to 5pm. Stores are open six days a week, with many open on Sunday, too; department stores usually stay open until 9pm at least one day a week.

**Climate**    See "When to Go" in Chapter 2.

**Currency**    See "Money" in "Preparing for Your Trip," earlier in this chapter.

**Currency Exchange**    You will find currency exchange services in major airports with international service. Elsewhere, they may be quite difficult to come by. Thomas Cook Currency Services offers a wide variety of services: more than 100 currencies; commission-free traveler's checks, drafts, and wire transfers; check collections; and precious metal bars and coins. Rates are competitive and service is excellent. Call 800/582-4496 for information. Many hotels will exchange currency if you are a registered guest. (Also see "Money" earlier in this chapter.) If you need a foreign-exchange service, the Chicago consumer Yellow Pages lists names and numbers of foreign-exchange groups under the heading "Foreign Exchange Brokers." In the Loop, try World Money Exchange, Inc., 6 E. Randolph, Suite 204 (☎ 312/641-2151 or 800/441-9634).

**Drinking Laws**    The legal drinking age in Chicago (and everywhere in the U.S.) is 21. Depending on the nature of their license and the day of the week, bars may remain open until anywhere from 2 to 5am. It is a serious criminal offense to drink and drive.

**Electric Current**    The U.S. uses 110–120 volts, 60 cycles, compared with 220–240 volts, 50 cycles, used in most of Europe. Small appliances of non-American manufacture, such as hair dryers or shavers, will require both a 100-volt converter and a plug adapter with two flat parallel pins. Such converters may be hard to find in the United States; it's better to bring one along from home.

**Embassies and Consulates**    All embassies are located in the national capital, Washington, D.C.; some consulates are located in Chicago. Most nations have a mission to the United Nations in New York City.

Listed here are the embassies (all in Washington, D.C.) and the Chicago consulates of the major English-speaking countries. Travelers from other countries can get telephone numbers for their embassies and consulates by calling directory assistance in Washington, D.C. (☎ 202/555-1212).

The **Australian** embassy is at 1601 Massachusetts Ave. NW, Washington, DC 20036 (☎ 202/797-3000). There is no consulate in Chicago.

The **Canadian** embassy is at 501 Pennsylvania Ave. NW, Washington, DC 20001 (☎ 202/682-1740). The consulate in Chicago is located at 180 N. Stetson Ave., Suite 2400, Chicago, IL 60601 (☎ 312/616-1870).

The **Irish** embassy is at 2234 Massachusetts Ave. NW, Washington, DC 20008 (☎ 202/462-3939). The consulate in Chicago is located at 400 N. Michigan Ave., Room 911, Chicago, IL 60611 (☎ 312/337-1868).

The **New Zealand** embassy is at 37 Observatory Circle NW, Washington, DC 20008 (☎ 202/328-4800). The consulate in New York is at 780 Third Ave., Suite 1904, New York, NY 10017-2024 (☎ 212/832-4038). The consulate in Los Angeles is located at 10960 Wilshire Blvd., Suite 1530, Los Angeles, CA 90024 (☎ 213/477-8241). There is no consulate in Chicago.

The **British** embassy is at 3100 Massachusetts Ave. NW, Washington, DC 20008 (☎ 202/462-1340). The consulate in Chicago is located in the Wrigley Building, 400 N. Michigan Ave., Suite 1300, Chicago, IL 60611 (☎ 312/346-1810).

**Emergencies**    Call 911 for fire, police, and ambulance. If you encounter sickness, accident, or lost or stolen baggage, call Traveler's and Immigrant's Aid (☎ 312/629-4500), an organization that specializes in helping distressed travelers, whether American or foreign.

**Gasoline [Petrol]**    One U.S. gallon equals 3.75 liters, while 1.2 U.S. gallons equals one Imperial gallon. You'll notice there are several grades (and price levels) of gasoline available at most gas stations. And you'll also notice that their names change from company to company. The unleaded ones with the highest octane are the most expensive (most rental cars take the least expensive "regular" unleaded), and leaded gas is the least expensive. Only older cars can take leaded gas, so check if you're not sure.

**Holidays**    On the following national legal holidays, banks, government offices, post offices, and many stores, restaurants, and museums are closed: January 1 (New Year's Day); third Monday in January (Martin Luther King Day); third Monday in February (Presidents Day); last Monday in May (Memorial Day); July 4 (Independence Day); first Monday in September (Labor Day); second Monday in October (Columbus Day); November 11 (Veterans Day/Armistice Day); last Thursday in November (Thanksgiving Day); and December 25 (Christmas Day).

The Tuesday following the first Monday in November, Election Day, is a legal holiday in presidential-election years.

**Information**    Before British visitors leave home, they can obtain information on Chicago from the United States Travel and Tourism Administration, P.O. Box 1EN, London W1A 1EN (☎ 071/495-4466).

A multilingual information desk operates in Terminal 3 at O'Hare Airport (☎ 312/686-2304). The Chicago Office of Tourism distributes a "Chicago Welcomes" brochure in five languages—English, Spanish, French, German, and Japanese. A section of the excellent CTA (Chicago Transit Authority) map is written in Spanish.

**Languages**    The Chicago Tour Guides Institute, 101 N. Wacker, Suite CM 285, Chicago, IL 60606 (☎ 312/276-6683; fax 312/252-3729), organizes tours in many languages; some 24 different languages are listed on their brochure, including Tagalog.

Finally, many hotels have concierges who are multilingual.

**Legal Aid**    The foreign tourist, unless positively identified as a member of the Mafia or of a drug ring, will probably never become involved with the American legal system. If you are pulled over for a minor infraction (for example, of the highway code), never attempt to pay the fine directly to a police officer or you may wind up arrested on the much more serious charge of attempted bribery. Pay fines by mail, or directly into the hands of the clerk of the court. If accused of a more serious offense, it's wise to say and do nothing before consulting a lawyer. Under U.S. law, an arrested person is allowed one telephone call to a party of his or her choice. Call your embassy or consulate.

**Mail**    If you want your mail to follow you on your vacation and you aren't sure of your address, your mail can be sent to you, in your name, c/o General Delivery at the main post office of the city or region where you expect to be. The addressee must pick it up in person and produce proof of identity (driver's license, credit card, passport, etc.). Chicago's main post office is at 433 W. Van Buren.

Generally to be found at intersections, mailboxes are blue with a red-and-white stripe and carry the inscription U.S. MAIL. If your mail is addressed to a U.S. destination, don't forget to add the five-figure postal code, or ZIP (Zone Improvement Plan) Code, after the two-letter abbreviation of the state to which the mail is addressed (CA for California, FL for Florida, IL for Illinois, NY for New York, and so on).

**Medical Emergencies**    If you become ill, consult your hotel concierge or desk staff for a physician recommendation. The best hospital emergency room in Chicago is, by consensus, Northwestern Memorial Hospital, right off North Michigan Avenue at 233 E. Superior (☎ 312/908-2000). For an ambulance, dial 911.

**Newspapers/Magazines**    National newspapers include the *New York Times, USA Today,* and the *Wall Street Journal.* National news weeklies include *Newsweek, Time,* and *U.S. News & World Report.* The two daily Chicago papers are the *Chicago Tribune* and the *Chicago Sun-Times.*

**Radio and Television**   Audiovisual media, with four coast-to-coast networks—ABC, CBS, NBC, and Fox—along with the Public Broadcasting System (PBS) and the cable network CNN, play a major part in American life. In big cities, televiewers have a choice of about a dozen channels (including the UHF channels), most of them transmitting 24 hours a day, without counting the pay-TV channels showing recent movies or sports events. All options are usually indicated on your hotel TV set. You'll also find a wide choice of local radio stations, each broadcasting particular kinds of talk shows and/or music—classical, country, jazz, pop, gospel—punctuated by news broadcasts and frequent commercials.

**Safety**   See "Safety" in "Preparing for Your Trip," above.

**Taxes**   In the United States there is no VAT (Value-Added Tax) or other indirect tax at a national level. Every state, and each city in it, has the right to levy its own local tax on all purchases, including hotel and restaurant checks, airline tickets, and so on. Chicago sales tax is 8.75%.

**Telephone, Telegraph, Telex**   The telephone system in the U.S. is run by private corporations, so rates, especially for long-distance service, can vary widely—even on calls made from public telephones. Local calls in the U.S. usually cost 25¢ when made from public phones.

Generally, hotel surcharges on long-distance and local calls are astronomical. You are usually better off using a public pay telephone, which you will find clearly marked in most public buildings and private establishments as well as on the street. Outside metropolitan areas, public telephones are more difficult to find. Stores and gas stations are your best bet.

Most long-distance and international calls can be dialed directly from any phone. For calls to Canada and other parts of the U.S., dial 1 followed by the area code and the seven-digit number. For international calls, dial 011 followed by the country code, city code, and the telephone number of the person you wish to call.

For reversed-charge or collect calls, and for person-to-person calls, dial 0 (zero, *not* the letter *O*) followed by the area code and number you want; an operator will then come on the line, and you should specify that you are calling collect, or person-to-person, or both. If your operator-assisted call is international, ask for the overseas operator.

For local directory assistance ("information"), dial 411; for long-distance information, dial 1, then the appropriate area code and 555-1212.

Like the telephone system, telegraph and telex services are provided by private corporations like ITT, MCI, and above all, Western Union. You can bring your telegram to the nearest Western Union office (there are hundreds across the country), or dictate it over the phone (☎ 800/325-6000). You can also telegraph money, or have it telegraphed to you, very quickly over the Western Union system.

**Telephone Directory**   There are two kinds of telephone directories available to you. The general directory is the so-called White Pages, in which private and business subscribers are listed. The inside front cover lists the emergency number for police, fire, ambulance, and other vital numbers (like the Coast Guard, poison-control center, crime-victims hotline, and so on). The first few pages are devoted to community-service numbers, including a guide to long-distance and international calling, complete with country codes and area codes.

The second directory, printed on yellow paper (hence its name, Yellow Pages), lists all local services, businesses, and industries by type of activity, with an index at the back. The listings cover not only such obvious items as automobile repairs by make of car, or drugstores (pharmacies), often by geographical location, but also restaurants by type of cuisine and geographical location, bookstores by special subject and/or language, places of worship by religious denomination, and other information that the tourist might otherwise not readily find. The Yellow Pages also include city plans or detailed area maps, often showing postal ZIP Codes and public transportation routes.

**Time**  The United States is divided into four time zones (six, if Alaska and Hawaii are included). From east to west, these are: eastern standard time (EST), central standard time (CST), mountain standard time (MST), Pacific standard time (PST), Alaska standard time (AST), and Hawaii standard time (HST). Always keep time zones in mind if you are traveling (or even telephoning) long distances in the United States. For example, noon in New York City (EST) is 11am in Chicago (CST), 10am in Denver (MST), 9am in Los Angeles (PST), 8am in Anchorage (AST), and 7am in Honolulu (HST).

Chicago is on central standard time. Daylight saving time is in effect from the last Sunday in April through the last Saturday in October (actually, the change is made at 2am on Sunday) except in Arizona, Hawaii, part of Indiana, and Puerto Rico. Daylight saving time moves the clock one hour ahead of standard time.

**Tipping**  The standard rates for tipping are 15% (before tax) to waiters for a well-served meal; 15% of the fare for a cab ride; $1 to the bellhop for carrying one bag ($1 per additional bag and a minimum of $3 in the first-class hotels); and a couple of dollars for maid service when you check out.

**Toilets**  Often euphemistically referred to as "restrooms," public toilets are non-existent on the streets of Chicago. They can be found, though, in bars, restaurants, hotel lobbies, museums, department stores, and service stations—and will probably be clean (although ones in the last-mentioned sometimes leave much to be desired). Note, however, that some restaurants and bars display a notice that "Toilets are for use of patrons only." You can ignore this sign, or better yet, avoid arguments by paying for a cup of coffee or soft drink, which will qualify you as a patron. The cleanliness of toilets at railroad stations and bus depots may be questionable; some public places are equipped with pay toilets that require you to insert one or two dimes (10¢) or a quarter (25¢) into a slot on the door before it will open. In restrooms with attendants, leaving at least a 25¢ tip is customary.

# 4 Getting to Know Chicago

The orderly configuration of Chicago's streets and the excellent system of public transportation make this city more accessible than most of the world's other large cities. This chapter provides an overview of the city's design, as well as some suggestions for how to maneuver within it. The chapter also lists some resources that travelers frequently require, from quick-service eyeglass repair to an all-night pharmacy.

## 1 Orientation

### VISITOR INFORMATION

The Chicago Office of Tourism staffs a **visitor information desk,** located in the old Water Tower, Michigan and Chicago Avenues, at the corner of North Michigan Avenue (☎ 312/280-5740 or 800/2CONNECT, or TDD 312/744-2947, or on the World Wide Web at http://www.ci.chi.il.us.). Its hours are Monday through Friday from 9:30am to 6pm, Saturday from 10am to 6pm, and Sunday from 11am to 5pm. Among its amenities are clean restrooms, a bank of pay telephones in a quiet corner, and a ton of pamphlets, including a *Loop Sculpture Guide* walking tour and a quarterly calendar of events listing festivals and other special events. Another tourism office visitors center is in the Chicago Cultural Center, 78 E. Washington (☎ 312/744-2400). Located in the Loop, convenient to many places you'll likely be visiting, the center is open Monday through Friday from 10am to 6pm, Saturday from 10am to 5pm, and Sunday from noon to 5pm. Closed holidays.

The **Illinois Bureau of Tourism,** 310 S. Michigan Ave. (☎ 800/2CONNECT or TDD 800/406-6418), operates a drop-in center convenient to anyone wandering or lodged within the Loop. Additionally, the bureau staffs an information booth in the State of Illinois Center, 100 W. Randolph St. (☎ 800/223-0121 for an information packet, or 800/822-0292 to speak directly with a vacation counselor), in the Helmut Jahn building at LaSalle Street in the Loop. The tourism bureau can provide general and specific information covering the entire state of Illinois. Other state-run information centers are in the Sears Tower (entrance on South Wacker Drive between Jackson and Adams) and at O'Hare and Midway Airports. The information centers are open weekdays from 8:30am to

5pm (except the information booth in the State of Illinois Center, which opens at 9am).

Local merchants along the State Street Mall (on State Street in the Loop, closed to auto traffic) staff an information center at the corner of State Street and Madison Avenue, open Monday through Saturday from 9am to 5pm.

**INFORMATION BY TELEPHONE**   The Events Hotline (☎ 312/744-3370) is a recorded hotline listing current special events occurring throughout the city.

The city of Chicago maintains a 24-hour information line for the hearing impaired who have TDD equipment. Call 312/744-8599.

The Chicago Architecture Foundation maintains a telephone line for information on the group's numerous tour offerings (☎ 312/922-TOUR).

**PUBLICATIONS**   Chicago's major daily newspapers are the *Tribune* and the *Sun-Times.* Both have daily cultural listings including movies, theaters, and live music, not to mention reviews of the latest crop of restaurants that are sure to have appeared in the city since this guidebook went to press. The Friday edition of the *Tribune* contains a special "Weekend" section with more detailed, up-to-date information on special events happening on Saturday and Sunday.

In a class by itself is the *Chicago Reader,* a free weekly that is an invaluable source of entertainment listings, classifieds, and well-written articles on contemporary issues of interest in Chicago. Published after 1pm every Thursday (except the last week of December), the weekly has a wide distribution downtown and on the North Side, and is available in many retail stores, building lobbies, and at the paper's offices, 11 E. Illinois St. (☎ 828-0350).

Most Chicago hotels stock their rooms with at least one informational magazine, such as *Where? Chicago,* that lists the city's entertainment, shopping, and dining locales.

## CITY LAYOUT

The Chicago River forms a Y that divides the city into its three geographic zones— North Side, South Side, and West Side (Lake Michigan is where the East Side would be). The downtown financial district is called the Loop.

The city's key shopping street is North Michigan Avenue, also known as the Magnificent Mile. In addition to department stores and vertical malls, this stretch of property north of the river houses many of the city's most elegant hotels. North and south of this downtown zone, Chicago stretches out along 29 miles of Lake Michigan shorefront that is, by and large, free of commercial development, reserved for public use as green space and parkland from one end of town to the other. Chicago proper today has about three million inhabitants living in an area about two-thirds the size of New York City; another four million make the suburbs their home. But the real trademark of Chicago is found between the suburbs and the Loop, where scores of residential neighborhoods give the city a character all its own.

**FINDING AN ADDRESS**   Having been a part of the Northwest Territory, Chicago is laid out in a grid system, with the streets neatly lined up as if on a giant piece of graph paper. Since the city itself isn't rectangular (it's rather elongated), the shape is a bit irregular, but the perpendicular patterns remain. Easing movement through the city are a half dozen or so major diagonal thoroughfares.

One thing that may seem goofy to visitors is that, while the city is divided into four geographical sections, the street numbering does not originate at the city's geographical midpoint. Instead, point zero is nearer to Chicago's historic and

*This is the greatest and most typically American of all cities. New York is bigger and more spectacular and can outmatch it in other superlatives, but it is a "world" city, more European in some respects than American. Chicago ... gives above all the sense that America and the Middle West are beating upon it from all sides.*

—John Gunther, *Inside U.S.A.,* 1947

*Chicago is as full of crooks as a saw with teeth.*

—Ibid.

commercial center, more north than south, and so far east as almost to border Lake Michigan. Point zero is located at the downtown intersection of State and Madison Streets. State divides east and west addresses, and Madison divides north and south addresses. From here, Chicago's highly predictable addressing system begins. Making use of this grid, it is relatively easy to plot the distance in miles between any two points in the city.

Virtually all of Chicago's principal north–south and east–west arteries are spaced by increments of 400 in the addressing system—regardless of the number of smaller streets nestled between them. And each addition or subtraction of 400 numbers to an address is equivalent to a half mile. Thus, starting at point zero on Madison Street, and traveling north along State Street for one mile, you will come to 800 N. State, which intersects Chicago Avenue. Continue uptown for another half mile and you arrive at the 1200 block of North State at Division Street. And so it goes right to the city line, with suburban Evanston located at the 7600 block north, 9 1/2 miles from point zero.

The same rule applies when traveling south, or east to west. Thus, heading west from State Street along Madison, Halsted Street—at 800 W. Madison—is a mile's distance, while Racine, at the 1200 block of West Madison, is 1 1/2 miles from the center. Madison then continues westward to Chicago's boundary along Austin Avenue, with the near suburb of Oak Park, which at 6000 W. Madison is approximately 7 1/2 miles from point zero.

The key to understanding the grid is that the side of any square formed by the principal avenues (noted in dark or red ink on most maps) represents a distance of half a mile in any direction. Understanding how Chicago's grid system works is of particular importance to those visitors who wish to do a lot of walking in the city's many neighborhoods and who want to plot in advance the distances involved in trekking from one locale to another.

The other ingeniously convenient aspect to the grid is that every major road uses the same numerical system. In other words, the cross street at 1200 N. Lake Shore Dr. is the same as at 1200 N. Clark St., is the same as at 1200 N. LaSalle St., etc. (Division Street).

**STREET MAPS**   A suitably detailed map of Chicago is published by Rand McNally, available at most newstands for $2.95.

## NEIGHBORHOODS IN BRIEF

**The Loop & Vicinity**   "Downtown," in the case of Chicago, means the Loop. The Loop refers literally to a core of primarily commercial, governmental, and cultural buildings contained within a corral of elevated subway tracks, but greater downtown Chicago overflows these confines and is bounded by the Chicago River to the north and west, by Michigan Avenue to the east, and by Roosevelt Avenue to the south.

# Central Chicago Neighborhoods

## NORTH SIDE NEIGHBORHOODS

**Magnificent Mile**    North Michigan Avenue is known as the Magnificent Mile, from the bridge to its northern tip at Oak Street. Here Chicago is at its most elegant. On and around North Michigan, many of the city's best hotels, shops, and restaurants are to be found.

**River North**    Adjacent to the Mag Mile's zone of high life and sophistication on the west is an old warehouse district called River North, increasingly gentrified and filled with great eateries, nightspots, and art galleries.

**The Gold Coast**    Some of Chicago's most desirable real estate and historic architecture run along Lake Shore Drive and its adjacent side streets of the Gold Coast. Despite trendy little pockets of real estate popping up elsewhere, the monied class still prefers to live by the lake.

**Old Town**    West of Dearborn, principally on North Wells between Division and North Avenue, is the nightlife district of Old Town, where many comedy clubs, such as Second City, have served up the lighter side of life to Chicagoans for more than a generation.

**Lincoln Park**    This fashionable residential neighborhood is north of North Avenue and bordered on the east by the huge park of the same name as far north as Diversey. The triangle formed by Lincoln Avenue, Halsted Street, and Armitage, where many of Chicago's in-spot bars and restaurants are located, is explored in detail in Chapter 8.

**New Town and Lakeview**    Midway up the city's North Side is the semigentrified/ bohemian quarter called New Town, which has become the neighborhood of preference for many gays and lesbians, artists, and urban homesteaders. The main thoroughfare is Belmont, between Broadway and Sheffield. Lakeview designates the onetime blue-collar neighborhood in the vicinity of Wrigley Field—home of the Chicago Cubs—at Sheffield and Addison (the area is also referred to as Wrigleyville). Many homesteaders have moved into this area in recent years, and a slew of nightclubs and restaurants have followed in their wake.

**Uptown and Andersonville**    Uptown, along the lake and about as far north as Foster, is where the latest wave of immigrants—including internal migrants from Appalachia and the Native American reservations—has settled. The "New Chinatown" is here, around Broadway and Argyle. Slightly to the north and west is the old Scandinavian neighborhood of Andersonville, whose main drag is Clark Street, between Foster and Bryn Mawr.

**Lincoln Square**    West of Andersonville, and slightly to the south, where Lincoln, Western, and Lawrence Avenues intersect, is Lincoln Square, the only identifiable remains of Chicago's once vast German-American community. The neighborhood hosts a big outdoor party on German-American Day in the fall. Lincoln Square now also has a distinctly Greek flavor, with several restaurants of that nationality to boot.

**Rogers Park**    Devon Avenue, on the northern fringes of the city bordering suburban Evanston, begins Rogers Park. It has been a Jewish neighborhood for decades, and now Asians, East Indians, and Russians live among the Orthodox Jews. The food options range from bagels and lox to tandoori.

## THE WEST SIDE

**Near West**    On the Near West Side, just across the Chicago River from the Loop, on Halsted between Adams and Monroe, is Chicago's old "Greek Town," and still

**Impressions**

*Chicago is stupefying . . . an Olympian freak, a fable, an allegory, an incomprehensible phenomenon . . . monstrous, multifarious, unnatural, indomitable, puissant, preposterous, transcendent . . . throw the dictionary at it!*
—Julian Street, *Abroad at Home*, 1914

the Greek culinary center of the city. Much of the old Italian neighborhood in this vicinity was the victim of urban renewal, but remnants still survive on Taylor Street; the same is true for a few old delis and shops on Maxwell Street, dating from the turn of the century when a large Jewish community lived in the area.

**Milwaukee Avenue Corridor**   A rich variety of neighborhoods can be found stretched along Milwaukee Avenue from Racine to Diversey. The Bucktown/Wicker Park area is one of Chicago's hot spots of upward mobility and cultural development. Mexican/Central American enclaves fall between Western and California, and a Polish neighborhood, with several traditional restaurants, exists around Logan Square.

### THE SOUTH SIDE

**Pilsen**   This old Bohemian neighborhood, centered at Halsted and 18th Street, is now an artists' colony within a wider community that is largely Chicano. Visit by day only.

**Bridgeport and Canaryville**   Bridgeport, whose main crossroads is 35th and Halsted, is Mayor Daley's old neighborhood. After Comiskey Park was torn down, the Chicago White Sox stayed in Bridgeport, recently inaugurating their new stadium there. Nearby Canaryville, just south and west, is typical of the "back of the yard" blue-collar neighborhoods that once surrounded the Chicago Stockyards. Neither area offers much to the typical visitor; "outsiders," in fact, aren't all that welcome.

**Hyde Park**   Hyde Park is like an independent village within the confines of Chicago, right off Lake Michigan, and roughly a 30-minute subway ride from the Loop. Fifty-seventh Street is the main drag, and the University of Chicago—with all its attendant shops and restaurants—is the neighborhood's principal tenant. Hyde Park's main attraction, however, is the world-famous Museum of Science and Industry.

**Pullman**   Pullman is the historic district on Chicago's Southeast Side, site of the former planned community—now preserved as a living museum—of the Pullman Palace Car Company.

## 2 Getting Around

The best way to savor Chicago (or any city) is by walking its streets. I realize, however, that walking is not always practical, particularly when moving between distant neighborhoods. In those situations, Chicago's public train and bus systems are efficient modes of transportation.

### BY PUBLIC TRANSPORTATION

The Chicago Transit Authority (CTA) operates an extensive system of trains and buses throughout the city of Chicago. The sturdy system carries more than two million passengers a day. Subways and elevated trains (known as the El) are generally safe and reliable, though it's advisable to avoid long rides through unfamiliar neighborhoods late at night.

# Chicago Transit System

## Lake Street/ Dan Ryan Route

### LAKE STREET

- [AB] Harlem
- [AB] Oak Park
- [AB] Ridgeland
- [AB] Austin
- [AB] Central
- [AB] Laramie
- [AB] Cicero
- [AB] Pulaski
- [B] Homan
- [A] Kedzie
- [A] Ashland
- [B] Halsted
- [AB] Clinton
  (see Downtown Stations map)
- [B] Cermak/Chinatown
- [AB] Sox/35th St.
- [A] 47th St.
- [B] Garfield
- [A] 63rd St.
- [AB] 69th St.
- [AB] 79th St.
- [AB] 87th St.
- [AB] 95th St.

### DAN RYAN

## O'Hare/Congress/ Douglas Route

### O'HARE

- [AB] O'Hare
- [AB] River Road
- [AB] Cumberland
- [AB] Harlem
- [AB] Jefferson Park
- [A] Montrose
- [AB] Irving Park
- [B] Addison
- [AB] Belmont
- [AB] Logan Square
- [A] California
- [B] Western
- [AB] Damen
- [AB] Division
- [AB] Chicago
- [B] Grand
  (see Downtown Stations map)
- [AB] Clinton
- [AB] Halsted/U of I
- [AB] Racine

### LEGEND:

- [A] A Train stop
- [B] B Train stop
- [AB] A & B Trains stop

### Polk [B]    18th St. [B]

| CONGRESS | DOUGLAS |
|---|---|
| [A] Medical Center | [B] Hoyne |
| [A] Western | [B] Western |
| [A] Kedzie/Homan | [B] California |
| [A] Pulaski | [B] Kedzie |
| [A] Cicero | [B] Central Park |
| [A] Austin | [B] Pulaski |
| [A] Oak Park | [B] Kildare |
| [A] Harlem | [B] Cicero |
| [A] DesPlaines | [B] 54/Cermak |

1-0435

**To EVANSTON**

**To SKOKIE**

**Howard/Englewood/
Jackson Park Route**

**HOWARD** [AB]

**Jarvis** [A]

**Morse** [AB]

**Loyola** [AB]

**Granville** [B]

**Thorndale** [A]

**Bryn Mawr** [AB]

**Berwyn** [B]

**Argyle** [A]

**Lawrence** [B]

**Wilson** [AB]

**Sheridan** [A]

**Addison** [B]

**Belmont** [AB]

**Fullerton** [AB]

**North/Clybourn** [A]

**Clark/Division** [AB]

**Chicago** [AB]

**Grand** [AB]

(see Downtown Stations map)

**Roosevelt** [AB]

**Tech/35th St.** [AB]

**Indiana** [A]

**43rd St.** [AB]

**47th St.** [AB]

**51st St.** [AB]

**Garfield** [AB]

**58th St.** [A]

**To ENGLEWOOD**

**To JACKSON PARK**

## LEGEND:

[A]  A Train stop

[B]  B Train stop

[AB]  A & B Trains stop

### Ravenswood Route

**Kimball** [AB]

**Kedzie** [AB]

**Francisco** [A]

**Rockwell** [B]

**Western** [AB]

**Damen** [A]

**Montrose** [B]

**Irving Park** [AB]

**Addison** [A]

**Paulina** [A]

**Southport** [B]

**Belmont** [AB]

**Wellington** [A]

**Diversey** [AB]

**Fullerton** [AB]

**Armitage** [AB]

**Sedgwick** [B]

**Chicago** [AB]

(see Downtown
Stations map)

1-0436

# Downtown Stations

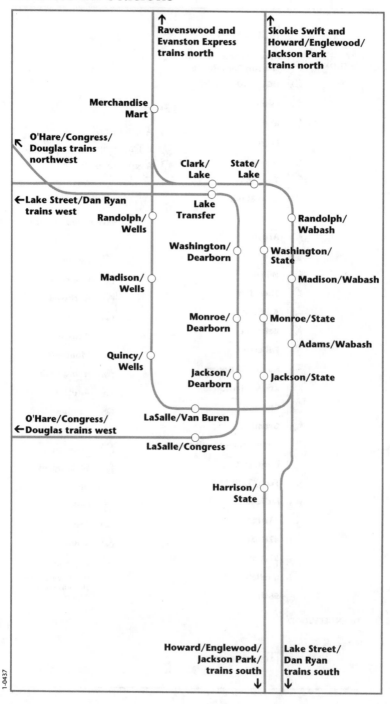

↑ Ravenswood and Evanston Express trains north

↑ Skokie Swift and Howard/Englewood/Jackson Park trains north

Merchandise Mart

↖ O'Hare/Congress/Douglas trains northwest

Clark/Lake

State/Lake

← Lake Street/Dan Ryan trains west

Lake Transfer

Randolph/Wells

Randolph/Wabash

Washington/Dearborn

Washington/State

Madison/Wells

Madison/Wabash

Monroe/Dearborn

Monroe/State

Adams/Wabash

Quincy/Wells

Jackson/Dearborn

Jackson/State

O'Hare/Congress/
← Douglas trains west

LaSalle/Van Buren

LaSalle/Congress

Harrison/State

Howard/Englewood/Jackson Park/trains south ↓

Lake Street/Dan Ryan trains south ↓

1-0437

40

Fares are $1.50, with an additional 30¢ for a transfer that must be used within two hours of receipt. A package of 10 tokens may be purchased for $12.50 at Jewel and Dominick supermarkets and at some token booths; tokens are accepted for both the El and buses. Children under 7 ride for free, while those between the ages of 7 and 11 pay 90¢ (15¢ for transfers), as do senior citizens over 65 (☎ 312/814-0700 to obtain appropriate ID).

Buses are equipped with machinery that accepts $1 bills. Fares are $1.50, 25¢ for a transfer. Seniors pay 75¢, 10¢ for a transfer, and can buy a pack of 20 tokens for $12.

**CTA INFORMATION**   The CTA operates a useful telephone information service (☎ 312/836-7000) that functions daily from 4:45am to 1am. When you want to know how to get from where you are to where you want to go, call the CTA. Make sure you specify any conditions you might require—the fastest route, for example, or the simplest (the route with the fewest transfers or least amount of walking), and so forth.

An excellent CTA map is available at subway or El fare booths, or by calling 312/ 836-7000.

**BY THE EL & THE SUBWAY**   The rapid transit system operates four major lines, north–south, west–south, west–northwest (the O'Hare train), and a zigzag northern route called the Ravenswood line. A separate express line services Evanston, while a smaller, local line in Skokie is linked to the north–south train. Skokie and Evanston are adjacent suburbs on Chicago's northern boundary.

Study your CTA map carefully before boarding any train. During the working day (6am to 7pm) A and B trains on all lines make alternate stops. Major stations, however, including all downtown stations (except State/Harrison), are combined AB stops throughout the day. While most trains run around the clock, decreasing in frequency in the off-peak and overnight hours, some stations close after work hours (as early as 8:30pm) and remain closed on Saturday, Sunday, and holidays. Other stops remain open on weekends and holidays despite the fact that their fare booths are closed. Simply climb to the platform and board the train; a conductor will collect your fare and provide necessary transfers on the train itself. Please note that you may not use your transfer on the line where you first obtained it.

**BY BUS**   Add to Chicago's gridlike layout a comprehensive system of public buses, and there is virtually no place in the city that isn't within close walking distance of a bus stop. Other than on foot or bicycle, the best way to get around Chicago's warren of neighborhoods—the best way to actually see what's around you—is while riding a public bus. (The view from the elevated trains can be pretty dramatic too; the difference is that on the trains you get the backyards, while on the bus you see the buildings' facades and the street life.) A couple of buses that are particulary handy for many visitors are the No. 151 Sheridan, which passes through Lincoln Park onto North Lake Shore Drive and then along Michigan Avenue as far south as Adams Street, where it turns west into the Loop, and the No. 156 LaSalle, which goes through Lincoln Park and then down the Loop's main drag of LaSalle Street.

PACE buses (☎ 312/836-7000) service the suburban zones that surround Chicago. They run every 20 to 30 minutes during rush hour, operating until midevening Monday through Friday, and early evening on weekends. Suburban bus routes are marked nos. 208 and above, and vehicles may be flagged down at intersections since few of the lines have bus stops that are marked.

**BY TRAIN** The Metra commuter railroad (☎ 312/322-6777 Monday through Friday from 8am to 5pm; at other times call RTA at 312/836-7000), which services the suburban zones that surround Chicago, has terminals at several downtown locations, including Union Station at Adams and Canal, LaSalle Street Station at LaSalle and Van Buren, Northwestern Station at Madison and Canal, and Randolph Street Station at Randolph and Michigan. To visit some of the most affluent suburbs in the country, take the Northwestern train and select from among the following destinations: Kenilworth, Winnetka, Glencoe, Highland Park, and Lake Forest. The Illinois Central–Gulf Railroad, known locally as the IC, runs close to Lake Michigan on track that occupies some of the most valuable real estate in Chicago. It will take you to Hyde Park and Pullman, both of which are described in this guidebook. Commuter trains have graduated fare schedules based on the distance you ride.

## BY TAXI

Taxis are very affordable for getting around Chicago on short runs—moving around the downtown area, for example—or for excursions to Near North Side neighborhoods, such as Old Town or Lincoln Park, or to the Near West Side's Greektown, for example. But for longer distances, the fares will really add up. Taxis are easy to hail in the Loop, on the Magnificent Mile and the Gold Coast, in River North, and in Lincoln Park, but if you go much beyond these key areas, you may need to call.

At this writing, the flag drops at $1.50 in Chicago cabs, increasing by $1.20 for each added mile, with a 50¢ surcharge for each additional rider age 12 to 65.

Some cab companies are American (☎ 312/248-7600), Flash (☎ 312/561-1444), and Yellow/Checker (☎ 312/829-4222 or 312/TAXI-CAB). *Note:* Unlike New York, where all taxis are painted yellow, Chicago's taxis can come in several colors and still be legitimately licensed.

## BY CAR

Chicago is spread out so logically that even for a visitor, driving around the city is relatively easy. Rush-hour traffic jams are not as daunting as in many other U.S. cities. Traffic runs fairly smoothly at most times of the day. The combination of wide streets and strategically spaced expressways makes for generally easy riding (although construction on the Dan Ryan over the past several years is said to have slowed things down a bit on that particular roadway, with no end in sight).

The great diagonal corridors violate the grid pattern at key points in the city, and shorten many a trip that would otherwise be tedious on the checkerboard surface of the Chicago streets. Lake Shore Drive (also known as the Outer Drive) has to be one of the most scenic and useful urban thoroughfares to be found anywhere. You can travel the length of the city (and beyond), never far from the great lake that is Chicago's most awesome natural feature.

**RENTALS** **Hertz** (☎ 800/654-3131) has an office downtown at 9 W. Kinzie (☎ 312/372-7600); at O'Hare Airport (☎ 312/686-7272); and at Midway Airport (☎ 773/735-7272). **Avis** (☎ 800/831-2847) has an office downtown at 214 N. Clark (☎ 312/782-6825); at O'Hare Airport (☎ 312/694-5600); and at Midway Airport (☎ 773/471-4495). **National** (☎ 800/227-7368) has an office downtown at 203 N. LaSalle (☎ 312/236-2581); at O'Hare Airport (☎ 312/694-4640); and at Midway Airport (☎ 773/471-3450). **Budget** (☎ 800/527-0700) has an office downtown at 1025 N. Clark (☎ 708/968-6661 for reservations); at O'Hare Airport (☎ 312/686-6800); and at Midway Airport (☎ 773/686-6780).

**DRIVING RULES** One bizarre anomaly in the organization of Chicago's traffic is the occasional absence of signal lights off the principal avenues. Thus, a block east or west of the Magnificent Mile (North Michigan Avenue)—one of the most traveled streets in the city—you will in some cases encounter only stop signs to control the flow of traffic. Once you've become accustomed to the system, it works very smoothly, with everyone—pedestrians and motorists alike—advancing in their proper turn. Unless otherwise posted, a right turn on red is allowed after stopping and signaling.

**PARKING**   Parking regulations are vigorously enforced throughout the city. Beware of tow zones, and, if visiting in winter, make note of curbside warnings regarding snow plowing. If you can't find a spot, a public garage is usually nearby, but you may have to pay the premium prices common in any metropolitan area. (Several garages connected with malls or other major attractions offer discounted parking with a validated ticket.)

Some convenient public parking lots are available at the following locations: Grant Park Parking, Michigan Avenue at Congress, and Michigan at Monroe (☎ 312/294-2437); MAP Parking, 350 N. Orleans (☎ 312/986-6822); McCormick Place Parking, 2301 S. Lake Shore Dr. (☎ 312/294-4600); Midcontinental Plaza Garage, 55 E. Monroe (☎ 312/986-6821); and Navy Pier Parking, 601 E. Grand (☎ 312/791-7437).

## BY BOAT

A shuttle boat operates daily from April through October between a dock adjacent to the Michigan Avenue bridge and Northwestern Station, a commuter train station across the river from the Loop. The ride, which costs $1.25 each way and takes about 10 minutes, is popular with both visitors and commuters. The service operates in the morning from 7:45 to 8:45am from the station, and in the afternoon from 4:45 to 5:27pm from the bridge.

## BY BICYCLE

**Turin Bicycle Shop,** 435 E. Illinois (☎ 312/923-0100), conveniently located at North Pier, offers 21-speed mountain bikes at a rate of $10 per hour, $40 maximum for the day. Renters must leave a $350 deposit on their Visa, MasterCard, or Discover cards; helmets and locks are provided at no additional charge. Open Monday through Thursday from 10am to 9pm, Friday and Saturday from 10am to 10pm, and Sunday from noon to 6pm.

**Bike Chicago** (☎ 800-915-BIKE) has six locations: Oak Street Beach, Buckingham Fountain in Grant Park, Navy Pier, Irving Park at the lake, North Avenue at the lake, and Fullerton and Cannon Drive in Lincoln Park. The company rents all sorts of bikes, including tandems and kids' sizes, for $8 an hour, or $30 a day, and offers free downtown delivery for daily rentals. Bike Chicago also rents in-line skates.

## FAST FACTS: Chicago

**American Express**   Travel service offices are located at the following locations: 34 N. Clark (☎ 312/263-6617); 122 S. Michigan (☎ 312/435-2595); 230 S. Clark (☎ 312/629-0685); and 625 N. Michigan (☎ 312/435-2570). All are open Monday through Friday from 9am to 5pm, and the office at 625 N. Michigan is also open on Saturday from 10am to 3pm.

**Area Codes**   As of press time, the phone company was still in the process of changing the city's area code system. The 312 long held by the whole city proper now applies to the Loop and the neighborhoods closest to it, including River North, North Michigan Avenue and the Gold Coast. The rest of the city now has 773 for an area code. We have tried to list the most up-to-date numbers, and we regret any errors. A toll-free number, ☎ 800/988-5888, provides the correct area codes both for the city and the suburbs, which also underwent changes.

**Babysitters**  Check with the concierge or desk staff at your hotel, who are likely to maintain a list of reliable sitters with whom they have worked in the past.

**Business Hours**  Shops generally keep normal business hours, opening around 10am and closing by 6pm Monday through Saturday. These days, however, most stores generally stay open late at least one evening a week. And certain businesses, such as bookstores, are almost always open during the evening hours all week long. Most shops (other than in the Loop) are now open on Sunday as well, usually from noon to 5pm. Malls, including Water Tower Place at 835 N. Michigan Ave., are generally open until 8pm, and are open Sunday as well.

Banking hours in Chicago are normally from 9am (8am in some cases) to 3pm Monday through Friday, with select banks remaining open later on specified afternoons and evenings.

**Camera Repair**  Central Camera, 232 S. Wabash (☎ 427-5580), has been a Chicago institution since 1899.

**Car Rentals**  See "Getting Around" in this chapter.

**Currency Exchange**  The Chicago consumer Yellow Pages list the names and numbers of groups offering this service under the heading "Foreign Exchange Brokers." In the Loop, try the World Money Exchange, Inc., 6 E. Randolph, Suite 204 (☎ 312/641-2151 or 800/441-9634).

**Dentists**  Chicago's Dental Emergency Service number is 312/836-7300; this service can refer you to an area dentist. You might also try your hotel concierge or desk staff, who often keep a list of dentists.

**Doctors**  In the event of a medical emergency, your best bet—unless you have friends who can recommend a doctor—is to rely on your hotel physician or go to the nearest hospital emergency room.

**Driving Rules**  See "Getting Around" in this chapter.

**Embassies and Consulates**  See Chapter 3.

**Emergencies**  The city of Chicago proclaims the following policy: "In emergency dial 911 and a city ambulance will respond free of charge to the patient. The ambulance will take the patient to the nearest emergency room according to geographic location." If you desire a specific, nonpublic ambulance, call the Vandenberg Ambulance Service (☎ 773/248-2712).

For fire or police emergencies, call 911.

**Eyeglass Repair**  Pearle Vision Center, 134 N. LaSalle (☎ 312/372-3204), offers one-hour service in many cases. Glasses Ltd. has two locations downtown: 49 E. Oak (☎ 312/944-6876) and 900 N. Michigan (☎ 312/751-0073), and offers same-day service in most cases.

**Faxes**  You can probably send or receive a fax from your hotel. Kinko's Copies is a copy center with a fax service and has several locations throughout the city, including 843 W. Van Buren (☎ 312/421-7373), 444 N. Wells (☎ 312/670-4460), and 2451 N. Lincoln (☎ 773/327-7770).

**Hairdressers and Barbers**    Deluxe and first-class hotels for the most part maintain the tradition of in-house beauty salons. For an inexpensive cut, you might also try Supercuts, at 745 N. Wabash (☎ 312/649-0234), and at 1628 N. Wells (☎ 312/944-7778).

**Hospitals**    By consensus, the best emergency room in Chicago is at North western Memorial Hospital, 233 E. Superior (☎ 312/908-2000), right off the Magnificent Mile.

**Hotlines**    For help with alcoholism, call 800/395-3400. The drug-abuse hotline in Chicago is 773/278-5015. There are also two crisis hotlines in Chicago: 773/769-6200 or 312/908-8100; the latter number is the Institute of Psychiatry, which accepts referrals and walk-ins.

**Laundry and Dry Cleaning**    If you want to pay the premium, you may make use of the services provided by your hotel. Otherwise, find the neighborhood laundromat and dry cleaner and make like a local.

**Libraries**    The Chicago Public Library's main branch is in the Harold Washington Library Center at 400 S. State (☎ 312/747-4300).

**Liquor Laws**    Most bars and taverns have a 2am license, allowing them to stay open until 3am on Sunday ("Saturday night"); some have a 4am license and may remain open until 5am on Sunday.

**Lost Property**    There is a lost-and-found service at O'Hare International Airport (☎ 312/686-2201).

**Luggage Storage and Lockers**    These may be found in limited numbers at O'Hare and Midway airports, at Union Train Station, and at the Greyhound Bus Station.

**Maps**    See "City Layout" earlier in this chapter.

**Newspapers and Magazines**    The *Chicago Tribune* (☎ 312/222-3232) and the *Chicago Sun-Times* (☎ 312/321-3000) are the two major dailies. The *Chicago Reader* (☎ 312/828-0350) is a free weekly, with all the current entertainment and restaurant listings. *Chicago Magazine* is a monthly widely read for its restaurant reviews.

**Pharmacies**    Walgreens, 757 N. Michigan Ave. (☎ 312/664-8686), is open 24 hours. Osco Drugs has a toll-free number (☎ 800/654-6726) that you can call to locate the 24-hour pharmacy nearest to you.

**Police**    For emergencies, call 911.

**Post Office**    The main post office is at 433 W. Van Buren (☎ 312/765-4357); a convenient branch is at 540 N. Dearborn (☎ 312/644-7603).

**Radio**    WBEZ (91.5 FM) is the local National Public Radio station. WFMT (98.7 FM) specializes in talk radio and classical music, and for years has been the home of Studs Terkel's syndicated interview show. WLUP (97.9 FM and 1000 AM) and WXRT (93 FM) play rock.

**Religious Services**    Times are usually posted outside the houses of worship. Consult your hotel staff or a telephone directory for the nearest location of the denomination or religion of your choice.

**Restrooms**    There is a clean restroom in the visitor information center located in the old Water Tower, at the corner of Michigan and Chicago Avenues. The Chicago Historical Society on Clark Street at North Avenue has a restroom downstairs, accessible without entering the museum itself. The department stores also have public restrooms, as do the malls.

**Safety** To be safest, refrain from using the El much after rush hour in the evening. The buses, however, particularly No. 151 running along Michigan Avenue and into Lincoln Park, are safer. In general, don't walk alone at night; stick to populated areas. Michigan Avenue, because it is well lit and well populated, is one of the safer areas at night. The Lincoln Park neighborhood is also generally safe (stay out of the park proper after dark, though), as are the Gold Coast, River North, and Wrigleyville. Stay out of the Loop's interior at night, and that also goes for Hyde Park and Pilsen. Consult your hotel concierge or personnel if in doubt.

**Shoe Repairs** Sam the Shoe Doctor has 11 locations, including one in the Sears Tower (☎ 312/876-9001), and will do repairs while you wait.

**Taxes** The local sales tax is 8.75%.

**Time Zone** All of Illinois, including Chicago, is located in the central time zone, so clocks are set one hour earlier than those on the East Coast and two hours later than those on the West Coast. Chicago switches to daylight savings time in early April, and back to standard time on the last Sunday in October. For the time, dial 976-1616.

**Transit Info** The CTA has a useful number to find out which El train to take to get to your destination: ☎ 312/836-7000.

**Traveler's Aid** A nationwide nonprofit service organization whose mission is to assist travelers in distress, Traveler's and Immigrant's Aid (☎ 312/629-4500) can provide food and shelter for those who are stranded, reunite family members who have become separated, locate lost luggage, and even furnish crisis counseling. In case of emergency after business hours (Monday through Friday from 8:30am to 5pm), call 312/222-0265.

**Weather** For the weather, dial 976-1212.

# Accommodations   5

Good hotels are in no short supply in Chicago. If anything, the city is on the overbuilt side, giving the visitor the edge when it comes to finding the best rate. During the week, Chicago's robust convention trade, individual business travelers, and a small minority of tourists fill hotels to capacity. But since the city's hospitality industry caters first and foremost to the business traveler, the hotels generally empty out significantly by Friday, and are therefore willing to slash prices— sometimes by as much as half—to push up their occupancy rates. If you're in the market for a weekend getaway, chances are you'll be able to find all sorts of extras, from free parking to complimentary breakfast to a split of champagne or even theater tickets.

If the city has a slow season, it's the depth of winter, when outsiders tend to shy away from the cold and the threat of being snowed in at O'Hare. So those who take pride in being serious bargain hunters may choose to visit then. Other travelers on tight budgets who prefer not to sightsee wearing heavy down coats may opt to stay in less expensive hotels—perhaps not right on the Magnificent Mile— during the week and move into swell digs for the weekend finale. The really inexpensive hotels and motels tend to be on the city outskirts, but I think most visitors will be able to find something that's both affordable and in a great location. Even with weekend bargains, though, expect to spend at least $70 per night for a single and $80 for a double in a hotel near the city center.

For the purposes of this chapter, I have divided the hotels into price categories that are roughly as follows: **Very Expensive,** over $185; **Expensive,** $140–$185; **Moderate,** $95–$140; **Inexpensive,** less than $95. The rates are per night and do no include taxes. Nor do they take into account corporate or other discounts. Since some hotels offer better special deals than others, these price headings are meant more as a guideline than an absolute. And if you're traveling alone, remember to ask if the hotel has special rates for single occupancy.

**RESERVE IN ADVANCE**   Whatever hotel or hotels you choose, regardless of season, making reservations well in advance will help ensure you get the best rate available. Most hotels have check-in times somewhere between 3 and 6pm; if you are going to be delayed, call ahead and reconfirm your reservation to prevent cancellation.

# Chicago Accommodations

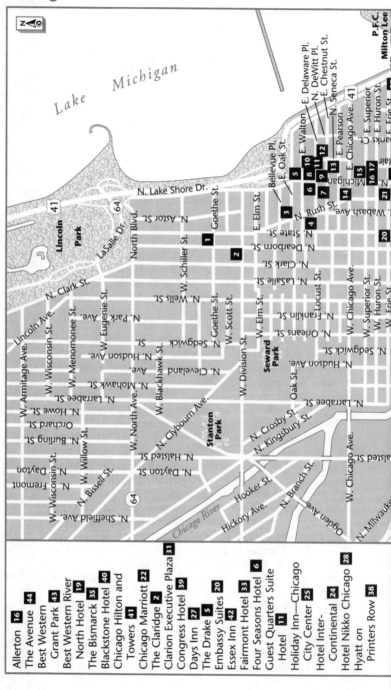

Allerton **16**
The Avenue **44**
Best Western Grant Park **43**
Best Western River North Hotel **19**
The Bismarck **35**
Blackstone Hotel **40**
Chicago Hilton and Towers **41**
Chicago Marriott **22**
The Claridge **2**
Clarion Executive Plaza **31**
Congress Hotel **39**
Days Inn **27**
The Drake **5**
Embassy Suites **20**
Essex Inn **42**
Fairmont Hotel **33**
Four Seasons Hotel **6**
Guest Quarters Suite Hotel **11**
Holiday Inn—Chicago City Center **25**
Hotel Inter-Continental **24**
Hotel Nikko Chicago **28**
Hyatt on Printers Row **38**

48

Chicago 32
Knickerbocker Hotel 10
Midland Hotel 36
Motel 6 23
Ohio House Motel 18
Omni Ambassador
East 1
Omni Chicago Hotel 21
Oxford House 30
Palmer House 37
Park Hyatt 14
Radisson Hotel
& Suites 17
The Raphael 12
Ritz-Carlton 13
Sheraton Chicago Hotel
and Towers 26
Stouffer Renaissance
Hotel 29
Summerfield Suites
Hotel 15
Sutton Place Hotel 3
Swissôtel 34
The Talbott 4
Tremont 9
Westin Hotel 8
Whitehall Hotel 7

1-0483

49

**CORPORATE DISCOUNTS**   Most hotels offer discounts of roughly 10% to individuals who are visiting Chicago on business. To qualify for this rate, your company must have an account on file at the hotel, or you may only be required to present some perfunctory proof of your commercial status, such as a business card or an official letterhead.

**BED & BREAKFAST RESERVATIONS SERVICE**   A centralized reservations service called **Bed & Breakfast/Chicago,** P.O. Box 14088, Chicago, IL 60614 (☎ 312/951-0085), lists more than 70 accommodations both in Chicago and in the North Shore suburbs. The possibilities range from rooms in private homes or apartments to guesthouses or inns. Rates generally run from $65 to $95 a night (continental breakfast included), but the service also offers several accommodations that are considerably more pricey.

## 1 Best Bets

- **Best Historic Hotel:** Having celebrated its 75th anniversary in 1995 with the completion of an extensive renovation, the **Drake** is a master at combining the decorous charm of yesteryear with every modern convenience.
- **Best for Business Travelers:** Both the **Ritz-Carlton's** and the **Four Seasons's** attention to detail and level of service make them the hotels of choice for most discerning business executives I know.
- **Best for a Romantic Getaway:** Its small size, European flavor, and soft, intimate rooms give the **Tremont** an edge in the romance category.
- **Best for Families:** With every room a suite, the **Embassy Suites** is ideal for families looking for a little more space than the typical hotel room provides. Rooms have Nintendo, there's an indoor pool, and the location is near some of kids' favorite eateries—Michael Jordan's, Planet Hollywood, and the Hard Rock Café.
- **Best Moderately Priced Hotel:** A couple of blocks off Michigan Avenue, the **Raphael** offers an appealing combination of price, location, and comfort.
- **Best Budget Hotel:** A little off the beaten path, the **City Suites** and **Surf Hotels** are spotless, cheap, and convenient to public transportation.
- **Best Location:** Most visitors would be more than happy with the location of any hotel on the Magnificent Mile of North Michigan Avenue.
- **Best Health Club:** The fitness center at the **Four Seasons** is sublime. Its dark paneling, discreet staff, and columned pool area could almost make exercise painless.
- **Best Hotel Pool:** With its dazzling all-tile junior Olympic-size pool constructed in 1929, the **Inter-Continental** takes this award easily.
- **Best Views:** This one's a toughy, and I must nominate several hotels for their mix of lake and city views—the **Swissôtel,** the **Four Seasons,** the **Drake,** and the **Ritz-Carlton.**

## 2 The Loop

Strictly speaking, "downtown" in Chicago means the Loop—the central business district, a six- by eight-block rectangle enveloped by elevated tracks on all four sides. An outer circle beyond this literal loop of tracks is bounded by the Chicago River and its south branch, forming an elbow on two sides, by Michigan Avenue running along the edge of Grant Park to the east, and by the Congress Expressway to the south. Within these confines are the city's financial institutions, trading markets, and municipal government, making for, as you might expect, quite a lot of hustle and bustle

Monday through Friday. Come Saturday and Sunday, however, the Loop is pretty dead, despite the fact that it is also home to major venues of music and theater and near the Art Institute. The Loop has an interesting selection of old Chicago hotels, no longer in the first rank perhaps, but with plenty of charm and character, and of undeniable convenience for those who prefer to be at the center of the city.

## VERY EXPENSIVE

### Stouffer Renaissance Chicago Hotel

One W. Wacker Dr., Chicago, IL 60601. ☎ **800/HOTELS-1** or 312/372-7200. Fax 312/ 372-0093. 553 rms. A/C MINIBAR TV TEL. $190–$230 deluxe double; $250 Club Level double; $550–$2,500 suite. Weekend rates $149 double. AE, DC, DISC, MC, V. Valet parking $19.

Comfort, service, scenic river view, amenities, convenient location—the Stouffer Renaissance has it all. Situated at the northeastern edge of the Loop, just across the bridge from the Magnificent Mile, the Stouffer Renaissance is right in between the Loop's attractions and the high-glitz shopping of North Michigan Avenue.

The rooms are tasteful, with a few surprising touches, such as the sweet white eyelet shower curtains. Terrycloth robes and hair dryers are in every bathroom, along with the usual lotions and fine soaps. These comforts, along with the wonderful views of the river and cityscape, make for a more than pleasant environment. On the Stouffer Renaissance's special business levels, called the Club Floors, the rooms are actually larger—a half a room larger—allowing for work space and a bigger sitting area. The Club Floors, which have their own concierge, provide a complimentary continental breakfast and evening hors d'oeuvres and pastries. Because of its proximity to the Loop theater district, the Stouffer Renaissance frequently offers weekend packages featuring show tickets.

**Dining/Entertainment:** The Great Street Restaurant and Bar, with its contemporary American menu and view over the Chicago River, is the hotel's main dining room. Another restaurant, Cuisines, specializes in lunches and dinners with a Mediterranean flavor. The Lobby Court serves cocktails and tea in the immense public space—to the sounds of the piano or a live jazz combo nightly.

**Services:** Complimentary coffee and newspaper delivered each morning with your wake-up call. Twice-daily maid service, complimentary shoe shines, concierge. One unusual treat: no telephone surcharge for toll-free, collect, or credit-card calls or for incoming faxes.

**Facilities:** Indoor swimming pool with skylights, plus a fully equipped health club, including sauna and whirlpool, with complimentary chilled water, juices, and fresh fruit.

## EXPENSIVE

### Clarion Executive Plaza

71 E. Wacker Dr., Chicago, IL 60601. ☎ **312/346-7100.** Fax 312/346-1721. 417 rms. A/C MINIBAR TV TEL. $185 double. Weekend rates $85–$129. AE, CB, DC, DISC, MC, V. Parking $18 with 24-hour in/out privileges.

This hotel is very modern, with a fabulous location on the river, facing the northern downtown zone centered around the Magnificent Mile. The rooms are furnished in tasteful contemporary detail. Tariffs for these rooms are higher than those at comparable Loop hotels, but at the Executive Plaza you are paying extra for the favored location and, perhaps, room spaciousness as well. The rooms have either a city or a river view. Club-floor rooms, where guests have access to a private lounge, are priced slightly higher.

## Hyatt on Printer's Row

500 S. Dearborn St., Chicago, IL 60605. ☎ **800/233-1234** or 312/986-1234. Fax 312/939-2468. 161 rms. A/C MINIBAR TV TEL. $157 double. Weekend rates (available Fri–Sun) $89 double. AE, CB, DC, DISC, ER, JCB, MC, V. Valet parking $18 on weekends, $22 on weekdays; self-parking $15, all with in/out privileges.

Here, in a national historic landmark amid buildings erected in the years immediately following the Great Fire, is the Hyatt on Printer's Row. The discreet and tasteful lobby announces your arrival at the Chicago hotel that can most honestly claim a certain sensibility usually found at fine European establishments. But, at the same time, what could be more American than a hotel that outfits each of its fashionably decorated rooms with two (count 'em, two) color TVs and a video cassette player?

For business travelers, the Hyatt offers extras such as in-room coffeemakers, newspaper delivery, express continental breakfasts, and workstations with computer modem jacks, all for an additional $15 per night. For visitors who want to see more than the inside of their hotel rooms, the Hyatt is an easy walk from the Art Institute, Grant Park, Orchestra Hall, the Harold B. Washington Library, and the city's financial district.

**Dining/Entertainment:** Prairie, one of the best restaurants in the city, is right here in the Hyatt (see Chapter 6).

**Services:** Complimentary coffee or tea daily for Gold Passport members, free daily newspapers in lobby. All rooms come with hair dryers, coffeemakers, irons, and ironing boards. The lobby is handicapped accessible, as are some rooms.

**Facilities:** The Hyatt recently installed a new fitness room in the basement, and for a complete health club, the hotel offers access to the nearby City Club.

## Midland Hotel

172 W. Adams St. (at LaSalle), Chicago, IL 60603. ☎ **800/621-2360** or 312/332-1200. Fax 312/332-5909. 257 rms. A/C TV TEL. $175–$240 double; from $350 suite. All rates include daily buffet breakfast and complimentary cocktail. Weekend package $99–$129 per night. AE, DC, DISC, MC, V. $6.50 credit toward nearby parking on Fri–Sat nights.

If you arrive in Chicago by train and are traveling light, you could easily walk to the Midland Hotel, a few short blocks across the river from Union Station. Once a private men's club, the Midland is a business hotel, though it's also a good base for visitors who wish to concentrate on the many attractions and distractions of the Loop.

The hotel's lobby is narrow but grandiose, designed primarily to speed guests to their rooms or to the public spaces. A number of deluxe rooms with large seating areas and king-size beds are available. At night, in place of a mint, a chocolate-dipped cookie is left at bedside.

**Dining/Entertainment:** The Midland has two restaurants: the Exchange, overlooking the lobby from the mezzanine, and the Ticker Tape Bistro, an art-deco dining room that serves a complimentary buffet breakfast.

**Services:** Guests receive complimentary copies of the *Wall Street Journal* and have use of the hotel's unique limo—an authentic English Austin taxi—to downtown destinations. The Midland offers its regular business clients membership in a corporate travel program called the Lion's Share, which allows members to upgrade their rooms at no added cost (depending on availability) and entitles them to special rates.

**Facilities:** The Midland's meeting facilities are legitimate curios in their own right, worth a detour; each meeting room is designed in the manner of some famous Chicago architect—Wright, Sullivan, and Adler among them. The hotel also has a fitness center and a 24-hour business center.

## Palmer House

17 E. Monroe St., Chicago, IL 60690. ☎ **800/HILTONS** or 312/726-7500. Fax 312/263-2556. 1,639 rms. A/C MINIBAR TV TEL. $145–$205 double; from $195 suite. Weekend rates (including continental breakfast) $89–$119. AE, DC, DISC, MC, V. Parking $9.75 weekdays, $8.75 weekends; self-parking across the street.

Not long before the Great Chicago Fire of 1871, a local merchant named Potter Palmer, who had profited handsomely in cotton speculation during the Civil War, purchased land along State Street. At that time, the area was peripheral to the city's commercial district. At one end of this strip, Palmer erected Field and Leiter, a retail and wholesale dry goods company (predecessor of Marshall Field & Co.). At the other end, he put up a hotel called the Palmer House. Both buildings were consumed by the fire. A second, even more splendid hotel was constructed soon thereafter, which in turn was replaced in 1925 by the current, grand Palmer House.

Entering the Palmer House at street level from either Monroe or State Street, guests pass the hotel's ground floor of arcade shops and more public restaurants, including Trader Vic's. In the center of this area stand several banks of escalators that lead to the second-floor lobby, an absolutely cavernous room, gilded in a way that modern architects can dream about but never re-create. Among the seven restaurants under the single roof of the Palmer House, the Empire Room still attracts a fashionable luncheon crowd.

Rooms are large, bright, and well furnished, but not special in the manner of the deluxe hotels. The hotel's top two floors, called the Palmer House Towers, are a private executive area where rooms cost slightly more. Amenities for guests of the Towers include private elevators, an exercise room with both steam and sauna compartments, and complimentary movies.

# MODERATE

## The Bismarck

171 W. Randolph St., Chicago, IL 60601. ☎ **800/643-1500** or 312/236-0123. Fax 312/236-3177. 500 rms. A/C TV TEL. $140 double. Weekend rates from $89. AE, DC, DISC, MC, V. Valet parking $17 with in/out privileges.

The Bismarck, located smack-dab in the middle of Chicago's financial quarter, is a few years past its centennial. The hotel boasts newly furnished rooms within walking distance of the Loop's centers of trade and culture. Guests may use the indoor pool and fitness facilities at a private club across the street. As with many of the Loop's other business-oriented hotels, the Bismarck offers a range of promotional packages to attract weekend visitors. A courtesy van transports guests to various stops within a 4-mile radius of the hotel.

## Oxford House

225 N. Wabash Ave. (at Wacker Drive), Chicago, IL 60601. ☎ **800/344-4111** or 312/346-6585. Fax 312/346-7742. 175 rms. A/C MINIBAR TV TEL. $89–$99 double; $175 one-bedroom suite; $200 two-bedroom suite. Weekend rates $55 double; weekend package $80 per person for three days. Monthly rates start at $960 single. Children under 16 stay free in parents' room. AE, DC, DISC, MC, V. Parking $10.25 daily with no in/out privileges.

Granted, the Oxford House is well situated, and it is considerably less pricey than other hotels in the area, but I found this place pretty scary. When I visited, the carpet was dirty, the windows were filthy, the Formica furniture looked decades old, the bathrooms were practically begging to be renovated, and the walls looked as though they hadn't been painted since the last time the Democratic Convention came to town. Staying here, however, is certainly affordable for most travelers, particularly because the rooms come equipped with kitchenettes. If you're not in the mood to cook, Café Angelo, off the lobby, is a restaurant of fairly good repute.

## 3 The Magnificent Mile

On the stretch of Michigan Avenue running north of the Chicago River to Oak Street, known as the Magnificent Mile, you'll find the premium hotels.

## VERY EXPENSIVE

### ✪ The Drake

140 E. Walton Place (at Michigan Avenue), Chicago, IL 60611. ☎ **800/55-DRAKE** or 312/787-2200. Fax 312/787-1431. 535 rms and suites. A/C MINIBAR TV TEL. $205–$265 double; $280–$310 executive floor; from $495 suite. Weekend rates start at $159 ($170 with continental breakfast) double. AE, CB, DC, DISC, ER, JCB, MC, V. Valet parking $21.50 with in/out privileges.

Formally opened on New Year's Eve in 1920, the Drake recently celebrated its 75th anniversary as Chicago's favorite hotel. The landmark building, which also fronts East Lake Shore Drive, remains a favorite spot for benefit balls and lavish weddings. The Drake looks over a quiet park beyond which—and very much in view—are the sands of Oak Street Beach, washed by Lake Michigan.

From the lobby through the corridors and on to the guest rooms, the sense that the Drake is a special place pervades. Touches like the benches in the elevators, the abundant fresh flowers, and the lobby ladies' room stalls that house their own sinks make it clear the Drake is an eminently civilized hotel. Some of my other favorite details are the extravagantly wide hallways, the new marble floors in the guest bathrooms, and the polished woodwork throughout.

A room at the Drake is priced in line with the city's other top hotels, but the Drake may have the best $205 room (for two) in the city. The typical bedroom is generous in size, lit with five table lamps, and furnished comfortably with a king-size bed; a sitting area with a well-stuffed settee, armchair, and coffee table; a writing desk with a separate chair; and a bathroom stocked with robes.

Two slightly more expensive "executive floors" reserve 51 rooms and five suites that provide such additional amenities as personalized stationery, a continental breakfast in a private lounge, free cocktails and hors d'oeuvres, plus a daily newspaper and valet assistance for polishing shoes, packing and unpacking, and securing theater tickets. The "concierge floors" (fourth and fifth) have some rooms with extra baths, plus a lounge open from 6:30am to midnight, where snacks, soft drinks, and fresh-brewed coffee are available without charge. In addition to minisuites and one-bedroom suites, the Drake has five immense boardroom suites, a bargain for the corporate set at $650 per night, each with separate conference room and bedroom, partial kitchen, and a spacious living area.

**Dining/Entertainment:** Even if you don't stay at the hotel, I recommend a visit to the Palm Court off the lobby for afternoon tea ($13.50 for a selection of finger sandwiches, currant buns, scones, whipped cream, strawberry preserves, pastry, and, of course, tea) or an after-dinner drink. The enormous room is an opulent one, resplendent in reds and golds, yards of fine draperies, and antique Oriental screens. Potted palms and seating clusters that offer privacy surround an ornate bubbling fountain. The hotel's restaurants include the Oak Terrace, a large dining room serving American fare and some great views of the lake and Michigan Avenue; the Cape Cod Room, a local favorite for seafood; and Coq d'Or, which has an eclectic menu.

**Services:** All rooms are provided with fresh fruit, Swiss chocolates at turndown, and newspapers each morning.

**Facilities:** Fitness center, meeting rooms, business center, shopping arcade, barbershop, beauty shop, and airline ticket office. The hotel has handicapped-accessible rooms.

## ✪ Four Seasons Hotel

120 E. Delaware Place, Chicago, IL 60611. ☎ **800/332-3442** or 312/280-8800. Fax 312/280-7585. 343 rms. A/C MINIBAR TV TEL. $300–$325 double; $325–$2,500 suite. Weekend rates from $265. AE, CB, DC, DISC, MC, V. Valet parking $22; self-parking $15.

Quite simply, you can't go wrong staying at the Four Seasons. The swanky new hotel is ensconced above the shops and offices of the 900 N. Michigan Ave. building, the city's most upscale vertical mall. The lobby's antique Italian marble fireplace (the only wood-burning fireplace in any Chicago hotel) and the intricate floral arrangements throughout the public spaces make for an atmosphere of elegance.

Being the tallest hotel in Chicago, the Four Seasons boasts spectacular views. The interiors are pretty snazzy, too. Guest rooms have English furnishings, custom-woven carpets and tapestries, and dark wood armoires. Everything is oh-so-tasteful. Each room has three two-line phones, a VCR, a CD player, and windows that open to let in the fresh air. The marble bathroom is equipped with a hair dryer, a lighted makeup mirror, oversized towels, and other indulgences from cotton balls to terry robes. Fifteen rooms are handicapped accessible.

My only objection is the smallness of the front desk and the concierge station, a situation that can create minor mayhem during the busier times.

**Dining/Entertainment:** An 18-foot white marble fountain marks the entrance to the opulent Seasons Restaurant, which serves elegantly presented American and continental fare. Sunday brunch is a favorite at the hotel. A piano player is usually on duty in the Seasons Lounge.

**Services:** Twice-daily maid service, complimentary shoe shine, 24-hour room service, newspaper and coffee delivered each morning. Guests also receive shopping cards that entitle them to discounts and special services at the mall's stores. Kid-friendly services include Nintendo and milk and cookies.

**Facilities:** The hotel's health spa is exquisite. The 50-foot indoor pool is framed by Roman columns and sheltered by a skylight. The Jacuzzi accommodates 20 people. The fitness center also has a sundeck, an outdoor jogging track, a steam room, and a sauna, in addition to all the standard equipment. The staff can arrange for personal trainers. The hotel also has a business center.

## ✪ Hotel Inter-Continental

505 N. Michigan Ave., Chicago, IL 60611. ☎ **800/327-0200** or 312/944-4100. Fax 312/944-1320. 844 rms. A/C MINIBAR TV TEL. $229 double. AE, CB, DC, DISC, MC, V. Valet parking $22 with in/out privileges.

Rivaling the best hotels in Chicago, the Hotel Inter-Continental is installed in a landmark building at the foot of the Magnificent Mile. Although it also occupies a more modern structure (formerly the Forum), the Inter-Continental truly shines in the adjoining tower, built in 1929 as a luxury men's club. There the feeling is both elegant, with its hand-painted ceilings and timeless quality, and intimate, with perhaps six rooms to a floor, each one spacious, comfortable, and attractive in muted tones. The bathrooms have sleek pedestal sinks and separate tubs and glass-enclosed showers. Each room also comes equipped with a refrigerator, three dual-line phones, a thick terry robe, and a large desk.

**Dining/Entertainment:** The Inter-Continental has both a casual restaurant, Cafe 525, and a fine Mediterranean one, The Boulevard. The Salon serves tea by day and cocktails by night with musical entertainment.

**Services:** Special amenities include twice-daily maid service, weekday newspaper, and complimentary overnight shoe shine. Rooms have coffeemakers, hair dryers, irons and ironing boards. The Inter-Continental also has a concierge and provides 24-hour room service.

**Facilities:** The hotel has a health club on the premises, featuring a spectacular all-tile, junior Olympic-size indoor pool, a gymnasium, an aerobics room, saunas, whirl-pools, and steam and massage rooms. Use of the pool is complimentary for guests, but the hotel charges $10 per day or $13.50 for the entire stay for use of the fitness center. Even if you don't have occasion while at the Inter-Continental to throw a party for 200 of your closest friends, take a peek at the ballrooms; they're some of the most beautiful around.

### Omni Chicago Hotel

676 N. Michigan Ave., Chicago, IL 60611. ☎ **312/944-6664.** Fax 312/266-3015. 347 rms (all suites). A/C MINIBAR TV TEL. $250–$280 suite. Weekend rates from $189. AE, CB, DC, DISC, MC, V. Valet parking $24 with in/out privileges.

Three floors up from Michigan Avenue is the lobby of the Omni Chicago Hotel, a business hotel with a fresh, modern interior. With its large, domed chandeliers, marble floors, and beautiful flower arrangements, the Omni is a lovely place to stay. All the rooms are suites with one king-size or two double beds. Each suite, tastefully decorated in deep greens and burgundies, has a living room with a sitting area, a dining table, a wet bar, and a refrigerator. Nice extras include a phone in the bathroom and two TVs. Most rooms have fax machines.

**Dining/Entertainment:** Off the lobby, overlooking Michigan Avenue with floor-to-ceiling windows, is the American/Mediterranean restaurant Cielo.

**Services:** Concierge, 24-hour room service, complimentary VCRs, and courtesy car available. Executive service offers complimentary newspaper, breakfast, and shoe shine.

**Facilities:** The Omni has a full health club, including a lap pool and a Jacuzzi.

### Park Hyatt

800 N. Michigan Ave. (on Water Tower Square), Chicago, IL 60611. ☎ **800/233-1234** or 312/280-2222 outside Illinois. Fax 312/649-2290. 255 rms. A/C MINIBAR TV TEL. $220–$250 double. Weekend rates $139–$155. AE, CB, DC, DISC, MC, V. Parking $24 overnight with in/out privileges.

Water Tower Square is not only the site of the Chicago landmark tower that survived the Great Fire of 1871, but it is also the address of the Park Hyatt, another gem among Chicago's smaller hotels. Set back from Michigan Avenue opposite this tree-shaded square, the Park Hyatt's two-story windows fill the lobby with light.

The rooms are on a par with those of the hotel's competitors, with such extras as modern pedestal sinks and small TVs in the bathrooms, Oriental touches in the furnishings, and fax machines on the upper floors. The eastern views are the best: a wall of windows overlooks the lake, Michigan Avenue, and the old Water Tower.

**Dining/Entertainment:** Open for breakfast, lunch, and dinner, Jaxx is a very good restaurant with a British accent.

**Services:** A Mercedes can often be seen parked at the entrance to the Park Hyatt, which guests may use without charge, on a first-come, first-served basis, for short local trips to restaurants, museums, and so forth. Maid service arrives three times daily, and the hotel offers complimentary shoe shines and packing assistance. The hotel will bring an Exercycle or a rowing machine to your room on request. Complimentary coffee and tea service is available for guests in the lobby until 9am daily.

**Facilities:** For $10, guests have access to a nearby full-service health club.

## ✪ Ritz-Carlton

160 E. Pearson St., Chicago, IL 60611. ☎ **800/621-6906** or 312/266-1000. Fax 312/266-1194. 431 rms, 82 suites. A/C MINIBAR TV TEL. $280–$380 double; $600–$2,500 suite. Weekend rates $185–$399. Valet parking $25.25 with in/out privileges; $23 self-parking with no in/out privileges.

Easily one of the best places to stay in Chicago, the Ritz-Carlton is a favorite of straightlaced businesspeople and the Grateful Dead alike. If you want to stay here, plan ahead: Management claims the hotel is booked every night, April through October, as much as six months in advance.

The reasons are numerous. One is the Ritz's excellent location adjacent to Water Tower Place. Another is the quality of the accommodations. The standard room has a king-size bed and a blue-and-white color scheme. The furnishings—a loveseat, an armoire, a desk—are traditional without being heavy. Touches like the little seat at the dressing table make for a very comfortable stay. So does the generously sized marble bathroom, stocked with a robe and a hair dryer. Lake views cost more but are spectacular.

Whether or not you stay here, the Ritz-Carlton is an elegant place for high tea, served from 3:30 to 5pm in the 12th-floor lobby. At the center of the wide-open lobby is a beautiful fountain, and at one end is the Greenhouse restaurant, designed with a glass roof and wall, that seems to jut out over the city. By the way, this particular Ritz-Carlton is part of the Four Seasons chain, not the Ritz-Carlton one.

**Dining/Entertainment:** Among the four restaurants is The Dining Room, one of the better hotel restaurants in Chicago, serving French cuisine in an elegant atmosphere.

**Services:** One-hour pressing, overnight dry cleaning, overnight shoe shine, 24-hour business services including in-room fax machines. Complimentary coffee is served in the lobby from 5:30 to 8am, and complimentary newspapers are available on request.

**Facilities:** Skylighted indoor lap pool, complete health and exercise facility are free of charge to Carlton Club members, $8 for other guests. Guests can use the pool and fitness facilities at the Four Seasons, its sister hotel a block away, at no charge.

## Sheraton Chicago Hotel and Towers

301 E. North Water St., Chicago, IL 60611. ☎ **312/464-1000.** Fax 312/464-9140. 1,204 rms. A/C MINIBAR TV TEL. $195–$230 double. Tower rates $168–$240 double. Weekend rates start at $99. AE, DC, DISC, MC, V. Valet parking $19 with in/out privileges.

A major convention center during the workweek, the Sheraton Chicago is a full-service leisure hotel on the weekends. Being the newcomer, the Sheraton had last pick of locations, and for that reason, it's a little out of the way compared with its peers—east of North Michigan Avenue along the Chicago River. Enormous only begins to define the Sheraton, and I acknowledge a certain wariness on my part of mega-hotels.

That said, the guest rooms are a nice size. A room with a king-size bed, for example, has a sitting area with a loveseat and a chair. The views are pretty. The bathrooms, on the other hand, are of the no-frills variety, and their ceilings are claustrophobically low. The 34-story building also has 96 tower rooms. Guests in the tower rooms have access to a courtesy lounge, where a complimentary continental breakfast is served daily.

**Dining/Entertainment:** The flagship restaurant at the Chicago Sheraton is the Streeterville Grille, featuring steaks and seafood with an Italian flavor. The Riverside Café offers a more informal dining option, and the Spectator Sports Bar provides a club atmosphere for sports fans. At ground level, along the river promenade both inside and out, is the Esplanade Express Café.

**Services:** Handicapped-accessible rooms are available. Each room is stocked with an iron and ironing board, a coffeemaker, and a hair dryer. Nintendo is available, and complimentary newspapers are delivered. The hotel also has a concierge.

**Facilities:** A complete business center with all services; a fully equipped health club and pool, and boat-docking facilities.

### Westin Hotel

909 N. Michigan Ave., Chicago, IL 60611. ☎ 312/943-7200 or 800/228-3000. Fax 312/943-9347. Telex 206593. 740 rms. A/C MINIBAR TV TEL. $195–$220 double; $190–$1,500 suite. AE, DC, JCB, MC, V. Parking $20 with in/out privileges.

The Westin has been looking a bit shabby of late, though recent renovations have improved things some. The guest rooms are in better condition, with merely adequate furniture but nice bathrooms. The Westin's location, at the corner of Michigan Avenue and Delaware Place (across the street from Bloomingdale's), makes up for most of the hotel's shortcomings.

**Dining/Entertainment:** Chelsea is one of the hotel's restaurants. A Starbucks coffee cart makes its home in the lobby.

**Services:** Concierge, valet service, 24-hour room service.

**Facilities:** Health club (free to guests).

### Whitehall Hotel

105 E. Delaware Place, Chicago, IL 60611. ☎ 312/573-6250. Fax 312/944-8552. 221 rms. A/C MINIBAR TV TEL. $215 double; from $575 suite. Weekend rates from $149. AE, CB, DC, DISC, JCB, MC, V. Parking $21.50 with in/out privileges.

The Whitehall Hotel has joined the pack of Chicago hotels catering to the business crowd. Its top four floors, called the Executive Floors, house a business center and a private lounge. The rooms on those floors all have fax machines, and guests receive complimentary breakfast. Rooms throughout the hotel are furnished in the style of 18th-century England, with Oriental accents.

Built in 1928 as a residential building, the Whitehall was converted to a hotel in 1972. After a full renovation, the Whitehall officially reopened in 1995. The hotel has chosen a traditional ambience, filling the small lobby with paintings of horses and dogs and hanging little lamps on either side of every guest-room door.

**Dining/Entertainment:** Whitehall Place, an American bistro, occasionally features live music. Pluses include sidewalk dining and high tea.

**Services:** Concierge, room service.

**Facilities:** Exercise room, business center (for upper floors).

## EXPENSIVE

### Chicago Marriott

540 N. Michigan Ave., Chicago, IL 60611. ☎ 800/228-9290 or 312/836-0100. Fax 312/836-6139. 1,172 rms and suites. A/C MINIBAR TV TEL. $194 double; $480 suite. Weekend rates $109–$129. AE, DC, DISC, MC, V. Valet parking $20.

Almost 1,200 rooms! Exactly the kind of hotel in which I don't want to stay. Although the Chicago Marriott has been the recipient of several awards by convention trade magazines, I find it to be your basic hotel with zero personality. The Marriott does have a great location.

**Dining/Entertainment:** Two restaurants and a sports bar/nightclub add to the hotel's self-contained environment.

**Services:** Room service (6:30am to 3am), same-day valet cleaning.

**Facilities:** A fitness center with four outdoor platform tennis courts, basketball courts, indoor swimming pool with whirlpool and exercise facilities, sundeck, rooftop putting green. The Marriott also has a business center, ample meeting space, and a beauty salon.

### ⑤ Guest Quarters Suite Hotel

198 E. Delaware Place, Chicago, IL 60611. ☎ **800/424-2900** or 312/664-1100. Fax 312/664-9881. 345 suites. A/C MINIBAR TV TEL. $235 double suite. Weekend and summer promotional rates start at $119. Children under 18 stay free in parents' room. AE, CB, DC, DISC, MC, V. Valet parking $20 per day with in/out privileges.

The Guest Quarters is a full-service all-suite hotel spread over 25 floors. Each suite features a separate living room and bedroom, deluxe bath, refrigerator, two telephones, and two TVs. The prices of the suites depend on bed size, floor (some have spectacular lake views), and furnishings. The rooms here aren't huge, but the hotel is spotless, and the Guest Quarters has not skimped on some of those little extras than can make a big difference, such as fresh flowers in the lobby and the complimentary coffee and newspaper every morning.

The Guest Quarters has a rooftop health club with a pool. Among its restaurants is the Park Avenue Cafe, an upscale establishment transplanted from New York. Most nights, the hotel also has live entertainment featuring jazz and contemporary music.

### Holiday Inn—Chicago City Center

300 E. Ohio St., Chicago, IL 60611. ☎ **800/HOLIDAY** or 312/787-6100. Fax 312/787-6238. 500 rms. A/C MINIBAR TV TEL. $145–$220 double. Weekend and promotional rates $119–$139. AE, CB, DC, DISC, MC, V. Parking $16.75.

Another hotel favored by conventioneers, north of the Chicago River, is the recently renovated Holiday Inn, located in an area east of the Magnificent Mile called City Center. Right next door to the hotel is the McClurg Court Sports Complex, where guests may enjoy the facilities free of charge. With its own fifth-floor outdoor pool and sundeck, and the hotel's proximity to such attractions as the new entertainment mall on nearby North Pier, and the Navy Pier—site of dozens of special events and open-air festivals—the Holiday Inn would make a good choice for summer visitors to Chicago.

### ⑤ Knickerbocker Hotel

163 E. Walton St., Chicago, IL 60611. ☎ **800/621-8140** or 312/751-8100. Fax 312/751-0370. 254 rms. A/C TV TEL. $125–$215 double. Weekend packages from $139. AE, DC, DISC, MC, V. Parking $20.25 with in/out privileges.

Built in 1927 and at one time part of Hugh Hefner's *Playboy* empire, the Knickerbocker has fallen out of the city's upper echelon of hotels. Perhaps because it is no longer among the most sought-after ballrooms for charity functions or weddings, the Knickerbocker is seeking a new image. It is attempting to get past its rep as a "social hotel" and replace it with the serious business hotel profile that so many Chicago hotels are adopting.

As part of a recent $10.5 million renovation, the Knickerbocker outfitted some rooms with fax machines and computers. All the guest rooms have a well-deserved fresh look. Too bad the overhaul couldn't do anything about the Knickerbocker's views, which, despite the hotel's good location a block from the 900 N. Michigan shops and right across the street from the Drake, are often rather dismal. One bonus for couples or families: about one-third of the rooms have two bathrooms, the result of a previous renovation that cut the number of rooms by 100.

### Radisson Hotel and Suites

160 E. Huron St., Chicago, IL 60611. ☎ **312/787-2900.** Fax 312/787-5158. 334 rms. A/C MINIBAR TV TEL. $175–$210 double. Corporate rate $155. Weekend rates $119–$149. AE, CB, DC, DISC, JCB, MC, V. Valet parking $19.50.

Formerly the Sheraton-Plaza, the Radisson was renovated in 1995. The project included a new lobby and new beds, case goods, and carpeting in the guest rooms. Since sleeping rooms begin on the 14th floor, the Radisson can boast some truly beautiful views of the lake and city. The rooms are spacious. In addition to a hair dryer, iron and ironing board, two phones and two lines, a computer modem hookup, and voice mail, a nice touch is the halogen lamp, which brightens the room to great effect. For an additional $25, a guest can upgrade to one of 88 suites, which feature microwave ovens.

Cassis is the hotel's French bistro and wine bar. The Radisson has an outdoor pool with a deck, where guests can arrange for barbecue or cocktail parties. The hotel also has a fitness center as well as a library/lounge area.

## Summerfield Suites Hotel

166 E. Superior St., Chicago, IL 60611. ☎ **800/621-8004** or 312/787-6000. Fax 312/787-4331. 120 suites. A/C MINIBAR TV TEL. $145 minisuite; $175 "Executive Parlour"; $195 one-bedroom suite. Weekend packages from $99 a night (including continental breakfast). AE, DISC, MC, V. Valet parking $17 with in/out privileges; $11.50 self-parking with in/out privileges.

Formerly known as the Barclay, Summerfield Suites underwent a $7 million renovation in 1995, updating the hotel's old-world feel and adding extras such as a full health club and a new sprinkler system. What Summerfield lacks in grand public spaces, it makes up for in coziness and room size. All the rooms are suites, and 80% of them have full kitchens, making Summerfield a good place to consider for long-term stays. The hotel even offers a grocery shopping service. Every suite has a VCR.

Although the hotel no longer has its own restaurant, it offers room service from Benihana of Tokyo and Gino's East pizzeria. A complimentary breakfast is now served in what used to be the Barclay Club. A stairwell from the paneled lobby leads downstairs to the appealing Bookmark Lounge, open from 4:30pm to about 1am. Stocked bookcases line the walls, and complimentary hors d'oeuvres are available during the cocktail hours.

The staff is efficient and attentive. Nice extras include the basket of fresh fruit on the reception counter, the complimentary shoe shine, and the small rooftop pool and sundeck. The hotel's biggest convenience may be its location, steps from North Michigan Avenue and two blocks from Water Tower Place.

## Talbott Hotel

20 E. Delaware Place, Chicago, IL 60611. ☎ **800/621-8506** or 312/943-0161. Fax 312/944-7241. 98 rms, 50 suites. A/C MINIBAR TV TEL. $180 double; $255–$395 suite. Weekend packages from $109. AE, DC, MC, V. Parking $11 across the street in a lot.

The Talbott is another one of those small, European-style gems that seem to thrive in Chicago, despite the city's reputation as a convention town. Constructed in the 1920s as an apartment building, the Talbott was converted to a hotel in 1989, making for spacious rooms, all of which contain either kitchenettes or full kitchens. Guests are treated to twice-daily maid service and a complimentary continental breakfast.

The lobby, decorated with leather sofas, a working fireplace, and numerous French horns used for fox hunts, is inviting. The cozy bar and complimentary evening coffee and brownies create an intimate, collegial atmosphere. A sidewalk café peps up the hotel during the summer months.

## ✪ Tremont

100 E. Chestnut St., Chicago, IL 60611. ☎ **800/621-8133** or 312/751-1900 outside Illinois. Fax 312/280-1304. 118 rms and suites. A/C MINIBAR TV TEL. $190–$255 double; from $450

suite. Weekend rates start at $175. AE, DC, DISC, MC, V. Parking $19.50 per day with no in/out privileges.

If you're looking for a small European-style hotel, the Tremont has great appeal. Built in 1921 as an apartment building and converted to a hotel in the late 1970s, the Tremont possesses an intimacy that most of its competitors lack. While almost every other hotel seems to be going with a color scheme of burgundy and forest green, the Tremont in its recent renovations opted for a very cheerful yellow and green, a nice complement to the bright sunshine that fills many rooms. The furnishings are tasteful without being somber; I especially liked the striped duvets and shower curtains. Every room comes with a VCR and a CD player, and the hotel offers rentals of both media. Of course, the hotel's size factor has its trade-offs. The Tremont does not have its own fitness center, but it does offer access to a nearby health club. The hotel has a restaurant off the lobby (though overpriced and with some obnoxious staff), offering 24-hour room service.

# MODERATE

### Allerton

701 N. Michigan Ave., Chicago, IL 60611. ☎ **800/621-8311,** 800/572-7839 or 312/440-1500 in Illinois. Fax 312/440-1819. 60 rms. A/C TV TEL. $119–$129 double; from $129 suite. Weekend rates $89 double; $99 suite. AE, JCB, MC, V. Parking next door for $21 for 24 hours with in/out privileges.

The Allerton has seen better days. The lobby is a little dingy, the furniture a little worn, and the halls a little dark. The service is not the most genteel (in place of a bell or buzzer, the front desk clerk simply yells to the bellman). On the other hand, I can't argue with the location. With the entrance on Huron, around the corner from Michigan Avenue, the Allerton is at the center of it all. The rooms and suites are fairly large and light, but by no means palatial, and some have kitchenettes. The hotel offers several attractive promotional packages, so be sure to inquire when you reserve your room.

### Days Inn

644 N. Lake Shore Dr., Chicago, IL 60611. ☎ **800/541-3223** or 312/943-9200. Fax 312/649-5580. 578 rms. A/C TV TEL. $85–$159 double. Weekend rates from $95. AE, DC, DISC, MC, V. Parking $12 per day.

The lakefront location of Chicago's Days Inn sets it apart from the city's other hotels, especially those in the moderate price range. A large hotel, the Days Inn's more expensive rooms overlook the lake. The hotel is three blocks from the newly redeveloped Navy Pier with its Children's Museum, Ferris wheel, and merry-go-round. There is a complete fitness center along with an outdoor pool, and a restaurant, the Lake Shore Cafe. The hotel also offers handicapped-accessible rooms.

### ⑤ The Raphael

201 E. Delaware Place, Chicago, IL 60611. ☎ **800/821-5343** or 312/943-5000. Fax 312/943-9483. 172 rms and suites. A/C MINIBAR TV TEL. $150–$185 double; $170–$185 suite. Weekend rates $110–$140. AE, CB, DC, DISC, MC, V. Parking $21 with in/out privileges.

If you're looking for a small hotel with an intimate feel, you might want to try the Raphael, ensconced among residential buildings a couple of blocks east of Michigan Avenue. The lobby of the Raphael, with its peculiar wood chandelier and gothic ambience, is about as old world as Chicago gets. Service at the reception desk is crisp and good-natured. Off the lobby are a small continental restaurant and the chummy Raphael bar and lounge. Decor varies in the hotel's rooms and suites from contemporary styling to the ornate. The rooms are spacious, if a little dark. And suites at the

Raphael cost less than some comparable hotels charge for their rooms. The hotel offers $10 day passes to a nearby health club.

## INEXPENSIVE

### Motel 6

162 E. Ontario St., Chicago, IL 60611. ☎ **312/787-3580.** Fax 312/787-1299. 191 rms. A/C MINIBAR TV TEL. $69 double; $53.10 AARP discounted rate. AE, DC, DISC, MC, V. Parking $11.75 with no in/out privileges.

Just east of North Michigan Avenue, Motel 6 is practically spitting distance from Crate & Barrel and the Tribune Tower. Formerly the Richmont Hotel, its rooms are on the small side, but they're comfortable. The lobby is clean and bright. The service isn't the Ritz, but then again, neither are the prices.

## 4 River North

The name "River North" designates a vast area parallel to the Magnificent Mile. The zone is bounded by the river to the west and south and roughly by Clark Street to the east and by Division Street to the north. The earthy red-brick buildings that characterize the area were once warehouses of various kinds and today form the core of Chicago's new art gallery district. The neighborhood also has spawned many of the city's trendiest restaurants. The hotels here span every price range, from the budget Ohio House Motel all the way up to the luxurious Hotel Nikko.

## VERY EXPENSIVE

### ✪ Hotel Nikko Chicago

320 N. Dearborn St., Chicago, IL 60610. ☎ **800/NIKKO-US** or 312/744-1900; reservations also through Japan Air Lines offices. Fax 312/527-2664. 425 rms. A/C MINIBAR TV TEL. $225 double; $240–$260 river-view room; from $300 suite. Weekend rate $135 per night based on two-night stay. Other packages available. AE, DC, DISC, JCB, MC, V. Valet parking $21 with in/out privileges.

On the northern bank of the Chicago River, the Hotel Nikko Chicago sets its own standard of luxury. The hotel's Japanese sensibility is apparent from the moment one enters the lobby; it's in the sleek design of the dark furniture, the horizontal lines, the minimalist fountain. In the back of the lobby is a small Japanese garden that separates the Nikko from its Riverfront Park, a 300-foot-long landscaped strip between Dearborn and Clark Streets.

On the guest floors, the hallways are wide and their walls are black. The typical guest room is well organized, with one all-purpose piece of furniture serving as desk, bureau, and armoire. For those who feel like splurging, a suite on the 19th floor more than satisfies, with three enormous rooms, including a huge marble bathroom, black-leather couches in the living room, and a large window offering a side view of the river.

**Dining/Entertainment:** The Hana Lounge, sunken in the center of the lobby, is open for lunch and drinks. Benkay is a first-rate Japanese restaurant, and it has a sake bar serving dozens of varieties of the rice wine. Every Sunday from 11am to 2pm, the Nikko plays host to an elaborate brunch in its Les Célébrités restaurant that has become the rage of Chicago. The $32 per person cost ($19 for children ages 5 to 12) includes a lavish spread of cold cuts, sausages, cheeses, breads, pastries, fruits, salmon and other seafoods, and hot and cold breakfast treats served from steaming chafing dishes. Also included in the price is a full menu of made-to-order dishes, such as eggs

Benedict, three-pepper omelets, vanilla flapjacks, stir-fry chicken and shrimp, and so forth, along with all the fresh-squeezed juices and cappuccino or caffè latte you desire to wash it all down. Twice monthly, radio station WNUA broadcasts its smooth jazz format live from its head table among the Nikko's well-stuffed and well-satisfied Sunday brunchers. Afternoon tea is served as well.

**Services:** Free daily newspaper and shoe shine.

**Facilities:** The fitness center costs $10 per session, which includes shorts, shirt, socks, plus free fruit and juices. For use of a pool, the hotel offers discounted sessions at a nearby health club.

# EXPENSIVE

### ⊗ Embassy Suites

600 N. State St., Chicago, IL 60610. ☎ **312/943-3800.** Fax 312/943-7629. 358 suites. A/C MINIBAR TV TEL. $159–$249 king suite; $169–$269 double suite. AE, DC, DISC, JCB, MC, V. Valet parking $20 with in/out privileges.

Although it bills itself as a business hotel and does a healthy convention business, the Embassy Suites is also a family-friendly hotel. All 358 suites have two rooms: a living room furnished with a sleeper sofa, a table, and four chairs, and a bedroom with either a king-size or two double beds. Each room has a TV and a phone with two lines. The suite also has a minikitchen outfitted with a refrigerator, microwave, coffeemaker, and minibar.

The suites all surround an expansive central atrium where, at one end, the hotel serves a complimentary cooked-to-order breakfast in the morning and, at the other end, supplies complimentary drinks and snacks in the evening. The Embassy Suites also has an indoor pool along with sauna, whirlpool, and workout room. And off the lobby is an excellent restaurant, Papagus Greek Taverna.

# MODERATE

### Best Western River North Hotel

125 W. Ohio St. (at the corner of LaSalle), Chicago, IL 60610. ☎ **800/528-1234** or 312/467-0800. Fax 312/467-1665. 152 rms. A/C TV TEL. $92–$132 double. Weekend rates from $69. AE, DC, DISC, JCB, MC, V. Free parking for guests.

This hotel is one of few that are right in the midst of some of the trendiest nightspots and restaurants in the city today. Theme restaurants such as Michael Jordan's and Ed Debevic's are within easy walking distance, as are the interesting Wells Street shops and River North's numerous art galleries. The hotel also has an all-season rooftop pool and a ground-floor restaurant called Great Plains. Rooms are designer-modern and large.

# INEXPENSIVE

### Ohio House Motel

600 N. La Salle St., Chicago, IL 60610. ☎ **312/943-6000.** Fax 312/943-6063. 50 rms. A/C TV TEL. $67–$75 king-size bed; $85–$105 four-person occupancy. AE, DC, DISC, MC, V. Free parking for guests.

The Ohio House Motel is a real bargain, especially considering its location in one of the hottest entertainment and restaurant districts in Chicago. This is a motel, folks—clean and well maintained, but with none of the luxuries of the Magnificent Mile places just east of here. The breakfast at the Ohio House Coffee Shop, served all day, is on the grand scale, however: two eggs, two strips of bacon, two sausages, and two pancakes for $2.95.

## 5  Near North

Near North refers to the area beginning at Division Street and extending north to North Avenue, bounded on the west by Clark Street and on the east by Chicago's fabled Gold Coast—a short strip of some of the city's priciest real estate along Lake Shore Drive. From the standpoint of social status, the streets clustered here are among the finest addresses in Chicago. It's a lovely neighborhood for a stroll among the graceful townhouses and the several lavish mansions that remain, relics from an even glitzier past. The hotels here tend to be upscale without hitting that peak that some of the nearby Michigan Avenue hotels reach.

## VERY EXPENSIVE

### Omni Ambassador East

1301 N. State Pkwy., Chicago, IL 60610. ☎ **800/843-6664** or 312/787-7200. Fax 312/787-4760. 275 rms and suites. A/C MINIBAR TV TEL. $215 double; $210–$230 executive suite. Weekend rates from $139. AE, CB, DC, DISC, MC, V. Parking $21.25 per day with in/out privileges.

The Omni Ambassador East blends in discreetly on the tree-shaded corner of State Parkway and Goethe Street in this quiet, residential neighborhood. Owned in its early days by Ernie Byfield—a great showman/hotelman who first attracted luminaries and stars to the Pump Room—the Ambassador East, following a decline throughout the sixties and seventies, has managed to regain some stature, though it's not in a league with the Ritz-Carltons, Four Seasons, or Drakes of the world.

As for the rooms, they are certainly clean and neat, but they could use a facelift. The hotel has yet to make any effort to be handicapped accessible, and the staff is on the obnoxious side. As you may imagine, the Ambassador East has the usual amenities—the terrycloth robes and a valet stand, for example. But you could probably do better elsewhere.

**Dining/Entertainment:** For the past 50 years, celebrities who have come to mingle with Chicago's Gold Coast society have done so most publicly from a designated booth in the Pump Room (see Chapter 6).

**Services:** At turndown, you'll find a bottle of Perrier with a bucket of ice, and a small jar of tasty Toll House cookies.

**Facilities:** A health-club facility five minutes away by cab costs around $10.

### Sutton Place Hotel

21 E. Bellevue Place, Chicago, IL 60611. ☎ **800/810-8666** or 312/266-2100. Fax 312/266-2141. 245 rms. A/C MINIBAR TV TEL. $245 double; $300 Junior Suite for one, $325 for two. Weekend rate (including breakfast and valet parking) $135 double. AE, DC, DISC, MC, V. Parking $22.

The fact that the Sutton Place is different from the city's other luxury hotels is evident before you even enter the building. Formerly Le Meridien Chicago, the Sutton Place stands between the pulsing Rush Street entertainment zone and the posh Gold Coast residential district. The lobby is small and dark, giving an effect of wearing your sunglasses indoors. Also contributing to that cool impression are the Robert Mapplethorpe art, the modern furniture, and the color scheme of black, gray, and burgundy. The glass-enclosed showers and separate sunken tubs set a certain tone. The rooms are equipped with VCRs, CD players, and three two-line phones. The hotel provides some sample CDs, mostly jazz and pop.

**Dining/Entertainment:** In addition to Brasserie Bellevue, the lobby restaurant and outdoor café, Sutton Place has a chocolate buffet every Saturday from 2:30 to 10pm.

**Services:** Car service to the Loop is available weekdays. As for the VCR in your room, the hotel has a video rental machine. Sutton Place also offers complimentary shoe shines, morning newspaper delivery, and 24-hour room service. Rooms come with terry robes and hair dryers.

**Facilities:** The hotel has a 24-hour exercise room, and for a full health club, including indoor pool and racquetball and tennis courts, Sutton Place offers discounted rates at the Gold Coast Multiplex.

## EXPENSIVE

### The Claridge

1244 N. Dearborn Pkwy., Chicago, IL 60610. ☎ **800/245-1258** or 312/787-4980 outside Illinois. Fax 312/266-0978. 168 rms. A/C MINIBAR TV TEL. $120 for a room with a queen-size bed; $150 for king-size; $165 for two doubles. Weekend rates $78–$93. All rates include continental breakfast. AE, DC, DISC, MC, V. Valet parking $15 with in/out privileges.

The only other "tourist-quality" hotel in the Near North, the Claridge is a block farther west than the Omni Ambassador East, but still only a brief stroll to the lakefront and the Oak Street Beach, and even closer to the north end of the Magnificent Mile, just across Division and east of Rush Street.

The Claridge is a small hotel; the lobby is meant only as a funnel to the rooms or to the restaurant, JP's Eating Place, in the rear of the building. Thanks to the competent desk staff, what could be a bottleneck functions fluidly. Some deluxe accommodations have sitting areas, and three executive suites on the 14th floor have working fireplaces. All guests receive complimentary morning newspapers.

# 6  Lincoln Park & the North Side

If you prefer the feel of living amid real Chicagoans in a residential neighborhood, several options await in Lincoln Park and further north. Not only do these hotels tend to be more affordable than those closer to downtown, but they also provide a different vantage point from which to view Chicago. If you stay at the City Suites Hotel or even the Surf Hotel, for example, you can join the locals on a pedestrian pilgrimage to Wrigley Field for a Cubs game. The area is flush with restaurants, and public transportation via the El or buses is a snap. On the Loyola University campus, on the city's far North Side, students will find an inexpensive bed for the night in Chicago's only youth hostel.

## INEXPENSIVE

### Chicago International Hostel

6318 N. Winthrop Ave., Chicago, IL 60660. ☎ **773/262-1011.** Fax 773/262-3673. $13 (payable in cash or traveler's checks). Length of stay at discretion of manager. No credit cards. Subway/El: Howard Street line north to Loyola Station; use Sheridan Road exit.

The Chicago International Hostel has dormitories for men and women, as well as some rooms for couples and disabled persons. The hostel is handicapped accessible. All prices include tax and linen; you must provide your own blanket or sleeping bag. Locked storage is available at $1 per day. A self-service laundromat and kitchen are on the premises. The hostel is open from 7 to 10am, closed from 10am to 4pm, and check-in is from 4pm to midnight. Midnight is the curfew. Some parking on the street. From the subway, enter the Loyola campus, following the path to the right for half a block south.

### ⑤ City Suites Hotel

933 W. Belmont Ave., Chicago, IL 60657. ☎ **773/404-3400.** Fax 773/404-3405. 45 rms. A/C TV TEL. $85 double; $99 suite. AE, DC, DISC, MC, V. Parking $6 in nearby lot. Subway/ El: Howard Street line to Belmont station.

A few doors down from the elevated train stop on Belmont Avenue, not far from the corner of Sheffield, an enterprising team has remodeled a transient dive called the Wilmont and turned it into a charming small hotel, something along the lines of an urban bed-and-breakfast.

Most of the rooms here are suites, with separate sitting rooms and bedrooms, all furnished with first-rate pieces and decorated in a homey and comfortable style. A bonus—or drawback, depending on your point of view—is the hotel's neighborhood setting, which runs from young professional families to gay couples to punks in full regalia. Blues bars, nightclubs, and restaurants abound hereabouts, making the City Suites a find for the bargain-minded and adventuresome. Room service is available from Ann Sather's, a neighborhood institution. The hotel is a $5 cab ride from the Belmont stop of the O'Hare–Douglas line from the airport.

### ⑤ Surf Hotel

555 W. Surf St., Chicago, IL 60657. ☎ **312/528-8400.** Fax 312/528-8483. 40 rms. A/C TV TEL. $89 suite. AE, DC, DISC, MC, V. Parking $7 in either of two nearby garages with no in/ out privileges. Bus: No. 151 from anywhere on Michigan Avenue (or Union Station) or No. 156 from LaSalle Street; get off at Sheridan and Surf and walk one block west.

Owned by the same group as the City Suites Hotel, and possessed of a similar history, the Surf was once an SRO building and has been converted into a neighborhood hotel. The company behind the hotel is purchasing a residential building to house former tenants of the hotel who lived there for many years.

In contrast to the City Suites, the Surf Hotel occupies a site on a quiet, tree-lined street several blocks east of its sibling, and relatively close to Lake Michigan. The developers are preserving and restoring most of the building's vintage 1920 architectural details while making the rooms modern and comfortable. The rooms, including the bathrooms, are immaculate, and rates include a continental breakfast.

## 7  The East Side

The term *East Side* is a relatively new one, describing the highrise/high-rent district that is east of Michigan Avenue, south of the river, and north of Grant Park. Don't be surprised if Chicagoans look at you a little funny when you ask directions to the East Side; it has yet to find its way into the geographical lexicon of the city. Most natives don't seem to have any name for the area at all. Don't expect happening restaurants or great stores; the area is essentially one of elite hotels, residential towers, and office buildings. The East Side is definitely a luxury "privacy zone," and the hotels here make the most of that mandate.

## VERY EXPENSIVE

### Fairmont Hotel

200 N. Columbus Dr., Chicago, IL 60601. ☎ **800/527-4727** or 312/565-8000. Fax 312/ 856-1032. 692 rms. A/C MINIBAR TV TEL. $199–$269 double. Weekend rates begin at $139. AE, CB, DC, DISC, JCB, MC, V. Valet parking $21.25 with in/out privileges.

There's something soothing about the Fairmont Hotel. Maybe it's the soft colors and warm lighting in the sunken lobby. Or perhaps it's the marble bathroom of each guest room, with its separate vanity area, doored toilet, TV, and telephone, all of which,

I am convinced, ease spousal fights. Whatever the elusive quality is, the Fairmont provides a luxury environment in a well-run facility.

**Dining/Entertainment:** Among the four restaurants and bars are Primavera, an Italian restaurant featuring the Primavera Singers, and Metropole, an art-deco lounge with evening entertainment. The Lobby Bar serves high tea every afternoon.

**Services:** Concierge, 24-hour room service, fur vaults, and safe-deposit boxes. All suites and rooms with king-size beds have fax machines.

**Facilities:** A full-service fitness center is connected to the hotel. Handicapped-accessible rooms available.

### Hyatt Regency Chicago

151 E. Wacker Dr., Chicago, IL 60601. ☎ **800/233-1234** or 312/565-1234. Fax 312/565-2966. Telex 256237. 2,019 rms. A/C MINIBAR TV TEL. $224 double; $249 Regency Club double. Weekend rates start at $109. AE, DC, DISC, MC, V. Valet parking $20 with in/out privileges.

Occupying two tall modern towers connected by a glass skyway, the Hyatt Regency is a convention hotel on the mega scale. On the upside, if you're desperate to find a room, it's hard to believe this place is ever *completely* sold out. But on the downside, the walk from the front desk to your room may seem more like a trek across the Himalayas. The lobby, in the east tower, covers half an acre and rises four stories to a greenhouse roof. At the center, a moat surrounds one of the hotel's restaurants.

With its considerable meeting facilities, high-tech check-in, and other streamlined services, the hotel caters heavily to exhibitions and conventions. The Hyatt's "Business Plan" creates a workstation in the guest room, including a desk, a telephone line with no extra access charge that is also PC compatible, and an in-room fax machine.

On the top two floors of the west tower, 45 rooms are reserved for the Regency Club, with its private lounge serving a complimentary continental breakfast in the morning and cocktails at the end of the workday. For some major luxury, book a penthouse Monarch Suite some winter night and stretch out near the fireplace before the 1,600-square-foot parlor space (rates available on request).

**Dining/Entertainment:** Restaurants and cafés occupy three different levels, all connected by walkways.

**Services:** 24-hour room service; irons and ironing boards in each room.

**Facilities:** Sports club a half-block away ($10 fee for adults) with Olympic-size swimming pool. A shopping arcade and beauty salon are on the premises.

### ⑤ Swissôtel Chicago

323 E. Wacker Dr., Chicago, IL 60601. ☎ **800/654-7263** or 312/565-0565. Fax 312/565-0540. 630 rms. A/C TV TEL. $195–$215 double. Weekend rates begin at $109. AE, CB, DC, DISC, JCB, MC, V. Parking $18.

Attention, all you golf nuts out there. If you stay at the Swissôtel Chicago, you're virtually an elevator ride away from a round of golf. That's right, the nine-hole, par-three Illinois Center Golf awaits you next door to this modern Swiss-owned hotel, smack-dab in the middle of town. Arrange for tee times through the concierge; green fees run $22, and a 45-minute session at the driving range costs $9.

For those of you who prefer your greens in your salad, the Swissôtel also has plenty to offer. The guest room views—of either the lake or Grant Park—are out of this world, and the fitness center atop the triangular tower has just about every gizmo you could possibly want. The guest rooms are lovely and generously sized, with marble bathrooms that have separate glass showers, hair dryers, and terry robes.

Following the trend of most Chicago hotels, Swissôtel is aggressively pursuing the business traveler. In Swissôtel's favor is its location, equally convenient to the Loop,

North Michigan Avenue, and River North. The rooms are equipped for homework or business meetings, with oversized writing desks, separate seating areas, two-line telephones, and TV monitors with access to financial markets. The hotel also has a full-service business center.

**Dining/Entertainment:** The Swissôtel has five eateries, including the East Side Terrace, an outdoor café with a view, open for lunch during the summer months.

**Services:** Multilingual concierge, complimentary newspaper delivered on request, 24-hour room service, full business center.

**Facilities:** Health club with full-size pool and the works, even exercise classes, all with sweeping views. Handicapped-accessible guest rooms available. An underground pedestrian concourse links the hotel to the Illinois Center's shops, restaurants, and office and residential buildings.

## 8 Along South Michigan Avenue

Unlike its northern Magnificent Mile half, South Michigan Avenue is less about glamor and more about old Chicago. Running the length of Grant Park, South Michigan Avenue is ideal for a long city stroll, passing grand museums, imposing architecture, and the park's greenery and statuary. Two blocks to the west is State Street, address of Marshall Field's and Carson Pirie Scott & Co.'s giant flagship stores. The lodging possibilities on the avenue fit all budgets.

### EXPENSIVE

#### Chicago Hilton and Towers

730 S. Michigan Ave., Chicago, IL 60605. ☎ **800/HILTONS** or 312/922-4400. Fax 312/922-5240. 1,620 rms. A/C MINIBAR TV TEL. $130–$230 double. Weekend rates start at $109 double, $149 for a Tower room. AE, CB, DC, DISC, JCB, MC. V. Valet parking $19 per day; self-parking $16.

Mammoth it may be, but the Chicago Hilton and Towers is easily the loveliest place to stay in the southern section of the city. From its gray-and-white marble lobby with sweeping staircase to the ubiquitous fresh flower arrangements, the Chicago Hilton takes its job as a luxury hotel seriously.

Depending on the itinerary you wish to follow, this hotel may actually be more convenient than its neighbors to the north. Located only five blocks from the Art Institute of Chicago, the Chicago Hilton is only a 10-minute walk from the Shedd Aquarium, Field Museum, and Adler Planetarium. If you're in town for a concert or festival in Grant Park, the Chicago Hilton is ideal.

As a result of a 1987 renovation that doubled the typical room size, most of the standard rooms at the Chicago Hilton have two bathrooms, a real treat when traveling with a companion or family. One of the marble baths has a tub, and the other, a shower. Another design convenience is the mirrored closet. The hotel's Tower section, which was renovated in early 1995, consists of three floors of rooms with hair dryers, bathrobes, irons and ironing boards, upgraded amenities, and a lounge open from 5:30am to 11pm, serving complimentary continental breakfast and evening hors d'oeuvres.

**Dining/Entertainment:** Four restaurants provide culinary options, from prime aged steaks at Buckingham's to snacks and sandwiches at the Fast Lane Deli. Sunday brunch in the form of an everything-you-could-imagine buffet is very popular.

**Services:** Concierge, 24-hour room service, complimentary transportation to the stores of the Magnificent Mile.

**Facilities:** A complete fitness center, featuring a lap pool with glass doors opening to a deck in summer, an indoor track, two hot tubs, a sauna, a steam room, and a host of exercise machines. The hotel has an enormous ballroom that has become a favorite on the black-tie charity circuit. The Chicago Hilton also maintains a boggling amount of convention space, which often handles the overflow from conventions at McCormick Place. Several shops, including a florist, lease space in the hotel.

# MODERATE

### Best Western Grant Park

1100 S. Michigan Ave., Chicago, IL 60605. ☎ **800/528-1234** or 312/922-2900. Fax 312/922-8812. 172 rms. A/C TV TEL. $108–$118 double. AE, DC, DISC, ER, JCB, MC, V. Valet parking $9 with in/out privileges.

Although no longer the daily bargain it was during its years as a dive called the Ascot, the Best Western Grant Park offers various weekend packages that fit many a tourist's budget. The regular rates are also reasonable, and the recently renovated rooms are up to mid-range tourist standards. Some have kitchenettes. The hotel has an outdoor swimming pool and workout facilities are available.

### ⊛ Blackstone Hotel

636 S. Michigan Ave., Chicago, IL 60605. ☎ **800/622-6330** or ☎/fax 312/427-4300. Telex 721507. 305 rms. A/C TV TEL. $119–$159 double. Weekend rates $69–$99 double. Rates include continental breakfast. AE, DC, DISC, JCB, MC, V. Valet parking $16.

When a suitable location was needed for the banquet scene in the movie *The Untouchables*, the Blackstone Hotel was the clear choice. Al Capone once actually holed up at the old Metropole Hotel, a mile or so farther south, but the Blackstone is of the same era. Makers of a host of other films, including *The Hudsucker Proxy*, *The Package*, and *The Babe*, evidently also found themselves attracted to the Blackstone's period style. A reference or two to the Blackstone may also be culled from literary sources. The Blackstone, for example, is the setting for a New Year's party in James T. Farrell's novel *Studs Lonigan*, a trilogy about the Chicago Irish at the beginning of the century.

Today the genteel Blackstone holds its own among the hotels of this quarter. But the Blackstone offers more than merely past glory. Most of the rooms are large and comfortable enough, and some are relatively inexpensive. Views are first-rate. One room, for example, looks out on Navy Pier and the harbor lighthouse to the north, Grant Park with its fountain and gardens in front, plus the Field Museum, Shedd Aquarium, and Adler Planetarium, the latter two occupying a promontory that juts out into the lake.

The Blackstone provides guests with a simple continental breakfast each morning, a good excuse for hanging out in the lobby and appreciating its rich details: the highly worked plaster ceiling, the dark hardwood walls trimmed in gold-leafed molding, giant brass wall sconces, a grand black marble fireplace set off by empire mirrors, crystal chandeliers, black-and-white marble floors, crimson velvet settees, and an imposing central staircase leading to the Mayfair Theater and banquet rooms. The Blackstone also boasts a game-and-billiards room, and a health club available to guests at $10 a day.

### Congress Hotel

520 S. Michigan Ave., Chicago, IL 60605. ☎ **800/635-1666** or 312/427-3800. Fax 312/427-7264. 830 rms. A/C MINIBAR TV TEL. $135–$165 double. Weekend rates start at $79 double. AE, CB, DC, DISC, MC, V. Valet parking $17 per day; self-parking $13.

Operating since the days of the World Columbian Exposition, which opened near Hyde Park in 1893, the Congress Hotel has a colorful history. The hotel was once a favorite venue for presidential political conventions, at least among candidates named Roosevelt. Teddy opened his Bull Moose convention at the Congress in 1912, and cousin FDR accepted the Democratic nomination here in 1932. Taking a look around, I think it's fair to say the Congress has seen better days. The hotel truly is on the shabby side these days; it's as if the ghosts of its more fortunate past were crying out from the few remaining elements of grandeur—the lobby's mosaic ceiling, the gold leaf—for a renovation.

Although one management company runs the place, the Congress is divided into three parts: a Days Inn with 80 rooms, a Ramada Inn with 500 rooms, and the Congress with 280. The Days Inn is the most modern. Many of the other rooms, though, are small, with tiny, unattractive bathrooms and chipped furniture. One thing the Congress does have going for it is the clear eastern view of Lake Michigan and Grant Park. The hotel also has several restaurants.

### Essex Inn

800 S. Michigan Ave. (at 8th St.), Chicago, IL 60605. ☎ **800/621-6909** or 312/939-2800. Fax 312/939-1605. 225 rms. A/C MINIBAR TV TEL. $99 double. Weekend rates start at $69. AE, CB, DC, DISC, MC, V. Parking $9.

The Essex is far from fancy, but a good medium-priced choice, well managed and accommodating. The Essex is particularly imaginative in its appeal to weekend visitors, offering special packages that are subject to availability from May to September. Rooms are clean and of a decent size, if decidedly no-frills (the closet has no door, just a space in the wall). Minibars are available on request.

## 9  The South Side

### Ramada Inn Lakeshore

4900 S. Lake Shore Dr., Chicago, IL 60615. ☎ **800/228-2828** or 773/288-5800. Fax 773/288-5745. 184 rms. A/C TV TEL. $89–$119 double. AE, DC, DISC, MC, V. Free parking.

Hyde Park has been described as a city within a city, and quite accurately so. Site of the Columbian Exposition of 1893 and the birthplace of nuclear fission, it's home to the Museum of Science and Industry, the Afro-American DuSable Museum, architecture by Frank Lloyd Wright, and the culture-packed campus of the elite University of Chicago.

Hyde Park can also feel like its own city because of its relative isolation from other attractive Chicago neighborhoods. Many adjacent areas have yet to be touched by urban renewal, and Hyde Park is a 20-minute train ride from downtown (half an hour by express bus). If the idea of staying somewhere less glitzy than the Magnificent Mile appeals to you, though, the Ramada Inn Lakeshore is worth checking out. Bright and very modern, the newly renovated Ramada has many of the accoutrements of a resort, including a large outdoor swimming pool and sun patio. The restaurant boasts a great view of the Chicago skyline and the lake, most dramatic at night. If you do tire of Hyde Park, the Ramada provides a complimentary hourly shuttle bus to the North Michigan Avenue shopping and dining district.

## 10  Near O'Hare Airport

The stretch of highway leading to and from O'Hare is lined with lodging choices, some of them quite nice, others not so. Combined, they account for more than 2,500 rooms in the immediate vicinity of the airport. Business travelers, especially, find these hotels and motels convenient, but so might people visiting friends or relatives in the suburbs. Those folks, though, need not limit themselves to this one section of Chicagoland to find a good hotel. As much of suburbia has evolved from bedroom community to semi-self-sufficient cities, with office parks popping up not far from residential subdivisions, hotels have moved in. For more information on the suburban hotels, including those near O'Hare, call the toll-free numbers of the major chains, such as Embassy Suites, Hilton, Hyatt, Marriott, Radisson, and Ramada, as well as Howard Johnson, Holiday Inn, Quality Inn, and TraveLodge. But if you're traveling to Chicago to see the city itself, I strongly recommend staying in or near the center.

## EXPENSIVE

### Hotel Sofitel

5550 N. River Rd., Rosemont, IL 60018. ☎ **800/233-5959** or 847/678-4488. Fax 847/678-4422. 363 rms. A/C MINIBAR TV TEL. $185 double. Weekend rate $89. AE, DC, MC, V. Free parking.

Linked by a heated tunnel to the O'Hare Exposition Center, the Hotel Sofitel is part of a French-owned chain now making its appearance in the American market. Touches in the hotel's decor suggest inspiration from the era of Louis XIV. The lobby recalls the monumental, with its marble floor, muraled walls, and bubbling fountain. Among the hotel's facilities are two restaurants, a bakery, and a health club with a swimming pool.

### Westin Hotel O'Hare

6100 N. River Rd., Rosemont, IL 60018. ☎ **800/228-3000** or 847/698-6000. Fax 847/698-4591. 525 rms. A/C MINIBAR TV TEL. $208 double. Weekend rate $91.50. AE, CB, DC, DISC, JCB, MC, V. Free parking.

In addition to its downtown branch, the chain has a Westin Hotel directly adjacent to O'Hare. In decorous, sleek surroundings, guests are offered such distractions as aerobics classes, racquetball courts, Nautilus equipment, and a swimming pool. Each guest room is spacious, with an oversized desk, two telephones, and two TVs (one is in the bathroom). The Westin's Bakery Café restaurant, specializing in chicken pot pie, is said to have a strong local following. Other facilities include an additional restaurant and two bars.

# 6 | Dining

Chicago's culinary reputation has expanded considerably since its steak-and-potato days. The city now boasts restaurants—Ambria, Charlie Trotter's, and Everest, to name a few—that can hold their own with the nation's best.

In recent years the dining scene has witnessed a virtual explosion in Italian eateries. Some are almost of the cookie-cutter variety, but the trend has also given Chicago some innovative and excellent restaurants. At the same time, some local chefs have found inspiration in their native locale, creating a cuisine that pays homage to the Midwest and its bounty. This new Midwestern cuisine puts a sophisticated twist on traditional comfort foods, and makes use of regional fruits, vegetables, and game.

But Chicago remains a city of neighborhoods (something on the order of 77, in fact). For that reason diners can still find ethnic foods—from German, Swedish, and Ukrainian to Thai and Vietnamese—that, while perhaps less chic than the American, French, and Italian cuisine of Chicago's top spots, are an essential element of the city's character.

Two other features of dining here seem to be peculiar to Chicago. First, although many seasoned travelers are scornful of hotel restaurants, several of Chicago's most worthy eateries happen to be housed in hotels, including Prairie (in the Hyatt on Printer's Row), Jaxx (in the Park Hyatt), and the Cape Cod Room (in the Drake). Second, a man by the name of Richard Melman has built an empire of more than two dozen restaurants under the Lettuce Entertain You umbrella. As you will see from the listings below, they vary in price and formality from the offbeat food court of foodlife to the family-style tradition of Maggiano's to the unmatched elegance of Ambria. Although a few of the Lettuce Entertain You members don't measure up in my estimation, I'd be surprised if any of them served up a perfectly awful meal or let you walk away feeling ripped off.

The restaurants in this guidebook are listed in neighborhood clusters. I've begun with those located near the Loop and the Magnificent Mile, then I've ventured into a few of the surrounding neighborhoods that you're most likely to explore during your stay.

Of course, "expensive" and "inexpensive" are relative terms, but here's a rough breakdown of how I've categorized the restaurants (the prices per person include at least two courses at dinner but do not include wine or other alcohol): **Very Expensive,** more than $40; **Expensive,** $25 to $40; **Moderate,** $15 to $25; **Inexpensive,** less than $15.

## 1 Best Bets

- **Best Spot for a Romantic Dinner:** Few activities are more intimate than dipping lobster tails in fondue by candlelight at **Geja's,** with a classical guitarist playing softly in the background.
- **Best Spot for a Business Lunch:** With great food, great service, and a central location in the Loop, **Trattoria No. 10** tops my list.
- **Best Spot for a Celebration:** At **Bossa Nova,** the music's Latin beat and the Spanish tapas will keep you in a festive mood for hours. Order the tapas a couple at a time and extend the merriment even longer.
- **Best View:** Forty stories above Chicago, **Everest** astounds with a spectacular view—and food to match. In the daytime, another winner is **Spiaggia,** overlooking Lake Michigan's Oak Street Beach. Sunday brunch at Days Inn puts you in the **Pinnacle,** a revolving top-floor lounge, also with a close-up view of the lake. One brilliant view day or night is at **The 95th** atop the John Hancock building. I recommend it for a drink—at the beginning or the end of the evening.
- **Best Value:** A mere $14.95 gets you a full slab of **Carson's** incredible baby back ribs, accompanied by a bowl of its almost-as-famous coleslaw and a choice of potatoes. The complimentary chopped liver in the bar area eliminates any need for an appetizer.
- **Best for Kids:** A meal at **Michael Jordan's Restaurant** and a trip to Niketown will keep most kids happy for hours.
- **Best American Cuisine:** **Zinfandel** offers a refreshing take on hearty American comfort food of all regions, along with an equally interesting, equally American wine list.
- **Best French Cuisine:** For fine French dining, **Ambria** has few rivals—anywhere in the world. Nestled in an elegant Lincoln Park dining room, Ambria's kitchen does not disappoint.
- **Best Italian Cuisine:** Despite its super-trendy ambience and buzz, **Centro** offers truly first-rate cooking, from the pasta to the chicken Vesuvio.
- **Best Steakhouse:** **Eli's** broils a mean steak, and if that's not enough, its multiple varieties of cheesecake will send you into cholesterol overdrive.
- **Best Burgers & Beer:** **R. J. Grunts'** burgers are big and juicy, cooked however you want them, and presented in a basket with perfect, thin french fries.
- **Best Pizza:** The crispy crust and golden brown cheese at **Barnaby's** wins my vote for the best thin pizza in town, while the chewy, gooey deep-dish version of **Gino's East** is the best of its kind.
- **Best Pretheater Dinner:** A local favorite, the **Italian Village**—actually three restaurants run by one family under one roof—knows how to get its clientele seated and fed (very well) in time for a show. A good choice if you're headed for the symphony, opera, or other downtown destination. If you're seeing a play at Steppenwolf or another off-Loop theater, try nearby **Carlucci** for an excellent Italian meal.
- **Best Fast Food:** Serving top-notch pasta, pizza, and salads, **Sopprafina** would never let you guess that it's a fast-food place were it not for its lack of a wait staff.
- **Best Ice Cream:** While many Chicago restaurants have top-notch dessert menus, I have found a shortage of good ice cream parlors in the city. The best is probably

the **Ben and Jerry's** at 338 W. Armitage in Lincoln Park (☎ 281-5152). The **Ice Cream and Yogurt Club** at 32 E. Oak St. between Michigan and Rush Streets (☎ 280-1224) scoops a decent product and features low-fat and no-fat options. **D. B. Kaplan's,** on the mezzanine level of Water Tower Place, 845 N. Michigan (☎ 280-2700), offers a full fountain of sweet delights, as does **Mrs. Levy's** in the Sears Tower, 233 S. Wacker (☎ 993-0530).

## 2 Restaurants by Cuisine

### ALSATIAN

Everest (The Loop, *VE* )

### AMERICAN

Ann Sather's (Wrigleyville/
the Mid-North Side, *I* )
The Berghoff (The Loop, *I* )
Blackhawk Lodge (Magnificent
Mile/Gold Coast, *E* )
Carson's (River North, *M* )
Eccentric (River North, *M* )
Ed Debevic's (River North, *I* )
Four Farthings (Lincoln Park, *M* )
Goose Island Brewing Company
(Lincoln Park, *I* )
Gordon (River North, *E* )
Hard Rock Café (River North, *M* )
Lou Mitchell's (The Loop, *I* )
Michael Jordan's (River North, *M* )
Mity Nice Grill (Magnificent
Mile/Gold Coast, *M* )
Nookies, Too (Lincoln Park, *I* )
Northside Tavern and Grill
(Wicker Park/Bucktown, *I* )
The Original A-1 (Magnificent
Mile/Gold Coast, *M* )
Planet Hollywood
(River North, *M* )
Printer's Row (The Loop, *E* )
Pump Room (Magnificent
Mile/Gold Coast, *E* )
R. J. Grunts (Lincoln Park, *I* )
Urbus Orbis (Wicker
Park/Bucktown, *I* )
Zinfandel (River North, *E* )

### ASIAN

Big Bowl Café (River North, *I* )
Saigon Vietnamese
Restaurant & Shabu
Shabu (Chinatown, *M* )

### BARBECUE

Carson's (River North, *M* )
The Original A-1 (Magnificent
Mile/Gold Coast, *M* )

### BISTROS

Escada Cafe (Magnificent
Mile/Gold Coast, *M* )
Marche (The Loop, *M* )

### BREAKFAST

Ann Sather's (Wrigleyville/
the Mid-North Side, *I* )
Benkay (River North, *VE* )
Billy Goat Tavern (Magnificent
Mile/Gold Coast, *I* )
Bongo Room (Wicker
Park/Bucktown, *I* )
Corner Bakery (River North, *I* )
Heaven on Seven (The Loop, *I* )
Lou Mitchell's (The Loop, *I* )
Oo La La! (Wrigleyville/
the Mid-North Side, *M* )

### BURGERS

Billy Goat Tavern (Magnificent
Mile/Gold Coast, *I* )
Green Door Tavern (River North, *I* )

### CAFÉ FARE

Big Shoulders Cafe (Lincoln Park, *I* )

### CAJUN

Heaven on Seven (The Loop, *I* )

### CALIFORNIAN

Big Bowl Café (River North, *I* )

### CHINESE

Dee's Mandarin Restaurant
(Lincoln Park, *M* )
Three Happiness (Chinatown, *I* )
Won Kow (Chinatown, *I* )

**Key to abbreviations:** *VE* = Very Expensive, *E* = Expensive, *M* = Moderate, *I* = Inexpensive.

## COFFEE SHOP

Heaven on Seven (The Loop, *I*)

## CONTINENTAL

Bistro 110 (Magnificent
Mile/Gold Coast, *M*)
Exchange Restaurant
(The Loop, *E*)

## CREOLE

Bub City (Lincoln Park, *M*)

## CUBAN

Cafe Bolero (Wicker
Park/Bucktown, *I*)

## DELI

Mrs. Levy's (The Loop, *I*)

## ECLECTIC

Cafe Absinthe (Wicker
Park/Bucktown, *E*)
foodlife (Magnificent
Mile/Gold Coast, *I*)

## FONDUE

Geja's (Lincoln Park, *E*)

## FRENCH

Ambria (Lincoln Park, *VE*)
Café Bernard (Lincoln Park, *M*)
Marche (The Loop, *M*)
Oo La La! (Wrigleyville/
Mid-North Side, *M*)
Yoshi's Cafe (Wrigleyville/
Mid-North Side, *VE*)

## GERMAN

The Berghoff (The Loop, *I*)
Zum Deutschen Eck
(Wrigleyville/
Mid-North Side, *M*)

## GREEK

Costas (Greektown, *I*)
Greek Islands (Greektown, *I*)
Papagus Greek Taverna
(River North, *M*)
Parthenon (Greektown, *I*)

## INTERNATIONAL

Gordon (River North, *E*)

## ITALIAN

Avanzare (Magnificent
Mile/Gold Coast, *M*)
Bella Vista (Wrigleyville/
Mid-North Side, *M*)
Bice (Magnificent
Mile/Gold Coast, *E*)
La Cantina (The Loop, *M*)
Carlucci (Lincoln Park, *M*)
Centro (River North, *E*)
Club Lucky (Wicker
Park/Bucktown, *M*)
Coco Pazzo (River North, *E*)
Harry Caray's (River North, *M*)
Maggiano's Little Italy
(River North, *M*)
Mia Francesca (Wrigleyville/
the Mid-North Side, *M*)
Mr. Beef (River North, *I*)
Oo La La! (Wrigleyville/
the Mid-North Side, *M*)
Parrinello (River North, *E*)
Ranalli's Pizzeria, Libations &
Collectibles (Lincoln Park, *I*)
RoseAngelis (Lincoln Park, *I*)
Rosebud on Rush (Magnificent
Mile/Gold Coast, *E*)
Rosebud on Taylor (Little Italy, *I*)
Scoozi (River North, *M*)
Sopraffina (The Loop, *I*)
Spiaggia (Magnificent
Mile/Gold Coast, *E*)
Trattoria No. 10 (The Loop, *M*)
Tucci Benucch (Magnificent
Mile/Gold Coast, *I*)
Tucci Milan (River North, *M*)
Tuttaposto (River North, *M*)
The Village (The Loop, *M*)
Vinny's (Wrigleyville/
the Mid-North Side, *M*)
Vivere (The Loop, *M*)
Vivo (The Loop, *M*)

## JAPANESE

Benkay (River North, *VE*)
Hatsuhana (Magnificent
Mile/Gold Coast, *E*)

## LATIN AMERICAN

Mambo Grill (River North, *M*)

## MEDITERRANEAN

Tuttaposto (River North, *M*)

## MEXICAN

Frontera Grill & Tobolobampo
(River North, *E*)
Hat Dance (River North, *M*)

## MIDWESTERN

Prairie (The Loop, *E*)

## NOUVELLE

Charlie Trotter's
(Lincoln Park, *VE*)
Yoshi's Cafe (Wrigleyville/
Mid-North Side, *VE*)

## PIZZA

Barnaby's
Barry's Spot (Wrigleyville/
the Mid-North Side)
Edwardo's (Lincoln Park)
Gino's East (Magnificent
Mile/Gold Coast)
Leona's Pizzeria (Wrigleyville/
the Mid-North Side)
Lou Malnati's Pizzeria
(River North)
Pat's Pizzeria (Wrigleyville/
the Mid-North Side)
Pizzeria Due (River North)
Pizzeria Uno (River North)
Ranalli's Pizzeria,
Libations & Collectibles
(Lincoln Park)

## POLISH

Mareva's (Wicker Park/
Bucktown, *M*)

## RUSSIAN

Russian Tea Time (The Loop, *I*)

## SEAFOOD

La Cantina (The Loop, *M*)
Cape Cod Room (Magnificent
Mile/Gold Coast, *E*)
Nick's Fishmarket (The Loop, *VE*)
Shaw's Crab House and Blue
Crab Lounge (Magnificent
Mile/Gold Coast, *M*)

## SPANISH

Café Ba-Ba-Reeba! (Lincoln Park, *M*)

## STEAK/CHOPS

Eli's the Place for Steak
(Magnificent Mile/Gold Coast, *E*)
The Saloon (Magnificent
Mile/Gold Coast, *E*)

## SWEDISH

Ann Sather's (Wrigleyville/
the Mid-North Side, *I*)

## TAPAS

Bossa Nova (Lincoln Park, *M*)
Café Ba-Ba-Reeba! (Lincoln Park, *M*)

## TEX-MEX

Bub City (Lincoln Park, *M*)

## THAI

Arun's (Wrigleyville/
the Mid-North Side, *M*)
P. S. Bangkok 2 (Lincoln Park, *I*)
Thai Borrahn (Magnificent
Mile/Gold Coast, *I*)

## VIETNAMESE

Saigon Vietnamese Restaurant &
Shabu Shabu (Chinatown, *M*)

## YUGOSLAVIAN

Cafe Bolero (Wicker Park/
Bucktown, *I*)

## 3 The Loop

In keeping with their proximity to the towers of power, many of the restaurants in the Loop and its environs—namely Printer's Row and the tragically trendy Randolph Street Market District—feature expense-account style prices. But it's still possible to dine here for less than the cost of your hotel room. Keep in mind that several of the best downtown spots are closed on Sunday.

# VERY EXPENSIVE

### ✪ Everest

440 S. La Salle St. ☎ **312/663-8920.** Reservations required. Main courses $26.50–$32.50; fixed-price meal from $69; three-course pretheater dinner $39, including complimentary parking. AE, DC, DISC, MC, V. Tues–Thurs 5:30–8:30pm; Fri–Sat 5:30–10pm. ALSATIAN.

Forty stories above the Chicago Stock Exchange, in the elite La Salle Club, is the lovely dining room of Everest. Its windows overlook the shimmering nightscape of downtown Chicago, and its culinary experience is one of the finest in the world. Chef (and owner) Jean Joho, a baker in his youth in Strasbourg, France, has paired his earthy appreciation of the home-style cookery of the Rhine country with his determination to procure North American foodstuffs, creating a menu with a rare delicacy of touch and imagination.

On a given evening, the menu degustation might consist of an appetizer of cauliflower and caviar, followed by an exotic plate of chilled barnacles from British Columbia, bathed in a vegetable vinaigrette. Then comes a napoleon of razor clams and a strudel of marinated cabbage. A more-than-credible foie gras from New York State is served next on a bed of marinated turnips, giving way to the seafood entrée, a rich Maine lobster roasted with ginger in a brine of Gewürztraminer wine. The pièce de résistance: a Texas-bred saddle of venison with wild huckleberries and gray shallots, sweet, tender, and gamey as if it had come directly from the larder of a superior huntsman.

The assortment of desserts is more traditional, but equally sublime, and the whole extravaganza is accompanied by a variety of fine American and Alsatian wines. His inspiration as varied as the peasant's pantry and the craggy sea bottom, Chef Joho spins an extraordinary and memorable culinary event.

### Nick's Fishmarket

First National Bank Plaza at Monroe and North Dearborn. ☎ **312/621-0200.** Reservations recommended. Main courses $14–$45.50; fixed-price lunch $19.96. AE, CB, DC, DISC, JCB, MC, V. Mon–Fri 11:30am–3pm and 5:30–11:30pm; Sat 5:30pm–midnight. SEAFOOD.

Taking the elevator down below street level to Nick's feels a little like plunging underwater in a submarine. Once submerged, you'll find yourself in one of the best fish and seafood places in the city.

Known for the Pacific specials flown in daily from Hawaii, Nick offers everything from California abalone, Maine lobster, and Dover sole to Atlantic swordfish, catfish, and salmon. Nick's also serves Beluga caviar with frozen vodka. If you're not in the mood for seafood, the menu still offers you more than a dozen choices, such as veal chop with Barolo wine truffle sauce and lamb chops with mint sauce.

The atmosphere at Nick's, though comfortable, is a bit on the stodgy side, but, with a piano player tickling the ivories Tuesday through Saturday evenings, it's a lovely choice for an old-fashioned, dressed-up evening of good food and music.

# EXPENSIVE

### Exchange Restaurant

In the Midland Hotel, 172 W. Adams. ☎ **312/332-1200.** Reservations required. Main courses $16.95–$23.95. AE, DC, DISC, MC, V. Mon–Fri 11:30am–2pm and 5–9pm. Private dinner parties can be arranged through the hotel's sales department. CONTINENTAL.

Gaining in reputation among the noon-hour corporate set is the diminutive Exchange Restaurant, which occupies one wing of the atrium mezzanine above the lobby of the Midland Hotel. On its beautifully decorated beaux-arts perch, the clublike Exchange is suitably above the fray.

# Dining in & Around the Loop

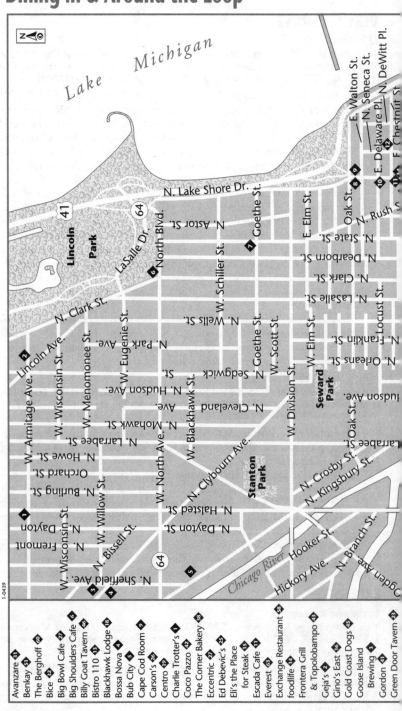

Avanzare 31
Benkay 57
The Berghoff 30
Bice 42
Big Bowl Cafe 27
Big Shoulders Cafe 6
Billy Goat Tavern 45
Bistro 110 44
Blackhawk Lodge 40
Bossa Nova 4
Bub City 5
Cape Cod Room 9
Carson's 26
Centro 12
Charlie Trotter's 1
Coco Pazzo 42
The Corner Bakery 30
Eccentric 22
Ed Debevic's 23
Eli's the Place for Steak 15
Escada Cafe 47
Everest 49
Exchange Restaurant 58
foodlife 43
Frontera Grill 43
Geja's 7
Gino's East 16
Gold Coast Dogs 55
Goose Island Brewing 3
Gordon 8
Green Door Tavern 29
& Topolobampo

1-0439

78

Heaven on Seven 63
The Italian Village 57
Lou Mitchell's 62
Maggiano's 3
Little Italy 46
Mambo Grill 48
Marche 53
Michael Jordan's 54
Mity Nice Grill 51
Mr. Beef 42
Mrs. Levy's 61
Nick's Fishmarket 44
The Original A-1 16
Papagus Greek
Taverna 49
Parrinello 56
Pizzeria Uno 50
Planet Hollywood 28
Prairie 64
Printer's Row 65
Pump Room 7
Rosebud on Rush 47
Russian Tea Time 59
The Saloon 42
Scoozi 21
Shaw's Crab House 48
Sopraffina 55
Spiaggia 8
Thai Borrahn 43
Trattoria No. 10 55
Tucci Benucch 10
Tucci Milan 43
Tuttaposto 22
Vivo 42
Zinfandel 57

79

In this relatively tiny space, which seats perhaps two dozen patrons, a different menu is provided for each season. Typical offerings are smoked chicken salad, seafood stir-fry, chilled poached salmon, and boiled whitefish with lemon and dill. Among the more exotic appetizers is the plate of New Zealand green-tipped mussels with garlic sauce. The dessert tray carries many tempting, freshly baked sweets, including a creamy carrot cake topped with fresh raspberries. In all, a very satisfactory lunch, in very pleasant surroundings, for a reasonable price.

### ✪ Prairie

In the Hyatt on Printer's Row, 500 S. Dearborn. ☎ **312/663-1143.** Reservations required. Main courses $13.50–$21.50; Sun brunch $15. Half portions of many dishes available for lunch. AE, CB, DC, MC, V. Mon–Fri 6:30am–10pm; Sat 7am–11pm; Sun 7am–10pm. MIDWESTERN.

In the section of the South Loop known as Printer's Row is Prairie, a tribute to the culinary traditions of the Midwest. The interior of the restaurant is inspired by Frank Lloyd Wright, the colors and wood trim forming patterns like those on a Native American blanket. All ingredients used to prepare the meals here come from the 14 Midwestern states, as do all the wines. Prairie also emphasizes seasonal specialties.

Don't expect, however, that anything arriving at the table will look homespun and plain. For starters, Prairie has a multitoned tomato soup, in swirls of yellow, red, and green, with sour cream and sturgeon caviar floating in the center. The tarragon-smoked chicken soup is a very healthy and tasteful brew. The grilled, beer-braised Sheboygan bratwurst embodies the Teutonic ideal of the great sausage. Among the main courses, the must-sample is the buffalo steak, served in its natural juices. My brother, a frequent diner here, adores the duck, cooked in a delicious dried cherry port wine sauce. For dessert, have a great hot-fudge sundae with real bittersweet chocolate.

### Printer's Row

550 S. Dearborn. ☎ **312/461-0780.** Reservations required. Main courses $13.50–$24.50. AE, CB, DC, DISC, MC, OPTIMA, V. Daily 11:30am–2:30pm; Mon–Thurs 5–10pm, Fri–Sat 5–10:30pm. AMERICAN.

Printer's Row is another citadel of new-wave American cuisine catering to the hip clientele who now live in buildings where Chicago's publishing industry was once centered. But if the neighborhood has lost its ink-stained commercial character, the Loop in general has gained by the return of inner-city dwellers, and the creation of some interesting and innovative restaurants.

Printer's Row has built a solid reputation over the past few years, mostly through chef Michael Foley's imaginative cooking. Among the chef's novelties are his various preparations of New York State foie gras. Venison, Foley's signature dish, is also regularly featured on the menu, as are tasty fish and poultry dishes, and all meals are accompanied by a healthy assortment of fresh vegetables. The game, incidentally, is New Zealand farm-raised, and may be accompanied by a sun-dried blueberry-and-brandy sauce, or by a sauce of honey-glazed wheatberries and lemon-rosemary. Homemade desserts and ice creams are also first-rate.

## MODERATE

### Russian Tea Time

77 East Adams St. ☎ **312/360-0000.** Reservations recommended. Main courses $10–$16. AE, CB, DC, DISC, MC, V. Sun–Mon 11am–9pm; Tues–Thurs 11am–11pm; Fri–Sat 11am–midnight. RUSSIAN.

This restaurant has a been a favorite pre- and posttheater place to dine ever since it opened as the Russian Tea Cafe in 1993. Its customers include both patrons and personnel of the Chicago Symphony, operagoers, and hosts and guests from the television and radio stations nearby. The atmosphere is old world and cozy, with lots of woodwork, and a friendly staff.

House specialties include blini with Russian caviar, goriachaya zakuska (an appetizer platter for two), stuffed quail with pomegranate sauce, and for vegetarians, mushrooms filled with spinach, onion, and cheese. The beef stroganoff and kulebiaka (meat pie with ground beef, cabbage, and onions) are great. Roast pheasant is served with a brandy, walnut, and pomegranate sauce and brandied prunes. For dessert try the homemade apricot-plum strudel.

## ✪ Trattoria No. 10

10 N. Dearborn. ☎ **312/984-1718.** Reservations recommended. Main courses $10.95–$21.95. AE, CB, DC, DISC, MC, V. Mon–Thurs 11:30am–2pm and 5:30–9pm; Fri 11:30am–2pm and 5:30–9pm; Sat 5:30–10pm. ITALIAN.

One of my personal favorites, Trattoria No. 10 is always at the top of my list of Loop eateries. The burnt orange tones and ceramic floor tiles are straight out of Tuscany, and the food is contemporary Italian, with such touches as sun-dried-tomato butter sauce and plenty of pine nuts. Each ravioli dish, the house specialty, is better than the next and can be ordered as an appetizer or as a main course. The ravioli al tre funghi with crimini caps and wild mushroom ricotta in a porcini cream sauce, priced at $6.95 for an appetizer portion and $10.95 for an entrée, is splendid. You could also start with gamberi aromatici, grilled shrimp with thyme and vegetable reduction, or rotolo di melanzane, a dish of eggplant rolled with roasted peppers, wild mushrooms, and Parmesan served in a roasted plum tomato sauce.

If you're not in the mood for ravioli, Trattoria No. 10 offers a group of other interesting pasta dishes, such as farfalle con anatra with duck confit, asparagus, caramelized onions, and pine nuts. While it serves lamb, veal, and chicken dishes, Trattoria No. 10's strength is clearly pasta.

## THE ITALIAN VILLAGE

The building at 71 W. Monroe houses three separate Italian restaurants, collectively known as the Italian Village. The Village was the first to open, back in 1927, followed shortly by La Cantina, and, in the early '90s, by Vivere. All three are owned by the Capitanini family, now in its third generation of management. But each has a unique take on Italian ambience and cooking.

### La Cantina

71 W. Monroe. ☎ **312/332-7005.** Reservations recommended. Main courses (including soup, salad, dessert, and coffee) $11.75–$25.50; salads $9.95–$10.95; sandwiches $6.95–$7.95. Lunch prices slightly lower. Mon–Fri 11:30am–3pm and 5pm–midnight; Sat 5pm–1am. ITALIAN/SEAFOOD.

La Cantina is the most moderately priced of the trilogy. It makes the most of its basement location by creating the feel of a wine cellar. The restaurant attracts a daily regular clientele of lawyers, judges, and the like, many of whom eat at the bar. Specializing in seafood, La Cantina offers at least five fresh varieties every day.

The dinner menu offers a big-time bargain: à la carte dishes (most of which are under $20) include a salad, and for $2 more, you also get soup, dessert, and coffee. As for the cuisine, no surprises where the pasta is concerned—all the reliable standards are here.

### The Village

71 W. Monroe. ☎ **312/332-7005.** Reservations recommended (accepted for parties of three or more). Main courses (including salad) $9.25–$23.75; salads $4.50–$10.25; pizza $9.25–$13.75; sandwiches $6.25–$13.95. Lunch prices slightly lower. AE, CB, DC, DISC, MC, V. Mon–Thurs 11am–1am; Fri–Sat 11am–2am; Sun noon–midnight. NORTHERN ITALIAN.

Upstairs is The Village, with its charmimg interpretation of al fresco dining in a small Italian town, complete with a midnight-blue ceiling and strings of white lights. It's the kind of pan-Chicago place where you might see one man in a tux and another in shorts. With 200 items, the menu is so big and broad that it's sure to satisfy. Those old-time, hearty northern Italian standards are all here, and at a great value. I'm talking chicken Vesuvio (with garlic and herbs), veal marsala (with marsala wine and mushrooms), eggplant parmigiana, tortellini alla bolognese (meat sauce) and, yes, even pizza. The lunch menu is somewhat abbreviated but still offers an enormous selection of salads, pasta, meats, and sandwiches.

### Vivere

71 W. Monroe. ☎ **312/332-4040.** Reservations recommended. Main courses $10.25–$20.50. AE, CB, DC, DISC, MC, V. Mon–Thurs 11:15am–2:15pm and 5–10pm; Fri 11:15am–2:15pm and 5–11pm; Sat 5–11pm. ITALIAN.

On the main floor is Vivere, the Italian Village's take on gourmet cooking. The chic interior, with rich burgundies, textured walls, spiraling bronze sculptures, and fragmented mosaic floors, complement the modern cuisine. In addition to excellent daily risotto and fresh fish dishes, Vivere presents interesting preparations of game and a particularly good petto d'anatra, a duck breast with escarole sautéed in red wine and balsamic vinegar. Pastas, which at lunch are available either in "primi" appetizer size or as the entrée, range from the basic linguine alla bolognese to the slightly daring agnolottini di fagiano (pheasant-filled pasta with butter, sage, and Parmesan).

## RANDOLPH STREET MARKET DISTRICT

Either that old real estate axiom "location, location, location" has its limits, or the owners of Vivo and Marche, two restaurants that practically define the word *hip* in Chicago, have proved that the more unexpected, the more out-of-the-way the spot, the more people will want to come. "It's *where?*" was the refrain I heard when Vivo opened back in 1991. Now this little stretch of Randolph Street west of the Loop has become a culinary neighborhood all its own.

Transportation to the Market District is easy, by the way—about a $5 cab ride from Michigan Avenue, or a slightly longer trek by bus (nos. 8 or 9) or El, with stops at Halsted and Lake, a block from the restaurant. The walk from the Loop is very pleasant, and totally secure in the daytime, but at night I'd save my stroll for Michigan Avenue.

### Marche

833 W. Randolph St. ☎ **312/226-8399.** Reservations recommended. Main courses $9–$16. AE, DC, DISC, MC, V. Mon–Wed 8am–2:30pm and 5pm–midnight; Thurs–Fri 8am–2:30pm and 5pm–2am; Sat 5pm–2am. FRENCH BISTRO.

The basic idea behind Marche is derivative of the popular and cavernous Paris café. The menu is also a by-product of French inspiration, but the execution is pure Americana. Co-owner and furniture designer Jerry Kleiner created an interior as a visual potpourri of mixed-media materials that favor the eclectic, the postmodern, and the outrageous. Multilevel seating enhances the effect and suggests a perpetual fiesta.

To ensure that Marche will outlast the impact of its perishable aesthetic, Michael Kornick, a dynamic young chef with some impressive power credits already notched on his resume (Gordon in Chicago, Four Seasons in Boston), was brought in to create the menu and supervise the kitchen, which is visible to diners from behind a glass barrier along one corner of the building. Chef Kornick seems to handle every idiom, whether the ordinary or the exotic, with equal ease and grace. There's still nothing like a steaming bowl of good onion soup to remove that inner chill on a blustery day.

Thè coriander-crusted tuna with horseradish and arugula is as delicious as it is original, and ditto the seasonal offering of spring morels served with wild leeks.

The entrées the night I dined at Marche were divided almost equally between meat
and fish, plus a couscous of grilled vegetables (only $9) and two pasta dishes for veg-
etarians. My grilled veal chop was delicate yet hearty, and my companion chose that
old bistro standby, steak with pommes frites. After sating our respective sweet tooths
with a chocolate pot de crème and a scoop of vanilla-bean ice cream doused with a
compote of rhubarb, we rolled off into the rainy night, leaving Marche to party on,
no doubt for some time to come.

### Vivo

838 W. Randolph. ☎ **312/733-3379.** Reservations accepted. Main courses $12.95–$17.95.
AE, CB, DC, MC, V. Mon–Wed 11:30am–2:30pm and 5:30–10pm; Thurs 11:30am–2:30pm and
5:30–11pm; Fri 11:30am–2:30pm and 5:30pm–midnight; Sat 5:30pm–midnight; Sun 5–9pm.
SOUTHERN ITALIAN.

Before there was Marche, there was Vivo, pioneer and prototype of the genre, half
the size, and hot, hot, hot since the day it opened. Vivo's mock-market ambience is
enhanced by fragments of the old warehouse that are allowed to peek through the
artsy decor.

Vivo's kitchen may have been somewhat underrated by the local food mavens in
the glare of publicity that has surrounded the place since its opening in the fall
of 1991. I have always enjoyed the food, but if you're simply in search of the best
Italian fare in town, head to Taylor Street or to Centro (in River North). Go to Vivo
for its one-of-a-kind combination of people-watching and filling food.

For starters, the portobello alla griglia and the antipasto della casa are both
positively first-rate. I have tried several pasta dishes, each of which is more than
satisfying.

## INEXPENSIVE

### The Berghoff

17 W. Adams. ☎ **312/427-3170.** Reservations recommended. Main courses $6.50–$9.95 at
lunch, $8.75–$13.95 at dinner. AE, MC, V. Mon–Thurs 11am–9:30pm; Fri–Sat 11am–10pm.
GERMAN/AMERICAN.

Closing in on its 100th anniversary in 1998, the Berghoff is a Chicago landmark. The
immense 700-seat restaurant is housed in one of the first buildings constructed in the
Loop after the Chicago Fire, and one of the only remaining buildings in the city with
a cast-iron facade. The Berghoff holds Chicago liquor license no. 1, issued at the close
of Prohibition, and it still serves its own brand of beer at $2.25 a stein.

While the menu rotates seasonally, the German standard-bearers are always available. The Berghoff serves hundreds of orders of Wiener schnitzel every day, plus
bratwurst, sauerbraten, corned beef, and the like. Because some of us have arteries
to worry about, the third generation of family management has added some lighter
fare in the form of salads, broiled fish, and vegetarian dishes.

If the food sounds somewhat manly, it's no coincidence. The stand-up bar at the
Berghoff didn't even admit women until 1969, when a group of NOW activists
staged a protest. The bar, where men used to drink nickel beers and eat free sandwiches, is still overwhelmingly male.

### Heaven on Seven

111 N. Wabash, 7th floor. ☎ **312/263-6443.** Reservations not accepted. Menu items
$2.50–$9.95. No credit cards. Mon–Fri 7am–5pm; Sat 10am–3pm. First and second Fri of month
5:30–9pm. CAJUN MEETS COFFEE SHOP.

When you take the elevator to the seventh floor of the Garland Building, just across from Marshall Field's, don't be scared off by the lunchtime line that extends all the way down the hall. It moves pretty quickly. And once you're inside you'll be in one of the working locals' favorite joints. Heaven on Seven is loud, it's crowded, and it serves a mean gumbo for $3.75. The Cajun and Creole specialties, most of which run about $8 or $9 and come with a cup of soup, include such Louisiana staples as red beans and rice, a catfish po' boy sandwich, and jambalaya. If you don't have a taste for tabasco, the enormous coffee-shop-style menu covers all the traditional essentials: grilled cheese sandwiches, omelets, tuna, the works. On the first and second Fridays of the month, Heaven on Seven hosts special dinners from 5:30 to 9pm, enlivened by a Cajun band.

### Mrs. Levy's

Sears Tower, concourse level, 233 S. Wacker Dr. ☎ **312/993-0530.** Reservations not accepted. Sandwiches $4–$6.99. No credit cards. Mon–Fri 6:30am–3pm. DELI.

To paraphrase the well-known slogan of rye-bread fame, "You don't have to be Jewish to like Mrs. Levy's," an eat-in delicatessen. It's all here at Mrs. Levy's in the Loop: matzoh-ball soup, bagels with lox and cream cheese, gefilte fish, latkes (potato pancakes), pastrami and corned beef, and much, much more. The food is good, not great, and the service is friendly, with no pressure if you want to linger a bit over your meal.

Take-out orders for Mrs. Levy's can be placed by calling Chef's Express at 842-LEVY. The service also takes orders for its several other Sears Tower eateries, which include a Mexican cantina and an Italian trattoria.

### Sopraffina

10 N. Dearborn. ☎ **312/984-0044.** Reservations not accepted. Pizza $3.95 for a half portion, $6.95 for a whole; pasta $5.50; sandwiches $4.25–$6.95. AE, CB, DC, DISC, MC, V. Mon–Fri 11am–4pm. ITALIAN.

Leave it to the folks at Trattoria No. 10 to create a first-rate fast-food Italian restaurant. Sopraffina somehow manages to offer low-priced fare without sacrificing creativity. We're not talking simple spaghetti with ketchup-impersonating marinara here. Instead, Sopraffina features funky pizzas on tasty crusts, including the one with chicken, mushrooms, broccoli, provolone, and Parmesan; a lasagna with a choice of Parmesan cream or marinara sauce; and a shrimp or chicken caesar panino (Italian sandwich). The antipasto is sold in 4-ounce servings and includes salad niçoise, marinated green beans, and couscous. Sopraffina does not have table service, but that's where the similarity to any other fast-food joint ends.

## 4 Ethnic Dining Near the Loop

All of the dining choices below are an easy cab ride from the convention center.

## CHINATOWN

Chicago's Chinatown, about 20 blocks south of the Loop and about two long blocks west of the McCormick convention complex, is expanding. For the moment, most of the commerce, which includes approximately 50 restaurants, plus several colorful food-and-vegetable markets and import houses, is strung along two thoroughfares, Cermak Road and Wentworth Avenue as far south as 24th Place. The Cermak stop on the Lake/Dan Ryan train is right on the edge of the Chinatown commercial district.

Many shops in Chinatown provide interesting browsing, especially the dry goods and fresh vegetable markets. You might also want to visit a Chinese bakery, such as **Keefer Bakery,** 249 W. Cermak (☎ 312/326-2289). Chinese baked goods are made with less sugar than is used in Western bakery products, and many pastries are filled with lotus or red-bean paste. The Keefer Bakery also has a line of dumplings, one filled with pork, another with ham and egg. The red-bean snowball is a typical pastry. As for the store's non-Chinese-sounding name, it comes from a street in Hong Kong! It's open daily from 8am to 7pm.

In the mezzanine-level dining room at **Won Kow** at 237 S. Wentworth (☎ 312/842-7500), you can enjoy dim sum from 10am to 3pm daily. Most of the dumplings cost between $1.50 and $2 an order. Other house specialties include Mongolian chicken, and 8 Treasure Duck with seafood.

### INEXPENSIVE

### Three Happiness

209 W. Cermak Rd. ☎ **312/842-1964.** Reservations not required. Main courses $4.75–$12. AE, DC, MC, V. Daily 9am–2am. CHINESE.

Three Happiness has enjoyed a reputation over many years of providing consistently reliable dishes from several regions of China. City residents come back to Three Happiness year after year during their once- or twice-annual visit to Chicago's traditional Chinatown. There is another Three Happiness at 2130 S. Wentworth (☎ 312/791-1228).

### Saigon Vietnamese Restaurant & Shabu Shabu

232 W. Cermak. ☎ **312/808-1318.** Reservations not needed. Main courses $4.95–$14.95. AE, DISC, MC, V. Daily 11am–3am. VIETNAMESE/ASIAN.

The food here is eclectic, and there aren't as many authentic Vietnamese dishes as one might wish. You can't blame the restaurant's owners, however; the American dining public simply has never acquired a taste for this very special cuisine. The spring rolls are Vietnamese style, though, and go down nicely with a bottle of Chinese beer. Shabu shabu is a kind of Japanese fondue where you construct a soup: to a steaming bowl of hot broth, you add the shrimp, fish, and veggies. Another soup, rice noodle, is a very generous serving for the price.

## LITTLE ITALY

Convenient to most downtown locations, a few blocks' stretch of Taylor Street is home to a host of traditional, hearty Italian restaurants.

### ✪ Rosebud on Taylor

1500 W. Taylor St. ☎ **312/942-1117.** Reservations recommended, especially on weekends. Lunch items $4.95–$14.95; main courses $9.95–$25.95. AE, DC, DISC, MC, V. Mon–Thurs 11am–3pm and 5–10:30pm; Fri 11am–3pm and 5–11:30pm; Sat 5–11:30pm; Sun 4–9:30pm. ITALIAN.

Expect to wait well beyond the time of your reservation, but fear not: Your hunger will be satisfied. The original Rosebud serves up enormous helpings of pasta in white bowls. Almost everyone walks out with a bag of leftovers. But the portions aren't just large, they're delicious. The deep-dish lasagna ($12.95) is intense, and the fettuccine Alfredo defines the word *rich*. Rosebud also offers a tempting selection of "secondi," meat, fish, and poultry dishes.

## GREEKTOWN

If you wander on South Halsted roughly from Van Buren to Washington Streets, you'll find a cluster of moderately priced and inexpensive Greek restaurants. **Greek Islands,** 200 S. Halsted (☎ 312/782-9855), **Parthenon,** 314 S. Halsted (☎ 726-2407), and **Costas,** 340 S. Halsted (☎ 312-263-0767) are all good bets for gyros, Greek salads, shish kebob, and moussaka, a sort of Greek lasagna.

## 5 The Magnificent Mile (North Michigan Avenue) & the Gold Coast

I suspect a great many tourists who visit Chicago never stray far from the Magnificent Mile and the adjoining Gold Coast area. From the array of restaurants, shops, and pretty streets in the area, it's not hard to see why.

I'm all in favor of exploring, so if you have at least a couple of nights in the city, I encourage you to venture out to, say, Wicker Park for dinner one evening. But the restaurants I've chosen along or near the Magnificent Mile are undeniably some of the best in the city.

## EXPENSIVE

### Bice

158 E. Ontario St. ☎ **312/664-1474.** Reservations required. Main courses $10–$17 at lunch, $13–$23 at dinner. AE, DC, MC, V. Daily 11:30am–midnight. NORTHERN ITALIAN.

Direct from Milan comes Bice, which first opened its doors in 1926 as a small hole-in-the-wall, and now has fashionable affiliates in New York and Beverly Hills, where it continues to be one of the hottest lunch spots in town. Bice occupies a lovely two-story building just minutes from North Michigan Avenue. Seating begins with open-air tables on the street level and moves through a series of raised platforms to the more or less formal interior dining room. The Bice menu, which changes daily, emphasizes northern Italian tastes.

During a recent lunch at Bice, I first sampled and enjoyed the insalata d'aragosta, a lobster salad with arugula, Belgian endive, and hearts of palm. A unique and intriguing appetizer is carpaccio of either tuna or swordfish. I was very satisfied with my misto di pasta della casa main course, a selection of four exquisitely prepared pastas, and likewise the simple scaloppine di vitello, veal scaloppine sautéed with roasted peppers, oregano, and basil. Desserts are special at Bice, and are all made on the premises, including the ice cream. Highly recommended is the tiramisù della Bice, ladyfingers with mascarpone cheese flavored with espresso and Kahlúa.

### ✪ Blackhawk Lodge

41 E. Superior St. ☎ **312/280-4080.** Reservations recommended. Main courses $10.95–$21.95. Lunch prices slightly lower. AE, CB, DC, DISC, MC, V. Mon–Thurs 11:30am–3pm and 5–10pm; Fri–Sat 11:30am–3pm and 5–11pm; Sun 5–10pm. REGIONAL AMERICAN.

New Executive Chef Scott Birch prepares comfort food with a twist. He picks up where his predecessor, Glenn Wielo, left off, livening up Blackhawk's regional American menu with treats such as grilled pork chops with sautéed apples, shoestring potatoes with mustard sauce, and pan-fried Idaho brook trout with pecan rice and lime butter.

The rustic setting of early American furniture and pine-knot paneling is reminiscent of a cabin in the North Woods. Blackhawk offers a nice range of appetizers, from terrific crab cakes to pumpkin ravioli. Servings are generous: my lineman-sized brother-in-law couldn't finish the enormous portion of fried chicken. The service is excellent—from the moment reservations are honored, even on a busy Saturday night, to the prompt pickup of credit cards for processing.

### Cape Cod Room

In the Drake Hotel, 140 E. Walton Place. ☎ **312/787-2200.** Reservations recommended. Main courses $16.75–$31. AE, CB, DC, DISC, ER, JCB, MC, V. Daily noon–11pm. Closed Christmas Day. SEAFOOD.

The Cape Cod Room is usually filled to capacity even during the middle of the week, underscoring its perennial popularity. The large, multilevel room, with tables and booths covered in red-and-white checkerboard cloths, is wood-beamed and stuffed with nautical paraphernalia. Since the fresh seafood catch from Lake Michigan and nearby rivers is minimal, the Dover sole—the dish favored by Paul Newman, who is said to dine here often when in Chicago—is flown in fresh every two days from its native channel waters off the coast of England. The sole is broiled to a light, crusty golden brown and served in a superb almond meunière sauce. The waiter performs the delicate surgery of deboning the fish at tableside into four delectable strips. The sole is accompanied by au gratin potatoes and a mixed salad, though the iceberg lettuce is a reminder that there is nothing nouvelle about the Cape Cod Room.

For starters, the delicious, hearty Bookbinder red snapper soup is flavored to taste with dry sherry brought to the table. Or you might order a mixed seafood appetizer of shrimp, bay scallops, salmon, and lobster in a creamy tarragon sauce. For the main course, you can choose from pike, Wisconsin largemouth (freshwater) bass, turbot from the coast of France, pompano from Florida, Gulf swordfish, and Pacific salmon. Shellfish include bay and sea scallops, shrimp, and Maine lobster. And if you want the works, try the bouillabaisse. The menu also offers a small selection of prime meat cuts, steaks, and chops. All main courses at the Cape Cod Room are à la carte. For dessert, try a simple bowl of fresh red raspberries and cream in season.

### Eli's the Place for Steak

215 E. Chicago Ave. ☎ **312/642-1393.** Reservations recommended. Main courses $17.95–$29.95. AE, DC, DISC, MC, V. Mon–Thurs 11am–2:30pm and 4–10:30pm; Fri 11am–2:30pm and 4–11pm; Sat 4–11pm; Sun 4–10:30pm. STEAK/CHOPS.

Every big town has its short list of restaurant institutions—Eli's is definitely on Chicago's. But Eli's is much more than a traditional steak joint where an occasional big-name celebrity shows up for a meal and a photo session. The restaurant has some deep roots of its own. The potato pancakes, the sautéed liver and onions, and the chicken fricassee are variations on the Central European comfort foods that found their way here by way of a neighborhood delicatessen where the late Eli Schulman got his start in Chicago 50 years ago. Add to this solid pedigree an element of friendly formality, a commitment to quality, and servings generous enough to ensure that you have something left for tomorrow's lunch, and you have in a nutshell the formula that has kept Eli's at the forefront of Chicago eateries since 1966.

The meal begins with a scoop of delicate chopped liver, accompanied by diced eggs and onions, a colorful crudité of fresh vegetables, and a basket of various breads and rolls. The restaurant's signature appetizer is the shrimp de jonghe, baked to succulent perfection with garlic and bread crumbs ($9.25, but also available as an entrée for $22.95). Now about those steaks—Eli's does not disappoint. The 20-ounce T-bone ($29.95) is perfect—full-flavored, juicy, and not too rich. And liver connoisseurs will appreciate the calf's liver Eli, a truly delicate and palate-pleasing selection.

Be sure to save some room for a slice of Eli's famous cheesecake, rapidly becoming a superstar dessert retailed throughout the country. A dozen or so of the 50 varieties are always available at the restaurant at $3.95 a slice. For something on the lighter side, try the pumpkin cheesecake, or go for broke with the mud pie version, a creamy chocolate concoction. The only problem is how to choose just one!

### Hatsuhana

160 E. Ontario. ☎ **312/280-8808.** Reservations accepted. Main courses $20–$25. AE, CB, DC, DISC, MC, V. Mon–Fri 11:45am–2pm and 5–10pm; Sat 5–10pm. JAPANESE.

Hatsuhana has one of the most popular sushi bars in Chicago. For you novices out there, traditional Japanese sushi is made of raw fish rolled in seaweed and rice. A typical sushi meal consists of several varieties of raw fish and other sea creatures. In the U.S., several types of cooked sushi, such as the aptly named California Roll, have become standards. The restaurant also offers tempura and teriyaki dinners, but I recommend sitting at the sushi bar to watch the skilled chefs at work. You can sample both the old and new sushi.

## Pump Room

In the Omni Ambassador East Hotel, 1301 N. State Pkwy. ☎ **312/266-0360.** Reservations required. Main courses $16.50–$26. AE, DC, DISC, MC, V. Mon–Thurs 7am–10pm; Fri–Sat 7am–midnight; Sun 10:30am–2:30pm (brunch) and 5–10pm. AMERICAN.

Back when celebrities journeyed by train between Hollywood and New York, stopping in Chicago to court the press, they would come to the Pump Room. Diners at Booth One inevitably showed up in the morning papers. Today the closest the Pump Room gets to most celebrities are the photographs of movie stars lining the walls.

Under the stewardship of Richard Melman and his Lettuce Entertain You enterprise, the restaurant remains a good place for a meal, though it's not the Pump Room of old. The selection on the dinner menu is limited to four appetizers—two are soups—a seafood salad, and three main courses: two varieties of grilled fish and a sautéed filet of beef. Though the menu is limited, the kitchen will try to accommodate special requests if possible. Five very potable wines are also offered on the menu. The roast eggplant soup, with basil and red pepper, and the twin filets of beef with wild mushrooms in bourbon sauce are superb. The fried calamari with roast garlic-tartare sauce is very good, but the Florida red snapper is only fair. Someone with a sense of humor conceived at least one of the Pump Room's desserts: one of the world's smallest hot-fudge sundaes, its ingredients served in individual shot glasses.

## Rosebud on Rush

55 E. Superior. ☎ **312/266-6444.** Reservations recommended, especially on weekends. Main courses $12.95–$29.95. AE, DC, DISC, MC, V. Mon–Thurs 11am–3pm and 5–10:30pm; Fri 11am–3pm and 5–11:30pm; Sat noon–11:30pm; Sun noon–9:30pm. ITALIAN.

If you don't feel like trekking to the original Rosebud on Little Italy's Taylor Street, the Gold Coast version offers delicious food in a trendier atmosphere. The wait can be long—as in three hours long—and here's a warning to summer travelers: Rosebud has been known to turn away hungry people wearing shorts. (The restaurant claims women are welcome to dine in shorts, just not men.)

Assuming you swing a table—either in the covered outdoor eating area or inside—you might try the minestrone soup, followed by the scrumptious rigatoni with broccoli in garlic and olive oil. The other pasta dishes fall nicely between boring and unnecessarily complicated. If you're craving protein, Rosebud offers plenty of veal, chicken, and seafood, plus pork and lamb chops. All in all, good food in a great location, if a tinge overpriced. If you want a more watery slant on Italian cooking, Rosebud's owners recently opened Carmine's Clamhouse a few blocks north at 1043 N. Rush St.

## The Saloon

200 E. Chestnut St. ☎ **312/280-5454.** Reservations recommended. Main courses $9.95–$26.95. AE, MC, V. Mon–Sat 11am–midnight; Sun noon–midnight. STEAK.

Forget the prosaic name. The Saloon is no diamond in the rough. Its setting, a few steps below sidewalk level in one of the neighborhood's most elegant apartment buildings, is all tone, with superb food. You wouldn't think there are many spins you could give to a meal of honest meat and potatoes, but the Saloon has managed to turn a corner or two, as it lives up to its claim to be a "steakhouse for the '90s." The Kansas City Bone-in Strip ($18.95), served "black 'n' blue," was a knockout, rich as butter under its outside crust, and just as tender. The Saloon's bargain taste treat is a thick slab of smokey barbecued meatloaf ($8.95). The menu also has a wide selection of seafood dishes. And let's not forget those potatoes—six varieties from mashed to hashed, all $1.95 as sides when they don't accompany a given entrée. Standouts for me were the puffy cottage fries and the mashed potatoes blended with scallions and bacon. Within a year of its opening, the Saloon has already managed to climb into one prominent Chicago food critic's list of the city's top 10 steakhouses. Lunch here, incidentally, is popular and quite reasonable.

### ✪ Spiaggia

980 N. Michigan Ave. ☎ 312/280-2750. Reservations required. Main courses $9.95–$18 at lunch, $26–$29 at dinner. AE, CB, DC, DISC, MC, V. Mon–Thurs 11:30am–2pm and 5:30–9:30pm; Fri–Sat 11:30am–2pm and 5:30–10:30pm; Sun 5:30–9pm. ITALIAN.

Picture a long, narrow room, colored in soft desert pastels and sharply contoured, with a ceiling two stories high. Against the outer wall, a curtain of tall, segmented windows with a spectacular view of Lake Michigan and Oak Street Beach gives the illusion that the entire room is curved and in motion. This is Spiaggia, a restaurant across from the Drake, whose boldness and novelty of design matches its innovative cuisine. A pianist provides nightly entertainment.

Spiaggia recognizes that pizza is a suitable appetizer, no matter how elegant the restaurant, if the dough is treated as pastry. The small pizza margherita with fresh tomato sauce, basil, and mozzarella is thin, crisp, and delicious. It's not unreasonable to make a lunch at Spiaggia exclusively from side dishes, adding to the pizza, say, an order of tender carpaccio (sun-dried beef) or zuppa di gamberi e fagioli (shrimp and white bean soup). The insalata normale, an interesting variety of leaves dressed with a light coating of herb vinegar and olive oil, is the best salad I have eaten in any Chicago restaurant.

Among the many pasta dishes are pappardelle con salsiccia e pollo (wide pasta with Italian sausage, chicken, mushrooms, tomatoes, and herbs) and agnolotti di vitello (veal-filled pasta crescents with tomato-basil sauce). Or if fish appeals, you might select the mista griglia di pesce (mixed seafood grill).

Lovers of sweets unite, and confront your finest struggle at Spiaggia! Try the hot zabaglione with seasonal fruits; the cannoli, an almond cone filled with ricotta/chocolate-chip gelato, and covered with orange and pistachio sauces; or the cioccolato bianco e nero, semisweet chocolate layers filled with white-chocolate mousse and seasonal fruits. Such a feast demands a finale, an apéritif from Spiaggia's list of fine grappas. The Nonino Grappa is as smooth as velvet.

Adjacent to the restaurant in another narrow, window-dominated space is the Café Spiaggia (☎ 280-2764), a more informal but equally spiffy trattoria serving pizzas, pastas, and antipasti.

## MODERATE

### Avanzare

161 E. Huron. ☎ 312/337-8056. Reservations required. Main courses $10.50–$17.25 at lunch, $10.75–$27.75 at dinner. AE, DC, DISC, MC, V. Mon–Thurs 11:30am–2pm and 5:30–10pm; Fri 11:30am–2pm and 5–11pm; Sat 5–11pm; Sun 5–9:30pm. NORTHERN ITALIAN.

Avanzare is one of those hangar-size continental-style cafés with wraparound windows overlooking the street. The space at ground level is fitted out with banquettes, trimmed in hardwood and padded with green-leather cushions. An upper-level balcony houses a few individual linen-covered tables for more private dining. But on most days during the lunch and dinner hours, downstairs is like a public square on a Saturday night in summer. Reasonable prices ensure a crowd of regulars.

I recommend the pollo al rosmarino (breast of chicken in rosemary sauce with mushrooms), the tortellini di pollo affumicato (smoked chicken–filled pasta with a sauce of provolone and spinach), and the spiedini di manzo con aglio (a skewer of sirloin tips rubbed with garlic)—all of gourmet quality. The linguine with shrimp sautéed in garlic, basil, and chilis is merely "good."

With one of the restaurant's tasty sweets or pastries for dessert, plus drink or beverage, the bill probably won't come to more than $45 for two—not cheap, but a fair exchange at Avanzare.

### Bistro 110

110 E. Pearson St. ☎ **312/266-3110.** Reservations accepted for lunch, not accepted for dinner. Main courses $9.95–$21.95. AE, CB, DC, DISC, MC, V. Mon–Thurs 11:30am–midnight; Fri–Sat 11:30am–1am; Sun 11:30am–11pm. CONTINENTAL.

One of the few restaurants in Chicago with a year-round sidewalk café (al fresco during the warm season and enclosed the rest of the year) is half a block west of North Michigan Avenue. Here, patrons sitting outdoors have a close-up view of Chicago's historic Water Tower, the spindly edifice of yellow stone that miraculously escaped destruction despite being directly in the path of the Great Fire. Inside, Bistro 110 is divided into several environments—the sidewalk enclosure, a bar area, and a large back room where most diners are seated. An activities chalkboard covers one whole side wall near the front of the restaurant, listing such bulletins as the daily news headlines, weather forecasts, movie and theater information, market quotes, and sports results. Neighborhood cronies tend to congregate here, drawn by the familiar faces and the reasonably priced daily specials.

A sample dinner might begin with half a dozen raw oysters or a novel baked Brie with sliced apples. Move on to classic main courses like steak au poivre or filet of salmon, served with a whole squadron of veggies: a wedge of orange bell pepper, a plum tomato, new potatoes, a section of corn on the cob, carrots, and asparagus. And for dessert try the crème brûlée, a cream custard topped with caramelized sugar and flavored with Tahitian vanilla beans; fresh fruit; or a white-chocolate terrine, a creamy white-chocolate mousse with a fresh raspberry sauce.

### Escada Cafe

840 N. Michigan Ave. ☎ **312/915-0500.** Reservations required. Main courses $9–$14. AE, MC, V. Mon–Sat 11:30am–3pm. BISTRO.

When Plaza Escada opened here in 1993, it brought to North Michigan Avenue not only the full range of the German firm's designer fashion and accessories, but also a small café with a privileged view of the Magnificent Mile that puts one in the perfect mood for shopping or strolling. From its tiny fourth-floor perch, surrounded by the elegant, well-made clothing, all is right with the world. The food itself is quite good. You might begin with the yellow pepper soup, followed by the lemon chicken Caesar salad or the gratin of crab with fricassee. Escada Cafe is also a civilized place to pause over a pot of tea and something sweet in midafternoon.

### Mity Nice Grill

835 N. Michigan Ave. (Water Tower Place). ☎ **312/335-4745.** Reservations not required. Main courses $7.95–$18.95. AE, DC, DISC, MC, V. Mon–Thurs 11am–10pm; Fri–Sat 11am–10pm; Sun 11am–9pm. AMERICAN.

Ensconced in the mezzanine of the busy vertical shopping mall at Water Tower Place, Mity Nice is a good place to go for a consolation meal after a frenzied bout of shopping. Being a Lettuce Entertain You restaurant, Mity Nice is certainly reliable in the kitchen, but it falls short of exciting. The price of a meal, though, is quite reasonable, making it a more service-oriented alternative to the foodlife food court (see below) just outside its doors. Most dinner entrées are in the $10 to $14 range, and the hot lunches rarely exceed $9. One lunchtime treat not on the dinner menu is grilled lemon chicken with capers, a large and lightly breaded filet of chicken breast. On both menus is the house specialty, a generous slice of meatloaf served with mashed potatoes and green beans ($8.95 at lunch, $10.95 at dinner). Other comfort foods, such as roast turkey and pot roast, rotate daily. Among the Italian selections, the toasted macaroni and cheese, made with penne instead of egg noodles, is terrific.

### The Original A-1

401 E. Illinois St., North Pier. ☎ **312/644-0300.** Reservations not required. Sandwiches $5.25–$6.50; main courses $6.95–$14.95. AE, DC, DISC, MC, V. Mon–Thurs 11:30am–10pm; Fri–Sat 11:30am–11pm; Sun 11:30am–9pm. TEXAS BARBECUE/AMERICAN.

If you happen to find yourself at North Pier for one reason or another (bike rental, river architectural tour, shop-hopping), you could look on a meal at the Original A-1 as an unexpected bonus. I heartily recommend the tender, tasty, baby back ribs ($9.95); the jalapeño mashed potatoes, and the lethal frozen margaritas ($3.75). If all that doesn't fill you up, a chuck wagon circulates offering barbecue beans and various salads at no additional cost.

### Shaw's Crab House and Blue Crab Lounge

21 E. Hubbard. ☎ **312/527-2722.** Reservations not accepted. Main courses $12.95–$18.95. AE, CB, DC, DISC, MC, V. Mon–Thurs 11:30am–10pm; Fri–Sat 11:30am–11pm; Sun 5–10pm. SEAFOOD.

This is a moderately priced–to–expensive fish house, organized continental style, with plush red banquettes along the walls and linen-covered tables in the center. For business lunches, Shaw's is right up there with any of its downtown rivals (though it's popular for dinner, too). For starters, if you're in luck, there are fresh oysters (based on availability at market prices). Other appetizers include baked oysters Alexander, blue crab fingers, and popcorn shrimp; and for soup there is a house gumbo by the bowl or the cup. Shaw's menu offers a number of side dishes, both traditional and exotic, like broccoli and asparagus, both topped with hollandaise, or Cajun-style four-grain wild rice. Main courses include dishes such as Calico Bay scallops and a pound of fresh Texas stone crab claws. Other popular specials are crab cakes and french-fried shrimp. The theme at Shaw's, layered on ever so lightly, is that of Key West and Papa Hemingway, suggested subtly by the restaurant's trademark dessert, key lime pie, and by the suave strains of such '30s tunes as "Begin the Beguine" playing in the background. Tuesday and Thursday evenings feature live jazz and blues, 7–10pm.

## INEXPENSIVE

### Billy Goat Tavern

430 N. Michigan Ave. ☎ **312/222-1525.** Reservations not accepted. Menu items $3–$6. No credit cards. Mon–Sat 7am–3am; Sun 7am–11pm. BREAKFAST/BURGERS.

"Cheeseborger, Cheeseborger—No Coke . . . Pepsi." Viewers of the original "Saturday Night Live" will certainly remember the classic John Belushi routine, a moment in the life of a crabby Greek short-order cook. The comic got his material from the Billy Goat Tavern, located under North Michigan Avenue near the bridge that crosses to the Loop. Just "butt in anytime," says the sign on the red door with the picture of the billy goat on it. The tavern is a hangout for the newspaper workers and writers who occupy the nearby Tribune Tower and Sun-Times Building. Offering beer and greasy food in the kind of dive journalists love to haunt, it's a good place to watch a game, chitchat at the bar, and down a few beers.

### foodlife

835 N. Michigan Ave (Water Tower Place). ☎ **312/335-3663.** Reservations not accepted.
Most items $4.50–$8. AE, DISC, DC, MC, V. Juice, espresso, and corner bakery Sun–Thurs
7:30am–9pm, Fri–Sat 7:30am–10pm; all other kiosks Sun–Thurs 11am–9pm, Fri–Sat 11am–
10pm. ECLECTIC.

From Lettuce Entertain You's Rich Melman, the man who brought Chicago the
world-class cuisine of Ambria and the family-style Maggiano's, comes foodlife, a food
court with a healthy twist. Located on the mezzanine of Water Tower Place, just
outside the entrance of the Mity Nice Grill, foodlife consists of a dozen or so kiosks
offering both ordinary and exotic specialties. Four hundred seats are spread out café-
style in a very pleasant environment under realistic boughs of artificial trees festooned
with strings of lights in the shapes of grapes and other fruits.

The beauty of a food court, of course, is that it tries to offer something for every-
body. At foodlife, the burger and pizza crowd will be satisfied, but so will vegetarians and diners looking for, say, a low-fat fresh Caesar salad. Diners here can also
choose south-of-the-border dishes and an assortment of Asian fare. Special treats include the Miracle Juice Bar's fresh orange juice and raspberry fruit smoothy, as well
as a host of healthy and/or gooey desserts and, at a booth called Sacred Grounds, various espresso-based beverages. A lunch or a snack at foodlife is basically inexpensive,
but the payment method (each diner receives an electronic card that records each
purchase for a total payment upon exit) makes it easy to build up a big tab while
holding a personal taste-testing session at each kiosk.

### Gino's East

160 E. Superior. ☎ **312/943-1124.** Reservations not required. Pizza $6.95–$17.40. AE, CB,
DC, DISC, MC, V. Mon–Thurs 11am–11pm; Fri–Sat 11am–midnight; Sun noon–10pm. PIZZA.

Gino's East is perhaps the only Chicago restaurant where patrons wait outside
nightly—even in the dead of winter—for pizza. Considering that Gino's can seat
about 600 patrons, the steady line is even more astounding. Then again, Gino's East
is the place *People* magazine once called the "pizza de résistance."

From the outside Gino's looks like a condemned building. Inside is even worse.
But the prerenovation look is purposeful, a studied part of Gino's "ambience." Diners
sit in dark-stained booths, surrounded by paneled walls covered with graffiti. Each
of these effects is craftily fashioned as a form of construction art, so well done in some
cases that you don't realize they are all around you unless you look closely. As for the
graffiti, you are allowed to indulge, but "if it isn't clean," the earnest young manager
confided, "we don't allow it."

As for the pizza, it's elaborate and tasty, "a banquet served on a lush, amber bed
of dough," or so one critic described it in a burst of rhapsodic prose. A small cheese
pizza is enough for two unless you're binging. A better bet for a satisfactory dinner
is the small supreme, with layers of cheese, sausage, onions, green pepper, and mushrooms; or the vegetarian, with cheese, onions, peppers, asparagus, summer squash,
zucchini, and eggplant.

Next to the restaurant is Gino's carry-out, with its own telephone number
(☎ 988-4200); pizzas take 30 to 40 minutes' cooking time.

### Thai Borrahn

247 E. Ontario St., 2nd floor. ☎ **312/642-1385.** Reservations accepted only for large groups.
Main courses $6.25–$16.50. AE, MC, V. Mon–Thurs 11am–10pm; Fri 11am–11pm; Sat 4–11pm;
Sun 4–10pm. THAI.

Terrific, authentic Thai fare is served in a lovely tranquil setting, where a few tables
allow you to sit on the floor (on comfortable cushions, with the floor cut away under the table) and dine in traditional style. Start with the classic tom yum soup, a

spicy broth that came brimming with real lemon grass, straw mushrooms, crushed chili peppers, cilantro, lime, and huge tender prawns. I ordered the classic pad thai and found it a wonderful combination of flavors and textures. My companion ordered squid sautéed in a hot pepper sauce, and we enjoyed generous portions accompanied by Singha beer.

There's only a narrow staircase leading to this second-floor restaurant, so it's not recommended for travelers with disabilities.

### Tucci Benucch

900 N. Michigan Ave., 5th floor. ☎ **312/266-2500.** Reservations recommended. Pizza $7.95–$8.95; pasta $8.50–$10.95; main courses $11.95–$12.95. AE, DC, DISC, MC, V. Mon–Thurs 11:30am–10pm; Fri–Sat 11:30am–11pm; Sun noon–9pm. ITALIAN.

In the vertical mall that houses Bloomingdale's and Henri Bendel, Tucci Benucch was created by the Rich Melman gang to resemble an Italian country villa. Each dining area is a replica of a typical room—kitchen, living room, sun room, and so forth—complete with all the domestic details, including garden plants and clothes on the line. The decor tries so hard to appear country Italian that it almost winds up resembling a movie set, and the effect is a little jarring in this sleek, upscale mall.

The inexpensive fare showcases different regions of Italy, and portions are generous. For about $20 total, a couple can dine on any variety of thin-crust pizzas, delicately sauced pastas, or garlic-roasted chicken, and that includes a glass of Chianti with the meal.

## 6  River North

River North, the area north of the Loop and west of Michigan Avenue, has become home in the last several years to the city's most prominent cluster of art galleries as well as to some of its most fashionable restaurants. The clientele is sophisticated; the food (for the most part), Italian.

## VERY EXPENSIVE

### Benkay

In the Hotel Nikko, 320 N. Dearborn St. ☎ **312/836-5490.** Reservations required. Main courses $10–$38; full meals $45–$100. AE, CB, DC, DISC, MC, V. Tues–Sat 7–10am, 11:30am–2pm, and 5:30–10pm. JAPANESE.

Benkay is a fine Japanese restaurant named for a legendary warrior-monk, whose life provides the tale for a 15th-century romance entitled *Gikeiki*. Aside from the sushi bar, we are rarely exposed in America to the wide range of Japanese cuisine. But at the Nikko's Benkay, if such familiar plates as teriyaki and sukiyaki are even listed, they are buried among the dozens of other specialties that appear on the extensive menu.

In one room, the table rests just above the floor and is surrounded by *tatami* (straw mats), on which diners normally sit cross-legged at their meals. To accommodate the more stiff-jointed Westerners, there is a cutaway under the table where you can stretch your legs. The small room is sparse, containing only an ebony-stained table, some flowers, and an art scroll hung on walls painted in subdued winter tones. The single window, shuttered with sliding rice-paper panels, overlooks the Chicago River and frames a close-up view of Helmut Jahn's controversial State of Illinois Building.

Begin with a glass of ozeki (hot sake), the proper cocktail before eating Japanese food. For appetizers, the menu lists soups—fish and miso—along with platters, such as beef sashimi, or a "combination" of Japanese specialties that varies with the season. Main courses are listed by type: nimono (stewed dishes), yakimono (from the grill), agemono (fried specialties), and sunomono (vinaigrettes). The sushi, with tuna, eel, and seaweed-wrapped cylinders of rice, are also filled with Japanese cucumber, avocado, and flying fish roe. For lunch, Benkay has a shokado bento, a partitioned bamboo box each of whose small compartments contains an item of traditional Japanese cooking, all fish or vegetables. To drink, there's a very dry cold sake, called otokoyama, that is quite potent. Brown tea is served throughout the meal. Dessert can be a Japanese confection, ice cream, or fruit, and green tea is served with the check.

# EXPENSIVE

### ✪ Centro

710 N. Wells St. ☎ **312/988-7775.** Reservations recommended. Main courses $8.95–$24.95. AE, CB, DC, DISC, MC, V. Mon–Thurs 11am–3pm and 5–10:30pm; Fri 11am–3pm and 5–11:30pm; Sat 5–11:30pm. ITALIAN.

From the folks who brought Chicago the Rosebud restaurants on Taylor and Rush Streets comes Centro, a more slick interpretation of dining in the '90s. Centro is where you're more likely to see suits attached to cell-phones, a fact that, combined with the acoustics and the lively crowd, makes for a rather loud experience.

But it's also a tasty one. For starters, you might try the insalata di fagioli, a salad of cannellini beans, tomatoes, and red onions in a garlic vinaigrette, or you could opt for focaccia or stuffed artichoke. The healthy portions of pasta range from baked cavatelli with marinara sauce and ricotta and mozzarella cheeses to linguine with clams, mussels, or calamari. The meat dishes are excellent as well, my favorite being the garlic-drenched chicken Vesuvio. If you can, save room for the tiramisù.

### ✪ Coco Pazzo

300 W. Hubbard. ☎ **312/836-0900.** Reservations accepted. Main courses $10–$11.50 at lunch, $12.50–$26 at dinner. AE, DC, MC, V. Daily 11:30am–2:30pm; Mon–Thurs 5:30–11pm; Fri–Sat 5:30–11:30pm, Sun 5–10:30pm. REGIONAL ITALIAN.

From Milan to Chicago by way of New York, the Coco Pazzo reputation has traveled well. Italian food has become something of a rage in the '90s, so diners have to be careful to single out the few select sheep from the more numerous goats among the restaurants specializing in this cuisine. Coco Pazzo can certainly be counted among the select. At its best, the food of northern Italy is simple and allows the ingredients to shine through. So a lot depends on the deft touch of the cook staff and the quality of their ingredients. Coco Pazzo wins high marks on both accounts, as it does for its open, light, and airy atmosphere. I have found its service, on the other hand, to be rather slow—so much so that at some business lunches I have not had time for my favorite course, dessert.

Coco Pazzo's menu, naturally, undergoes periodic changes, but there is always a tempting risotto del giorno, and at lunchtime, a focaccia, a thin-crust pizza filled with delectables, in addition to a tempting list of pastas, pizzas, seafood, veal, and chicken dishes. To begin, both the fresh vegetable antipasto and grilled portobello mushrooms are excellent. The manager is helpful in introducing the house wines, sold by the glass, one Barbera red being particularly memorable. The selection of tasty breads on the table is accompanied by top-quality virgin olive oil for dipping, which goes especially well with alternating swallows of the rich and robust wines.

The focaccia alla gene, a thin-crust white pizza filled with prosciutto, fontina cheese, and fresh tomatoes, is one of lunch's high points, but I am also very fond of the daily risotto. The desserts also are special. One day's list might include a tart filled with fresh raspberries and topped with a dreamy, champagne-spiked zabaglione, or, if you're really lucky, the fondente cioccolato, a flourless chocolate cake with a warm mousse center, chocolate sauce, and cappuccino ice cream. Coco Pazzo is an easy cab ride from downtown Chicago; it's also a pleasant walk from Michigan Avenue along Hubbard Street.

### ✪ Frontera Grill & Topolobampo

445 N. Clark St. ☎ **312/661-1434.** Reservations accepted at Frontera Grill only for parties of five or more; accepted at Topolobampo. Main courses $8.95–$21. AE, DC, DISC, MC, V. Tues–Thurs 11:30am–2pm and 5:30–10pm; Fri 11:30am–2pm and 5–11pm; Sat 10:30am–2:30pm and 5–11pm. MEXICAN/MESOAMERICAN.

Testimony to Frontera Grill's unique cuisine is Chicagoans' willingness to brave the restaurant's no-reservation policy. Granted, the margaritas are mighty fine, but the draw is still the food. Owners Rick and Deann Groen Bayless have brought authentic Mexican cooking to the U.S., so don't come here looking for tacos or burritos. Instead, you'll find such fare as the tacos al carbón, a generous portion of grilled beef, pork, duck, or catfish, folded into hot corn tortillas—by the diner to prevent the shells from becoming soggy. On the lighter side are the Mexico City–style quesadillas, corn turnovers filled with melted cheese and accompanied by fried black beans (a southern Mexican specialty) and guacamole.

To reinforce the fact that Mexican food is not all Chi-Chi's, the Baylesses opened Topolobampo, a more formal and more expensive establishment, under the same roof. Topolobampo has an intimate atmosphere and a menu all its own. The sopa de hongos y nopales (wild mushrooms and cactus paddles) is very subtle, and for the main course you may choose from a number of intriguing dishes, including grilled, marinated, free-range baby chicken with salsa for lunch, and fresh sea scallops with smoky chipotle-honey glaze and braised black beans for dinner. Another option is the ensaladas surtidas, a tasting plate of salads with many exotic ingredients. Or, if you just can't decide, try the chef's "tasting dinner" of five courses for $39.

### Gordon

500 N. Clark St. ☎ **312/467-9780.** Reservations required. Main courses $17.95–$25.95; chef's five-course tasting menu $48.95. AE, DC, DISC, JCB, MC, V. Mon 5:30–9:30pm; Tues–Thurs 11:30am–2pm and 5:30–9:30pm; Fri 11:30am–2pm and 5:30pm–12:30am; Sat 5:30pm–12:30am; Sun 11am–2pm and 5:30–9:30pm. AMERICAN/INTERNATIONAL.

Gordon's "Americanized international cuisine" epitomizes a blending of continental flare and sophistication with the quality control and freshness of the American kitchen. The roast loin of lamb with orange couscous, for example, hints of Spain, but the accompanying onion marmalade and asparagus bring the platter back to the heartland. Presentations of the meals at Gordon, moreover, are as artful as the food is delicious.

You can drop a bundle for dinner here, the quintessential Gordon experience, or sample the same fare under more mundane conditions at lunch for roughly half the price. I enjoyed the restaurant's signature appetizer, the superb artichoke fritters, went on to a very palatable sirloin plate, and ended with a trio of crèmes brûlées. Weekend diners can come to dance Friday and Saturday nights from 8:30pm to midnight. And the Sunday brunch ($19.95) consists of a drink and several courses. Another Gordon trademark is the nightly wine tasting, three 5-ounce samples of selected wines ($10 to $13).

## MODERATE

### ✪ Carson's

612 N. Wells. ☎ **312/280-9200.** Reservations not accepted. Main courses $8.95–$25.95. Carry-out prices slightly lower. AE, CB, DC, DISC, MC, V. Mon–Thurs 11am–11pm; Fri–Sat 11am–12:30am; Sun 4pm–12:30am. Closed Thanksgiving. AMERICAN/BARBECUE.

A true Chicago institution, Carson's calls itself "The Place for Ribs," and boy, is it ever. The barbecue sauce is sweet and tangy, and the ribs are meaty. Included in the $14.95 price for a full slab of baby backs are coleslaw and one of four types of potatoes (the most decadent are the au gratin), plus right-out-of-the-oven rolls. Carson's also barbecues chicken and pork chops.

For dinner, there's often a wait, but don't despair. In the bar area you'll find a heaping mound of some of the best chopped liver around and plenty of cocktail rye to go with it. When you're seated at your table in the darkly lit dining room with the large booths and white tablecloths, tie on your plastic bib—and indulge.

In case you don't eat ribs, Carson's steaks also have an exellent reputation, although I must confess that in the almost two decades that I've been eating here, I have never been able to tear myself away from the ribs. If by some remarkable feat you have room left after dinner, the candy bar sundaes are a scrumptious finale to the meal. Carson's popularity has led to something of a factory mentality among management, which evidently feels the need to herd 'em in and out, but the wait staff is responsive to requests not to be hurried through the meal.

### Hard Rock Café

63 W. Ontario. ☎ **312/943-2252.** Reservations not accepted. Main courses $5.95–$12.95. AE, MC, V. Sun–Fri 11am–2am; Sat 11am–3am. AMERICAN.

Around the corner from Ed Debevic's (see below) is another establishment replicated by franchise in various cities, here and abroad—the Hard Rock Café. This version of the temple of Rock looks more like a branch of the public library, except for the trademark globe twirling over the portico. It offers shakes, burgers, and fries to all who might dig the memorabilia and the loud rock soundtrack that typifies the Hard Rock style, regardless of location. If you don't binge, you can get away with $10 to $15 per person.

### Harry Caray's

33 W. Kinzie. ☎ **312/828-0966.** Reservations accepted for lunch; accepted at dinner only for parties of eight or more. Main courses $7.95–$29.95. AE, DC, DISC, MC, V. Mon–Thurs 11:30am–3pm and 5–10:30pm; Fri 11:30am–3pm and 5–midnight; Sat 11:30am–4pm (sandwich menu/bar only) and 5pm–midnight; Sun noon–4pm (sandwich menu/bar only) and 4–10pm. ITALIAN.

Harry Caray's is a sports bar masquerading as an Italian restaurant. Harry, of course, is the dean of baseball's play-by-play announcers, and he has amassed a sizable collection of memorabilia. In fact, it covers almost every square inch of the place. If you're a baseball fan, particularly a Cubs fan, go for a drink. Harry himself is actually a frequent patron of the bar. But skip the food.

If you're famished, munch on Harry's own brand of potato chips, made on the premises and dubbed—what else?—Holy Cow Chips. But then go to one of the other area restaurants. Or, come in after dinner and soak up the macho sports bar atmosphere—five TVs are stationed in the giant barroom, which sometimes stays open until 3am, depending on the crowd.

### Hat Dance

325 W. Huron St. ☎ **312/649-0066.** Reservations required. Main courses $7.95–$15.95. AE, DC, DISC, MC, V. Mon–Thurs 11:30am–2pm and 5:30–10pm; Fri 11:30am–2pm and 5:30–11:30pm; Sat 11:30am–3:30pm and 5–11:30pm; Sun 5–9pm. MEXICAN.

Another of Rich Melman's Lettuce Entertain You restaurants, Hat Dance is not one of his best. The food rarely rises above the ordinary. Most memorable are the simpler items: an appetizer called *un ostión*, a single oyster in a shot glass filled with salsa; roasted corn on the cob smothered in hot-and-sour sauce; and a fresh corn tamale filled with shredded chicken and coated with mole poblano. All of which points to a positive outcome: You can make the scene at Hat Dance and not spend a fortune if you avoid the pricey main courses.

## Maggiano's Little Italy

516 N. Clark St. ☎ **312/644-8100.** Reservations recommended. Main courses $7.50–$13.95 at lunch, $8.50–$26.95 at dinner. AE, DC, DISC, MC, V. Mon–Thurs 11:30am–2pm and 5:30–10pm; Fri 11:30am–2pm and 5pm–midnight; Sat 5pm–midnight; Sun 4–9pm. CLASSIC ITALIAN.

The benchmark at Maggiano's is large portions, served family style. The other novelty is tradition; many Chicago diners are turning away from the skimpy, lighter fare of northern Italy to the classic food many Italian families still get at Mama's Sunday dinner. The key to Maggiano's success, of course, is that its kitchen also manages to maintain Mama's high standards of preparation and taste.

Two outstanding appetizers at Maggiano's are the zuppa di mussels, and the baked shrimp oreganata served with sliced tomato, mozzarella, and peppers. The pasta dishes and some main courses on the dinner menu come in two sizes, the larger of which usually satisfies at least two people. Even the salads are big enough for two. Favorites among the pastas are the spaghetti with meat ragù, the fettuccine Alfredo with broccoli, and the garlic shrimp with shells. The whole roast chicken with peppers and onions will certainly go around the table several times, while the smothered New York steak, cooked Maggiano style, is a house specialty.

## Mambo Grill

412 N. Clark St. ☎ **312/467-9797.** Reservations accepted for parties of five or more only. Main courses $8.95–$14.95. AE, DC, DISC, MC, V. Mon–Sat 11am–1am. LATIN AMERICAN.

If you want to see how the other half eats (other half of the Western Hemisphere, that is), check out this bright, colorful River North storefront eatery with its pan-Latino menu. What are listed as appetizers might better be viewed as tapas, perfect for small-platter midnight grazing. You can make a meal of these treats without ever getting near the list of the more substantial entradas.

You could go Cubano and Brasileiro with mojitos and caipirinhas to quench your thirsty demons, and tiritas (potato-crusted calamari with dipping sauces) and tostones (plantain chips with black bean dip) to tease the palate. Linger in the Caribbean for some Puerto Rican pasteles (tamales filled with shredded duck criollo and wrapped in banana leaves), then rumba 'round to Bogotá for some Colombian-style arepas (cornmeal cakes filled with sautéed mushrooms and manchego cheese). After that, if you just can't resist that cauldron of steaming, spicy Latin bouillabaisse, go for the zarzuela de mariscos (Cuban-style seafood stew). Dessert at the Mambo Grill can only mean the pumpkin flan.

## Michael Jordan's

500 N. La Salle St. ☎ **312/644-DUNK.** Reservations not accepted. Main courses $6–$12.50 at lunch, $12–$22 at dinner. AE, CB, DC, DISC, MC, V. Sun–Thurs 11:30am–10:30pm; Fri–Sat 11:30am–midnight. AMERICAN.

At 10am to noon, within 20 minutes of opening on an autumn Saturday, Michael Jordan's was already filling up rapidly. Such is the Jordan aura that the young people lunching there that day—mostly in the company of adults, but representing some three-quarters of the clientele—sat, ate, and acted as respectfully as if they were at a table in their girl- or boyfriend's home for the very first time, perhaps, on the longshot chance that Mike himself might suddenly make an appearance.

I don't mean to imply, however, that Michael Jordan's is a restaurant that would not appeal to a more mature crowd, which gathers primarily at night. I found the food surprisingly good, and very affordable at lunchtime, particularly from a family point of view. I began with a soup of the day, a very tasty chicken gumbo, so thick with big chunks of meat that it could have been a satisfying meal in itself. Next I sampled a side dish of Juanita's macaroni and cheese, a traditional preparation, followed by a super-size grilled chicken breast sandwich on herb focaccia with melted provolone. The children's menu is very economical, with items priced from $3.50 to $4.95. It was a comforting feeling that despite the restaurant's mass popularity (you might have to wait for some time to be seated), the owners have made Michael Jordan's accessible to those families whose budgets don't normally allow for dining in expensive, fashionable eateries.

### Parrinello

535 N. Wells St. ☎ **312/527-2782.** Reservations recommended. Main courses $8–$20; lunch prices a little lower. AE, CB, DC, MC, V. Mon–Thurs 11:30am–2:30pm and 5–10pm; Fri 11:30am–2:30pm and 5–11pm; Sat 6–11pm. Closed Labor Day, Thanksgiving, Christmas, and New Year's Day. ITALIAN.

Just down the street from Centro, Parrinello is another great Italian restaurant, with perhaps a pinch less attitude. Among the antipasti, the grilled portobello mushrooms and bruschetta are standouts, but if you're looking for something a little different, you might want to try the spicy sausage with beans and swiss chard. Parrinello offers a couple of risotto dishes and only about a half-dozen pasta selections, but the choices are worthy. No penne in marinara sauce here. Rather, you can taste tortellini with prosciutto, pine nuts, and peas, or trecce with portobello, gorgonzola, and mascarpone. The secondi are every bit as tempting, from the roasted duck breast with sun-dried cherries to the sautéed veal with hazelnuts and balsamic vinegar.

### Planet Hollywood

633 N. Wells. ☎ **312/266-9850.** Reservations accepted for parties of 15 or more. Main courses $6.50–$17.95. AE, DC, DISC, MC, V. Sun–Fri 11am–2am; Sat 11am–3am. AMERICAN.

Arnold Schwarzenegger, Sylvester Stallone, and Bruce Willis seem to have the golden touch—and not just at the box office. Their Planet Hollywood restaurant chain is packing them in, albeit with the same gimmicky fireworks that sell movie tickets. But movie buffs are sure to appreciate the memorabilia the Planet Hollywood chain has collected; some of the highlights in the Chicago restaurant are a Marilyn Monroe dress from *Gentlemen Prefer Blondes,* an Arnold Robot from *The Terminator,* and Batman and Robin costumes from the TV show. The menu is broad; the most popular items seem to be the pizza and pasta. But if you go, do it for the show, not the meal.

### Scoozi

410 W. Huron. ☎ **312/943-5900.** Reservations recommended. Pasta $6.95–$8.50 at lunch, $7.95–$11.00 at dinner; main courses $8.95–$14.95 at lunch, $9.95–$15.95 at dinner. AE, DC, DISC, MC, V. Mon–Thurs 11:30am–2pm and 5–10:30pm; Fri 11:30am–2pm and 5–11:30pm; Sat 5–11:30pm; Sun 5–9pm. ITALIAN.

Scoozi has been one of the most popular eateries in this city since opening in December 1986. You can opt for a relatively calm luncheon at Scoozi or the madcap people-scene at night. On the weekends there is often a wait of up to two hours before being seated. The management, however, distributes pizza and beverages among the waiting masses.

With its lively strains of classical music buzzing in the background, Scoozi has its own élan, every bit as important a factor in making it a Chicago mainstay as the very good food.

For an appetizer, you might begin with a pizza smothered with asparagus, mushrooms, and three types of cheese. Or select from the antipasti bar. Next you might try salmaccio, smoked salmon with melon and chives, and then panzanella, antipasto salad on friselle bread. Main courses include pollo stefano, chicken breast with steamed vegetables; tricolored mezzaluna bandiera, cheese-filled pasta with separate servings of pesto, tomato, and Alfredo sauces; and a very rich mastaccioli al formaggio, with broccoli, walnuts, and a sauce of four cheeses. Finish your meal with tiramisù, a bing cherry tart, or the granita (chipped ice flavored with cantaloupe).

## Tucci Milan

6 W. Hubbard. ☎ **312/222-0044.** Reservations required. Main courses $4.95–$20. AE, DC, DISC, MC, V. Mon–Thurs 11:30am–10pm; Fri–Sat 11:30am–11pm; Sun 5–9pm. ITALIAN.

You might say that Tucci Milan is the city cousin of its country kin, Tucci Benucch (see above), but this place is a good deal more sophisticated. Hundreds of tiny white lights hang above the tables and banquettes, which are laid out to resemble a traditional Italian trattoria. Tucci Milan has a good, if somewhat inconsistent, kitchen.

For a light snack, I recommend a pizza monte napoleone, a very tasty item said to be a favorite low-calorie lunch choice among Milan's high-fashion models. The crust is very thin, with the consistency of matzoh, and topped with arugula, black olives, and thin strips of mozzarella. For dessert, try the espresso tiramisù cake, consisting of layers of chocolate mousse and an Italian cream cheese filling; the incredibly delicious bread pudding with caramel sauce; or the zuccotto, a mixed-layer cake of crushed hazelnuts and white-chocolate mousse. The lunch and dinner menus at Tucci Milan are the same, and offer the usual selection of antipasto, salads, and pastas.

## Tuttaposto

646 N. Franklin. ☎ **312/943-6262.** Reservations recommended. Pizza $9–$15; main courses $12–$25; five-course menu degustation $39; seven-course menu degustation $45. Lunch prices slightly lower. AE, CB, DC, DISC, MC, V. Mon–Thurs 11:30am–2pm and 5–10pm; Fri 11:30am–2pm and 5–11pm; Sat 5–11pm; Sun 5–9pm. MEDITERRANEAN/ITALIAN.

Tuttaposto's Mediterranean cruise may begin and end in Italy, but its ports of call stretch from Greece to Tunisia. The menu rotates every few weeks, but on a given evening you'll find a brief selection of pizza with thin, crunchy crusts cooked in a wood-burning oven. Tuttaposto offers a dozen or so salads and vegetarian dishes, such as grilled vegetables with Israeli zhoug sauce, Spanish roast garlic and coriander soup, and Greek salads. For a main course, the long, rectangular ravioli stuffed with goat cheese and potato in a tomato basil sauce is a nice light choice. The gnocchi, prepared with wild mushrooms, is also pleasing.

Among the many meat, poultry, and seafood choices, the charcoal-grilled lamb chops are standouts. Friends have praised the sesame-crust sea bass with couscous and tahini, and I have many next-times on my list, the garlicky ginger shrimp and the roast pancetta-stuffed rabbit with polenta and portobello mushrooms among them.

The lunch menu has an appealing mix of light dishes (lots of salads) and more hearty selections (pasta, rotisserie chicken, couscous). The gourmet sandwich choices, served on fresh-baked focaccia, include grilled swordfish and wood-roasted sesame chicken. My friends have had some bad experiences at the bar, but I'd still recommend Tuttaposto for the food and for the trendy, vaguely industrial atmosphere.

## Zinfandel

59 W. Grand Ave. ☎ **312/527-1818.** Reservations accepted. Main courses $12.50–$17.95. AE, DC, MC, V. Tues–Thurs 11:30am–2:30pm and 5:30–10pm; Fri 11:30am–2:30pm and 5:30–11pm; Sat 10:30am–2:30pm and 5:30–11pm. AMERICAN.

Yes, the name accurately implies you'll find an extensive and interesting wine list at Zinfandel, one of the most welcome recent additions to Chicago's restaurant scene. It's a joint venture between the Baylesses of Frontera Grill/Topolobampo fame (see above) and Susan and Drew Goss (she's the chef, he's the wine buyer).

Zinfandel's food is at once totally familiar and unique. Using many of her grandmother's "basic" recipes as a starting point, Ms. Goss crafts such home-comfort standbys as buttermilk biscuits, but these are far from prosaic, and each batch is cooked to order in a hot iron skillet. The menu changes seasonally, but if you're lucky, it will include the cheese sampler with marinated salads and grilled farmhouse bread or the "wilted" field greens with strips of Smithfield ham, Stewart pecans, sweet red onions, and a warm maple dressing.

The crispy hazelnut corn cakes are grainy and delicious, served with a tangy relish of woodland mushrooms, dried cherries, and maple sugar. The smoky roast chicken breast, with cheesy corn grits, braised greens, and roasted chili relish, presented with all the artsy flourish of the nouvelle-style kitchen, is a masterpiece of juices, tastes, and textures. And on and on go the variations on Zinfandel's inspired menu.

While Prairie and the Blackhawk Lodge (see above) celebrate the Midwest, Zinfandel studies the entire nation, drawing inspiration from the Carolinas to Oklahoma. Each month, the kitchen devises a special menu based on ethnic specialties, such as Creole and Acadian. One other feature to recommend Zinfandel: The Americana decor nicely complements the American cuisine.

## INEXPENSIVE

### Big Bowl Café

159 W. Erie St. ☎ **312/787-8279.** Reservations not required. Little bowls $1.95–$4.95; big bowls $4.95–$8.95. AE, DC, DISC, MC, V. Mon–Thurs 11:30am–10pm; Fri–Sat 11:30am–11pm; Sun 5–9pm. CALIFORNIAN/ASIAN.

The Big Bowl Café, attached to another Lettuce Entertain You Restaurant called Wild Fire, but a completely separate entity, is the ideal place for a light lunch or an after-show snack or supper. It's set up like a long, narrow dining car along the sidewalk, with two large windows that stretch to the ceiling, creating an open-air atmosphere when the weather permits. The food is steamed hot with each order. And although the presentation and the use of certain ingredients, such as fresh ginger, lend a definite Asian accent to the dishes, there is also an unmistakable link to the health-food-and-salad tradition of California.

All dishes are served in bowls, large or small, and may be eaten with chopsticks if desired. One real bargain is a Big Bowl Chicken Salad, a generous order of shredded chicken combined with many fresh greens and vegetables. The Smokin' Shrimp is also an exotic and tasteful treat, with good-size, succulent butterfly shrimp served over a wild rice pilaf in a rich beef broth.

### Ed Debevic's

640 N. Wells (at Ontario). ☎ **312/664-1707.** Reservations not accepted. Menu items $1.50–$6.95. AE, DC, DISC, MC, V. Mon–Thurs 11am–midnight; Fri–Sat 11am–1am; Sun 11am–11pm. AMERICAN.

Ed Debevic's is a temple to America's hometown lunch-counter culture. The whole idea behind Ed's is to put you on. The waitresses play the parts of gum-chewing toughies with hearts of gold who could hail from Anywhere, USA. Most are very consciously costumed to fit the image. It's all a performance—but it works.

A more basic reason for Ed's success is that the food is kept simple and reasonably priced. In addition to the diner staples, the menu offers chili and Chicago hot dogs, plus daily blue-plate specials, from meat loaf to turkey with dressing and gravy. Then there are the soda fountain temptations—milkshakes, malts, black cows. Ed's also serves as a cocktail lounge. Wherever you sit you are surrounded by '50s nostalgia, while tunes like "Duke of Earl" or other vintage goldies fill the air.

## Green Door Tavern

678 N. Orleans. ☎ **312/664-5496.** Reservations not accepted. Main courses $6.50–$7.95. AE, DC, MC, V. Mon–Sat 11:30am–midnight. BURGERS.

Across the street from Hat Dance (see above) is the Green Door Tavern, looking for all the world like an old off-campus hangout. The old wood-frame building was put up temporarily after the 1871 fire, presumably just before the city ordinance that banned such construction inside the newly designated "fire zone," and the Green Door has been there since 1921. Apparently the original framing crew went light on the bracing timbers in a few places, because the whole building leans to the right. Typical of the items on the sandwich menu are the hickory burger, the triple-decker grilled cheese, and the Texas chili. There's even a veggie burger, and the menu includes some Cajun fare and pasta. Dinner specials are also posted daily and are served after 5pm.

## Mr. Beef

666 N. Orleans. ☎ **312/337-8500.** Sandwiches from $3.40. No credit cards. Mon–Sat 9am–6pm. ITALIAN BEEF SUBS.

Something the Midwest can boast of (or maybe it's only Chicago?) that is lacking on either coast is Italian beef sandwiches. Italian beef is thinly shredded slices of roast beef marinated in a tasty brine and distributed to both food stands and the public in two-gallon jars. "Want good Italian beef? Go to Mr. Beef" is the common wisdom. What could be better than a juicy sandwich for $3.40?

## Papagus Greek Taverna

620 N. State St. (on the ground floor of the Embassy Suites Hotel). ☎ **312/642-8450.** Reservations recommended for dinner on weekends. Main courses $4.75–$13.95. AE, DC, DISC, MC, V. Mon–Thurs 11:30am–10pm; Fri–Sat noon–midnight; Sun noon–10pm. GREEK.

Papagus is a sprawling and attractive restaurant decorated with the colorful artifacts typical of a Greek tavern or café. And as with most authentic Greek taverns, you don't have to go near the main courses at Papagus to sample a wide range of dishes and flavors and come away satisfied. You can make a meal—especially lunch—from a combination of delicious hot and cold appetizers.

Every table is equipped with a stack of small plates, which you use to sample each of the items you have selected. From the list of cold appetizers, you might enjoy the whipped feta cheese or the roasted eggplant, both of which can be spread on the excellent, crusty house bread.

Most of the hot appetizers come in two sizes—the small serving is more than adequate for two persons who are sampling various dishes. Among the choices are a tasty moussaka, ground beef layered with lamb, eggplant, and squash, and an exceptional pastitsio, baked macaroni with ground meat wrapped in phyllo pastry. The spinach pie is a must, and the spicy lamb-and-beef meatballs possess a uniquely Greek flavoring. Finish off the meal with a shot of ouzo, a cup of espresso or thick Greek coffee, and a slice of Papagus's divine baklava.

## Pizzeria Uno

29 E. Ohio St. (at the corner of Wabash). ☎ **312/321-1000.** Reservations not accepted. Pizza $3.35–$11.85. AE, CB, DC, DISC, MC, V. Mon–Thurs 11:30am–1am; Fri–Sat 11:30am–2am; Sun 11:30am–11:30pm. PIZZA.

Pizzeria Uno invented Chicago-style pizza, and many deep-dish aficionados still refuse to accept any imitations. You can't miss it. The ornate trim is smartly painted in deep green. You may eat in the restaurant itself on the basement level or, weather permitting, in the outdoor patio right off the sidewalk. Daily pizza specials are featured, with any topping you choose, and salads, sandwiches, and a house minestrone are also available.

Uno was so successful, but lacking in room for expansion, that the owners opened **Pizzeria Due** in a lovely, gray-brick Victorian townhouse nearby at 618 N. Wabash Ave. (at the corner of Ontario; ☎ 943-2400). Due stays open a half hour later than does Uno on Monday through Saturday.

One popular feature at both places is the express lunch: a choice of soup or salad, and a personal-size pizza, all served up within five minutes for $4.95.

## 7 Lincoln Park

Lincoln Park, the neighborhood roughly defined by North Avenue on the south, Belmont on the north, the park on the east, and Halsted Street on the west, is inhabited by singles and young families—folks who were commonly referred to as yuppies a few years back. No surprise then that the neighborhood has spawned a dense concentration of some of the city's best restaurants.

## VERY EXPENSIVE

### ✪ Ambria

2300 Lincoln Park West. ☎ **773/472-0076.** Reservations required. Main courses $19.50–$29.95; fixed-price meals $42–$55. AE, DC, DISC, MC, V. Mon–Thurs 6–9:30pm; Fri–Sat 6–10:30pm. FRENCH.

Near the Lincoln Park Conservatory and housed in the impressive former Belden Stratford Hotel, Ambria is ensconced in several large rooms off the old lobby. It is, quite simply, one of Chicago's finest restaurants. The dimly lit, wood-paneled interior is refined and intimate, almost clublike, and eminently civilized. On one national survey after another honoring the nation's finest restaurants, the name Ambria appears. There is not much room at the top, but Ambria maintains its position with grace and consistency.

The menu changes frequently, of course, so the dishes described here are simply examples of the style of the preparations you will encounter while dining at Ambria. On one recent occasion, my companion and I began our meal with a flaky, mouthwatering napoleon of lobster, bacalhao, and crispy potato, and a pastry stuffed with escargot and summer vegetables that was equally successful. This was followed by an imaginative salad comprised of tender squab with red cabbage, endive, and bacon. For our main courses, we chose a roasted rack of lamb with stuffed baby eggplant, couscous, and artichoke chips, served in the lamb's herb-scented natural juices; and the roasted medallions of New Zealand venison with wild rice pancakes, caramelized rhubarb, and root vegetables, accompanied by a blackberry sauce. Both dishes were superb.

The wine steward provided us with an excellent recommendation, a California cabernet, one of those wonderful private cellar selections for which the Napa Valley is justly famous. We first chose our desserts from the daily pastry creations, a concoction rich with cream and dark chocolate, then exercised a bit more discretion in our second selection, the bowl of firm and sweet fresh red raspberries.

### ✪ Charlie Trotter's

816 W. Armitage. ☎ **773/248-6228.** Reservations required. Fixed-price dinners $65 and $85. AE, CB, DC, MC, V. Tues–Sat from 5:30pm. NOUVELLE.

He has been called the greatest American-born (in nearby Wilmette) chef of his generation. Splurge on a meal at Charlie Trotter's and judge for yourself. The grand

# Lincoln Park/Wrigleyville Dining

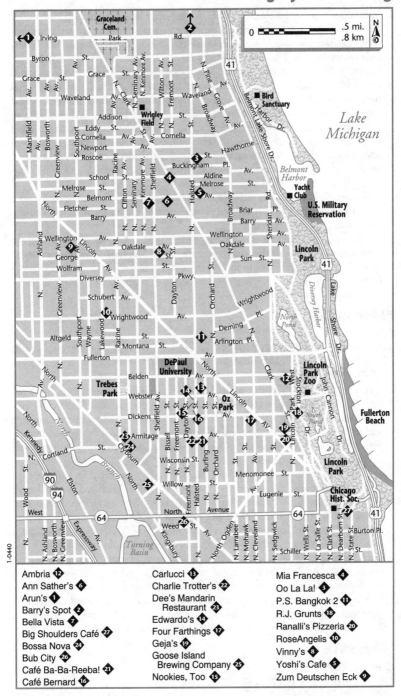

Ambria 12
Ann Sather's 6
Arun's 1
Barry's Spot 2
Bella Vista 7
Big Shoulders Café 27
Bossa Nova 24
Bub City 26
Café Ba-Ba-Reeba! 21
Café Bernard 16

Carlucci 13
Charlie Trotter's 22
Dee's Mandarin
  Restaurant 23
Edwardo's 14
Four Farthings 17
Geja's 19
Goose Island
  Brewing Company 25
Nookies, Too 15

Mia Francesca 4
Oo La La! 3
P.S. Bangkok 2 11
R.J. Grunts 18
Ranalli's Pizzeria 20
RoseAngelis 10
Vinny's 8
Yoshi's Cafe 5
Zum Deutschen Eck 9

menu degustation, which changes daily, is the perfect introduction to the innovative creations of the owner/chef who has given his name to this critically acclaimed palace of a cuisine not easily classified. It clearly has roots in the French style, but Trotter feels no constraints. The evening I dined here, the meal began with a terrine lightheartedly dubbed the amuse bouche. Next followed a very colorful serving of striped artichoke cannelloni cooked in a saffron oil of roasted garlic and aged chèvre, and then a seafood course, smoked sea scallops with a timbale of lobster. The greens were a sheaf of shredded Belgian endive accompanied by bits of Stilton cheese, apricot, watercress, and almond slivers. A dish of seared salmon in a sesame crust was followed by a meat course of spit-roasted free-range veal with zucchini. Dessert was a chocolate mousse with bananas in a caramel-rum sauce, and an assortment of petits fours, accompanied by coffee freshly brewed at tableside. The wine was a 1979 BV Burgundy Reserve, a superior California selection.

A vegetarian degustation menu ($55) is also available and no doubt represents a similar lush parade of highly stylized presentations as that of the big production to which I was so happily treated.

The waiter boasted that 80% of the produce used at Charlie Trotter's is grown organically, and most of the meat is pasture raised. The restaurant also recycles all plastics and paper generated in its operation. The ambience of the renovated 1908 brownstone is pleasant; the real show is best seen from the table for four in the kitchen.

## EXPENSIVE

### Geja's

340 W. Armitage. ☎ **773/281-9101.** Reservations required. Main courses $18.50–$29.50. AE, CB, DC, DISC, MC, V. Mon–Thurs 5–10:30pm; Fri 5pm–midnight; Sat 5pm–12:30am; Sun 4:30–10pm. FONDUE.

Geja's (pronounced "*Gay*-haz") was the first wine bar in Chicago, opened in 1963 by John Davis, who is very active in this Lincoln Park community. The specialty here is fondue, a culinary anachronism that was quite fashionable a quarter century ago and still makes for a romantic evening. Fortunately, Mr. Davis has single-handedly preserved the fondue experience in Chicago, providing a fun and welcome break from the ordinary mode of dining.

If there are at least two in your party (all main courses are served for two or more), choose the connoisseur fondue dinner, the best Geja's has to offer. The meal begins with a cheese fondue appetizer, a dish of imported Gruyère and kirsch, kept melted over a burner at your table, into which you dip apple wedges and chunks of dark bread; the flavorful Gruyère is the key to the tastiness of this delicious dish. Next, a huge platter arrives, brimming with squares of beef tenderloin, lobster tails, and jumbo shrimp—all raw—and a caldron of boiling oil to cook them in. These delicacies are accompanied by a variety of raw vegetables, such as green pepper, mushroom, broccoli, and small potatoes, which are also softened in the oil. And when the flaming chocolate fondue arrives for dessert, with fresh fruit and pound cake for dipping, you want to beg for mercy. As an added incentive, Geja's usually has a flamenco or classical Spanish guitarist to provide the background music.

## MODERATE

### ✪ Bossa Nova

1960 N. Clybourn Ave. ☎ **773/248-4800.** Reservations recommended. Tapas $3.95–$7.95; main courses $9.95–$14.95. AE, DISC, MC, V. Tues–Thurs 5:30–11pm; Fri 5:30pm–1:30am; Sat 5:30pm–2:30am. TAPAS.

You're in the mood for some hip Latino music, maybe a little dancing, but you're also hungry. If Chicago were Toon Town, you'd see a neon sign from miles away, with rounded cartoon finger flashing above the entrance to Bossa Nova, proclaiming, "This is the place!"

Bossa Nova is a supper club that promises to deliver a memorable evening. Its location on Clybourn Avenue, the very western edge of Lincoln Park, is a bit off the beaten track, but that only adds to the adventure. The dining area is spacious, with sleek hardwood surfaces all around.

The tapas menu is conducive to dining with a bunch of friends—order a lot, taste it all, pass it around. All the dishes are at least satisfactory, and a few are outstanding. We were not knocked out by the spring rolls, for example, but the polenta more than made up for it, with huge, perfectly cooked prawns adorning the top. We reached a split decision on the ribs, but the scallops were of the melt-in-your-mouth variety, the jerk chicken was nicely tender, and the calamari had a nice spicy zing.

While we were sampling all this food, a live band took the stage around 10:30pm and the party shifted gears as they began belting out tunes that ranged from covers of Gypsy Kings to traditional Mexican favorites. It didn't take long for diners to abandon their tables and crowd onto the dance floor. The rhythm is irresistible and no one will care if you're out there doing your own thing. Bossa Nova is a great place for a memorable night on the town. Call ahead to see what band is playing—it could be salsa, samba, African, reggae, or anything in between. There's a $5 cover on Friday and Saturday after 10pm.

## Bub City

901 W. Weed St. ☎ **773/266-1200.** Reservations not accepted. Main courses $9.95–$19.95. AE, DC, DISC, MC, V. Mon–Thurs 11:30am–4pm and 5–11pm; Fri 11:30am–4pm and 5pm–midnight; Sat 5pm–midnight; Sun 4–10pm. CREOLE/TEX-MEX.

At the tip of the Clybourn Corridor, just south of North Avenue, the Melman restaurant chain has installed Bub City, a Disney-style interpretation of an edge-of-town roadhouse. I find the big-barn look and the frat-boy crowd tedious; the food, mediocre.

If you like Tex-Mex, try the Texas torpedoes (fried jalapeños); a mumbo-jumbo combo of oysters, shrimp, crab claws, and blue crab fingers; Ralphy Boy baked oysters; gumbo; or mushrooms stuffed with crab and shrimp in lemon-butter sauce. Main courses include the salmon barbecue, or the mixed grill with salsa pepino, consisting of blackened lamb chop, chicken breast, and boneless pork chop with pepper jelly.

When I asked the waitress if they had espresso, she replied, "No, but we have really old coffee." It's that kind of place. The bar stocks Texas beer (Rattlesnake and Lone Star) and Muther Margaritas. On Friday and Saturday, the bar is open until 2am.

## Café Ba-Ba-Reeba!

2024 N. Halsted. ☎ **773/935-5000.** Limited number of reservations accepted. Tapas $1.95–$7.50; main courses $8.95–$11.95. AE, DC, MC, V. Mon 5:30–11pm; Tues–Thurs 11:30am–2:30pm and 5:30–11pm; Fri 11:30am–2:30pm and 5:30–midnight; Sat 11:30am–3pm and 5:30pm–midnight; Sun 5–10pm. SPANISH/TAPAS.

Located at the southern end of Halsted Street's Restaurant Row, near Armitage, is Café Ba-Ba-Reeba!, marked by a neon sign announcing *tapas* and frequented by a young Lincoln Park crowd. Ba-Ba-Reeba is a valiant attempt to popularize the merits of this unique Iberian snack tradition with a selection of some 45 hot and cold tapas of the restaurant's own creation.

Inside, the café includes a covered patio, two bars, and several dining rooms. The bright acrylic and oil paintings, mostly pop portraiture and other representations, are some of the most delightful you will see gathered in one room anywhere in Chicago.

The plato de la casa is a plate of very satisfactory traditional meats and cheeses. The queso con albahaca, slices of fresh mozzarella on plum tomato topped with fresh basil leaf, is excellent. Among the hot tapas, the pincho de pollo y chorizo, chicken and chorizo sausage brochettes with a dip of garlic-cumin mayonnaise, was economical and very tasty.

For dessert you might try the tarta de chocolate or a concoction served with ice cream called profiteroles de chocolate.

### Café Bernard

2100 N. Halsted. ☎ **773/871-2100.** Reservations recommended. Main courses $10–$19. AE, CB, DC, MC, V. Sun–Thurs 5–10:30pm; Fri–Sat 5–11:30pm. FRENCH.

The Café Bernard features French country fare at moderate prices—many dishes are in the $12 to $14 range. This little French restaurant on the corner, incidentally, has the authentic look and feel of a Parisian back-street bistro, with low lighting and a casually dressed clientele. Its main courses range from steak au poivre to stuffed breast of pheasant to venison and other game.

### Carlucci

2215 N. Halsted. ☎ **773/281-1220.** Reservations recommended. Main courses $10.95–$18.95. AE, CB, DC, DISC, MC, V. Mon–Thurs 5:30–10:30pm; Fri–Sat 5:30–11:30pm; Sun 5–10pm. ITALIAN.

Behind a simple storefront awning is Carlucci, one of the best Italian restaurants in Chicago. The restaurant is actually quite large, with several rooms, including an interior open-air courtyard. During your dinner, try a glass of Spanna, a dry red wine squeezed from the nebbiolo grape in Italy's Piedmont region. Carlucci sells 20 Italian wines by the glass.

Crusty, soft-centered bread to dip in a puddle of virgin olive oil spiked with hot chili peppers begins each meal at Carlucci. The many antipasti on the menu include several varieties of pizza. I chose an insalata quattro colori of radicchio, arugula, endive, and tiny yellow pear tomatoes, flavored with walnuts and Gorgonzola, and dressed with lemon juice and olive oil—a superb combination. Half orders are permitted, so you can sample both a pasta and a main meat course. The fazzoletti, triangular ravioli filled with zucchini, leeks, and carrots, is topped with fresh prawns sautéed with tomato and balsamic vinegar. The paillard di vitello ai ferri consists of scaloppine of veal seasoned with lemon sage and grilled to tender perfection.

### Dee's Mandarin Restaurant

1114 W. Armitage Ave. (Racine). ☎ **773/477-1500.** Reservations recommended. Main courses $9–$13. AE, CB, DC, DISC, MC, V. Mon–Thurs 5–11pm; Fri–Sat 5pm–midnight; Sun 4:30–10:30 pm. CHINESE.

A solid, reliable Chinese restaurant in the Lincoln Park neighborhood, Dee's offers a typical menu that includes all the old standbys—moo shu, Peking duck, and Mandarin beef.

### Four Farthings

2060 N. Cleveland. ☎ **773/935-2060.** Reservations accepted. Main courses $9.95–$17.95. AE, CB, DC, DISC, MC, V. Mon–Fri 11:30am–2am; Sat 11:30am–3am; Sun 11am–2am. AMERICAN.

Several blocks in from the park along Dickens (at a triangle formed by Lincoln and Cleveland Avenues) is a tavern and restaurant owned by Bill and Jon Nordhem that has been a Lincoln Park institution for many years. At the Four Farthings, the restaurant and bar clientele are completely different, the former catering to a some-what upscale gourmet set, the latter to a sports crowd who likes to gather for Bears and Cubs games. In warm weather, locals enjoy the outdoor seating. A delicious shrimp Caesar salad and an equally tasty appetizer of smoked-salmon ravioli might start your meal. Four Farthings's menu features fresh seafood, as well as chops and steaks. The restaurant's wine selection is also quite extensive, with many excellent varieties sold by the glass.

## INEXPENSIVE

### Big Shoulders Cafe

Clark St. and North Ave. at the Chicago Historical Society. ☎ **312/642-4600.** Reservations accepted. Main courses $6.95–$7.95. AE, DC, MC, V. Mon–Fri 9:30am–4:30pm; Sat–Sun noon–5pm. CAFÉ FARE.

Here's an option for a nice light meal, whether or not you are tying the occasion into a swing through the Chicago Historical Society. Big Shoulders is not just a cafeteria serving the museum; it is a popular restaurant in its own right, and it remains open even when the Historical Society is closed.

Soon after you are seated in Big Shoulders, your waiter will appear with a plate of owner Jerome Kliejunas's trademark tasty cornbread, generously sprinkled with flecks of jalapeño and millet. A very nice lunch or supper can then be made of the Caesar salad with grilled chicken breast or strips of sirloin; or the double Sheboygan bratwurst with grilled onions, roasted potatoes, and a small vegetable salad. Those who wish to drop in for coffee or tea and dessert are also welcome. Occasionally the café is closed for private parties during the dinner hours, so it is best to call ahead if that is the time frame you have in mind.

### Edwardo's

2120 N. Halsted. ☎ **773/871-3400.** Reservations not accepted. Pizzas $9.50–$22; all-you-can-eat pizza and salad served Mon–Sat 11:30am–3pm for $4.95. AE, MC, V. Mon–Thurs 11am–midnight; Fri–Sat 11am–1am; Sun 11am–11:30pm. El: From the Fullerton stop of the Ravenswood or Howard line, walk south on Halsted; from the Armitage stop on the Ravenswood line, walk north on Halsted. PIZZA.

Some locals claim that Edwardo's has the best pizza in Chicago. The chain has sev-eral locations, and the all-you-can-eat pizza special is the only one in Chicago.

### Goose Island Brewing Company

1800 N. Clybourn Ave. ☎ **312/915-0071.** Reservations accepted. Sandwiches $5.25–$7.50; main courses $7.95–$13.95. AE, CB, DC, DISC, MC, V. Mon–Thurs 11am–1am; Fri–Sat 11am–2am; Sun 11am–midnight; kitchen closes two hours before the bar. AMERICAN.

Some of the best beer in Chicago is manufactured at this modest microbrewery on the Clybourn corridor. Don't take my word for it. An impressive cast of professional beer mavens and critics have arrived at the same conclusion. In the course of a year, Goose Island brewmeister Greg Hall (whose dad John is the pub/brewery's owner) mixes up some 2,500 barrels a year of about 30 different varieties of lagers, ales, stouts, pilsners, and porters that change with the seasons. Normally a pint costs $3.25, but a 6-ounce sampler glass is only $1, making a tasting session a fun evening's entertainment.

As for the food, the cup of jalapeño chicken soup is good, as is the corn chowder. The tangy, delicate fresh mussels are drenched in garlic butter. But I recommend sam-pling the beer and then dining at another of the neighborhood's more accomplished restaurants. To stave off the hunger, though, munch on the free homemade potato chips, better even than Harry Caray's. Goose Island goes through 3,000 pounds of spuds a week; after all, what goes better with beer? What else goes great with a brewsky? A game of pool, and Goose Island has seven tables.

### Nookies, Too

2114 N. Halsted. ☎ **773/327-1400.** Reservations not accepted. Menu items $1.95–$8.95. CB, DC, MC, V. Mon–Thurs 6:30am–11pm; Fri–Sat 24 hours; Sun 6:30am–9pm. AMERICAN.

Nookies, Too is open for breakfast, lunch, and dinner, serving hash and eggs, eggs Benedict, omelets (over a dozen varieties), blintzes, pancakes, burgers, sandwiches, and blue-plate specials. Cheery, well lighted, and with a big counter, it's an appealing place for a good, solid, everyday meal.

### P.S. Bangkok 2

2521 N. Halsted. ☎ **773/348-0072.** Reservations not accepted. Main courses $3.50–$12.95. AE, DC, DISC, MC, V. Mon–Thurs 11:30am–10pm; Fri–Sat 11:30am–11:30pm; Sun 4:30–10pm. THAI.

This is a Thai restaurant with oodles of dishes, mostly in the $5 to $8 range. With a menu of 20 appetizers, 10 soups, and more than 24 main courses, you ought to be able to find something to tempt your palate—though for many of us, practically any Thai platter is a tasty treat.

### Ranalli's Pizzeria, Libations & Collectibles

1925 N. Lincoln. ☎ **312/642-4700.** Reservations not accepted. Main courses $6.50–$12.95. AE, CB, DC, DISC, MC, V. Sun–Fri 11am–2am; Sat 11am–3am. PIZZA/ITALIAN.

Yards from the farm in the Lincoln Park Zoo is Ranalli's and its three-score tables spread out on an open-air patio. Acres of memorabilia (the "collectibles") line the walls of the adjoining indoor restaurant and bar, though in the proper weather the festive potential of the outside setting far outshines the cavelike atmosphere inside and under cover (unless you're a sports fan glued to the big game). Thin crust (as opposed to "Chicago" deep-dish) pizza is the specialty, along with Philadelphia-style "hoagie" sandwiches, salads, pasta, ribs, and steak. The main attraction, though, is the seemingly endless roster of beers.

### ✪ R. J. Grunts

2056 Lincoln Park West. ☎ **773/929-5363.** Reservations accepted for parties of six or more. Sandwiches and main courses $5.95–$14.95. AE, DC, DISC, MC, V. Mon–Thurs 11:30am–10pm; Fri–Sat 11:30am–11pm; Sun 10am–2:30pm (brunch) and 3–10pm. AMERICAN.

For Richard Melman and his Lettuce Entertain You restaurant empire, it all began in relative modesty at R. J. Grunts, located at the corner of Dickens Street, just north of Armitage, directly across from Lincoln Park. Grunts is one of those restaurant/bars that somehow manages to be all things to all people. The neighborhood crowd hangs out here, as do the cops on the beat. Grunts boasts, in my opinion, the best burger and fries in the city. Other favorites are the French onion soup and the chili. In my countless meals here with friends and family (I used to live nine floors above it), no companion has ever had a bad meal, whether it was one of several chicken or vegetarian dishes or several trips to the salad bar (reportedly the first in the city). One big draw at Grunts, which began as a salad and veggies eatery at the dawn of the health-food movement, is the Sunday brunch, an all-you-can-eat feast from the salad bar, plus such dishes as omelets or eggs Benedict.

### RoseAngelis

1314 W. Wrightwood Ave. (Lakewood). ☎ **773/296-0081.** Reservations accepted for parties of eight or more. Main courses $7.95–$9.95. DISC, MC, V. Tues–Thurs 5–10pm; Fri–Sat 5–11pm; Sun 4:30–9pm. ITALIAN.

Two former lawyers traded in their law books for pots and pans, opening RoseAngelis about five years ago. Ensconced in an old house in a residential section of Lincoln

Park, the restaurant charms with its series of small dining rooms and garden patio. Then it delights with its exceptional and affordable Italian food. Try the outstanding, garlicky chicken Vesuvio (not offered on Friday and Saturday nights because of preparation time), browned to perfection, or the substantial lasagna, my mom's favorite in the city. The specials also tend to be worth sampling, as is the tiramisù.

## 8  Wrigleyville & the Mid-North Side

The area surrounding Wrigley Field has a long history as a neighborhood of working-class families. Wrigleyville has gentrified to an extent, as developers have built new townhouses and apartments, and with that affluence has come a group of new, very popular restaurants.

### VERY EXPENSIVE

#### ✪ Yoshi's Cafe

3257 Halsted St. ☎ **773/248-6160.** Reservations required. Main courses $17–$25. AE, MC, V. Tues–Thurs 5:30–10pm; Fri–Sat 5:30–10:30pm; Sun 5–9:30pm. NOUVELLE FRENCH.

Despite having won raves from *Conde Nast Traveler, Zagat's,* and other high-profile publications, Yoshi's is surprisingly low-key—you don't have to be celebrating an elaborate occasion to dine here. It looks plain and unassuming from the outside, but once you step past the bar, you'll discover a restaurant decorated with understated elegance and simplicity, an intimate spot that serves only 48 patrons. It's such a comfortable place, in fact, that when Steve Martin discovered it while in town performing a stint at a local theater, he became hooked and dined here every night. This is unquestionably one of Chicago's top spots.

My waiter was extremely knowledgeable and friendly—happy to suggest a wine from the extensive list and to explain the preparations in detail. And the preparations are intriguing, with very light sauces and combinations chosen to enhance the flavors and textures of the ingredients. The menu, which frequently changes, lists predominantly seafood choices, and dishes reflect a strong Japanese influence and are exquisitely presented in the Japanese tradition. I enjoyed a filet of fluke that was lightly coated with crushed almonds, and my companions were taken with the tuna tartare, served on a bed of avocado and created with such fresh fish that each piece seemed to melt in your mouth. Our desserts were imaginatively conceived, including a delicate white and dark chocolate mousse, served in a "demitasse" created from a sheet of rich dark chocolate. And chef Yoshi Katsumura himself came out from the kitchen to visit each table and make sure everyone was happy. Highly recommended.

### MODERATE

#### ✪ Arun's

4156 N. Kedzie (Irving Park). ☎ **773/539-1909.** Reservations recommended. Main courses $13.95–$24.95. AE, CB, DC, DISC, MC, V. Tues–Sat 5–10pm; Sun 5–9pm. THAI.

It's been called the best Thai restaurant in the city—possibly the country. Chef/owner Arun Sampanthavivat prepares a refined traditional cuisine that's authentic and flavorful without being tastebud-burning. Try the hot-and-sour shrimp soup, the three-flavored red snapper, the garlic prawns, and, of course, the pad thai. House specialties also include khao kriab (steamed rice dumplings filled with crabmeat, shrimp, chicken, peanuts, and garlic with a tangy vinaigrette) and golden baskets (flower-shaped bite-size pastries filled with shrimp, chicken, sweet corn, and shiitake mushrooms).

The decor is just as beautiful, with Thai artwork—paintings, artifacts, and antiques—as the backdrop.

## Bella Vista

1001 W. Belmont Ave. ☎ **773/404-0111.** Reservations recommended for dinner on weekends. Main courses $9.25–$17.95. AE, DC, MC, V. Mon–Thurs 11:30am–11pm; Fri–Sat 11:30am–midnight; Sun 5–10pm. El: Belmont stop on the Howard line. ITALIAN.

Near the corner of Sheffield, the Bella Vista was installed in an old bank building. The former financial institution's glorious and ornate interior decor of columns, painted plaster, and marble—not to mention a skylight covering virtually the entire ceiling of one room—have been totally preserved. As the name implies, it is indeed a beautiful view.

The food at Bella Vista—the in-spot along the Belmont entertainment strip— is classic Italian, with a slightly nouvelle accent. Among the appealing selections are the antipasti di giorno, with seven different items daily; the pasta del mare, black-pepper linguine with prawns, clams, mussels, and roasted peppers; and the bisteca griglia, strip steak with garlic and portobello mushrooms and potato ravioli.

## Mia Francesca

3311 N. Clark St. ☎ **773/281-3310.** Reservations not accepted. Main courses $8.95–$16.95. MC, V. Daily 5–10:30pm. ITALIAN.

From the time it opened about five years ago, Mia Francesca has been one of the hardest tables to get in Chicago. Unless you plan on arriving as the doors open, be prepared to wait. By 7pm, that wait often exceeds an hour (people have been known to wait for three). No, it's not just trendy, though fashionable people do frequent Mia Francesca, and it's popular with young professionals. The decor is simple, and the place tends to be noisy.

But it's the food—unpretentious but never dull—that keeps locals coming back. The menu changes daily, but you can count on thin-crust individual pizzas, chicken, veal, and fish dishes nightly. The pastas are out of this world.

## Oo La La!

3335 N. Halsted St. ☎ **773/935-7708.** Reservations accepted. Main courses $8.95–$15.95. AE, MC, V. Dinner daily 5:30–11pm; Sun brunch 10am–3pm. FRENCH/ITALIAN.

It happens sometimes in big cities where there's a surplus of both creativity and storefronts. Wait-in-line restaurants spring up in modest spaces that in prior incarnations might have housed the neighborhood dry cleaner or the corner hardware store. In such a space, Oo La La! provides both scene and substance for the 60 lucky patrons who squeeze into its swank and chummy confines on a given night.

Oo La La! calls itself a border bistro, referring to the binational inspiration of Chef Jill Dietz-Rosenthall's dishes, which may be traced to the typical workaday Parisian bistro or Roman trattoria, but which have been modified and pampered to satisfy the more demanding palates of those who dine out frequently. So, at Oo La La!, you may have your grilled chicken or roasted lamb shank, and eat it too, so to speak, not only with gusto but with pleasure. The pasta dishes, on the other hand, have evolved somewhat further from the homeland trattorias. But pasta is like that, because nine-tenths of the challenge is in the sauce, and Chef Jill's alchemy in this medium is on a par with the best Chicago has to offer. Her emphasis is on simplicity and preparation, rather than novelty for its own sake. Take the penne with smoked eggplant in a tomato and basil sauce with goat cheese—the pasta is embraced, not smothered. Even the outrageous tomato pumpkin ravioli—tomato pasta stuffed with pumpkin in a sage cream sauce—however arch, is food first and foremost. Oo La La!, just north of Belmont, about an $8 cab ride from downtown, is definitely in, definitely fun, and definitely good.

### Vinny's

2901 N. Sheffield Ave. ☎ **773/871-0990.** Reservations recommended, especially for dinner on Fri–Sat. Main courses $7.95–$22.95. AE, DC, MC, V. Sun–Fri 5–10pm; Sat 5–11pm. El: Ravenswood line to Diversey; then walk north on Sheffield. CLASSIC ITALIAN.

Vinny's is in! An old warehouse has been converted into a family restaurant on the scale of a continental café, and though the space is enormous with its two hall-size separate rooms, you will still have to wait for a table during peak dinner hours. How to explain Vinny's success? The time-honored formula of quality and quantity.

Vinny's has locked step with the new Chicago "tradition" of serving family-style portions that can easily stretch for three or four people. For starters, try spicy broccoli, or a generous platter of fried calamari. The Goomba chicken plate, with sausage, peppers, onions, and roasted potatoes, is certainly big enough to share; the platter would serve a small army. Don't miss Aunt Tessie's rum cake for dessert, or the homemade lemon ice if you're in the mood for something lighter.

### Zum Deutschen Eck

2914 N. Southport. ☎ **773/525-8389.** Reservations recommended. Main courses $11.95–$18.95. AE, CB, DC, DISC, MC, V. Mon–Thurs 11:30am–midnight; Fri noon–2am; Sat noon–3am; Sun noon–midnight. Take the Lincoln Avenue bus no. 11 to Southport, and walk a half-block south on Southport. GERMAN.

Zum Deutschen Eck (which translates as The German Corner) is housed in a large Bavarian-style chalet just north of Diversey and west of Lincoln Avenue. Its menu features the best of German and continental cooking.

After munching on the fresh rolls and breadsticks served at the beginning of each meal, try liver-dumpling consommé, accompanied by a crisp cucumber salad. Owner Al Wirth, Jr., whose father opened Zum Deutschen Eck in the late '50s, suggests the Ochsenmaul, which literally means calves' cheeks, and tastes something like a sweeter, more tender version of prosciutto. I ordered the German Schlact Platte, a selection of German wursts and smoked pork loin, served with parsley potatoes and sauerkraut. Never have I sampled a more delicious knockwurst or Thueringer bratwurst, which it turns out are procured from local butchers and contain no filler, but only pure meat. Dinners here include soup, appetizer, and salad. You can drink draft Dortmunder lager during your meal, and for dessert, there's a small but scrumptious Black Forest devil's food cake with fresh whipped cream. I don't know why anyone on a diet would go to a German restaurant, but just in case, the place has added a group of heart-healthy selections.

Ample parking is available at Zum Deutschen Eck, and the music—sing-along and schmaltzy, of course—never stops, as a duo of accordion and drums bang out one familiar beer-drinking song after another, alternating between German and English.

## INEXPENSIVE

### Ann Sather's

929 W. Belmont. ☎ **773/348-2378.** Reservations accepted for parties of six or more. Main courses $6.95–$11.95. AE, MC, V. Sun–Thurs 7am–10pm; Fri–Sat 7am–11pm. SWEDISH/AMERICAN.

A sign hanging by the door marks Ann Sather's with the following inscription: "Once one of many neighborhood Swedish restaurants, Ann Sather's is the only one that remains." It's a real Chicago institution, where you can enjoy Swedish meatballs with buttered noodles and brown gravy, or the Swedish sampler of duck breast with lingonberry glaze, meatball, potato-sausage dumpling, sauerkraut, and brown beans. All meals are full dinners, including appetizer, main course, vegetable, potato, and dessert. It's the sticky cinammon rolls, though, that make addicts out of diners.

On Monday night there are live performances upstairs at Ann Sather's in a cabaret setting. There is another branch at 5207 N. Clark ( ☎ 271-6677).

### Barry's Spot

5759 N. Broadway. ☎ **773/769-2900.** Reservations not accepted. Pasta dishes and sandwiches $3.95–$6.95; pizza $5.70–$17.95. AE, CB, DC, DISC, JCB, MC, V. Mon–Thurs 4pm–1am; Fri–Sat 4pm–2am; Sun 4pm–midnight. PIZZA.

Great-tasting pizza is the specialty here—thin, pan, or stuffed varieties with homemade sausage, fresh mushrooms, zucchini, eggplant, or sliced tomatoes. Barry's also has freshly baked lasagna, and vegetable-and-spaghetti parmigiana (eggplant, zucchini, and mushrooms with meat sauce), each complete with a healthy serving of salad and French bread. All main courses are served with minestrone soup as well. Owners Barry and Barbara Bernsen take the time to greet customers, and if you are an out-of-towner, they'll be happy to give you directions.

## 9 Wicker Park/Bucktown

Now that the yuppies have conquered Lincoln Park and are making definite inroads in Wrigleyville, Wicker Park has become the neighborhood of contention. Artists, photographers, musicians, and the like began moving in a few years back, drawn by the light-drenched studios, the cheap rents, and the "real people" feel of the place. It didn't take long for wannabes to follow. The armies have splintered into factions, with artists fighting artists—some apparently think it's a crime to sell a painting—and entrepreneurs battling developers. But from the muck has risen a really happening scene.

A great evening out is to have dinner at one of Wicker Park's many interesting restaurants and then catch some music at a neighboring club. If you start at the intersection of North, Damen, and Milwaukee Avenues, you won't have to walk more than a couple of blocks in any direction to find a hot spot. Cab fare's not too bad from downtown, or you can take the El's O'Hare line to Damen.

## EXPENSIVE

### Cafe Absinthe

1954 W. North Ave. ☎ **773/278-4488.** Reservations recommended. Main courses $12.50–$22. AE, DC, MC, V. Mon–Thurs 5:30–10pm; Fri–Sat 5:30–11pm; Sun 5:30–9pm. ECLECTIC.

For most Chicagoans, alleys function as a place to store garbage until the sanitation crews come along, keeping the sidewalks clear. Cafe Absinthe uses its alley as the restaurant entrance. Looks can be deceiving, for Absinthe is no dive. On the contrary, it's becoming one of Chicago's hippest eateries, both because its out-of-the-way location is attracting trendy types and because the dining experience is interesting and elegant.

The darkly lit interior sets the mood. Along one wall, draperies divide the tables. One or two dishes are rotated daily, but on a typical evening Absinthe will offer such appetizers as wild boar leg salad with sushi rice roll and apple wasabi relish, or grilled quail with polenta, portobello mushrooms, and port wine sauce. Main courses include grilled tuna with garlic mashed potatoes and beef tenderloin with acorn squash and roasted garlic Roquefort sauce. The dessert menu is every bit as tempting, from the hazelnut dacquoise with chocolate and caramel sauces to the kiwi, papaya, mango, and coconut sorbets with passion fruit soup.

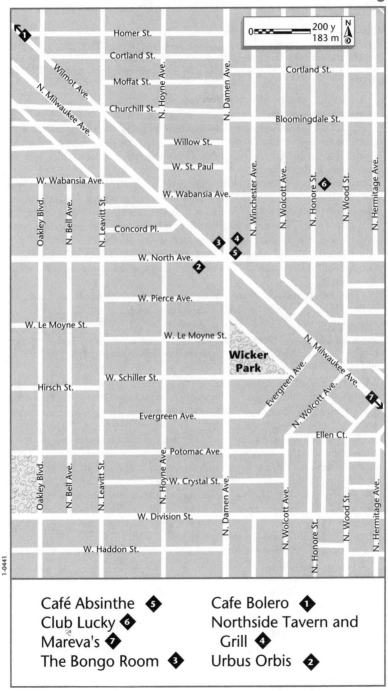

# Bucktown/Wicker Park Dining

Café Absinthe ◆5  Cafe Bolero ◆1
Club Lucky ◆6  Northside Tavern and
Mareva's ◆7  Grill ◆4
The Bongo Room ◆3  Urbus Orbis ◆2

1-0441

# MODERATE

### Club Lucky

1824 W. Wabansia (at the corner of Honore, near North and Damen). ☎ **773/227-2300.** Reservations accepted only for parties of six or more. Main courses $5.95–$18.95. MC, V. Mon–Thurs 11:30am–11pm; Fri 11:30am–midnight; Sat 5pm–midnight; Sun 4–10pm. TRADITIONAL ITALIAN.

Club Lucky is one of the hottest spots in Chicago. The scene here is youngish, and very dress-up; expect to wait for a seat.

Club Lucky seems to have been carved from a local '50s-era corner tavern with a catering business in the back room. In fact, the place was designed to look like that, with plenty of Naugahyde banquettes, a Formica-topped bar and tables, and Captain Video ceiling fixtures.

You may or may not take to the scene, but the food does not disappoint. Prices overall are moderate, and the family-style portions are generous. The large calamari appetizer—"for two," the menu says—will almost certainly keep you in leftover land for a day or two. The menu offers real Italian home-style cooking, such as pasta e fagioli (thick macaroni-and-bean soup—really a kind of stew). You might also order the rigatoni with veal meatballs, served with steamed escarole and melted slabs of mozzarella; or the spicy, grilled boneless pork chops served with peppers and roasted potatoes.

The lunch menu includes about a dozen Italian sandwiches for about $5 each, such as scrambled eggs and pesto, meatball, and Italian sausage.

### Mareva's

1250 N. Milwaukee Ave. ☎ **773/227-4000.** Reservations required. Main courses $8–21.95. AE, DC, MC, V. Fri 5pm–midnight; Sat 11:30am–3pm and 5pm–midnight; Sun 11:30am–3pm and 5–10pm. POLISH.

A very fine Polish restaurant is located on the fringes of Wicker Park. Before they opened the restaurant, Stanley and Irene Idzik had managed the family catering business part-time. When their children grew up, Irene was able to launch the restaurant of her dreams, Mareva's.

Mareva's offers sophistication and continental charm, celebrating the best of Polish culture and cookery with considerable dignity. Wednesday through Sunday a pianist plays Chopin and other classical pieces at both lunch and dinner.

In Slavic fashion, you might begin your dinner with shots of frozen vodka, then follow with your choice of pirogi. There is one stuffed with a chicken mousse flavored with cognac, leeks, and cream; and another with a mousse of swordfish and sole, served with homemade yogurt, dill, and pear sauce. The traditional pirogi, with veal, potato, and cabbage and served with sour cream, is also on the menu. Next, try one of the borschts, the clear beet or the Ukrainian, both of which are savory and salutary. Follow this with a perfect Caesar salad. From the game dishes, you might choose the lean duck breast that is first grilled and then baked in a juice of oranges and champagne, or the venison in a sauce of mushrooms and herbs over a bed of wild rice. For dessert, you might choose the fruit compote à la polonaise, fresh fruit served hot over vanilla ice cream with a dash of brandy; or one of several pastries.

The luncheon menu at Mareva's is more modestly priced, which makes the restaurant a bargain as well as a culinary standout. And from the banqueting side of the operation, which still hosts and caters weddings and other social functions on the upper stories of the same building, there is a unique carry-out service. The main intention of this service is to provide a Polish meal for home-catered parties, but individuals giving a day's notice may also take out this well-packed "nine-course" special, which includes clear borscht or assorted pirogi, fresh green beans and carrots, salad, new potatoes with parsley, butter-fried chicken, roast beef in gravy, potato dumpling, Polish sausage and sauerkraut, rolls and butter, and pastries. Valet parking for 350 cars is available.

# INEXPENSIVE

## Bongo Room

1560 N. Damen. ☎ **773/489-0690.** Reservations not required. Most items $1.50–$8. No credit cards. Mon–Fri 7am–3pm; Sat–Sun 9:30am–2:30pm. BREAKFAST/LIGHT LUNCH.

At about 7:30 in the morning, the commuters are streaming by this little storefront oasis, racing to the station next door to catch the downtown El. A fair number of them pop in here first for take-out, or pause long enough to enjoy their large cup of cappuccino or caffè latte with perhaps a home-baked muffin while seated at one of the handful of tables that line the plate-glass window. Buried behind their papers, they take in the rumbling of the trains through one ear, and the blaring arias that are the ambient music of the Bongo Room through the other. French toast, flapjacks, and other good fare are also served, all of it well prepared and reasonably priced. The menu changes every four months, and the decor, once a year.

## Cafe Bolero

2252 N. Western Ave. ☎ **773/227-9000.** Reservations not required. Main courses $4.95–$11.95. AE, MC, V. Tues–Sun 9:30am–10pm. CUBAN/YUGOSLAVIAN.

This is perhaps a bit farther west than most visitors will want to travel. But the more adventurous among you will be rewarded if you do. Cafe Bolero is the combined enterprise of a multicultural husband-and-wife team; he's Cuban, she's Serbian. The café was brand-spanking-new in 1994, very tastefully laid out, even possessing a touch of elegance. Most of the dishes lean toward the Caribbean; this is certainly one of the few restaurants west of the Appalachians where you can get a genuine Cuban sandwich (grilled pork and cheese on French-style bread). They also have tostones (fried plantains), but these are very special, cupped on top and filled with ground beef picadillo. One Slavic-style dish is the homemade grilled sausage, with feta cheese and marinated roasted peppers ($6.50 for one, $11.95 for two). And there's a daily entrée as well, like picadillo criollo or bifstec Palomilla. Espresso and cafe con leche are also available.

## Northside Tavern and Grill

1635 N. Damen. ☎ **773/384-3555.** Reservations not accepted. Menu items $4.95–$9.25. AE, DC, DISC, MC, V. Sun–Fri 11:30am–2am; Sat 11:30am–3am. AMERICAN.

One of the best cheap eats in the city, Northside cooks up great burgers and sandwiches, all for around $5 or $6. The back dining room looks like a rec room circa 1973, complete with fireplace, pinball machines, and a pool table. In nice weather, Northside opens up its large patio for dining. On Thursday night, you might be able to catch a local band. You're always sure to find entertainment in the form of people-watching: Northside attracts all sorts.

## Urbus Orbis

1934 W. North Ave. ☎ **773/252-4446.** Reservations not accepted. Menu items $1.75–$6.50. MC, V. Mon–Thurs 9am–midnight; Fri–Sat 9am–1am; Sun 10am–midnight. AMERICAN.

This coffeehouse says just about everything there is to say about Bucktown. It's full of artists, slackers, and others who just like to hang out in the comfy library chairs, maybe read one of the wildly diverse magazines Urbus Orbis stocks (from *Foreign Affairs* to the *Perot Periodical*), or play a game of chess. Huge windows overlook

North Avenue, and exhibits of local artists' work change every month or so. I once stopped in for a hot chocolate, and the guy at the table next to me was rapping with his dog.

As for the food and drink, Urbus Orbis has a full menu of coffee—cold and hot— as well as lemonade and Torani soda in a multitude of flavors. The food is mostly noshy, as in eggs, salads, sandwiches, muffins, and cookies. Urbus Orbis also has a theater space in back that holds several dozen spectators. Monday through Wednesday you might find live music, while Thursday through Sunday the entertainment is more typically theater or performance art. The scheduling is irregular, so your best bet is calling ahead; you could also check the *Reader,* Chicago's free weekly in-the-know paper.

## 10   Only in Chicago

### PIZZA

Now here's a topic about which Chicagoans are passionate. To the uninitiated: Chicago-style pizza, also known as "deep-dish," is thick-crusted and often demands a knife and fork. The thin-crusted variety favored in New York is also widely available; a third type, called "stuffed," is similar to a pie, with a crust both on top and bottom. Many pizzerias serve both thick and thin, and some make all three kinds.

Two of Chicago's gourmet deep-dish restaurants, **Pizzeria Uno,** at 29 E. Ohio, at the corner of Wabash (☎ 312/321-1000), and **Pizzeria Due,** 618 N. Wabash, at the corner of Ontario (☎ 312/943-2400), are listed earlier in this chapter under Section 5, "River North." **Gino's East,** 160 E. Superior (☎ 312/943-1124), is mentioned under Section 4, "The Magnificent Mile (North Michigan Avenue) & the Gold Coast."

In River North, **Lou Malnati's Pizzeria** at 439 N. Wells (☎ 312/828-9800) bakes both deep-dish and thin-crusted pizza and even has a low-fat cheese option. **Edwardo's** is a pizza chain that serves all three varieties. It has several Chicago locations, including one at 2120 N. Halsted (☎ 773/871-3400), which is mentioned in Section 6, "Lincoln Park." Also reviewed in Section 6 is **Ranalli's Pizzeria, Libations & Collectibles,** 1925 N. Lincoln (☎ 312/642-4700).

In Wrigleyville are **Leona's Pizzeria,** 3215 N. Sheffield (☎ 773/327-8861), and **Pat's Pizzeria,** 3414 N. Sheffield (☎ 773/248-0168), both of which serve all three kinds of pizza. Leona's also has a location in Little Italy at 1419 W. Taylor St. (☎ 312/850-2222), and Pat's has one at 211 N. Stetson (☎ 312/946-0220).

If you find yourself on the city's far north side, **Barry's Spot,** 5759 N. Broadway (☎ 773/769-2900), has great-tasting pizza (see Section 7 in this chapter, "Wrigleyville & the Mid-North Side"). My very favorite pizza is the crispy thin-crusted product at **Barnaby's,** 2832 W. Touhy (☎ 773/973-4550).

### HOT DOGS

Chicagoans take as much pride in their hot dogs as they do in their pizza. It's not as if the hot dog is foreign to this city where Armour and Swift once located their sprawling packing plants down by the stockyards. The facades of Chicago's hot-dog stands, as if by some unwritten convention, are all very colorful, with bright signs of red and yellow, exaggerated lettering, and comic illustrations of the wieners and fries.

Naturally, Chicago is home to a few designer hot-dog shops, such as **Gold Coast Dogs,** 418 N. State St., at Hubbard (☎ 312/527-1222). These are the smarty-pants of hot-dog gastronomy in Chicago. The setting of this storefront two blocks off North Michigan Avenue, just across the river from the Loop, is a mixture of residential and commercial blocks. At Gold Coast Dogs you can grab your food and run, or join the crowd on one of the stools around the counter. Choose your frank with hot peppers, celery salt, green relish, or veggies (someone from the store shops at Chicago's central market every day for fresh produce). Hot dogs start at $1.90 and burgers at $3.57. You can also have melted cheddar cheese on your french fries, and homemade brownies for dessert. It's open Monday through Friday from 7am to midnight, on Saturday from 8am to 8pm, and on Sunday from 11am to 8pm. A second branch of Gold Coast is located in Lincoln Park, about two blocks from the main entrance to the zoo, at 2100 N. Clark (☎ 773/327-8887).

## 11  Breakfast, Brunch & Afternoon Tea

You can get a good (and upscale) breakfast at one of the hotels near the Loop or the Magnificent Mile. On the seventh floor of the **Four Seasons Hotel,** 120 E. Delaware Place (☎ 312/280-8800), breakfast is served daily in the Seasons Dining Room from 6:30 to 9:30am, or in the Seasons Cafe from 8am to noon. Enjoy à la carte entrées from home-smoked salmon to French toast or complete meals that range from classic Midwestern fare to a Japanese breakfast. Prices range from $7 to $19.

At **The Drake,** 140 E. Walton Place at Michigan Avenue (☎ 312/787-2200), the Oak Terrace on the lobby level offers traditional morning meals from 7 to 11:30am on Monday through Saturday, and Sunday from 7 to 10:30am. Prices range from $3 to $15.75, which gets you the Chicagoan, complete with orange juice, two eggs, sirloin steak, hash browns or home fries, toast, and a beverage. Reservations are only necessary for parties of eight or more.

The Great Street Restaurant and Bar on the second floor of the **Stouffer Riviere Hotel,** 1 W. Wacker Dr. (☎ 312/372-7200), presents a breakfast buffet from 6 to 10am on Monday through Friday, until 11:30am on Saturday, and until noon on Sunday. For $10.95 per person, you can help yourself to sausage, bacon, eggs, French toast, cereal, danish, and more. No reservations are required.

A more informal choice in the Loop, just across from Marshall Field's, is **Heaven on Seven,** 111 N. Wabash, 7th floor (☎ 312/263-6443), where the Cajun and Creole specialties supplement an enormous diner-style menu that has anything you could possibly desire. Open weekdays from 7am, Saturday from 10am; closed on Sunday. See Section 2, "The Loop," for a complete listing.

You might also want to try **Ann Sather's,** at 929 W. Belmont (☎ 773/348-2378) and at 5207 N. Clark (☎ 773/271-6677), famous for their homemade cinnamon rolls, and open daily from 7am. See Section 7, "Wrigleyville & the Mid-North Side," for details. The **Nookies** restaurants are also a Chicago favorite for all the standard morning fare. One is at 2114 N. Halsted (☎ 773/327-1400).

**Oo La La!,** 3335 N. Halsted St. (☎ 773/935-7708), weighs in with a trendy brunch of its own, from 10am to 3pm, for those who want to wander north a bit on a Sunday morn. That walk up Halsted, from say, Armitage, would really get the day off to a pleasant start. See Section 7 for a complete listing.

If you're shopping on the Magnificent Mile and feel like having an elegant afternoon tea, complete with finger sandwiches, scones, and pastry, go to the the **Palm Court at the Drake,** 140 E. Walton Place (☎ 312/787-2200). A fine afternoon tea is served at the **Ritz-Carlton,** 160 E. Pearson St. (☎ 312/266-1000) in the 12th floor lobby. The Ritz-Carlton is conveniently located near the Water Tower.

## Corner Bakery

516 N. Clark St. ☎ **312/644-7700.** Breakfast $2.50–$6; sandwiches $3–$7. AE, DC, DISC, MC, V. Mon–Fri 7am–2pm; Sat–Sun 8am–noon. BREAKFAST/SANDWICHES.

Sunday morning is a nice time to come to Chicago's River North neighborhood, especially if the weather is agreeable; you could begin your day with a fine continental breakfast at the Corner Bakery, the honest-to-goodness bakery attached to Maggiano's Italian restaurant. The baked goods are exceptional, especially when accompanied by an oversized cup of creamy caffè latte. Many local office workers also come to the Corner Bakery during the week for their sandwiches, most of which are gone by 2pm. And, of course, all of Chicago—restaurants included—is starting to come to the Corner Bakery for the fabulous bread.

## ✪ Lou Mitchell's

565 W. Jackson. ☎ **312/939-3111.** Reservations not accepted. Breakfast items $1.50–$5.95. No credit cards. Mon–Sat 5:30am–3pm; Sun 7am–3pm. AMERICAN/BREAKFAST.

A favorite for breakfast among Chicagoans since 1923 is Lou Mitchell's, across the south branch of the Chicago River from the Loop, a block farther west than Union Station. A French food critic passing through Chicago rated Lou Mitchell's the number one breakfast spot in America, home of the "five-star breakfast." The owner greets you at the door with a basket of doughnut holes (milk duds for the ladies—don't ask), so you can nibble while waiting for a table. The wait is short, since turnover is continuous and service efficiently attentive. Here I had the best bowl of oatmeal I've ever eaten, deliciously creamy. An order of two double-yolk fried eggs with toasted homemade Greek bread, homemade orange marmalade, and hash browns is served at your table in the same skillet it was all cooked in. There are 14 different omelets, including one made with apples and cheddar cheese. Breakfast is served all day.

# In case you want to see the world.

At American Express, we're here to make your journey a smooth one. So we have over 1,700 travel service locations in over 120 countries ready to help. What else would you expect from the world's largest travel agency?

do more ®

**Travel**

# In case you want to be welcomed there.

We're here to see that you're always welcomed at establishments everywhere. That's why millions of people carry the American Express® Card – for peace of mind, confidence, and security, around the world or just around the corner.

do more

# In case you're running low.

**We're here to help with more than 118,000 Express Cash locations around the world. In order to enroll, just call American Express before you start your vacation.**

do more

**Express Cash**

# And just in case.

We're here with American Express® Travelers Cheques and Cheques *for Two*.® They're the safest way to carry money on your vacation and the surest way to get a refund, practically anywhere, anytime.

Another way we help you...

do more ®

**Travelers Cheques**

# What to See & Do in Chicago

Chicago may be the city that works, but it's also the city that plays. The parks are oversized, and many of the museums have gone interactive. Navy Pier is the latest facility, boasting everything from the Chicago Children's Museum to a concert stage, ice skating rink, and 15-story Ferris wheel. Most of the city's major sights are downtown, or close to it, making them within easy walking distance of (or a short cab ride from) the city's principal hotels.

## SUGGESTED ITINERARIES

### If You Have 1 Day

If you have only a day in Chicago, get a taste of a few things special to the city. Assuming you'll be visiting during the nicer weather, start the day in the Loop, either on a self-guided tour or on an organized one by the Chicago Architecture Foundation. Thanks to the Great Fire of 1871 and the determination to rebuild, Chicago has been a world leader in architecture for more than a century. Then, in the afternoon, take the El uptown (along with a whole lot of business types taking a "long lunch") to the sublime Wrigley Field for a Cubs game. To top off the day, catch an evening show at Second City, the comedy club that gave John Belushi and Bill Murray their start.

### If You Have 2 Days

Spend the first day in the downtown area. Walk around the Loop (as mentioned above) to see buildings as well as the city's extensive sculpture collection. Then select one or two museums, such as the Art Institute, the Field Museum of Natural History, the Shedd Aquarium, the Adler Planetarium, or a smaller institution of interest to you. Finish off the day either with a shopping trip up the Magnificent Mile of North Michigan Avenue or gallery-hopping in River North, which has plenty of excellent restaurants for dinner. On the second day, head for a neighborhood on the North Side, such as the Gold Coast, Lincoln Park, or Wicker Park, and explore. In the afternoon, you won't be far from Wrigley Field, where you can see the Cubs play. In the evening, try Second City or perhaps an offbeat theater not far from Wrigley.

## What's Special About Chicago

Architecture
- The first city of modern architecture, Chicago boasts buildings by the greats: Frank Lloyd Wright, Mies van der Rohe, Louis Sullivan, Daniel Burnham, and Philip Johnson, to name a few.

Lake Michigan
- Beaches on the Great Lake, right downtown, as well as miles of shoreline perfect for jogging, biking, in-line skating, or just strolling.

Museums
- World-class institutions that include the Museum of Science and Industry, the Shedd Aquarium, the Adler Planetarium, the Field Museum of Natural History, and the Art Institute of Chicago.
- Many small museums that focus on ethnic groups or special interests.

Parks
- Lincoln Park on the Near North Side, a long stretch of lakefront property that contains one of the last free zoos in America.
- Grant Park, between the lake and the Loop, hosting a summertime music series and a crammed calendar of events, including the Chicago Blues Festival in June, the Taste of Chicago food feast in late June and July, and the Jazz Festival in September.

Performing Arts
- From the high culture of the Chicago Symphony and the Lyric Opera to the groundbreaking drama of Steppenwolf and the uproarious antics of the Second City comedy troupe, the city has this area covered.

Sports
- At least one team for every major professional spectator sport—the basketball Bulls, football Bears, baseball's Cubs and White Sox, and the hockey Blackhawks.
- Numerous Park District golf courses, plus one privately run nine-hole course just east of the Loop, among other facilities for outdoor recreation.

### If You Have 3 Days

Begin the third day with a trip to Hyde Park, where you can see the University of Chicago and Frank Lloyd Wright's Robie House, among other sights. Then spend a few hours being fascinated by the Museum of Science and Industry. When you head back north, you could see another museum, or, if it's a beautiful day, I recommend going straight to Lincoln Park to stroll around the zoo or to rent rollerblades or a bike. Choose one of the neighborhood's many good restaurants for dinner and then one of its jazz or blues clubs for a finale.

### If You Have 5 Days or More

You've still only scratched the surface. You could hear great music at the Chicago Symphony or the Lyric Opera. You could also dine on Polish food north of Logan Square, German food on Lincoln Square, or Mexican food in Pilsen. You could visit the Board of Trade or the Chicago Historical Society or take an architectural river cruise. You could also venture out of the city center to suburban Oak Park, one half hour by El from downtown and a must for any fan of Frank Lloyd Wright's architecture.

# Ferris Bueller's Day Off

In the classic John Hughes film, with Matthew Broderick in the title role, a high school senior plays hooky for a day and takes off for Chicago with his best friend and girlfriend. In the course of a few hours, after parking their Ferrari in the Loop, Ferris and his buddies spend the morning at the Board of Trade, have lunch at a posh French restaurant, go uptown to a Cubs game, swing back downtown to the Art Institute, get stuck in traffic during a Loop parade, make a final stop at the beach, and still manage to make it back to their cushy suburb in time for dinner. A quick analysis of his itinerary might indicate that it is pure fiction, that you would need at least two days to accomplish everything (after all, you don't have the benefit of film editing). But under certain circumstances you might be able to swing a modified version of events: do it on a Tuesday, when the Art Institute is open until 8pm; or reverse the order a bit, stopping at the museum after the Board of Trade and choosing a day with a 3pm baseball game rather than the usual 1:15pm start. In either case, though, I recommend avoiding Loop parade traffic.

# 1  The Top Attractions

## IN & AROUND THE LOOP

The Loop's major museums form a cluster on South Michigan Avenue and Grant Park. The interior streets have a good deal to offer as well, primarily in the form of innovative architecture, such as the Rookery and the Sears Tower, and grand public sculpture by Picasso, Miró, and others. The heart of the Loop is also where you'll find such oddities as the Board of Trade, the world's largest commodities, futures, and options exchange. After dark the Loop is virtually empty, except on the perimeter, where you can spend an evening at Orchestra Hall, the Auditorium Theater, or the Civic Opera House, to name a few of the city's world-class performing arts centers.

### ✪ Art Institute of Chicago

Michigan Avenue (at Adams St). ☎ **312/443-3600.** Admission $6.50 adults; $3.25 children, students, and seniors. Admission free on Tues. Mon and Wed–Fri 10:30am–4:30pm, Tues 10:30am–8pm, Sat 10am–5pm, Sun and holidays noon–5pm. Closed Thanksgiving Day, Christmas Day. Bus: 3, 4, 60, 145, 147, or 151. Subway/El: Take the Lake/Dan Ryan, Evanston, or Ravenswood line to Adams, or the Howard line to Monroe or Jackson.

Chicago's temple of art houses a major collection—from medieval and early Renaissance to Rothko and all the modernists. It has a notable collection of impressionist art. A couple of the most famous works here are Grant Wood's *American Gothic* and Seurat's pointillist masterpiece *A Sunday on La Grande Jatte —1884.*

Just some of the museum's other attractions are exhibits of photography, furnishings, prints and drawings, ceramics, and Asian art, including a room of Japanese screens. Another popular attraction is the original Trading Room of the old Chicago Stock Exchange, salvaged when the Adler and Sullivan Stock Exchange building was demolished in 1972. Also be sure to see Marc Chagall's wonderful stained-glass windows.

### Sears Tower

233 S. Wacker Dr. (enter on Jackson). ☎ **312/875-9696.** Admission $6.50 adults, $4.75 seniors, $3.25 children ages 5–17, free for children under 5, $18.50 family (two adults and up to three children). Skydeck daily Mar–Sept 9am–11pm; Oct–Feb 9am–10pm. Bus: 7, 126, 151, or 156. Subway/El: Take the Ravenswood or Evanston line to Quincy.

# Chicago Attractions

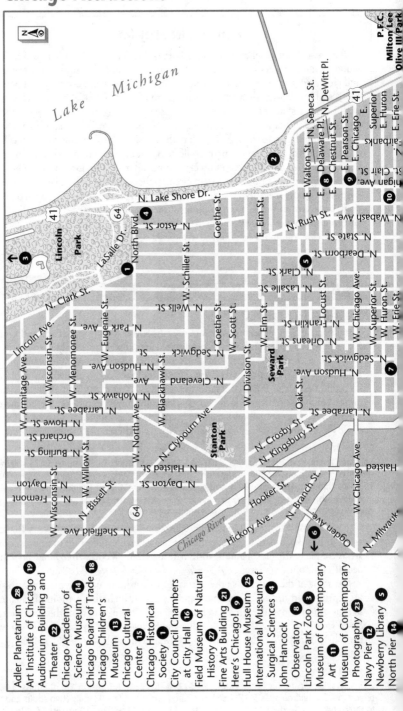

Lake Michigan

Lincoln Park

N. Lake Shore Dr.

Chicago River

Adler Planetarium 28
Art Institute of Chicago 19
Auditorium Building and
Theater 22
Chicago Academy of
Science Museum 14
Chicago Board of Trade 18
Chicago Children's
Museum 13
Chicago Cultural
Center 15
Chicago Historical
Society 1
City Council Chambers
at City Hall 16
Field Museum of Natural
History 27
Fine Arts Building 21
Here's Chicago! 9
Hull House Museum 25
International Museum of
Surgical Sciences 4
John Hancock
Observatory 8
Lincoln Park Zoo 3
Museum of Contemporary
Art 11
Museum of Contemporary
Photography 23
Navy Pier 12
Newberry Library 5
North Pier 14

Peace Museum **1**
Petrillo Music Shell **20**
Polish Museum of America **6**
Sears Tower **17**
Shedd Aquarium **26**
Spertus Museum of Judaica **24**
Terra Museum of American Art **10**

The view from the world's second tallest skyscraper is everything you'd expect it to be, a momentary suspension between earth and sky. From the Skydeck 100 floors up, the city is spread before you, both intimate and colossal. (The twin towers that surpassed the Sears Tower in height, in case you were wondering, are in Kuala Lumpur.)

## ○ Chicago Board of Trade

141 W. Jackson. ☎ **312/435-3590.** Free admission. Visitor center, Mon–Fri 9am–1:15pm. For groups of 10 or more, call for reservations. Bus: 1, 7, 60, 126, 151, or 156. Subway/El: Take the Ravenswood or Evanston line to Quincy or Van Buren.

The best live, improvisational acting in the city isn't necessarily at the theater. The Trading Pit at the Chicago Board of Trade, a massive citadel that stands at the foot of LaSalle Street, and the City Council chambers at City Hall (see below) can—on a given day—provide the best entertainment in town.

Watched over by a statue of Ceres, goddess of grain, the men and women inside frantically deal in commodities and financial futures and options. From a vantage point in the fifth-floor visitor center, you can watch the traders make their deals (*watch* is the operative word—try to figure out their hand signals), peaking in a shouting frenzy at the closing hour, after which these individual gamblers in pinstripes will count up their chips and learn if they've come out winners or losers for the day.

### City Council Chambers at City Hall

Washington, LaSalle, Randolph, and Clark Streets. ☎ **312/744-4000.** Free admission. Open when in session. Bus: 20, 56, 131, 156, or 157. Subway/El: Take the Lake Street line to Clark or the O'Hare/Congress/Douglas line to Washington.

Not far from the Board of Trade, power of a slightly different sort is being brokered during the public meetings of the equally volatile Chicago City Council, which meets in the square block that is City Hall. Although politics aren't nearly as colorful under Mayor Richard M. Daley as they were under his dad, when the right issue is being debated, factions can still get down and dirty, and the political posturing can make for the best kind of theatrics. Call ahead to find out when the council is in session (☎ 312/744-3081).

# IN SOUTHERN GRANT PARK

At Balbo Street and South Michigan Avenue, you can head east across Grant Park, trekking along the lakeshore route to the Field Museum, the aquarium, and the planetarium. Or you can make your approach by the wooden pedestrian bridge at Michigan Avenue and 12th Street that crosses the tracks in the general vicinity of the Field Museum (the other establishments lie just beyond). The CTA no. 146 bus will take you to all three of these attractions. Call 312/836-7000 for stop locations and schedule.

## ○ Field Museum of Natural History

Roosevelt Road and Lake Shore Drive. ☎ **312/922-9410.** Admission $5 adults; $3 children ages 3–17, students with ID, and seniors; free for children 2 and under, members, teachers, and armed forces personnel in uniform. Maximum family charge $16. Admission free on Wed. Daily 9am–5pm. Closed Thanksgiving, Christmas, and New Year's Day. Bus: 146.

For those who find the foundations of science—anthropology, botany, zoology, and geology—more intriguing than technology, the Field Museum of Natural History will be more compelling than the Museum of Science and Industry. Indeed, the Field Museum—endowed by the formidable Chicago prince of dry goods, Marshall Field I—was initially mounted in the old Palace of Fine Arts following the World Columbian Exposition of 1893, the very same complex in Hyde Park that now houses the Museum of Science and Industry. The current home of the Field

# South Michigan Ave./Grant Park

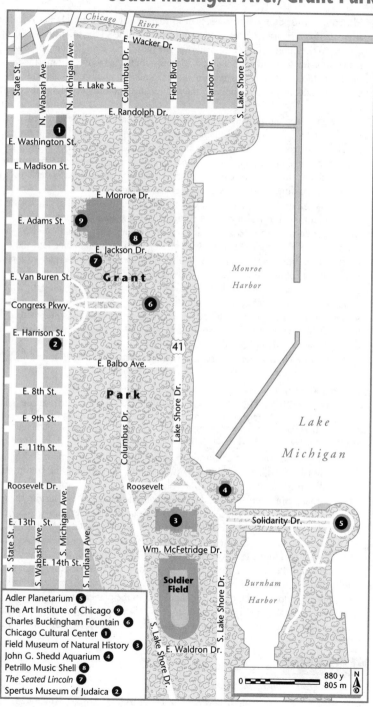

Chicago River

E. Wacker Dr.

State St.

N. Wabash Ave.

N. Michigan Ave.

E. Lake St.

Columbus Dr.

Field Blvd.

Harbor Dr.

S. Lake Shore Dr.

E. Randolph Dr.

**1**

E. Washington St.

E. Madison St.

E. Monroe Dr.

E. Adams St.  **9**

**8**

E. Jackson Dr.

**7**

Monroe
Harbor

**Grant**

E. Van Buren St.

Congress Pkwy.

**6**

E. Harrison St.

**2**

41

E. Balbo Ave.

**Park**

E. 8th St.

E. 9th St.

Lake
Michigan

E. 11th St.

Roosevelt Dr.

Roosevelt

**4**

Columbus Dr.

Lake Shore Dr.

Solidarity Dr.

**5**

E. 13th St.

S. State St.

S. Wabash Ave.

S. Michigan Ave.

S. Indiana Ave.

**3**

E. 14th St.

Wm. McFetridge Dr.

**Soldier
Field**

S. Lake Shore Dr.

Burnham
Harbor

Adler Planetarium **5**
The Art Institute of Chicago **9**
Charles Buckingham Fountain **6**
Chicago Cultural Center **1**
Field Museum of Natural History **3**
John G. Shedd Aquarium **4**
Petrillo Music Shell **8**
*The Seated Lincoln* **7**
Spertus Museum of Judaica **2**

E. Waldron Dr.

0        880 y
         805 m

N

1-0443

125

Museum, a tour de force of classicism in marble (designed by Daniel Burnham after the Erechtheum in Athens, but completed by others long after his death), was opened to the public in 1921. Spread over the museum's acres of floor space are the scores of permanent and temporary exhibitions—some interactive, but most requiring the old-fashioned skills of observation and imagination, notably those grand presentations in taxidermy and sculpture of the flora, fauna, and early peoples of the natural world.

One anthropological coup at the Field is a permanent exhibit entitled "Inside Ancient Egypt." In 1908 researchers in Saqqara, Egypt, excavated two of the original chambers from the tomb of Unis-ankh, son of the Fifth Dynasty ruler Pharaoh Unis, and transported them to the museum in Chicago. This *mastaba* (tomb) of Unis-ankh now forms the core of a spellbinding exhibit that realistically depicts scenes from Egyptian funeral, religious, and other social practices.

Visitors can explore aspects of the day-to-day world of ancient Egypt, viewing 23 actual mummies and realistic burial scenes, a living marsh environment and canal works, the ancient royal barge, a religious shrine, and a reproduction of a typical marketplace of the period. Many of the exhibits allow hands-on interaction, and there are special activities for kids, such as making parchment from living papyrus plants.

If Ancient Egypt doesn't get your kids going, try going back millions of years in the Field's dinosaur exhibit. Other permanent exhibits include "Traveling the Pacific" (employing hundreds of artifacts from the museum's oceanic collection to re-create scenes of island life in the South Pacific), dazzling gemstones, a Pawnee earth lodge for storytelling on Native American life and lore, and those appealing dioramas that depict the ways and customs of ancient peoples.

A welcome change here—instead of the traditional cafeteria found in most museums, there's a McDonald's.

### Adler Planetarium

1300 S. Lake Shore Dr. ☎ **312/322-0304,** or 312/922-STAR for a recorded message. Admission $3 adults, $2 children (ages 4–17). One admission fee for sky shows and exhibits. Free on Tues. Mon–Thurs 9am–5pm, Fri 9am–9pm, Sat–Sun 9am–6pm. Sky shows at numerous times throughout the day—call 922-STAR for current times. Bus: 146.

A causeway across one end of Burnham Park Harbor links the mainland here to Northerly Island, which is occupied by two tenants, Miegs Field, the landing strip for small, private aircraft, and the Adler Planetarium. The zodiacal 12-sided structure sits on a promontory at the end of ornamental Solidarity Drive, just up the road from the aquarium. The planetarium's founder, Sears, Roebuck executive Max Adler, imported a Zeiss projector, invented in Germany in 1923, to Chicago in 1930. He wanted to bring the sky closer to people, hoping the novelty of the artificial sky would redirect attention to the real experience of watching a night sky.

Today the Adler Planetarium offers a range of programs for both children and adults. Multimedia sky shows re-create the nighttime skies and current topics in space exploration. A closed-circuit monitor connected to the planetarium's Doane Observatory telescope allows visitors to view dramatic close-ups of the moon, the planets, and distant galaxies (only on Friday after the 8pm sky show). In addition, the Adler

---

### ❓ Did You Know?

- The two blue bars on the Chicago flag represent the two branches of the Chicago River.
- Chicago has more large-scale, free outdoor concerts than any other city in the world.
- Historic Wrigley Field and the Cubs themselves are owned by the Tribune Company, also publisher of the city's largest-circulation newspaper.
- The Chicago Board of Trade is the world's largest futures and options exchange.
- Second City, the famous improvisational theater, launched the careers of Alan Alda, Dan Aykroyd, John Belushi, Gilda Radner, and Joan Rivers.
- The Shedd Aquarium is the world's largest indoor marine mammal pavilion.
- Chicago has 29 miles of frontage along Lake Michigan.
- The yearly outdoor bash, Taste of Chicago, is the largest food and entertainment festival in the world.

---

has exhibits on navigation, space exploration, and "The Universe in Your Hands," incorporating the planetarium's History of Astronomy Collection.

To find out what to look for in this month's sky, call the Nightwatch 24-Hour Hot Line (☎ 922-STAR), or check in on the Internet at http://astro.vchicago.edv/adler.

### ❍ Shedd Aquarium

1200 S. Lake Shore Dr. ☎ **312/939-2438.** Admission to both Aquarium and Oceanarium, $8 adults, $6 children 3–11 and seniors, free for children under 3. Admission to Oceanarium on Thurs, $4 adults, $3 children 3–11 and seniors. Admission to original Aquarium galleries only, $4 adults, $3 children 3–11 and seniors; free to everyone on Thurs. Aquarium tickets available on a limited, first-come, first-served basis, so it's recommended you purchase tickets in advance at any Ticketmaster outlet. Daily 9am–6pm; last entry into Oceanarium 5:15pm. Bus: 146.

The third point of this museum triangle is the Shedd Aquarium, a marble octagon, whose Doric exterior is decorated with a motif of marine symbols, and whose interior galleries are populated by thousands of denizens of river, lake, and sea. The aquarium's most popular entertainment is the twice-daily (at 11am and 2pm; additional show at 3pm on Saturday and Sunday) feeding of the sharks and other creatures of the reefs, from the hands of divers who swim among them in a 90,000-gallon tank. It's also fun to watch the frolicking of the river otters in their naturalistic habitat, landscaped with plant life native to the Illinois prairie. But the true revelation comes from studying the collection of sea anemones, those odd flowerlike animals of the deep.

Already the world's largest indoor aquarium, the Shedd doubled its size a few years ago with the opening of the Oceanarium, a marine mammal pavilion that re-creates a Pacific Northwest coastal environment. As you follow a winding nature trail, you encounter whales, dolphins, sea otters, and harbor seals. A colony of penguins in a separate exhibit area inhabits a naturalistic environment meant to resemble the Mariana Islands in the southern sea off Argentina. You can observe all these sea mammals at play through large underwater viewing windows. On a fixed performance schedule in a large pool surrounded by an amphitheater, the whales and dolphins are put through their paces of leaps and dives by a crew of friendly trainers. However, after the death of the first set of Belugas, their presence in captivity became somewhat controversial, and on weekends there is often a line of protest picketers. If you want a good sit-down meal in a restaurant with a spectacular view overlooking Lake Michigan, check out Soundings, right there inside the aquarium.

# NORTH OF THE LOOP

### Terra Museum of American Art

666 N. Michigan Ave. ☎ **312/664-3939.** Admission $4 adults, $2 seniors, free for children under 14 and students with ID. Tues noon–8pm, Wed–Sat 10am–5pm, Sun noon–5pm. Bus: 3, 11, 125, 145, 146, 147, or 151. Subway/El: Take the Howard line to Grand or Chicago.

Housing the formerly private collection of industrialist Daniel J. Terra, the Terra Museum of American Art has assembled some 400 pieces of 18th-, 19th-, and 20th-century American art.

### John Hancock Observatory

94th floor of the John Hancock Center, 875 N. Michigan (enter on Delaware). ☎ **312/751-3681.** Admission $4.75 adults, $3.25 students, $4 seniors, free for children under 5 and military personnel in uniform or with active duty cards. Daily 9am–midnight. Subway/El: Take the Howard line to Chicago Avenue. Bus: 125, 145, 146, 147, or 151.

The John Hancock Observatory delivers an excellent panorama of the city and an intimate view over nearby Lake Michigan and the various shoreline residential areas. On a clear day you can see portions of the three states surrounding this corner of Illinois (Michigan, Indiana, and Wisconsin), for a radius of 80 miles. The view up the North Side is particularly dramatic, stretching from the nearby Oak and North Street beaches, along the green strip of Lincoln Park, to the line of highrises that you can trace up the shoreline until they suddenly halt just below the boundary of the northern suburbs. The lake itself seems like a vast sea without any boundaries at all. The view is also spectacular at night.

Three high-speed elevators carry passengers to the observatory in 40 seconds, and the entrance and observatory are handicapped accessible. If you prefer, you could stop in at the 95th, one floor up, and take in your views with a drink.

### Chicago Historical Society

1601 N. Clark St. (at North Avenue). ☎ **312/642-4600.** Admission $3 adults, $2 seniors and students, $1 children ages 6–17. Free admission on Mon. Mon–Sat 9:30am–4:30pm, Sun noon–5pm. Bus: 11, 22, 36, 72, 151, or 156.

At the southwestern tip of Lincoln Park stands one of Chicago's most interesting exhibition halls. Despite its name, this place is not only for scholarly types. In the society's new permanent second-floor exhibition, called "We the People," among the objects on display are an original copy of the Ephrata Cloister Hymnal, a memento of a little-known early communal religious group in colonial Pennsylvania, and the Bowles' New Pocket Map (1784), which depicts Mount Desert Island and Penobscot Bay along the coast of Maine in reverse order. Various other articles and documents reveal how the nation's mercantile interests prolonged the practice of importing slaves from Africa. Also rare—as both a document and the tale it refers to—is the copy of Herman Mann's 1866 biography of Deborah Sampson, the "female soldier in the war of Revolution." I had a hard time leaving because each time I started to go, my eye would catch something else, such as the touching painting of Washington's farewell to his staff at New York's Fraunces Tavern, which shows many of the officers openly and unashamedly weeping as they take leave of their commander-in-chief.

Perhaps the most exciting, emotionally charged exhibit on the Civil War you will ever see, "A House Divided" opened at the Historical Society in February 1990 and is scheduled to close in the year 2000. The exhibition is divided into eight sections and draws on the society's antebellum Lincoln and Civil War holdings. Through a display of more than 600 artifacts, it examines the major political and social forces of mid-19th-century America, with a strong emphasis on Abraham Lincoln. Some of the major artifacts include the "Railsplitter" painting of Lincoln, the Emancipation Proclamation table, the Appomattox table, Lincoln's deathbed, John Brown's Bible, and a diorama of the Lincoln–Douglas debates.

Adding to the museum's attractiveness is the recently opened restaurant, the Big Shoulders Café, on the ground floor past the gift shop, entered through a terracotta arch. Its facade is adorned with animals and historical figures in relief, and was removed intact from the old Stockyard Bank and reassembled here. The food is light, delicious, and imaginative.

## ✪ Lincoln Park Zoo

2200 N. Cannon Dr. ☎ **773/935-6700.** Free admission. Daily 8am–5:15pm. Zoo buildings 9am–5pm. Bus: 151 or 156.

The Lincoln Park Zoo is spread over 35 acres, is open 365 days a year, and is always free. The zoo is humanely and imaginatively designed, with the animals occupying separate habitats appropriate to their species. The seal tank, for example, has a lower passage with a wall of glass, so you can see the sleek arctic mammals swimming underwater as well as sunning and cavorting on their little rock island. The families of great apes in the ape house often study the humans as intently as we do them.

The best time to visit the zoo, of course, is in good weather, for that is when the park itself is at its most animated, overflowing with people strolling through the zoo as part of their daily constitutional. The zoo has a population of more than 1,200 animals, birds, and reptiles. Just the names of the large mammals are enough to excite interest: gorillas, rhinos, wolves, bears, camels, bison, gazelles, big cats, zebras, orangutans, elephants, and hippos. For the adjoining children's zoo, see "Especially for Kids" later in this chapter.

# HYDE PARK

Birthplace of atomic fission, home to the University of Chicago and to the Midwest's most popular tourist attraction, the Museum of Science and Industry, Hyde Park is also one of Chicago's most successfully integrated middle-class neighborhoods. You could easily set aside one full day to explore this southeast corner of Chicago.

**HISTORY**   When Hyde Park was settled in 1850, it became Chicago's first suburb. A hundred years later, in the 1950s, Hyde Park added another first to its impressive resume, one that the current neighborhood is not particularly proud of—it was selected as the prototype for the nation's first urban-renewal plan. At the time, a certain amount of old commercial and housing stock was demolished rather than rehabilitated—just those kinds of buildings that would be much prized today—and replaced by projects and small shopping malls that actually make some corners of Hyde Park look more suburban, in the modern sense, than they really are.

What Hyde Park does have to be proud of is that, in racially balkanized Chicago, this neighborhood has found an alternative vision. As Southern blacks began to migrate to Chicago's South Side during World War I, many whites fled. But most whites here, especially those who wanted to stay near the university, chose integration as the only realistic strategy to preserve their neighborhood. The 1980 census numbered 17,000 whites and 11,000 blacks in the neighborhood's population, a racial balance that nevertheless once earned Hyde Parkers a witty barb from the sharp tongues of Mike Nichols and Elaine May: "Hyde Parkers: white and black, arm in arm, united against the poor."

Hyde Park is decidedly middle class, with pockets of true affluence in Kenwood that reflect the days when the well-to-do moved here in the beginning of the century to escape the decline of Prairie Avenue. Among those old Chicago families who once occupied the estates in Kenwood were meat packer Gustavus Swift; lumber merchant Martin Ryerson; Sears, Roebuck executive Julius Rosenwald (who endowed the Museum of Science and Industry); John Shedd (the president of Marshall Field's who gave the city the aquarium that bears his name); and William Goodman (who sponsored the Art Institute and the theater to which his name is affixed). Among Hyde Park–Kenwood's well-known black residents in recent years were the late Elijah Muhammad and Muhammad Ali, along with numerous other Nation of Islam families who continue to worship in a mosque, formerly a Greek Orthodox cathedral, that is one of the neighborhood's architectural landmarks. The late Mayor Harold Washington also lived here. Surrounding this unusual enclave, however, are many marginal blocks where poverty and slum housing abound. For all its nobility, Hyde Park's achievement in integration merely emphasizes that even more unwieldy than racial differences are socioeconomic ones.

Through its fight for self-preservation, Hyde Park has gained a reputation as an activist community. A certain vitality springs from acts of coping with the world as you find it, and it is this element that distinguishes Hyde Park from other middle-class neighborhoods in Chicago. Hyde Park, in a word, is cosmopolitan.

The University of Chicago is widely hailed as one of the more intellectually exciting institutions of higher learning in the country, and has been home to some 58 Nobel laureates. The year the university opened its doors, 1892, was a big one for Hyde Park, but 1893 was even bigger. In that year, Chicago, chosen over other cities in a competitive international field, hosted the World Columbian Exposition, commemorating the 400th anniversary of Columbus's discovery of America.

To create a fairground, the landscape architect Frederick Law Olmsted was enlisted to fill in the marshlands along Hyde Park's lakefront and link what was to become Jackson Park to existing Washington Park on the neighborhood's western boundary with a narrow concourse called the Midway Plaisance. On the resulting 650 acres—at a cost of $30 million—12 exhibit palaces, 57 buildings devoted to U.S. states and foreign governments, and dozens of smaller structures were constructed under the supervision of architect Daniel Burnham. Most of the building followed Burnham's preference for the Classical Revival style and exterior surfaces finished in white stucco. With the innovation of outdoor electric lighting, the sparkling result was the "White City" that attracted 27 million visitors in a single season, running from May 1 to October 31, 1893. The exposition sponsors, in that brief time, had remarkably recovered their investment, but within a few short years of its closing, most of the fair's buildings were destroyed by vandalism and fire. Only the Palace of Fine Arts, occupying the eastern tip of the midway, survives to this day, and now houses the Museum of Science and Industry.

**GETTING THERE**    From the Loop, the ride to Hyde Park on the no. 6 Jeffrey Express bus takes about 30 minutes. The bus originates on Wacker Drive, travels south along State Street, and ultimately follows Lake Shore Drive to Hyde Park. Weekdays the bus runs from around 5am to 10:30pm, and on weekends and holidays from around 7am to 8pm. The southbound bus adds a surcharge of 30¢ to the normal fare of $1.50. The no. 1 local bus originates at Union Station on Adams and Canal Streets.

The Metra/Elevated train follows the old Illinois Central line—still referred to as the IC—arriving in Hyde Park in about 15 minutes from downtown. Trains run every hour Monday through Saturday from 5:15am to 12:50am, and at two-hour intervals on Sunday and holidays from 12:50am to 10:30pm. IC stations in the loop are at Michigan and Randolph and at Van Buren Street, where printed schedules are available. The fare is approximately $1.90 each way.

For CTA bus and Metra train information, call 312/836-7000.

For taxis, dial TAXI-CAB (☎ 312/829-4222) for Yellow or Checker cabs. The one-way fare from downtown is around $12.

**A SUGGESTED ITINERARY**   A *long* one-day itinerary for Hyde Park should include the following: a selected tour of the U of C campus, a visit to several museums and cultural institutions, a tour of the Kenwood mansions (preferably by car), a walk through the area's commercial center, and a stroll around the lakeshore Promontory Point. (See Chapter 8 for a walking tour of the neighborhood.)

## ATTRACTIONS

### ✪ Museum of Science and Industry

57th Street and Lake Shore Drive. ☎ **773/684-1414** or TDD 684-DEAF. Admission to museum only, $6 adults, $5 seniors, $2.50 children ages 5–12, free for children under 5. Free on Thurs. Museum and Omnimax Theater, $10 adults, $8 seniors, $5.50 children, $3 children under 5 (free if seated on an adult's lap). Omnimax Theater only, Thurs and evening shows $6 adults, $5 seniors, $4 children, children under 5 free if on adult lap. Summer daily 9:30am–5:30pm; fall–spring Mon–Fri 9:30am–4pm, Sat–Sun and holidays 9:30am–5:30pm. Bus: 151 or 156.

Hyde Park is probably already on your must-do itinerary of Chicago, in the form of a visit to this world-famous museum, the granddaddy of every interactive museum.

In statistical terms alone, the museum's collection is awesome: some 2,000 exhibits spread over 14 acres in 75 exhibition halls. The current headline attraction at the museum is the Henry Crown Space Center, where the story of space exploration, still in its infancy, is documented in copious detail, highlighted by a simulated space shuttle experience through sight and sound at the center's Omnimax Theater. Old hat now, but a favorite of mine since early childhood, is the descent into a full-scale replica of a southern Illinois coal mine. In 1995, the museum unveiled "AIDS: The War Within," the first permanent exhibit on the immune system and HIV, the virus that causes AIDS.

But whatever your particular technofetish—from submarines to space capsules, from special effects to the mysteries of the human organism—you will find the object of your curiosity somewhere in this amazing museum. There's even a 133-foot United Airlines 727 attached to the balcony. The Omnimax Theater offers Friday and Saturday evening showings at 7 and 8pm.

### DuSable Museum of African-American History

740 E. 56th Place. ☎ **773/947-0600.** Admission $3 adults, $1 children ages 6–13, $2 students and seniors. Free on Thurs. Mon–Wed and Fri–Sun 10am–5pm, Thurs 10am–6pm. Bus: 4. Subway/El: Take the Howard line to Jackson Park.

The DuSable Museum is a repository of the history, art, and artifacts pertaining to the African-American experience and culture. The exhibits the museum does have are very worthwhile, but unfortunately, the bulk of the collection dates only from the WPA period in the late '30s and the black arts movement of the '60s, with only sketchy exhibits tracing the earlier stages of the African-American experience in this country.

The museum, located on the eastern edge of Washington Park, also has a gift shop, a research library, and an extensive program of community-related events, including an annual carnival celebration.

# The Museum of Science & Industry

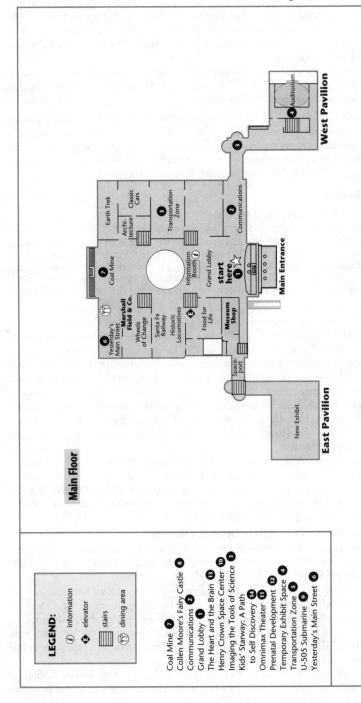

**Main Floor**

West Pavilion
Auditorium 4

3

Earth Trek
Classic Cars
Archi-tecture
Transportation Zone 5
Communications 2

Coal Mine 7

Information Booth (i)
Grand Lobby
**start here** 1
Main Entrance

Marshall Field & Co.
Wheels of Change
Santa Fe Railway
Historic Locomotives
Food for Life
**Museum Shop**

Yesterday's Main Street 6

Space-port

New Exhibit

East Pavilion

**LEGEND:**
(i) information
⬧ elevator
▥ stairs
⑰ dining area

Coal Mine 7
Collen Moore's Fairy Castle 8
Communications 2
Grand Lobby 1
The Heart and the Brain 13
Henry Crown Space Center 10
Imaging the Tools of Science 3
Kids' Starway: A Path to Self Discovery 14
Omnimax Theater 11
Prenatal Development 12
Temporary Exhibit Space 4
Transportation Zone 5
U-505 Submarine 9
Yesterday's Main Street 6

132

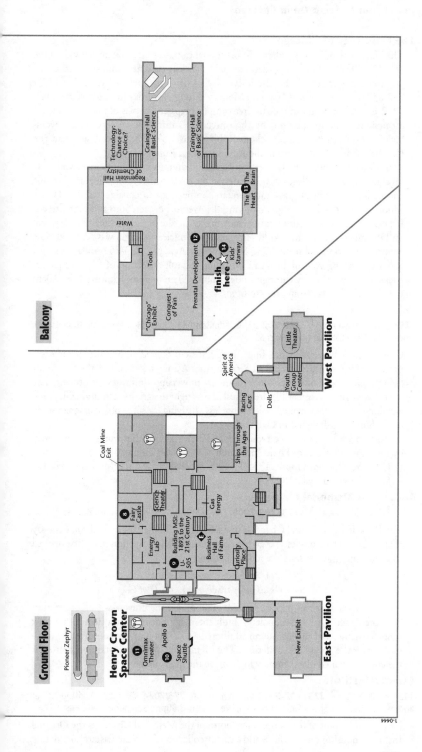

**Ground Floor**

Pioneer Zephyr

**Henry Crown Space Center**

11 Omnimax Theater
10 Apollo 8
Space Shuttle

Energy Lab

Coal Mine Exit

8 Fairy Castle

Science Theater

9 Building MSI: 1893 to the 21st Century
U-505

Business Hall of Fame

Gas Energy

Curiosity Place

Ships Through the Ages

Racing Cars

Spirit of America

Dolls

**West Pavilion**

Little Theater

Youth Group Center

**East Pavilion**

New Exhibit

**Balcony**

"Chicago" Exhibit

Conquest of Pain

Tools

Water

Technology: Chance or Choice?

Regenstein Hall of Chemistry

Grainger Hall of Basic Science

Grainger Hall of Basic Science

12 Prenatal Development

finish here ★

14 Kids' Starway

13 The Heart / The Brain

1-0444

133

## The University of Chicago

The University of Chicago offers visitors several campus tours, and an Activities Line (☎ 773/702-9559 for a recorded message) that lists current campus events. Campus tours are organized by the university's Office of Special Events (☎ 773/702-8374). Tours begin at 10am on Monday through Saturday from Ida Noyes Hall, 1212 E. 59th St. You can pick up free campus maps and copies of the "Chronicle," a calendar of events put out by the university's information service, at several locations on campus, among them Robie House, 5757 S. Woodlawn, and the Graduate Admissions Office in the Administration Building.

Just walking around the University of Chicago campus is bound to make you wistful about your own college days. Wander on the stone paths among the quads, or just choose a nice patch of grass and vegetate. Some stops to consider are the Henry Moore statue, *Nuclear Energy*, on South Ellis Avenue between 56th and 57th Streets. It's next to the Regenstein Library, which marks the site of the old Stagg Field, where on December 2, 1942, the world's first sustained nuclear reaction was achieved. The Seminary Co-op Bookstore, 5757 S. University Ave. (☎ 773/752-4381), has just about everything you might want, including the full collection of Penguin paperbacks. It's open Monday through Friday from 8:30am to 9pm, Saturday from 10am to 6pm, and Sunday from noon to 6pm.

### Robie House

5757 S. Woodlawn Ave. ☎ **773/702-2150.** Admission $3 adults, $1 seniors and students with student ID. Daily tours at noon. Bus: 55.

One of Frank Lloyd Wright's finest works, it's considered among the five masterpieces of 20th-century American architecture. A tour takes you to the first-floor living/dining room only (the other rooms are university administrative offices). The open layout and craftsmanship are typical of a Wright design. Its institutional-looking exterior, though, may make Robie House less satisfying for some observers than some of the homes he designed in Oak Park.

*Note:* In addition to Robie House, several of Wright's earlier works, still privately owned, dot the streets of Hyde Park, such as the Heller House, 5132 S. Woodlawn (1897); the Blossom House, 1332 E. 49th St. (1882); and the McArthur House, 4852 S. Kenwood Ave. (1892).

### Rockefeller Memorial Chapel

5850 S. Woodlawn Ave. ☎ **773/702-7000.** Free admission. Daily 9am–4pm. Bus: 55.

The Rockefeller Memorial Chapel is just across from Robie House. Did someone say chapel? This is false modesty, even for a Rockefeller. When the university first opened its doors, the students sang the following ditty:

> *John D. Rockefeller, wonderful man is he*
> *Gives all his spare change to the U of C.*

John D. was a generous patron, indeed. He founded the university (in cooperation with the American Baptist Society), built the magnificent minicathedral that now bears his name, and shelled out an additional $35 million in donations to the institution over the course of his lifetime. The Memorial Chapel's outstanding feature is the circular stained-glass window high above the main altar.

### Oriental Institute

1155 E. 58th St. ☎ **773/702-9521** for information, 773/702-9507 for special tours. Free admission. Tues and Thurs–Sat 10am–4pm, Wed 10am–8:30pm, Sun noon–4pm. Bus: 55.

Near the midpoint of the campus, just north of the Memorial Chapel, is the Oriental Institute, housing one of the world's major collections of Near Eastern art, dating from 9000 B.C. to the 10th century A.D. These ancient objects are extraordinarily beautiful to the eye, subtle in form, texture, and hue. As part of its educational commitment, the Oriental Institute occasionally offers one-day seminars for adults and Sunday family programs (call for information).

The gift shop at the Oriental Institute, called the Suq, is renowned in its own right as a shopper's treasure trove. Deck yourself with the jewelry of the Fertile Crescent . . . and walk like an Egyptian.

### David and Alfred Smart Museum of Art

5550 S. Greenwood Ave. (at E. 56th St.). ☎ **773/702-0200.** Free admission; donations welcome. Tues–Fri 10am–4pm, Sat–Sun noon–6pm. Closed holidays. Bus: 55.

The David and Alfred Smart Museum of Art is named for two of the founders of *Esquire* magazine, whose family foundation created the University of Chicago's fine arts museum. The Smart Museum houses a permanent collection of more than 7,000 works ranging from classical antiquity to the contemporary. In keeping with its university setting, the Smart also hosts an intriguing variety of temporary exhibitions with such names as "Selected Work from the Prinzhorn Collection of the Art of the Mentally Ill" and "The Earthly Chimera and the Femme Fatale: Fear of Woman in Late 19th Century Art."

## OUTDOOR ATTRACTIONS

Hyde Park is not only a haven for book lovers and culture aficionados—the community also has its open-air attractions. One unexpected corner of tranquility is the Bergen Garden, a one-acre formal garden three stories high built on the roof of the parking garage at the Regents Park apartment buildings, 5020–5050 S. Lake Shore Dr. (☎ 773/288-5050). Open to the public, the garden features lagoons (with 8 inches of water, but painted black to give the appearance of depth), live ducks, several fountains, a maze of pathways among scores of trees and 30,000 plants, and a small waterfall—a tour de force of urban landscape gardening that transformed a bleak concrete eyesore into a sanctuary.

A number of additional worthy outdoor environments are located near Lake Michigan, including Lake Shore Drive itself, where many stately apartment houses follow the contour of the shoreline. A very suitable locale for a quiet stroll during the day is Promontory Point, at 55th Street and Lake Michigan, a bulb of land that juts into the lake and offers a good view of Chicago to the north, and the seasonally active 57th Street beach to the south.

Farther south, just below the Museum of Science and Industry, is Wooded Island in Jackson Park, the site of the Japanese Pavilion during the Columbian Exposition, and today a lovely garden of meandering paths. The Perennial Garden in Jackson Park is at 59th Street and Stony Island Avenue, where more than 180 varieties of flowering plants display a palette of colors that changes with the seasons.

# 2 More Attractions

## ✪ A LOOP SCULPTURE TOUR

With the help of a very comprehensive pamphlet, "The Loop Sculpture Guide," you can guide yourself through Grant Park and much of the Loop to view some 65 examples of Chicago's monumental public art. The best-known of these works are by 20th-century artists, including Picasso, Chagall, Miró, Calder, Moore, and Oldenburg. The guide also highlights the more traditional park monuments of such 19th-century sculptors as Augustus Saint-Gaudens and Lorado Taft. It provides detailed descriptions of 30 major works, including photographs, and identifies them

---

**Impressions**

---

*SATAN (impatiently) to NEW-COMER: The trouble with you Chicago people is, that you think you are the best people down here; whereas you are merely the most numerous.*

—Mark Twain, "Pudd'nhead Wilson's New Calendar,"
in *More Tramps Abroad,* 1897

---

on a foldout map of the Loop. "The Loop Sculpture Guide" is distributed free at the Visitor Information Center in the Chicago Cultural Center, 78 E. Washington, conveniently located near the tour itself.

## ALONG SOUTH MICHIGAN AVENUE

Fashion and glamor may have moved north to the Magnificent Mile, but Chicago's grandest stretch of boulevard is still south of the river. From a little north of the Michigan Avenue Bridge all the way down to the Field Museum, South Michigan Avenue runs parallel to Grant Park on one side and the Loop on the other. A stroll along this boulevard in any season offers both visual and cultural treats. The attractions are listed from north to south.

### Chicago Cultural Center

78 E. Washington St. ☎ **312/744-6630,** or FINE-ART for weekly events. Free admission. Mon–Thurs 10am–7pm, Fri 10am–6pm, Sat 10am–5pm, Sun noon–5pm. Closed holidays. Bus: 3, 4, 20, 56, 60, 127, 131, 145, 146, 147, 151, or 157. Subway/El: Take the Ravenswood or Lake/Dan Ryan line to Randolph.

The Cultural Center bills itself as "an architectural showplace for the lively and visual arts." It offers various films, lectures, special events, and exhibitions; you may want to call to check if anything's scheduled that might appeal to you. The Cultural Center's building dates from 1897 (it's the former Chicago Public Library), a hodgepodge of Roman, Greek, and Italian Renaissance styles. The Chicago Office of Tourism is now located here, as is the Museum of Broadcast Communications (see listing under "More Museums" below).

The ground floor on the Randolph Street side of the Cultural Center houses a café, a good spot to hang out over a cup of gourmet coffee and baked goods.

### Fine Arts Building

410 S. Michigan Ave. ☎ **312/427-7602.** Free admission. Daily 8am–6pm. Bus: 3, 4, 60, 145, 147, or 151. Subway/El: Take the Ravenswood or Lake/Dan Ryan line to Madison.

Built as a showroom for Studebaker carriages in 1885, the landmark Fine Arts Building was converted at the turn of the century into a concert hall. Its upper stories sheltered a number of well-known publications *(Saturday Evening Post, Dial)* and provided offices for such luminaries as Frank Lloyd Wright, sculptor Lorado Taft, and L. Frank Baum, author of *The Wizard of Oz.* Harriet Monroe published her magazine, *Poetry,* here and first introduced American readers to Carl Sandburg, T. S. Eliot, and Ezra Pound. Movie buffs should take note that the two original ground-floor theaters have been converted into an art cinema with four separate screening rooms. Located throughout the building are a number of interesting musical instrument shops. Take at least a quick walk through the marble-and-wood lobby, which suggests something monastic and cloisterlike, or visit the top floor (10th) to see the spectacular murals.

# The Loop Sculpture Tour

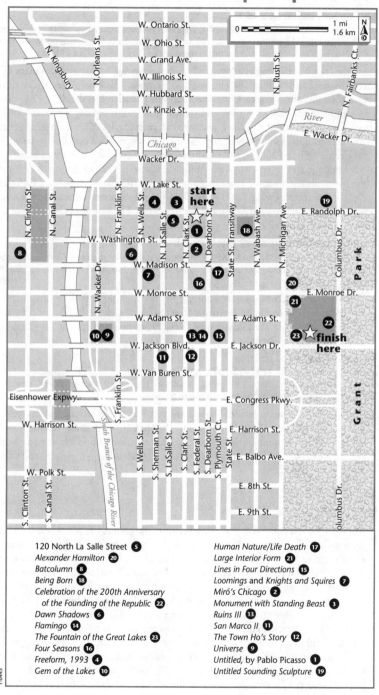

1-0445

137

### Auditorium Building and Theater

50 E. Congress Pkwy. ☎ **312/922-4046.** For ticket reservations or box office information, call 312/902-1500. Admission $4 adults, $3 seniors and students. Tours offered Mon–Thurs. Call 312/431-2354 for details and for group reservations. Bus: 145, 147, or 151.

On the corner of Congress Parkway and Michigan Avenue is a national landmark that was designed and built in 1889 by Louis Sullivan and Dankmar Adler, the Auditorium Building and Theater. Considered Sullivan's masterpiece, the theater's interior is a glittering display of mirrors and stained glass and is equally renowned for its excellent acoustics and sightlines, making good seats of all 4,000 within its confines. The Auditorium Building, formerly also a hotel, was the first building to be wired for electric light in Chicago, and the theater was the first in the country to install air-conditioning. In the days when the Auditorium was the leading theater of Chicago, the hydraulically operated stage could be lowered from view, creating a ballroom capable of accommodating 8,000 guests. Today the Auditorium attracts major Broadway musicals, such as *Miss Saigon* and *Les Miserables*. The building offers tours of the front public areas, but backstage is off-limits.

### Museum of Contemporary Photography

600 S. Michigan Ave. ☎ **312/663-5554.** Free admission. Mon–Wed and Fri 10am–5pm, Thurs 10am–8pm, Sat noon–5pm. Shorter hours in summer. Bus: 6, 146, or 151. Subway/El: Take the Howard line to Harrison.

The Museum of Contemporary Photography occupies the first floor of Columbia College, near the corner of Harrison Street. The museum exhibits, collects, and promotes contemporary photography. Related lectures and special programs are scheduled during the year.

### Spertus Museum of Judaica

618 S. Michigan Ave. ☎ **312/922-9012.** Admission $4 adults; $2 seniors, students, and children; $9 maximum family rate. Free on Fri. Sun–Thurs 10am–5pm, Fri 10am–3pm. Bus: 145, 147, or 151. Subway/El: Take the Howard line to Jackson.

The Spertus Museum of Judaica houses intricately crafted and historic Jewish ceremonial objects, textiles, coins, paintings, and sculpture, tracing 5,000 years of Jewish heritage. The museum has the Artifact Center, a simulated Middle Eastern archaeological site in which children can use authentic tools to dig for pottery and other pieces of the past.

## ON THE WATER

### NORTH PIER

Among Chicago's popular year-round leisure playgrounds is North Pier, 435 E. Illinois St. (☎ 312/836-4300), a two-block-long complex fronting the Chicago River's Ogden Slip. Having outgrown its mercantile role (it was built as warehouses around 1910), North Pier has been converted into an all-purpose entertainment center. Now it houses nightspots, museums, restaurants, and nearly four dozen specialty shops, boutiques, and galleries (see Chapter 9 for a selected list). I find it all a bit touristy—along the lines of Underground Atlanta and similar "festival marketplaces."

North Pier shopping hours are Monday through Saturday from 11am to 9pm, and Sunday from noon to 8pm. Parking is available in lots adjacent to the complex for $4 for four hours with a validation ticket obtained with a minimum purchase. Six CTA buses go directly to North Pier: nos. 29, 56, 65, 66, 120, and 121. Seasonal boat-docking facilities are also available; for information, call 312/836-4252.

*Note:* The Chicago Academy of Sciences Museum (see "Lincoln Park" below) will be temporarily located at North Pier through the life of this book.

## ☻ Navy Pier

Built during World War I, Navy Pier has been a ballroom, a training center for Navy pilots during World War II, and a satellite campus of the University of Illinois. It has just undergone yet one more transformation, one that has returned it—at least in spirit—to its original intended purpose, a place for Chicagoans to come to relax and to be entertained. Developers have resurrected the ballroom, and they also have installed a winter garden, an ice rink, a concert stage, and a giant, 15-story Ferris wheel. The 50 acres of pier and lakefront property also is home to the Chicago Children's Museum, a carousel, and about as many shops and restaurants as you'd expect. Navy Pier, which is at 600 E. Grand Ave. (☎ 312/595-PIER), also will continue to host the huge annual art show that kept many Chicagoans from forgetting about the place entirely.

# NORTH OF THE LOOP

North of the Chicago River are a number of attractions you should not overlook, including several museums and buildings, the city's greatest park, a zoo, and one of the world's most impressive research libraries. Most of these sites are either on the Magnificent Mile (North Michigan Avenue) and its surrounding blocks or not too far from there, on the Near North Side.

## THE MAGNIFICENT MILE

James T. Farrell writes of Chicago's famous Bughouse Square on Walton Street, between Dearborn and Clark in *Studs Lonigan,* calling it an "outdoor forum of garrulous hobohemia." In the 1920s an oddball collection of orators used to harangue each other and the crowds of onlookers on anything from free love to a stateless society. Officially called Washington Square, it was one of Chicago's first parks. The main attractions here today are some fine old mansions, renovated townhouses, and the glorious Newberry Library, which, incidentally, sponsors a revival of the Bughouse Square debates on a designated weekend each September, an event in which the public is heartily encouraged to participate.

### Here's Chicago

In the Water Tower Pumping Station, 163 E. Pearson (at the corner of North Michigan Avenue). ☎ **312/467-7114.** Show tickets $5.75 adults; $4.50 seniors, students, the handicapped, and children under 12; $12 family (including two adults with three or more children). Daily 9:30am–6pm. Shows presented every 30 minutes until 4pm Mon–Thurs, until 5pm Sat–Sun. Bus: 125, 145, 146, 147, or 151. Subway/El: Take the Howard line to Chicago Avenue.

For a quick and painless orientation to the city, stop in at *Here's Chicago,* a 45-minute sound-and-sight show. Both the Pumping Station and the Water Tower across the street—which one wag likened to a sandcastle at the bottom of a goldfish bowl, and which in 1892 Oscar Wilde dubbed a "monstrosity"—were in the path of the Great Fire of 1871. The architect must have done something right, for these two limestone monuments were the only ones that withstood the blaze when all the other buildings disintegrated around them.

The show begins with a brief tour of the Pumping Station's machinery—which Wilde, anticipating the high-tech fashion craze by nearly a century, is said to have loved. Next, patrons are treated to a few minor exhibits, one on the Chicago Fire, another a tableau of life-size figures representing the denouement of the St. Valentine's Day massacre (the mannequin corpses of the gangsters are laid out in a neat line). The remainder—and the best part of the show—is visual. First comes a computerized slide show showing the varied scenes and human faces of Chicago, and finally a 70mm film entitled *City of Dreams,* which takes you on a simulated helicopter ride over the city, particularly exciting as the chopper tunnels through downtown by way of the river.

In the Pumping Station lobby you'll find a gift shop, a few fast-food stands, and of particular importance to visitors who are wandering through unknown streets, a Chicago Office of Tourism information desk, clean restrooms, and a bank of pay phones.

## Newberry Library

60 W. Walton. ☎ **312/943-9090.** Tues–Thurs 10am–6pm, Fri–Sat 9am–5pm. Free 45-minute tours Thurs at 3pm and Sat at 10:30am. Bus: 22, 36, 125, 145, 146, 147, or 151. Subway/El: Take the Howard line to Chicago Avenue.

The Newberry Library is a bibliophile's dream. Established in 1887 at the bequest of the Chicago merchant and financier Walter Loomis Newberry, the noncirculating library today contains many rare books and manuscripts, as well as a vast depository of published resources for those who are seriously delving into American and European history and literature, as well as other aspects of the humanities from the late Middle Ages onward. The collections, many items of which are on display, include more than 1.5 million volumes and 75,000 maps, housed in a comely five-story granite building, designed in the Spanish-Romanesque style by Henry Ives Cobb and built for the library in 1893. Beyond being a sanctuary in which to conduct research, the Newberry has staked out a little piece of civilization, sponsoring a series of concerts, lectures, and children's story hours throughout the year.

## Museum of Contemporary Art

220 E. Chicago Ave. ☎ **312/280-2660,** or 312/280-5161 for a recorded announcement. Admission $6.50 adults; $4 children ages 12–16, students, and seniors; free for children under 12. Free admission on Tues. Tues and Thurs–Sun 11am–6pm, Wed and first Fri of month 11am–9pm. Café and store, Tues–Sat 11am–4:45pm. Bus: 151. Subway/El: Take the Howard line to Chicago Avenue.

Housed in a new $46 million building that first opened its doors in July 1996, the MCA emphasizes experimentation in a variety of media—painting, photography, video, dance, music, and performance. The new museum and sculpture garden, designed by Berlin's Josef Paul Kleihues (his first project in the U.S.), pays homage to Mies van der Rohe, Louis Sullivan, and other great Chicago architects. While the exhibits change frequently, the MCA also has a permanent collection of more than 3,300 pieces, highlighting the work of Chicago artists but gathered from all over the nation and the world as well. In addition to a range of special activities and educational programming, including films, tours, and lecture series, the MCA features the Site Cafe and a store with one-of-a-kind gift items.

If you're planning a trip for late summer, you may want to call to inquire about New Art, a River North street party thrown by the MCA's New Group (its version of a junior board) to inaugurate the gallery season. The hippest of young Chicago attends.

# MORE MUSEUMS

Chicago has a horde of smaller museums devoted to all manner of subjects. Many of their collections preserve the stories and heritage of a particular immigrant group that has become inseparable from the history of the city as a whole.

## American Police Center and Museum

1717 S. State St. ☎ **312/431-0005.** Admission $3.50 adults, $2.50 seniors, $2 children 6–11. Tours require a minimum of 20 people and reservations. Mon–Fri 8:30am–4:30pm, Sun noon–4pm. Bus: 29, 44, 62, or 164.

Carrying a mandate to help prevent crime by fostering better civilian understanding of law enforcement, the museum displays police equipment and memorabilia. It must have been where Nelson Algren brought Simone de Beauvoir to show her the electric chair, an event Algren refers to in an interview for the *Paris Review*.

## Balzekas Museum of Lithuanian Culture

6500 S. Pulaski Rd. ☎ **773/582-6500.** Admission $4 adults, $3 students and seniors, $1 children. Daily 10am–4pm. Bus: 53A.

The Balzekas Museum of Lithuanian Culture gives insight into the history and ancient culture of the tiny Baltic state that was absorbed into the former Soviet Union, and achieved independence in August 1991. The museum is located on the Far Southwest Side, home to the largest Lithuanian community outside of Lithuania. The collection contains a range of objects from books to artworks, arms and armor, maps, and decorative ornaments.

## Chicago Athenaeum: The Museum of Architecture and Design

6 N. Michigan Ave. ☎ **312/251-0175.** Suggested donation $3 adults, $2 seniors and students. Tues–Sat 11am–6pm, Sun 11am–5pm. Bus: 3, 4, 20, 56, 60, 127, 131, 145, 146, 147, 151, or 157. Subway/El: Take the Ravenswood or Lake/Dan Ryan to Madison.

The collection reaches across several fields of design, including architectural, industrial, and graphic, all with a special emphasis on Chicago. Only a small portion of the collection is on public view at once, but serious researchers can see more by appointment.

## Martin D'Arcy Gallery of Art

Loyola University, 6525 N. Sheridan Rd. ☎ **773/508-2679.** Free admission. Mon–Fri noon–4pm. Bus: 151. Subway/El: Take the Howard line to Loyola.

A treasure trove of medieval and Renaissance art, the Martin D'Arcy Gallery of Art covers the years A.D. 1100 to 1700. All the rich symbolism of Catholicism through the baroque era is embodied in such works as a gem-encrusted sculpture in silver and ebony of Christ's scourging, a head of John the Baptist on a silver platter, golden chalices, rosary beads carved with biblical scenes, and many other highly ornamented ritual objects.

## Hull House Museum

800 S. Halsted. ☎ **773/413-5353.** Free admission. Mon–Fri 10am–4pm, plus Sun in summer noon–5pm. Bus: 8. Subway/El: Take the O'Hare/Congress/Douglas line to Halsted/University of Illinois.

Three years after the Haymarket Riot, a young woman named Jane Addams bought an old mansion on Halsted Street that had been built in 1856 as a "country home" but was now surrounded by the shanties of the immigrant poor. Here Addams and her co-worker, Ellen Gates Starr, launched the American settlement-house movement with the establishment of Hull House, an institution that endured in Chicago until 1963. In that year all but two of the settlement's 13 buildings, along with the entire residential neighborhood in its immediate vicinity, were demolished to make room for the new University of Illinois at Chicago campus. The story of the opposition to this project is eloquently told in the words of the participants themselves, who appear among the scores of others interviewed by Studs Terkel for his book *Division Street America*.

Of the original settlement, what remains today is the Hull House Museum, the mansion itself, and the residents' dining hall, snuggled among the ultramodern, poured-concrete buildings of the university campus. Inside are the original furnishings, Jane Addams's office, and numerous settlement maps and photographs. Rotating exhibits re-create the history of the settlement and the work of its residents, showing how Addams was able to help transform the dismal streets around her into stable inner-city environments worth fighting over.

### International Museum of Surgical Science

1524 N. Lake Shore Dr. ☎ **312/642-6502.** Free admission, $2 suggested donation. Tues–Sat 10am–4pm, Sun 11am–5pm. Bus: 151.

Housed in a 1917 Gold Coast mansion, the museum has a collection of surgical instruments, paintings, and sculpture depicting the history of surgery. A turn-of-the-century apothecary shop and dentist's office are re-created in a historic street exhibit.

### Mexican Fine Arts Center Museum

1852 W. 19th St. ☎ **773/738-1503.** Free admission. Tues–Sun 10am–5pm. Bus: 9. Subway/El: Take the O'Hare/Douglas line to 18th Street or Hoyne.

The Mexican Fine Arts Center Museum features the work of Mexican and Mexican-American artists.

### Museum of Broadcast Communication

78 E. Washington St. ☎ **312/629-6000.** Free admission. Mon–Sat 10am–4:30pm, Sun noon–5pm. Bus: 3, 4, 60, 145, 147, or 151. Subway/El: Take the Ravenswood or Lake/Dan Ryan line to Madison.

Housed in the Chicago Cultural Center, the Museum of Broadcast Communication includes both the Radio Hall of Fame and the Kraft TeleCenter. Pay a visit if you'd like to listen to or watch the classic programs of yore, or if you've always dreamed of anchoring your own newscast.

### Peace Museum

314 W. Institute Place ☎ **312/440-1860.** Admission $3.50 adults; $2 seniors, students, and children. Tues–Wed and Fri–Sat 11am–5pm; Thurs noon–8pm. Bus: 11, 22, or 65. Subway/El: Take the Ravenswood line to Chicago Avenue.

Exhibits, performances, and other programs serve as vehicles for the ideas and messages on international and domestic peace, now collected in a permanent home.

### Polish Museum of America

984 N. Milwaukee. ☎ **773/384-3352.** Suggested donation $2 adults, $1 children. Daily 11am–4pm.

Located in the heart of the first Polish neighborhood in Chicago, this museum has one of the most important collections of Polish art and historical materials outside Poland. And it is also the largest museum in the country devoted exclusively to an ethnic group. PMA's programs include rotating exhibitions, films, lectures, and concerts.

### Swedish-American Museum

5211 N. Clark. ☎ **773/728-8111.** Free admission. Tues–Fri 10am–4pm, Sat–Sun 10am–3pm. Bus: 22. Subway/El: Take the Howard line to Bryn Mawr.

A storefront exhibit chronicles the Swedish immigrant contribution to American life and is also a gift shop for typical items of Scandinavian manufacture.

### Ukrainian National Museum

2453 W. Chicago Ave. ☎ **773/276-6565.** Donations requested. Mon–Wed by appointment, Thurs–Sun 11am–4:30pm. Bus: 49 or 66.

The Ukrainian National Museum possesses an unmistakably old-world atmosphere; few cultures seem to have changed as little over the ages as that of the Ukrainians. Throughout the two upper stories of this converted brownstone, you will find decorative Easter eggs, fine embroidery, wood carvings, artwork, crafts, and folk costumes, all of which reflect an incredible continuity in technique over the years.

**Morton B. Weiss Museum of Judaica, K. A. M. Isaiah Israel Congregation**
1000 E. Hyde Park Blvd. ☎ **773/924-1234.** Free admission. Call for an appointment, or visit following weekly services. Transportation: Take the Metra train to Hyde Park; then take a cab.

Among other fascinating artifacts of Jewish culture, you'll see some of the findings unearthed at digs in the Holy Land by amateur archaeologist Gen. Moshe Dayan. Also of note are the illustrated marriage contracts on parchment from the Middle Ages, and the Byzantine-style synagogue itself, built in 1924.

# CHICAGO'S PARKS
## GRANT PARK

Grant Park is really a patchwork of giant lawns pieced together by major roadways and a network of railroad tracks. Covering the greens are a variety of public recreational and cultural facilities. The immense Buckingham Fountain, accessible along Congress Parkway, is the baroque centerpiece of the park, patterned after—but twice the size of—the Latona Fountain at Versailles, with adjoining esplanades beautified by rose gardens in season. Throughout the late spring and summer, the fountain spurts columns of water up to 100 feet in the air, illuminated after dark by a whirl of colored lights.

Popular outdoor concerts are staged at the Petrillo Music Shell, at Jackson and Columbus Drives, over a 10-week summer period every Wednesday, Friday, Saturday, and Sunday evenings. Other favorite annual events are the free outdoor jazz festival (around Labor Day) and the blues festival (in June). The Taste of Chicago, purportedly the largest food festival in the world, takes place every summer for a week preceding and including July 4. Local restaurants' tents serve up more ribs, pizza, hot dogs, and beer than you'd ever want to see, let alone eat. For program information, call 312/294-2920.

At the north end of the park is a covered outdoor sports plaza with 12 lighted tennis courts, a rink for ice skating in the winter and roller skating in the summer, a cross-country ski trail that operates during January and February, and a field house.

Scattered about the park are a number of sculptures and monuments, including the Native American on horseback (at Congress and Michigan Avenue), which has become the park's trademark, as well as likenesses of Copernicus, Columbus, and Lincoln, the latter by the American genius Augustus Saint-Gaudens, located on Congress between Michigan Avenue and Columbus Drive. On the western edge of the park, at Adams Street, is the Art Institute, and at the southern tip are the Field Museum of Natural History, the Adler Planetarium, and the Shedd Aquarium (see Section 1, "The Top Attractions," earlier in this chapter).

To get to the park, take bus no. 3, 4, 6, 60, 146, or 151. If you want to take the subway or the El, get off at any stop in the Loop along State or Wabash.

## LINCOLN PARK

Lincoln Park is the city's largest, and certainly one of the longest, parks around. Straight and narrow, Lincoln Park begins at North Avenue and follows the shoreline of Lake Michigan northward as far as Ardmore Avenue (not far from the "new" Chinatown and Andersonville). Within its elongated 1,200 acres are a first-class zoo, a half-dozen bathing beaches, a botanical conservatory, two excellent museums, a golf course, and the usual meadows, formal gardens, sporting fields, and tennis courts typical of urban parks. To get to the park, take bus no. 22, 145, 146, 147, 151, or 156.

A group calling itself Friends of Lincoln Park, 900 W. Fullerton (☎ 773/472-7275), has an "adopt-a-monument" program, asking corporate sponsors to underwrite the cleanup and repair costs for a very fine selection of public statues honoring a group of great men: LaSalle, Schiller, Benjamin Franklin, U. S. Grant, Shakespeare, Hans Christian Andersen, Goethe, and, of course, Lincoln. The statue of Lincoln in the park that bears his name is one of two in Chicago by Augustus Saint-Gaudens (the other is in Grant Park). Saint-Gaudens also did the Bates Fountain near the conservatory. In the area near the conservatory is the bust of a contemporary figure, that of Sir Georg Solti, laureate music director of the Chicago Symphony, one of those rare cases in which a man is so honored before his death.

### Lincoln Park Conservatory

Fullerton Drive (at Stockton Drive). ☎ 312/294-4770. Free admission. Daily 9am–5pm (10am–6pm during flower shows). Bus: 151 or 156.

Inside are four great halls filled with thousands of plants, the closest thing (other than several smaller conservatories scattered in a few neighborhood parks) that Chicago has to a botanical garden within the city limits. The Palm House features giant palms and rubber trees, the Fernery nurtures the plants that grow close to the forest floor, and the Tropical House is a symphony of shiny greenery. A fourth environment is aptly named the Show House, for here the seasonal flower shows are held.

### Chicago Academy of Sciences Museum

North Pier, 435 E. Illinois St. ☎ 773/871-2668. Admission $3 adults, $2 seniors and children. Free on Tues. Daily 10am–5pm. Bus: 29, 56, 65, or 66.

The other nature-oriented institution in the park is the Chicago Academy of Sciences Museum, the oldest museum in Chicago. The museum is relatively small, but packs a lot in, and is particularly good at showing dioramas on the variety of ecosystems found in the Midwest. The Children's Gallery, open daily from 10am to 3pm, features puzzles, games, live animals, fossils, artifacts, and more for kids to explore.

*Note:* The above address is the temporary site of the museum, which is scheduled to move to a new, permanent home at Fullerton Parkway and Cannon Drive in 1998.

### Café Brauer

2000 N. Cannon Dr. ☎ 773/935-6700. Daily 10am–5pm. Bus: 151 or 156.

A onetime Chicago institution near the zoo, Café Brauer has reopened its doors to the public following a massive restoration costing more than $4 million. Operating a cafe and ice-cream parlor on the ground floor, and a banquet area called the Great Hall on the second floor, the Brauer's return restores some of the elegant atmosphere that characterized the park around the turn of the century, when this landmark building was erected.

## 3 Especially for Kids

Chicago has plenty of places to take the kids—places, in fact, that make every effort to turn a bored child into a stimulated one. All the city's museums are leaders in the "please touch me" school of interactive exhibitions, with buttons and lights and levers and sounds and bright colors, and activities for kids at special exhibitions. I have already described most of the attractions listed in this section, but I'm grouping them together for the sake of convenience. (I know most parents can use all the help they can get.)

The **Museum of Science and Industry,** 57th Street and Lake Shore Drive (☎ 773/684-1414), has high-tech, push-button exhibits for children, and kids are particularly awed by the large-screen Omnimax Theater. (See Section 1 of this chapter for a more detailed listing.)

The **Chicago Academy of Sciences Museum,** Fullerton and Cannon (☎ 773/871-2668), has a special Children's Gallery. (See above.)

The **Field Museum of Natural History,** Roosevelt Road and Lake Shore Drive (☎ 312/922-9410), has a "place for wonder" with many curiosities that children can touch. Most kids also go nuts over the dinosaurs and the mummies. (See Section 1 of this chapter for details.)

The **Adler Planetarium,** 1300 Lake Shore Dr. (☎ 312/322-0304), offers special "sky shows" for children on Saturday morning. (See Section 1 of this chapter for details.)

The **Shedd Aquarium,** 1200 S. Lake Shore Dr. (☎ 312/939-2426), shows divers hand-feeding sharks while swimming in the same tank and explaining everything via an underwater intercom. (See Section 1 of this chapter for details.)

The **Chicago Cultural Center,** 78 E. Washington St. (☎ 312/269-2820, or 312/744-6630 for a listing of current events), offers films for children every Saturday, and a special program of activities in the summertime. (See Section 2 of this chapter for details.)

The **Art Institute of Chicago,** Michigan Avenue at Adams Street (☎ 312/443-3600), has designated five galleries as a "junior museum" where children can engage in art projects of their own. (See Section 1 of this chapter for details.)

The **DuSable Museum of African-American History,** 740 E. 56th Place, in Hyde Park (☎ 773/947-0600), has a summer program offering cultural and educational activities for children. (See Section 1 of this chapter for details.)

The **Newberry Library,** 60 W. Walton (☎ 312/943-9090), has children's literature story hours many Saturday mornings. (See Section 2 of this chapter for details.)

Every kid should also get to go at least once to a **Cubs baseball game** at Wrigley Field. (See Section 6 of this chapter for details.)

## MORE ATTRACTIONS

### Chicago Children's Museum
Navy Pier, 600 E. Grand Ave. ☎ 312/527-1000. Admission $3.50 nonmember adults, $2.50 nonmember children and seniors; membership fee $35 a year per family. Tues–Fri 12:30–4:30pm, Sat–Sun 10am–4:30pm. Bus: 29, 56, or 65.

The Chicago Children's Museum has areas especially for preschoolers as well as older children. Several permanent exhibits allow kids a maximum of hands-on fun. "Amazing Chicago," for example, is a miniversion of Chicago represented by playhouse-size constructions of several well-known Chicago buildings where the kids can go in and play. In the miniature "Art Institute," they can draw and hang up their own art, and in the "Sears Tower" they learn about architecture and play with decorating materials. "Touchy Business" is a tactile tunnel for kids ages 3 to 7, where the labyrinth leads through a Lighted Forest to the pretend house of the Three Bears, with lots of stuff to touch and learn about along the way. Kids can also play dress-up with the museum's collections of masks and clothes, and they can make crafts, such as puppets or jewelry, to take home.

### Lincoln Park Pritzker Children's Zoo and Nursery
2200 N. Cannon Dr. (in Lincoln Park Zoo). ☎ 773/935-6700. Free admission. Daily 9am–5pm. Bus: 151 or 156.

The Children's Zoo is a delight for children and adults alike. Kids will have the opportunity to touch many of the animals, which are handled by zookeepers. Chicks, snakes, and rabbits are common residents of the Children's Zoo, and if you're lucky, you might find a baby chimp or some unusual species.

At the Farm-in-the-Zoo, kids will discover a working reproduction of a Midwestern farm, complete with a white-picket-fenced barnyard, chicken coops, and stalls filled with livestock, including cows, sheep, and pigs. Even the aroma is authentic.

## 4  Organized Tours

If you want someone else to organize your sightseeing, by bus or by boat, Chicago has a number of experienced companies that provide just about any kind of itinerary you can imagine.

## ORIENTATION TOURS

For a narrated city tour by bus, contact **American Sightseeing,** 530 S. Michigan Ave. (☎ 312/427-3100), which offers a varied selection of two- to five-hour tours covering daytime sights and nightlife.

"Double Decker Bus Rides," narrated one-hour tours of the Loop, downtown, and the lakefront, are offered daily from 9:30am to 5pm by **Chicago Motor Coach** (☎ 312/922-8919). Board the buses at the Sears Tower, the Water Tower, or Mercury Boat, and buy your ticket from the driver, who will then give you a brochure describing the day's stops. You can get off at any number of attractions along the way and reboard throughout the day. The cost is $7 for adults, $5 for children.

## SPECIAL-INTEREST TOURS

The **Untouchable Tours,** or so-called Gangster Tours, P.O. Box 43185, Chicago, IL 60643 (☎ 773/881-1195), is the only bus tour in Chicago of all the old hoodlum hangouts from the Prohibition era. See the old hotel where Capone had his command center, the site of O'Bannion's flower shop, and the site of the St. Valentine's Day massacre, plus much more; $20 for adults, $15 for children. Tours, which depart from 605 N. Clark St., run Monday to Wednesday at 10am; Thursday at 10am and 1pm; Friday at 10am, 1pm, and 7:30pm; Saturday at 10am, 1pm, and 5pm; and Sunday at 11am and 2pm. Untouchable also offers tours of the historic Beverly Hills/Morgan Park neighborhood of stately old homes (☎ 773/881-1831).

And, of course, don't forget the **Chicago Architecture Foundation,** 224 S. Michigan Ave. (☎ 312/922-3432), with its guided programs by foot, bike, and bus to more than 50 different architectural sites and environments in and around Chicago. Its "Chicago Architecture Highlights by Bus" trip on Saturdays at 9:30am covers the Loop, Hyde Park, and the Gold Coast, plus several other historic districts; $25 per person (call for reservations). Just a few of the other excursions offered are a Frank Lloyd Wright bus tour and walking tours of the Gold Coast, River North, Grant Park, Old Town, and the Jackson Boulevard Historic District. Most cost around $5 and last a couple of hours. The foundation also plans a series of 45-minute lunchtime tours, generally in the Loop area and often focusing on a particular landmark, such as the Fine Arts Building or the Monadnock Building.

### BUGGY RIDES

**Coach Horse Livery Ltd.,** Pearson Street and Michigan Avenue (☎ 312/266-7878), maintains a fleet of old-fashioned horse carriages stationed around Water Tower Square. Each driver has his or her own variation on the basic Magnificent Mile itinerary, and the charge is $30 for each half hour.

### RIVER TOURS

The **Chicago Architecture Foundation** (☎ 312/922-3432) organizes river trips that leave from the south side of the Chicago River, at Michigan Avenue and Lower Wacker Drive, and cruise for an hour and a half along both the north and south branches, accompanied by a lecturer. Although you can see the same buildings on your own by foot, the guides, or docents, provide an interesting historic perspective

# A River Runs Through It

With apologies to the late Norman Maclean for appropriating the title of his wonderful collection of fiction, *A River Runs Through It,* the words here refer to the river in Chicago, not to the one in the writer's native Montana. Chicago owes not only its name but also its existence to its river. Native Americans referred to the land around the river with a word—that to the ears of the early Europeans sounded like "chicago"—meaning "powerful," presumably owing to the strong odors of either the swampy decay or the plant life pervasive along the riverbank. Because the Chicago River provided a crucial link between the Great Lakes and the Mississippi River, the frontier city was destined to grow into the nation's great midcontinental hub of transportation and transshipment, facilitating travel and trade between the eastern settlements and the West.

Today the Chicago River remains one of the most visible yet enigmatic of Chicago's major physical features. It branches into so many neighborhoods that it's almost omnipresent. The effect is similar to that famous revolutionary-era flag of the segmented snake; you see the river only in isolated snatches, each of which usually includes one of the city's 50 some-odd bridges. An almost mystical moment occurs downtown when all the bridges spanning the main and south branches—connecting the Loop to both the Near West Side and the Near North Side—flap up and then down like the wave of spectators at a ball game. When the drawbridges are raised, allowing for the passage of some ship or barge or contingent of high-masted sailboats, automobile traffic in downtown Chicago grinds to a halt, but only briefly, because the choreography in Chicago is well practiced (it's the city that works).

The Chicago River has long outlived the critical commercial function it once performed for the city that developed along its banks. Most of the remaining millworks that still occupy these banks no longer depend on the river alone for the transport of their materials, raw and finished. The river's main function today is to serve as a fluvial conduit for sewage which, owing to an engineering feat that reversed its flow inland in 1900, no longer pollutes the waters of Lake Michigan. Recently Chicagoans have begun to discover another role for the river, that of leisure resource, providing short cruises on its water and park areas on its banks. Actually, today's developers aren't the first to wonder why the river couldn't be Chicago's Seine. A look at the early-20th-century Beaux Arts balustrades lining the river along Wacker Drive—complete with comfortably spaced benches—shows that Daniel Burnham knew full well what a treasure the city had.

and some fun Trivial Pursuit details (David Letterman once called the busts of the nation's retailing legends that face the Merchandise Mart the "Pez Hall of Fame").

Since the cruise opens on the main branch, right at the Michigan Avenue bridge, my docent took the opportunity to explain how the opening of the bridge, a part of Daniel Burnham's Plan of Chicago—nicknamed Paris on the Prairie—transformed the street from one of grand mansions to a major commercial thoroughfare. The cruise points out both landmark buildings, such as the Gothic 1925 Tribune Tower, designed by a New York architect who won a contest, and contemporary ones, including the very recent NBC Building, constructed in wedding-cake style in homage to the city's old zoning codes which mandated that sunlight reach down to the street.

The docents generally do a good job of making the cruise enjoyable for visitors with all levels of architectural knowledge. Mine, for example, gave a thumbnail sketch of the difference between the modern, function-as-form school of Mies van der Rohe's IBM Building and the postmodern look of 333 Wacker, which addresses its environment with its curved line that follows the river. In addition to pointing out famous buildings—Marina City, the Civic Opera House, Sears Tower, to name a few—the docents approach the sites thematically, explaining, for example, how Chicagoans' use of, and attitudes toward, the river have changed in the last two centuries.

The architecture foundation boat tour costs $15 on weekdays and $17 on weekends. In the height of the season, from June through September, it runs three times daily—at 9:30am, noon, and 2pm—and in May and October, the boat leaves at noon on Monday through Friday, and at noon and 2pm on weekends. The foundation recommends buying tickets in advance through TicketMaster (☎ 312/902-1500).

**Mercury Chicago Skyline Cruiseline** at Michigan Avenue and Wacker Drive (☎ 312/332-1353) also offers frequent water tours, usually combining the river and the lake. Tickets range from $4 to $6 for children under 12, and $8 to $12 for adults, depending on the length of the cruise.

The **Friends of the Chicago River,** 407 S. Dearborn St. (☎ 312/939-0490), is a nonprofit organization with a mission to foster the vitality of the river both for people and the ecosystems that depend on it. Each summer the organization sponsors walking tours, canoe trips, and boat tours. The organization also publishes and sells five excellent maps—"Chicago River Trails"—for self-guided walking tours along the north and south branches and the downtown section of the river.

The Friends of the Chicago River offers docent-guided walks along eight sections of the river, scheduled on many Saturdays and Sundays from May through October. All tours meet at 10am or 2pm at varying locations depending on the specific tour, are approximately two hours long, and cost $5 per person. Typical of the excursions is a walk around the perimeter of Goose Island, Chicago's only island.

## BOAT TOURS ON LAKE MICHIGAN

Tired of just looking out at the deep blue water from the top of the Hancock, the Shedd Aquarium, Oak Street Beach, and a host of other spots? Reverse your perspective. Take a sightseeing cruise and look at that incredible skyline from an offshore vantage point. Offering one- and two-hour water tours between late April and early October are the **Mercury Chicago Skyline Cruiseline** (☎ 312/332-1353) and the **Wendella Streamliner** (☎ 312/337-1446), both located under the Michigan Avenue Bridge, at Michigan and Wacker Drive. Both lines take in a stretch of the Chicago River and the area of the lake off the downtown district. Scheduling for these cruises depends on the season and the weather, so call ahead for the current hours. Prices range from $8 to $12 for adults, and $4 to $6 for children under 12, depending on the duration of the cruise. One of the most dramatic events during the boat tours is passing through the locks that separate river from lake.

For the kids, the Mercury Line also puts on a "Wacky Pirate Cruise," an hour of singing and surprises, departing from the dock at 10am every Thursday, Friday, Saturday, and Sunday from mid-June to early September. The cost is $8 for adults, $5 for kids. Reservations required through TicketMaster (☎ 312/902-1500).

**Shoreline Marine Sightseeing** (☎ 312/222-9328) schedules one-hour lake cruises from three different dock locations: the Shedd Aquarium, the Adler

Planetarium, and Buckingham Fountain in Grant Park. Cruises operate between Memorial Day and Labor Day, and tickets cost $6 for adults and $3.50 for children under 10.

**Chicago from the Lake Ltd.,** 455 E. Illinois (☎ 312/527-2002), home ports in the Ogden Slip adjacent to North Pier at the end of East Illinois Street. The company runs both architectural river tours and lake and river historical tours from May through September. Complimentary coffee, lemonade, cookies and muffins are served. Tickets are $18 for adults, $16 for seniors, $12 for children ages 7–18, and free for children under 7.

The *Spirit of Chicago* (☎ 312/836-7899) has evening dinner cruises that depart daily from Navy Pier at 7pm, offering dancing to a live band and a floor show, returning to port at 10pm. The price is $59.95 per person Sunday through Thursday, and $74.35 on Friday and Saturday, plus service. In addition, the boat offers weekday luncheon trips at $31.80, moonlight cocktail cruises on Friday and Saturday for $37.80, and a Sunday brunch sailing for $37.80.

## NATIONAL HERITAGE CORRIDOR

Another Mercury Line offering is a cruise along the river route that links Chicago with the Mississippi River, taking in everything from the cityscape to the prairielands. Spring and fall dates are to be announced; call for details (☎ 312/332-1353). Price is $39.50 per person, including coffee and breakfast pastries.

## CEMETERY TOURS

No, I'm not kidding. Cemeteries are fascinating places, whether in New Orleans, where the dearly departed aren't really buried at all but are enclosed in aboveground sarcophagi, or in Boston, where Revolutionary War heroes are crowded together, or here in Chicago, where some of the cemeteries are as pretty as parks.

One of the best is **Graceland,** which stretches along Clark Street in the Swedish neighborhood of Andersonville. The land between Irving Park Road and Montrose Avenue, running for about a mile along Clark, is occupied exclusively by cemeteries—primarily Graceland. Here you can view the tombs and monuments of many Chicago notables. When Graceland was laid out in 1860, public parks as such did not exist. The elaborate burial grounds that were constructed in many large American cities around this same time had the dual purpose of relieving the congestion of the municipal cemeteries closer to town and of providing pastoral recreational settings for the Sunday outings of the living. Indeed, cemeteries like Graceland (and Green-Wood in Brooklyn) were the precursors of such great municipal green spaces as Lincoln Park in Chicago and Central Park in New York. Much of Lincoln Park, in fact, had been a public cemetery since Chicago's earliest times. Many who once

---

**Impressions**

*I say God's Chicago, for who else will own it, complete it, and gather it to be the perfect city upon earth? Chicago has all the possibilities of becoming the earth's final city, the Babylon of the Plains.*

—Shane Leslie, *American Wonderland,* 1936

*The city that works.*

—Quoted in *The Economist,* March 3—9, 1979, as "Recently Traditional," without source

rested there were reinterred in Graceland when the plans for building Lincoln Park went forward.

The **Chicago Architecture Foundation** (☎ 312/922-3432) offers walking tours of Graceland on selected Sundays during August, September, and October. They cost $5 per person and last about two hours. Among the points of interest you will discover as you meander the paths of these 119 beautifully landscaped acres are the Carrie Getty and Martin Ryerson tombs, famous architectural monuments designed by Louis Sullivan. Sullivan himself rests here in the company of several of his most distinguished colleagues: Daniel Burnham, Ludwig Mies van der Rohe, and Howard Van Doren Shaw, an establishment architect whose summer home in Lake Forest, called Ragdale, now operates as a writers' and artists' colony. Some of Chicago's giants of industry and commerce are also buried at Graceland, including Potter Palmer, Marshall Field, and George Pullman. An ambiguous reference in the *WPA Guide to Illinois* (New York: Pantheon Books, 1983), reprinted without revisions, records that Graceland also contains the grave of Chicago's first white civilian settler, John Kinzie. The racial adjective is a reminder that Chicago's very first settler was a black man named DuSable.

The architecture foundation offers tours of some other cemeteries, as well, including the **Oak Woods Cemetery,** the **Rosehill Cemetery,** and the suburban **Lake Forest Cemetery.** Call for details.

## 5 Outdoor Activities

Perhaps because Chicago's winters can be so brutal, Chicagoans take their summers very seriously. In the warmer months, with the wide blue lake and the ample green parks, it's easy to think the city is one big grown-up playground. Whether your fancy is water sports or land-based ones, you'll probably be able to find it here.

**BEACHES**   Public beaches line Lake Michigan all the way up north into the suburbs and Wisconsin and southeast through Indiana and into Michigan. A few of the most popular in Chicago are **Oak Street Beach,** at the northern tip of the Magnificent Mile, which attracts the biggest percentage of Beautiful People; the **North Avenue Beach,** about six blocks farther north, which pulls in a somewhat more loose and laid-back crowd; and a couple miles north along the **Belmont Avenue strip,** where gays congregate. If you've brought the pooch along, you may want to take him/her for a dip at the doggie beach between Belmont and Irving Park Road. Here's my mother hen thing again, but please take note that the whole lakefront is not beach and don't go doing anything stupid like diving off the rocks.

**BIKING**   I've heard real die-hard cyclists complain that Chicago is too flat to be a good biking town, but I personally don't mind not having to pedal uphill, especially when I'm facing one of those major winds off the lake. Biking is a great way to see the city, particularly the lakefront, which has a bike path that extends for miles. To rent bikes, try **Bike Chicago** (☎ 800-915-BIKE), with four locations: Oak Street Beach, Buckingham Fountain in Grant Park, Navy Pier, and at Cannon Drive and Fullerton in Lincoln Park. Open from May through October (weather permitting), Bike Chicago stocks mountain and touring bikes, as well as tandems, kids' bikes, and strollers. Rates are $8 an hour, $30 a day; the company offers free downtown deliveries for day rentals. Twice a day, the company leads a two-hour bike tour designed for all fitness levels. It departs from Oak Street Beach and costs $20.

If you bring your own bike and you encounter mechanical trouble while riding, **Kozy's** has a repair shop at Diversey Point Center, at Diversey Parkway and the lake (☎ 773/525-0933).

**BOWLING**   Okay, bowling's not an outdoor activity, but what if it's raining? The bowling alley closest to the major hotels is **Spenser's Marina City Bowl,** 300 N. State St. (☎ 312/527-0747), in River North.

**GOLF**   It's amazing, astounding, but Chicago really does have a golf course right downtown. **Illinois Center Golf,** 221 N. Columbus Dr. (☎ 312/616-1234), is a nine-hole course east of Michigan Avenue. Open seven days a week, greens fees are $22; a bucket of about 45 balls at the driving range is $6, and a bucket of 80 balls is $9.

   The Park District also maintains a number of golf courses—I've heard more than any city in the country. Most convenient to the majority of visitors is **Sydney R. Marovitz,** 3600 N. Lake Shore Dr. Still referred to as Waveland by many Chicagoans, it's a nine-hole course right on the lake. If you feel like just hitting a bucket of balls, the **Diversey Driving Range,** 140 W. Diversey Pkwy. (at the lake), is right in Lincoln Park. For information on all the courses' hours, greens fees, and price per bucket of balls for driving ranges, or to make same-day tee-time reservations, call the Park District (☎ 312/245-0909).

**ICE SKATING**   With the opening of Navy Pier, 600 E. Grand Ave., Chicago has a new skating rink (☎ 312/595-PIER).

**IN-LINE SKATING**   The wheeled ones have been taking over Chicago's sidewalks, streets, and bike paths since the early '90s. Numerous rental places have popped up, and several sporting goods shops that sell in-line skates also rent them. The rentals generally include helmets and pads. One convenient place to try is **Kozy's,** Diversey Point Center at the lake (☎ 773/525-0933), which rents rollerblades for $7 an hour, or $19 a day; a $100 deposit is required. **Bike Chicago** (☎ 800-915-BIKE) also rents in-line skates from its four locations: Oak Street Beach, Buckingham Fountain in Grant Park, Navy Pier, and Cannon Drive and Fullerton in Lincoln Park. Bike Chicago charges $6 an hour, or $20 a day, and offers free delivery to downtown locations for day rentals. A third spot is **Londo Mondo Motionwear,** 1100 N. Dearborn (☎ 312/751-2794), on the Gold Coast, renting rollerblades for $7 an hour, or $20 a day. Every Wednesday at 6:30pm, Londo Mondo is the starting point for Blade Sessions, a skate-through-the-city party open to all. It ends at Melvin B's, where the first drink is on the house.

**JOGGING**   Despite all the bikers and skaters, runners still manage to hold their own on the pathways of Chicago's parks and lakefront. Many parks also have exercise stations with outdoor apparatus. For other information, call the Park District (☎ 312/294-2200).

   For information about competitive marathons, call the **Chicago Area Runners Association** (☎ 312/666-9836) and the Chicago Marathon (☎ 312/527-1105).

**SAILING**   It seems a shame just to sit on the beach and watch all those beautiful sailboats gliding across the lake. Go on, get out there. The **Chicago Sailing Club,** in Belmont Harbor (☎ 773/871-SAIL), rents J-22 boats from 9am to sunset, weather permitting. A J-22 holds four or five adults, and rates range from $30 to $40 an hour ($10 extra for a skipper), depending on the time and day of the week. If you want to take the boat out without a skipper, you need to demonstrate your skills first. Reservations are recommended.

**SKYDIVING**   Okay, all you thrill-seekers out there, how about skydiving? **Skydive Chicago** (☎ 815/433-0000)—the name's a little deceptive—is about an hour and a half southwest of the city in Ottawa, Illinois. It offers the first-time jumper a trip up—and back down—for $169. Before getting in a plane that takes you to 13,000 feet, you take an hour-long class. When you do jump, you're harnessed to an instructor. Experienced jumpers—those who can produce a license and a logbook—can make the jump for $16.

**TENNIS**   For the hundreds of tennis courts where you can personally lob the ball, call the Park District (☎ 312/294-2200).

## 6 Spectator Sports

With Michael Jordan the most recognized athlete in the world, Bears fans immortalized in Saturday Night Live's "Da Bears" sketches, and the country's annual late-summer sympathies directed at the collapse of the Cubs and White Sox, I wonder sometimes if outsiders think of Chicago in any other context than that of spectator sports. Chicago fans are nothing if not loyal, and for that reason attending a home game in any sport is an uplifting experience.

**AUTO RACING**   Go to **Raceway Park,** 130th Street and Ashland Avenue (☎ 773/385-4035), or the **Santa Fe Speedway,** 9100 S. Wolf Rd. (☎ 773/ 839-1050).

**BASEBALL**   Baseball is imprinted in the national consciousness as part of Chicago, not because of victorious dynasties, but rather because of the opposite—the Black Sox scandal of 1919 and the perennially pennant-chasing Cubs. Let's start with the **Cubs.** The fact that every fan knows the Cubbies will crumble by August makes their devotion that much stronger; it's easy to love a winning team, but it takes heart to love a losing one. And when the team plays in so perfect a place as **Wrigley Field,** with its ivy-covered outfield walls, its hand-operated scoreboard, its view of the shimmering lake from the upper deck, and its "W" or "L" flag announcing the outcome of the game to the unfortunates who couldn't attend, how could anyone stay away? After all the strikes and temper tantrums and other nonsense, Wrigley has managed to hold onto something like purity. Maybe it emanates from the retired no. 14 jersey of Ernie Banks, the legendary second baseman from the '50s and '60s, eras when the Cubs rarely climbed more than a rung or two out of the cellar in the standings. Banks once said, "It's a beautiful day, so let's play two," or words to that effect. One more great Cubs tradition: classy second basemen. Ryne Sandberg, MVP and multiple Golden Glove winner, gave up a megacontract to retire in 1994 because he didn't think he was playing well enough to earn his millions. But he, like MJ, has risen again.

Enough with the romanticizing. On to the practical matters. Yes, Wrigley finally installed lights almost a decade back, but by agreement with the residential neighborhood it occupies, the Cubs still play most games in the daylight, as they should. I wholeheartedly suggest you attend a day game, the price of which, including a hot dog, a beer, and, of course, a box of Crackerjack, will run you about $20. Because Wrigley is small, just about every seat is decent. A word of warning: If you're sitting in the bleachers and you happen to catch a home-run ball of the visiting team, throw it back or risk intense verbal abuse from 35,000 fans.

Wrigley Field, 1060 W. Addison St. (☎ 773/404-2827), is easy to reach. Take the B train on the north–south line to the Addison stop, and you're there. You could also take the no. 22 bus, which runs up Clark Street. Known as Wrigleyville, the entire area around the stadium is surrounded by souvenir shops, sports bars, and restaurants. One sandwich shop, the **Friendly Confines,** is actually located within the stadium itself, just off the sidewalk. **Sluggers,** a sports bar with real batting cages, is right around the corner from Wrigley at 3540 N. Clark St. (☎ 773/248-0055).

## Impressions

*Nothing missed by these Chicago papers. If world came to an end tomorrow Tribune would come out day after with illustrations and an interview with God Almighty.*

—John Foster Fraser, *Round the World on a Wheel,* 1899

The **Chicago White Sox** play at **Comiskey Park,** 333 W. 35th St. (☎ 773/924-1000), in the South Side neighborhood of Bridgeport; to get there by subway/El, take the Lake/Dan Ryan line to Sox/35th Street. As baseball legend has it, some young fan confronted Shoeless Joe Jackson with the words "Joe, say it ain't so!" hoping his idol would deny his role in the conspiracy labeled the Black Sox scandal, in which eight White Sox players allegedly sold out to the bookmakers and threw the 1919 World Series. That drama, emblematic of the end of the age of innocence for America after World War I, is very much a part of Bridgeport's story as well, since Comiskey Park is located a few blocks east, nestled in the shadow of the Dan Ryan Expressway. The new stadium, built to prevent the White Sox from fleeing the city, stands across from the original "baseball palace of the world," which opened on July 1, 1910. The new third base stands on the spot once occupied by a well-known baseball bar called McCuddy's saloon.

Game times and schedules for each month are available by writing to the Chicago Office of Tourism, 78 E. Washington, Chicago, IL 60602.

**BASKETBALL**  Michael's back. Need I say more? The **Chicago Bulls,** NBA Champs in 1991, 1992, 1993, and 1996, play at the **United Center,** 1901 W. Madison St. (☎ 312/455-4500). Tickets are tough to come by, particularly late in the season. If you're not lucky enough to have an old buddy with season tickets, try your concierge or a ticket broker, such as Gold Coast Tickets (☎ 312/644-6446) or Center Stage (☎ 312/233-8686).

The **De Paul Blue Demons,** the local college team, play at **Rosemont Horizon,** 6920 N. Mannheim Rd. (☎ 312/341-8010).

**BEACH VOLLEYBALL**  Call the **Association of Midwest Volleyball Professionals,** 1848 N. Mohawk St. (☎ 773/266-8580), for dates, times, and locations.

**CLINCHER**  In the summertime you may pass a park where two teams are engaged in a game that looks a lot like softball, but with an oversized 16-inch ball, and generally without gloves. This sport is clincher, and it's only played in Chicago (or in a few other places by former Chicagoans). Championship clincher, incidentally, is big business in Chicago, with players making a fair bundle in exchange for their services. Look for the tournaments at **Mount Prospect Park,** near O'Hare International Airport. Or catch a more informal game in **Oz Park,** in the western part of the Lincoln Park neighborhood.

**FOOTBALL**  The **Chicago Bears** play at **Soldier Field,** 425 E. McFetridge Dr. (☎ 312/663-5408). Just in case you weren't aware, Soldier Field is not one of those modern, enclosed, air-conditioned monstrosities. The Bears play the old-fashioned way—in the open air, which is usually below freezing and quite often wet, too.

The **Northwestern Wildcats** play Big Ten college ball at **Dyche Stadium,** 1501 Central Ave., in nearby Evanston (☎ 847/491-7070).

**GOLF**  The PGA's **Western Open** takes place at **Cog Hill Golf and Country Club,** 119th Street and Archer, in Lemont (☎ 773/242-1717), typically in early July.

**HOCKEY** Although Chicago isn't really a hockey town, its team, the **Blackhawks,** has a devoted following. The Blackhawks play at the **United Center,** 1901 W. Madison St. (☎ 312/455-7000).

**HORSE RACING** There's thoroughbred racing at **Arlington International Race Course,** Euclid Avenue and Wilke Road, Arlington Heights (☎ 847/255-4300), and at **Hawthorne Race Track,** 3501 S. Laramie, in Cicero (☎ 708/780-3700); thoroughbred and harness racing at **Balmoral Race Track,** Illinois Route 1 and Elms Court Lane, in Crete (☎ 708/568-5700); and harness racing at **Maywood Park Race Track,** 8600 W. North and Fifth Avenues, in Maywood (☎ 708/343-4800).

**TENNIS** Chicago has a number of international tennis tournaments throughout the year, including the **Virginia Slims Women's Pro Tournament.** Call the **Chicago District Tennis Association** (☎ 312/834-3727) for information.

# Chicago Strolls 8

Rushing around from one attraction to another can sometimes leave travelers feeling that, while they've seen a lot, they've seen nothing. There is something very satisfying about mastering a city, about sensing that, if you were to return, you'd be able to find your way back to that favorite bistro or little jazz club. In my experience, that mastery comes not by taking taxis or buses, but by walking. The sidewalks carry a certain rhythm that vehicles just don't.

Being a city of neighborhoods—by one count 77—Chicago is an opportune place to put on a pair of comfortable shoes and explore. Now I'm not saying that all 77 are equally worth visiting; some, in fact, having fallen into decay, are worth keeping your distance from. But others, though appearing to be simply rows of neat bungalows, may hold in store untold adventures. On the Far Southwest Side, for example, is the largest Lithuanian community outside of Lithuania. And on the North Side, in West Rogers Park along Devon Avenue from Western to Kedzie, is a mishmash of Hasidic Jews, Russians, Asians, and other ethnic groups, forming a virtual United Nations.

In this chapter are detailed walking tours of three popular areas to visit and narrative descriptions of several others. As Nelson Algren writes in *Chicago: City on the Make,* "It isn't hard to love a town for its greater and its lesser towers, its pleasant parks, or its flashing ballet. Or for its broad boulevards. . . . But you can never truly love it till you can love its alleys too."

## WALKING TOUR 1
## The Loop

**Start:** Sears Tower, 233 S. Wacker Dr.
**Finish:** Fine Arts Building, 410 S. Michigan Ave.
**Time:** Two and a half hours, not counting food stops or prolonged visits at individual sites, such as the Sears Tower observation deck.
**Best Times:** Daytime, on weekdays. During business hours, you'll witness the city's business district in full swing. On weekends, the Loop is very quiet, a nice time for a long walk, but it won't have the same kind of energy. And on weekends, keep in mind that some restaurants and attractions will not be open.
**Worst Times:** Nighttime. The Loop, except for its seedier fringes, is virtually abandoned after dark, and is not the safest place to be

wandering. The strip of South Michigan Avenue covered in this tour, with its hotels and cultural centers, remains active in the evenings. Even so, I strongly recommend taking this stroll before the sun sets.

Begin this tour at the:

1. **Sears Tower,** the world's largest skyscraper, where the sky deck is open daily at 9am and the last ticket is sold at 10:30pm (enter on Jackson Street). From the 103rd floor, you can orient yourself pretty well as to where you'll be walking during the rest of your tour.

🍵 **STARTING OUT**   To make sure you have enough energy for the long walk, you could head a few blocks to the west, across the Chicago River near Union Station, to **Lou Mitchell's,** 565 W. Jackson (☎ 312/939-3111), one of the great breakfast-all-day spots in Chicago, open Monday through Saturday from 5:30am and Sunday from 7am. You can arrive close to the restaurant by the no. 151 or 157 public bus, both of which run down North Michigan Avenue and turn into the Loop.

From the Sears Tower, begin walking north along:

2. **Wacker Drive,** which follows the contour of the Chicago River and borders two legs of this tour. While you're strolling you can observe the architectural gems that line the riverside and see many of the bridges that cross it at strategic points. The first building of note is:

3. **The Chicago Mercantile Exchange,** 30 S. Wacker. The "Merc" has been the great commodities exchange of the heartland since 1919. Visitors are welcome during trading hours.

Just north of the Merc, you'll see the:

4. **Civic Opera House,** at Madison and Wacker, where the Lyric Opera of Chicago performs. The building is grand and imposing, just as an opera house should be. The opera season runs from September through February, and the box office is open Monday through Friday from 9am to 5pm.

Wacker Drive now curves to the east. As it does, take a glance at that enormous building across the river. It's the:

5. **Merchandise Mart,** still owned by the Kennedy family (one of Robert Kennedy's sons, Christopher, is an executive there). If you look into the green glass of 333 Wacker, you'll see a stunning reflection of the Mart and the river.

At LaSalle Street, enter to the right and walk two blocks to Randolph Street. Occupying this entire block is:

6. **The James R. Thompson Center (formerly the State of Illinois Center),** 100 W. Randolph, built in 1985 from a design by Chicago architect Helmut Jahn, and named for the long-serving governor. The orange-and-blue glass-and-steel structure is still controversial among Chicagoans. The monumental sculpture near the entrance is by Jean Dubuffet.

Return to Wacker Drive, and continue east. As you approach Wabash Avenue, note the:

7. **Herald Square Monument,** Lorado Taft's final work, dedicated on December 15, 1941, the anniversary of the ratification of the Bill of Rights. The statue, a symbol of tolerance and unity, shows American Revolution heroes Robert Morris and Haym Salomon, with George Washington between them.

The next block brings you to the:

8. **Michigan Avenue bridge,** across which you can see the Tribune Tower (to the east) and the Wrigley Building (on the west). As you approach the bridge, you may

# Walking Tour—The Loop

1. Sears Tower
2. Wacker Drive
3. The Chicago Mercantile Exchange
4. Civic Opera House
5. Merchandise Mart
6. The State of Illinois Building
7. Heald Square Monument
8. Michigan Avenue Bridge
9. 360 N. Michigan Bldg.
10. Carbon & Carbide Bldg.
11. Stone Container Building
12. Chicago Cultural Center
13. Art Institute of Chicago
14. State Street Pedestrian Mall
15. Orchestra Hall
16. Sante Fe Building
17. Chicago Board of Trade
18. The Rookery Building
19. Monadnock Building
20. The Fisher Building
21. The Old Colony Building
22. The Manhattan Building
23. Printer's Row
24. Dearborn Station
25. Harold Washington Library Center
26. Auditorium Building and Theater
27. Fine Arts Building

1-0446

157

see signs for river tour boats and the double-decker tour bus that makes a circuit of this area.

Turn to the right on Michigan Avenue, and note—on the left—the:

9. **360 N. Michigan building,** an architectural landmark in Chicago since 1923. Notice the domed roof supported by columns, and the building's trapezoidal shape. The building occupies the spot where Fort Dearborn stood from 1803 to 1812, when its occupants abandoned it and were massacred by American Indians.

Continue south along Michigan Avenue until Washington Street; half a block west is the:

10. **Carbide and Carbon Building,** 230 N. Michigan. Notice its elegant gilded facade.

A block or so south is the:

11. **Stone Container Building,** 150 N. Michigan. Its slanted, diamond-shaped top is best seen from a few blocks' distance. Try looking back at it, say, from the steps of the Art Institute of Chicago.

Before you get to the museum, though, you'll come across the:

12. **Chicago Cultural Center,** 78 E. Washington, with many programs of interest to the public, and the new home of the Museum of Broadcasting.

Three more blocks south along Michigan Avenue, at Adams Street, is the:

13. **Art Institute of Chicago,** the city's most prestigious museum. It sits on the edge of Grant Park, which accompanies this walk the entire length south along Michigan Avenue. If you don't have time now, be sure to come back to the museum to see some of its wonderful collections.

☕ **TAKE A BREAK**  Turn right on Adams and walk two and a half blocks to The Berghoff, 17 W. Adams (☎ 312/427-3170), a favorite Chicago watering hole and restaurant from nearly the turn of the century. Have a light pick-me-up here at the bar. A glass of Maibock beer and a bratwurst will cost about $6.

On the way back to Michigan Avenue, make a digression northward along the:

14. **State Street Mall.** One of the most famous department stores along this strip is Carson Pirie Scott, 1 S. State, a Chicago architectural gem designed by Louis Sullivan. Two blocks further north is Marshall Field's landmark building. Return to Michigan Avenue and continue south to:

15. **Orchestra Hall,** 220 S. Michigan, home of the Chicago Symphony, and one of the avenue's grandest buildings, dating from 1905. One door down from here you can drop in on the:

16. **Sante Fe Building,** 224 S. Michigan Ave. When it was built in 1904 by Daniel Burnham, it was one of the first highrises (it has 17 stories). Burnham liked his handiwork so much that he moved his offices here. The building has recently been restored, so go inside and check out the skylit lobby court, with its polished mahogany, detailed grillwork, and marble floors. Fittingly, the Chicago Architecture Foundation's ArchiCenter gift shop and tour center are here (☎ 312/922-TOUR for a recorded message of available tours). Here you can arrange for a more intensive tour of the downtown architectural highlights. The Chicago Symphony's shop is also in the building.

A digression to the interior streets will pick up some of the outstanding architectural sights in the Loop. Walk west along Jackson to LaSalle. On the northeast corner is a plaque commemorating the adoption of standard time in the U.S. in 1883—before that more than 100 different local times were in use, an Excedrin headache for the railroads. On the left you'll see the:

**17. Chicago Board of Trade,** 14 W. Jackson, facing north, looming over LaSalle.

Walking north now on LaSalle, you'll approach:

**18. The Rookery Building,** 209 S. LaSalle, a Root and Burnham building. Take a peek at the lobby, designed by Frank Lloyd Wright and recently restored.

Return east along Jackson to see the:

**19. Monadnock Building,** 53 W. Jackson, the north half of which was designed in 1891 by Burnham and Root, the south half by Holabird and Roche. It's the tallest masonry building in Chicago.

Continue south along Dearborn Street and note some other standout relics of Chicago's revival after the Great Fire of 1871:

**20. The Fisher Building,** 343 S. Dearborn, built by Burnham in 1896, with an addition dating from 1907.

**21. The Old Colony Building,** 407 S. Dearborn, constructed in 1894.

**22. The Manhattan Building,** 431 S. Dearborn, erected in 1891. It's Chicago's oldest surviving steel-frame building, an innovation that, along with elevators, made skyscrapers possible.

Cross Congress Parkway to enter:

**23. Printer's Row,** as this stretch of old Dearborn Street is known, where the oldest concentration of the city's postfire buildings is found. Today this neighborhood has undergone a revival, becoming a trendy alternative to living on the Gold Coast or in Lincoln Park. Many interesting shops and restaurants line the row.

**☕ TAKE A BREAK** **Prairie,** at 500 S. Dearborn (☎ 312/663-1143), is an ideal place for lunch or dinner, offering gourmet dishes from heartland recipes and ingredients (see complete listing in Chapter 6).

Continue south along Dearborn to:

**24. Dearborn Station,** the oldest surviving train station in Chicago, but now converted into a small mall of shops and restaurants.

Head back north to Congress and go one block east to see the:

**25. Harold Washington Library Center,** the block-square red-brick building built in 1991.

Continue east on Congress to the:

**26. Auditorium Theater,** 50 E. Congress. Dankmar Adler and Louis Sullivan designed this masterpiece and supervised its construction in 1889. Much of the building now houses Roosevelt University, but the theater is still in use, and it is considered to be one of the most acoustically perfect performing spaces in the world.

Make a left on Michigan, heading north, to see the:

**27. Fine Arts Building,** 410 S. Michigan, and maybe take in a foreign flick. From here you could also cross the street into Grant Park to relax or to watch Buckingham Fountain. Or, if you have any energy left, you could walk (or take a quick cab ride) to the three great museums at the lower end of Grant Park—the Field, the Shedd Aquarium, and the Adler Planetarium.

## WALKING TOUR 2
### Lincoln Park

**Start:** Moody Bible Church, 1609 N. LaSalle St.
**Finish:** Ben and Jerry's, 338 W. Armitage.

**Time:** Two to three hours or more, depending on how long you linger in Lincoln Park and at the various museums, whether or not you elect the digression to the Clybourn Corridor, and how long you stop to relax. You might want to make this tour by bike or rollerblades.

**Best Times:** Anytime after 11am, when most of the stores, restaurants, and attractions are open, until dark. The weekends are preferable, since that's when the streets are liveliest.

**Worst Times:** After dark. Lincoln Park is busy then, with its healthy supply of restaurants and bars, and I recommend spending an evening in the neighborhood, but walking tours are generally better taken in the daytime.

This tour will take you through a series of neighborhoods on the Near North Side, but primarily through the area called Lincoln Park and DePaul. The heavily gentrified area is the neighborhood of choice for singles in their 20s and marrieds in their 30s, and as such, it is loaded with shops, restaurants, and nightspots. Some of the highlights are the Chicago Historical Society, Lincoln Park—with its zoo, beach, and conservatory—and the North Halsted Street shopping and restaurant strip.

Begin at:

1. **Moody Bible Church,** 1609 N. LaSalle St., an enormous house of worship. Its predecessor, built in 1864, was wiped out in the Great Fire. Dwight L. Moody was a founder of the Young Men's Christian Association (YMCA). Public transportation runs close to this location. The no. 151 bus running through the Loop and along North Michigan Avenue (from the north it follows Sheridan Road through Lincoln Park) will bring you to North Avenue and the Inner Drive. You can also take the no. 156 bus, which stays on LaSalle Street and then enters the park.

   Just east across the street is the:

2. **Chicago Historical Society,** North Avenue and Clark Street (☎ 312/642-4600). For details on the exhibits housed in the historical society, see Chapter 7.

   After leaving the historical society, head north on Clark Street. At the Lincoln Avenue intersection, look to the right for the:

3. **Farm in the Zoo,** a section of Lincoln Park Zoo that is especially great for urban and suburban kids who've never milked a cow and who think eggs are laid by the dozen. You could enter the farm here (it and the entire zoo are free) and do a whole zoo visit. The feeding of the seals and sea lions, by the way, takes place around 2pm daily right near the main entrance, which is several blocks north at Webster.

   Picking up from the farm, you could also continue north on Clark, feeding into Lincoln Park West, which, as the name suggests, runs along the park.

   ☕ **TAKE A BREAK** On the corner of Dickens, one block north of Armitage, is **R. J. Grunts,** 2056 Lincoln Park West (☎ 773/929-5363). The restaurant has the best burgers in town, plus chili, vegetarian and heart-healthy meals, and a salad bar brimming over with a wide variety of fresh items. For all you trivia buffs out there, I used to live nine floors up from this local hangout.

   If you have the kids along, after lunch you can take them across the street to the new and very nice:

4. **Cummings Playground,** which stretches between Dickens and Webster on Lincoln Park West.

   Continue north on Lincoln Park West until Belden, where another choice awaits you. Just inside the park is an interesting:

5. **Statue of William Shakespeare.** And just beyond the monument, signs mark another entrance to the zoo, and the:

# Walking Tour—Lincoln Park

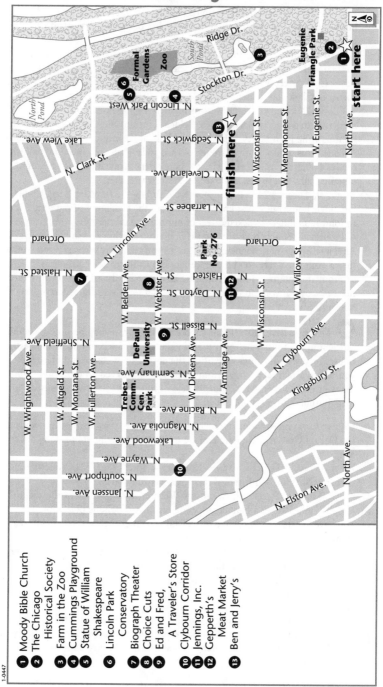

1. Moody Bible Church
2. The Chicago Historical Society
3. Farm in the Zoo
4. Cummings Playground
5. Statue of William Shakespeare
6. Lincoln Park Conservatory
7. Biograph Theater
8. Choice Cuts
9. Ed and Fred, A Traveler's Store
10. Clybourn Corridor
11. Jennings, Inc.
12. Gepperth's Meat Market
13. Ben and Jerry's

1-0447

6. Lincoln Park Conservatory, with its permanent botanical displays and periodic floral shows. In season, the lawn that stretches between the zoo and the conservatory is a beautiful garden.

Across from the park, the Belden-Stratford houses two very fine restaurants, Ambria and Le Grand Café. Turn left here on Belden and walk west to the corner of Clark Street, where you will note the huge branch of Tower Records on the corner of Clark and Belden.

Cross Clark and continue west on Belden for the residential view along this attractive, tree-shaded block. Where Belden, Lincoln, and Orchard intersect, turn right past the John Barleycorn Memorial Pub, and continue north along Lincoln Avenue. This somewhat drab stretch of road ends when you reach Halsted, which crosses Fullerton, as will you. Halsted here offers many appealing choices of restaurants, bars, and stores, and one very historic site, the:

7. Biograph Theater, 2433 N. Lincoln (☎ 773/348-4123), which is still a functioning movie house but is best known as the place the fledgling FBI put a violent end to John L. Dillinger's wicked career of murder and crime.

From here, double back and recross Fullerton, continuing south along Halsted. After a relatively long, nondescript stretch as you approach Webster Street, you will see on your left a very good Italian restaurant, Carlucci (see Chapter 6).

From this point, you can continue down Halsted and pick up this tour at no. 11 below, or you can turn right on Webster for a long digression west to Clybourn Avenue.

☕ TAKE A BREAK    If you choose the detour, it may be time for another quick stop, and just when you need it, there's a branch of one of the best java houses in town, **Starbucks,** right on the corner of Webster and Halsted. Treat yourself to a rich espresso, a creamy cappuccino, or even an o.j. before continuing west on Webster, where immediately in from the corner you will see a lovely neighborhood flower shop, called:

8. Choice Cuts. As you wander down Webster, you will pass the north boundary of the DePaul University campus. Among the other interesting shops along this street are:

9. Ed and Fred, A Traveler's Store, 1007 W. Webster (☎ 773/477-6220), near the corner of Sheffield, outfitters of travel gadgets and books.

At Magnolia Street, which crosses Webster, more or less in the vicinity of Charlie's Ale House, a banner suspended from a telephone pole announces that you have left the neighborhood of DePaul and entered that of Sheffield. In a few short blocks, you will have arrived at the:

10. Clybourn Corridor. Clybourn Avenue is one of the shorter of the diagonal streets that punctuate the Chicago grid. Along this "corridor," formerly a warehouse and light industrial district, a growing number of fashionable shops and restaurants have opened in recent years.

☕ TAKE A BREAK    Right on the corner of Webster and Clybourn is a one-of-a-kind enterprise called **Batteries Not Included,** 2201 N. Clybourn (☎ 773/472-9920); it's a storefront restaurant featuring an intriguing menu of French-Caribbean dishes.

Walking south from here, you can explore the Clybourn Corridor and rejoin the tour near the end on Armitage. Some visitors may not feel completely comfortable on the corridor, though you're not very likely to have a problem during the day. If you're uneasy, you could explore the intersection's offerings and then head back east on Webster.

From here, pick up the tour back on Webster and Halsted, heading south to explore the many shops, including a branch of Banana Republic.

☕ **TAKE A BREAK**   One oh-so-popular stop for locals is **Café Ba-Ba-Reeba!,** 2024 N. Halsted (☎ 773/935-5000), a Chicago version of a Spanish tapas bar. Tapas are appetizer-size portions featuring inventive combinations of foods, both hot and cold. Best to go with a group and order a bunch.

A few of the other good restaurants to consider along North Halsted, depending on your appetite and mood, are **Café Bernard** for French food bistro style, **Edwardo's** for pizza, and **Nookies, Too** for breakfast anytime (open 24 hours over the weekend). (Each of these restaurants is detailed in Chapter 6.)

As you descend North Halsted Street, you will come to Armitage. You will eventually turn left, or east, here, but many other interesting shops are to be found as Halsted continues south, including:

11. **Jennings, Inc.,** 1971 N. Halsted (☎ 773/587-7866), an accessories "bar" that serves complimentary cappuccino and espresso.
12. **Gepperth's Meat Market,** 1970 N. Halsted (☎ 773/549-3883), a specialty food market I mention for anyone considering a picnic in nearby Lincoln Park.

One of the most highly praised and elegant restaurants in Chicago, **Charlie Trotter's** (see Chapter 6), open for dinner only, is located on Armitage just west of Halsted Street. You might want to file away the location for later.

As we approach Lincoln Park, not far from where the tour began, stop in for a well-deserved ice-cream cone at:

13. **Ben and Jerry's,** 338 W. Armitage. If you can't make up your mind, you won't go wrong with the chocolate chip cookie dough.

## WALKING TOUR 3
### Hyde Park

**Start:** 53rd Street station of the Metra Railroad.
**Finish:** Museum of Science and Industry, 57th Street and Jackson Park.
**Time:** Three hours, depending on stops and digressions.
**Best Times:** Any day of the week before dusk. Check with the Hyde Park–Kenwood Development Corporation (☎ 773/667-3932) about special programs that may be taking place in the neighborhood during the time of your visit, and schedule your tour accordingly.
**Worst Times:** After dark. This walking tour must be taken during daylight hours, since the experience is largely visual, and you may not feel entirely safe walking around here at night.

Hyde Park is described in detail under "The Top Attractions" in Chapter 7. Assuming you are staying in or near downtown Chicago, you may get to Hyde Park in a half hour or less on one of several modes of public transportation or by cab.

This tour begins at the:

1. **53rd Street station of the Metra train.** The Metra train has two stops on South Michigan Avenue. Make sure you board the South Chicago train; otherwise you may have to ride to the 57th Street station, still in Hyde Park, but several long blocks from where the tour begins.

⚫ **STARTING OUT**  If you're going to make a day of it in Hyde Park, you might as well start off with a traditional breakfast at **Valois,** 1518 E. 53rd St. (☎ 773/667-0647). "See Your Food" is the slogan that greets you on the sign outside Valois, a small cafeteria-style restaurant and hangout for the whole Hyde Park community for several generations. Short-order meals are the specialty here. An alternative for a refueling stop at this point is near the tour's first stop, a Starbucks coffee shop on the corner of Harper and 53rd.

After leaving the train station, or Valois, as the case may be, start heading west on 53rd Street until you come to:

2. **Harper Court,** a complex of interesting shops and restaurants. For a sampling of the shops, see Chapter 9.

From Harper Court, continue west on 53rd Street until you reach Dorchester Avenue, where, on the southeast corner, directly beyond a vacant lot, you will see:

3. **The oldest house in Hyde Park,** circa 1840. Actually it is the rear section of a more recent structure, with a steep roof and something of the shed or outbuilding about it.

Continue west on 53rd. Just past Kenwood, you will see:

4. **Nichols Park,** a pretty little park where only recently an ugly lot stood.

Make a left on Kimbark, heading south. At the corner of 55th Street, notice:

5. **St. Thomas Apostle School and Church.** The lacy terracotta trim at the church entrance was designed in 1922 by an apprentice of Frank Lloyd Wright.

Hang right on 55th and cross it one block west at Woodlawn (okay, I'm being a mother hen here—I want you to cross at the light because Hyde Park drivers are notorious). Here you're entering the:

6. **Golden rectangle,** an area bordering the U of C campus where the neighborhood's priciest real estate is located. On the west corners, on both sides of 56th Street, is a complex of homes called:

7. **Professor's Row,** dating from 1904 to 1907, some of the most desirable residences in Hyde Park. Migratory parrots, which have somehow drifted here from the South American rain forests, have nested within the confines of Professor's Row, causing a heated controversy in recent years between local "Friends of the Birds" and Illinois farmers who claim the presence of the parrots is a danger to crops.

Now walk one block west to Woodlawn to see one of the prettiest residential streets in the neighborhood. If you're a physics fanatic, you might want to scoot back north to see:

8. **No. 5537 Woodlawn,** the former home of Enrico Fermi, the physicist responsible for the first sustained nuclear chain reaction.

Otherwise, head south to 56th Street. At the northeast corner is the:

9. **McCormick Theological Seminary,** and on the southwest corner is the Hyde Park Union Church.

Still heading south on Woodlawn, at 58th Street you will reach a highlight of the tour:

10. **Robie House,** 5757 S. Woodlawn Ave., perhaps the ultimate expression of Frank Lloyd Wright's Prairie School style. Robie House can be toured every day at noon, $3 for adults, $1 for seniors and students.

On the southwest corner of this intersection is the:

11. **Oriental Institute,** 1155 E. 58th St., an extraordinary collection of ancient art and artifacts dating from 9000 B.C. The institute is closed Monday.

Continue south on Woodlawn one block to:

# Walking Tour—Hyde Park

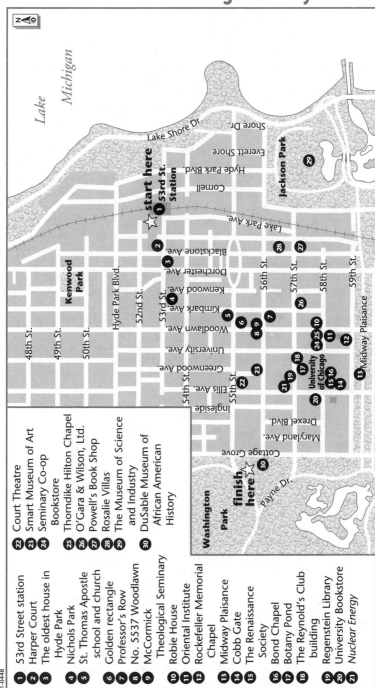

1. 53rd Street station
2. Harper Court
3. The oldest house in Hyde Park
4. Nichols Park
5. St. Thomas Apostle school and church
6. Golden rectangle
7. Professor's Row
8. No. 5537 Woodlawn
9. McCormick Theological Seminary
10. Robie House
11. Oriental Institute
12. Rockefeller Memorial Chapel
13. Midway Plaisance
14. Cobb Gate
15. The Renaissance Society
16. Bond Chapel
17. Botany Pond
18. The Reynold's Club building
19. Regenstein Library
20. University Bookstore
21. Nuclear Energy
22. Court Theatre
23. Smart Museum of Art
24. Seminary Co-op Bookstore
25. Thorndike Hilton Chapel
26. O'Gara & Wilson, Ltd.
27. Powell's Book Shop
28. Rosalie Villas
29. The Museum of Science and Industry
30. DuSable Museum of African American History

**12.** **Rockefeller Memorial Chapel,** at 59th and Woodlawn, a tour de force of modern Gothic architecture, housing the world's second-largest carillon. Carillon concerts may be heard Sunday at 11:30am and Monday through Friday at 6pm.

That wide stretch of green in front of you is the:

**13.** **Midway Plaisance,** which divides the main campus from the law school and other satellite buildings, many of which were designed by well-known modernist architects such as Eliel Saarinen, Edward Durell Stone, and Ludwig Mies van der Rohe.

Make a right in front of Rockefeller Chapel and head west along 59th Street. After you pass University Avenue, the University of Chicago campus will be on your right. Enter through:

**14.** **Cobb Gate.** You have two options here. Either continue on this self-guided tour or, depending on the time of day, take the official university tour, which departs from Ida Noyes Hall, 1212 E. 59th St., Monday through Saturday at 10am. The main attractions for those continuing on the self-guided tour are listed below. Given the campus layout, you'll probably have to ask directions. At some point, I strongly recommend just lying down on the grass and soaking up some of that academia. For you movie buffs, near the center of the Quad is where Harry and Sally met for the first time, before that long drive to New York. Near where you entered the campus is:

**15.** **The Renaissance Society,** on the fourth floor of Cobb Hall, which introduced such artists as Klee, Miró, and Matisse to the Midwest and continues to exhibit vanguard artists. Between Classics and Harper Quads, you must visit the:

**16.** **Bond Chapel,** with its ornate stained glass and carved wood. On the opposite side of the Quad is the peaceful:

**17.** **Botany Pond,** designed by the two sons of Frederick Law Olmsted. This section of the campus houses many of the science buildings.

If you exit the Quad here (the big gate near the pond is apparently Hull Gate, but most students don't seem to call gates by their names), a few steps to the east is the:

**18.** **Reynolds Club,** housing the student union and the University Theater.

Across the street and half a block to the west is the:

**19.** **Regenstein Library,** the main undergraduate library, a modern—some would say monstrous—facility built where Stagg Field once stood, the university's stadium.

Take 57th Street west to Ellis Avenue. A block or so south is the:

**20.** **University Bookstore,** a good place to shop for U of C souvenirs—T-shirts, caps, and the like. It also has books.

Reversing direction and heading north, between 57th and 56th Streets, you will come to the famous bronze sculpture:

**21.** *Nuclear Energy* by **Henry Moore.** It is built over the site where, in 1942, Enrico Fermi conducted the first self-sustaining, controlled nuclear chain reaction.

Continue north on Ellis and make a right on 55th Street. Here is the:

**22.** **Court Theatre,** an Equity house of some 250 seats.

Go east on 55th to the corner and make a right on Greenwood Avenue, heading south one block to the:

**23.** **Smart Museum of Art,** 5550 S. Greenwood Ave., where the university's impressive collection of nearly 7,000 works is housed.

From here another lengthy digression is possible. If you'd like to see the elegant Kenwood neighborhood, walk north here about five blocks, preferably along Woodlawn (two blocks to the east). Or you may make a prior contact with the Hyde Park–Kenwood Development Corporation (☎ 773/667-3932) for information on organized or self-guided tours of Kenwood. Now return south along University Avenue to 57th Street, where you can drop in at the:

24. **Seminary Co-op Bookstore,** 5757 S. University Ave., on the northeast corner of 58th Street, making sure to also take a peek into the lovely and diminutive:

25. **Thorndike Hilton Chapel,** in the same building.

We will now begin to head east again. Either walk down 57th Street, taking note of two interesting bookstores, first:

26. **O'Gara & Wilson, Ltd.,** 1311 E. 57th St. (☎ 773/363-0993), Chicago's oldest book dealer, and then farther down the street:

27. **Powell's Book Store,** 1501 E. 57th St. (☎ 773/955-7780), crammed with used titles in every subject from the classics to the social sciences.

Or, follow 59th Street and take Harper up to 57th to see the:

28. **Rosalie Villas,** where the cottages once formed a miniature planned community constructed in the 1880s.

From here, continue into Jackson Park until you reach the final stops on this tour:

29. **The Museum of Science and Industry,** 57th Street and Lake Shore Drive, one of the most popular tourist attractions in Chicago.

For those of you with a different academic bent, a short cab ride away is the:

30. **DuSable Museum of African-American History,** 740 E. 56th Place (see Chapter 7 for complete listing).

## STROLLING AROUND OTHER NEIGHBORHOODS

## EXPLORING THE GOLD COAST

In Chicago the "Gold Coast" refers not only to the lakefront highrises between Oak Street and North Avenue but also to the interior blocks off this strip. Although the Gold Coast has its share of restaurants and shops, it is primarily a residential neighborhood, and for this reason, it makes for a peaceful walk on a weekday. Weekends are a bit busier, as the professionals who work hard all week tend to play just as hard in their off-time.

### SUNRISE ON THE DRIVE

People on "the other side" (that is, the east side of Lake Michigan, which happens to be the state of Michigan) like to boast that they have the sunset, while Chicagoans have to get up before dawn to see the sun do its thing over the water. True, but a morning person won't mind rising early to take a stroll along Oak Street Beach or Lake Shore Drive as the sun rises.

As the morning progresses, the path that borders the street side of the beach can be precarious. In-line skaters have joined the bike enthusiasts of late, giving the path something of a roller derby effect. The slow lane is on the sand.

If you opt for the jogging route—which takes you north into nearby Lincoln Park—still exercise caution; wheeled ones have been known to invade. Among the sights you will pass are the Chess Pavilion, the zoo, the conservatory, an exercise station with outdoor apparatus (south of Diversey), and various harbors, beaches, tennis courts, and athletic fields.

### HISTORIC GOLD COAST ARCHITECTURE

This stretch of Lake Shore Drive, as well as those streets in the immediate vicinity, first received the appellation "Gold Coast" because many of Chicago's wealthiest families built their mansions here in the years following the Chicago fire. The fire had virtually destroyed all of the Near North Side, once a prosperous neighborhood of artisans and craftspeople, primarily German immigrants. State Street merchant Potter Palmer began the trend in 1882 with his million-dollar castle at what is now 1359 N. Lake Shore Dr. Other affluent Chicagoans followed Potter's lead, but with the exception of several survivors like those now housing the International College of Surgeons (no. 1516) and the Polish Consulate General (no. 1530), most of these shoreside estates have long been replaced by elegant apartment buildings.

A winding, self-guided architectural tour through the interior streets of the Gold Coast is a must to appreciate the eclectic variety of building styles that flowered in Chicago after the Great Fire of 1871. On these streets, the preservation of Chicago's oldest mansions and fine townhouses has fared better than on the drive itself, though the architectural relics here are likewise sheltered beneath the shadows of modern highrises.

A block from the water is Astor Street, a designated landmark along its entire length between Division Street and North Avenue, with many well-preserved fine houses. Some of the standouts to look for are nos. 1316 to 1322, which show a Romanesque influence in the manner of the Boston architect H. H. Richardson's style. (The only actual sample of Richardson's work in Chicago, however, is the South Side's Glessner House in the Prairie Avenue Historical District, which today serves as headquarters for the Chicago Architecture Foundation; it's discussed later in this chapter.) Charnley House, on the other hand, at 1365 N. Astor St., at the corner of Schiller Street, is distinctly Chicago, built in 1892 by Adler and Sullivan during the period when Frank Lloyd Wright (who could have had a hand in the design) worked for the firm.

On a side street off Astor, at 20 E. Burton, is the Patterson–McCormick Mansion. The original building, an Italianate palazzo, was designed by Stanford White as a wedding present for the daughter of the *Chicago Tribune*'s publisher, and later expanded in 1927 by David Adler for Cyrus McCormick II. Today the complex has been broken up into condos. At 1406 N. Astor St. is the Ryerson House, also by David Adler, whose design in this case was inspired by the hotels of Paris constructed during the Second Empire. Another sturdy example of the Romanesque style is the May House, at 1443 N. Astor, built in 1891, while the Russel House, at no. 1449, constructed 40 years later by Holabird and Root, is distinctly art deco, and the Tudor house at no. 1451 was designed by architect Howard Van Doren Shaw.

On the corner of North Boulevard, between Astor and North State Parkway, is Chicago's Catholic Archbishop's Residence, 1555 N. State Pkwy. The Queen Anne–style red-brick mansion with many chimneys was one of the first houses built in the district, erected in the 1880s on land that had previously been a cemetery. At 1550 N. State is a building where each of the 10 floors originally housed a single apartment of 9,000 square feet, designed by Benjamin Marshall, the architect for the Blackstone and Drake hotels. At 4 W. Burton St. is the Madlener House (ca. 1900) by the firm of Richard E. Schmidt, one of the city's earliest examples of the horizontal architecture that would come to characterize the Prairie School and the work of Frank Lloyd Wright. Today the building is home to the Graham Foundation for Advanced Studies in Fine Arts. The George S. Isham House at 1340 N. State St., built in 1889, has been better known in recent years as Hugh Hefner's Playboy Mansion, and is now a women's dormitory for the School of the Art Institute.

Half a block farther south, at 1301 N. State, at the corner of Goethe, is the Omni Ambassador East Hotel and its famous Pump Room restaurant. You may want to walk into the Pump Room to scan the celebrity photos lining the walls. Finally, near

# The Gold Coast

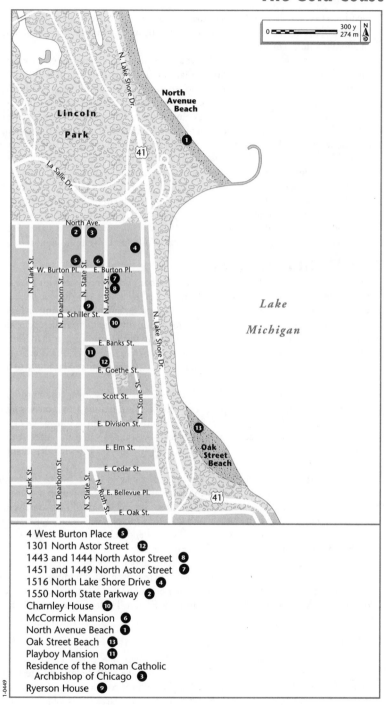

4 West Burton Place **5**
1301 North Astor Street **12**
1443 and 1444 North Astor Street **8**
1451 and 1449 North Astor Street **7**
1516 North Lake Shore Drive **4**
1550 North State Parkway **2**
Charnley House **10**
McCormick Mansion **6**
North Avenue Beach **1**
Oak Street Beach **13**
Playboy Mansion **11**
Residence of the Roman Catholic
  Archbishop of Chicago **3**
Ryerson House **9**

1-0449

Division Street are the Frank Fisher Apartments, 1207 N. State, a small white-brick building with a curved, glass-block facade in the art moderne tradition, built around an appealing inner courtyard.

Continuing up North Dearborn Street are several notable examples of early Chicago architecture, beginning with the landmark Three Arts Club, at 1300 N. Dearborn, built in 1912 by Holabird and Root, and still functioning as a residence for women students enrolled in music and arts classes. St. Chrysostom's Episcopal Church, at 1424 N. Dearborn, often enlivens the neighborhood with its 43-bell carillon. Above North Avenue begins Lincoln Park (see Chapter 7 and the walking tour earlier in this chapter), and to the northeast is the neocolonial brick structure of the Chicago Historical Society standing alone in a large meadow (see Chapter 7).

Three additional architectural sites close to the south end of the park, along Lincoln Park West, should not be overlooked. They are Tonk House, 1817 N. Lincoln Park West, noteworthy for its carved wooden doors; the Louis Sullivan Town Houses, nos. 1826 to 1834, built in 1885 and still in very good repair; and no. 1838, the 1874 boyhood home of Charles Wacker, whose idea it was to create a double-decker street along the edge of the Chicago River, today called Wacker Drive in his honor.

## THE DIVISION STREET AREA

Two blocks south from the Claridge Hotel, Dearborn Street intersects with Division Street. Division Street is also the name Studs Terkel used as the title for his best-selling chronicle about the lives of mostly ordinary Chicago folk. The name, he says, is meant to stand not for a real street, but for a kind of geographic archetype of the American reality. It is easy to imagine that it was on this Division Street that Terkel, who grew up in what was the boardinghouse district around nearby LaSalle Street, first heard the voices of Chicago's working stiffs that he transmits so faithfully to his readers.

Some of Chicago's rougher edges are still evident on this street (the notorious Cabrini Green housing project is only a few blocks west), but the area is increasingly succumbing to the forces of gentrification that surround it. But as long as Division Street is the number one address for singles bars—yes, this is where the characters of *About Last Night . . .* came to drink and to meet—it's not going to shed that slightly seedy feel.

To the north of Division, State *Parkway* is strictly Gold Coast, but to the south it's State *Street* once again, and all commercial—not in the downtown sense of department stores, as in "State Street, that Great Street," but lined with storefronts such as the neighborhood dry cleaner and the mom-and-pop newsstand. Rush Street doesn't actually extend all the way to Division but ends a block to the south, where it stems diagonally into State at the corner of Bellevue.

Not to be overlooked while in the vicinity is the opportunity for some serious high-fashion window shopping along Oak Street, where most of the buildings have been remodeled to accommodate a host of designer boutiques (see Chapter 9). One hold-over from Oak Street's less glamorous past is the Esquire Theater, now a rehabilitated six-screen cinema.

## OLD TOWN

West of LaSalle Street stretches a strip of old Chicago bohemia called Old Town, separating the Gold Coast from Cabrini Green. LaSalle itself, before the street was widened in the 1930s to accommodate Loop-bound car commuters, was an elegant quarter of private residences considered the western boundary of the Gold Coast. For years thereafter, many a foreshortened structure along LaSalle, whose facade was

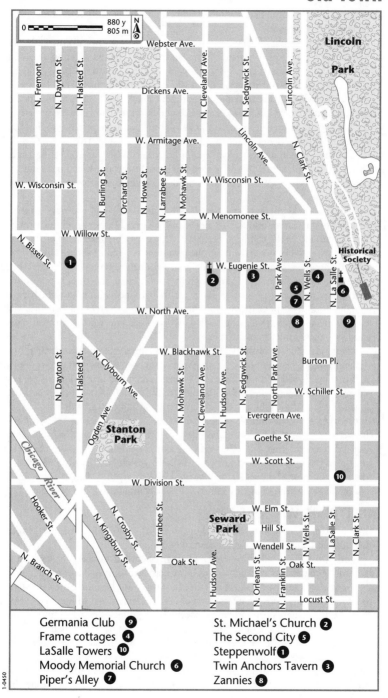

0 ——— 880 y
805 m
N

Webster Ave.

Lincoln
Park

N. Fremont

N. Dayton St.

N. Halsted St.

Dickens Ave.

N. Cleveland Ave.

N. Sedgwick St.

Lincoln Ave.

W. Armitage Ave.

Lincoln Ave.

N. Clark St.

N. Burling St.

Orchard St.

N. Howe St.

N. Larrabee St.

N. Mohawk St.

W. Wisconsin St.

W. Wisconsin St.

W. Menomonee St.

W. Willow St.

N. Bissell St.

❶

Historical
Society

† W. Eugenie St.

N. Park Ave.

N. Wells St.

N. La Salle St.

❷    ❸    ❺    ❹    † ❻

❼

W. North Ave.    ❽    ❾

W. Blackhawk St.

Burton Pl.

N. Mohawk St.

N. Cleveland Ave.

N. Hudson Ave.

N. Sedgwick St.

North Park Ave.

W. Schiller St.

N. Clybourn Ave.

Ogden Ave.

Evergreen Ave.

Goethe St.

Stanton
Park

W. Scott St.

❿

N. Dayton St.

N. Halsted St.

Chicago River

W. Division St.

W. Elm St.

N. Larrabee St.

N. Crosby St.

N. Kingsbury St.

Seward
Park

Hill St.

Wendell St.

N. Wells St.

N. LaSalle St.

N. Clark St.

Hooker St.

N. Branch St.

Oak St.

N. Hudson Ave.

N. Orleans St.

N. Franklin St.

Oak St.

Locust St.

| | |
|---|---|
| Germania Club ❾ | St. Michael's Church ❷ |
| Frame cottages ❹ | The Second City ❺ |
| LaSalle Towers ❿ | Steppenwolf ❶ |
| Moody Memorial Church ❻ | Twin Anchors Tavern ❸ |
| Piper's Alley ❼ | Zannies ❽ |

1-0450

lopped off to accommodate the broadened avenue, functioned as a rooming house or a hotel for transients.

Today this stretch of LaSalle is attempting a revival toward upscale housing as development presses westward on the North Side. One old building, the LaSalle Towers, on the northeast corner of Division and LaSalle, seems itself a wry commentary on the latest transformation of LaSalle. The artist Richard Hass has painted the exterior walls of this circa-1920s apartment hotel with a series of trompe l'oeil murals as an homage to Chicago's architectural heritage. On the front of the building Hass has re-created an image of Louis Sullivan's archway entrance to the Transportation Building designed for the Columbian Exposition of 1893.

Old Town's main drag is a block west of LaSalle on Wells Street, covering a stretch three-quarters of a mile long between Division Street and Lincoln Avenue, the diagonal extension of Wells that heads northwest right out of the city and into suburban Skokie.

Old Town, like much of the Near North Side of Chicago, was once a German neighborhood. But around the beginning of the Great Depression in the early '30s, the area around Wells had begun to fray, attracting a new generation of artists and writers trying to eke out a living on the government's Works Progress Administration. Under these circumstances, Old Town became the center of Chicago's bohemian life, a status it maintained through the hippie era of the '60s and on until the recent onslaught of gentrification. Today, although lined with boutiques, bars, restaurants, and nightspots, the neighborhood still emanates artsy, quasi-radical vibes, an aura enhanced each year in mid-June, when Wells Street is transformed into an outdoor gallery for its annual Art Fair.

The residential part of the neighborhood, sometimes referred to as the Old Town Triangle, begins roughly above North Avenue, only two blocks west of Lincoln Park at this point. A walk through these quiet streets is rewarded by a vision of Old Town the way it was around the turn of the century and earlier. Many of the wood-frame houses built after the Chicago Fire are still standing and coexist with residential creations of more recent vintage, notably the 10 luxury townhouses on Sedgwick Street between Wisconsin and Menomonee, designed by nine of Chicago's top contemporary architectural firms. On the corner of nearby Eugenie and Cleveland Streets is an enormous Bavarian baroque church, St. Michael's, rebuilt from its standing walls after the fire. For most of the second half of the 19th century, St. Michael's was the parish center of Chicago's largest German Catholic community.

## BUCKTOWN/WICKER PARK

Even a decade ago, this neighborhood west of the Gold Coast was a mix of working-class housing and light industrial buildings.

Today, if you're really hip—say, a photographer or a musician, or you just like renovating slightly decayed houses—you live here. Artists in search of good light and low rent were the first outsiders to move into what had become a Hispanic neighborhood radiating from the intersection of North, Damen, and Milwaukee Avenues. Next came the merely artsy, followed shortly by the wanna-bes. The rent isn't quite so low anymore. What's more, the original artists are appalled by their new neighbors, some of whom have begun to commercialize the area with art galleries and trendy eateries (see Chapter 6 for some recommendations). Some residents even object to Round the Coyote, the weekend in the early fall when artists open up their studios to the public. Recently it has taken on a festival atmosphere, as the area businesses have tried to cash in on the crowds.

If you miss Round the Coyote, when detailed maps of artists' workspaces are available, I suggest going to the main intersection and strolling from there down the main arteries. A good starting point is the landmark Flatiron Building, now housing several artists and galleries. You may want to go early enough to catch some daylight, then stay on for Bucktown's lively night scene, catching an alternative rock band at one of the music clubs.

## THE NEAR WEST SIDE

Late Sunday evening on October 8, 1871, a fire broke out somewhere near the O'Leary home. Legend has it that the fire began in the O'Learys' barn, a freak accident caused when a cow upended an oil-filled lantern. The fire raged mostly to the east and north, jumping the Chicago River in both directions, leveling all of downtown Chicago and most of the Near North Side as far as the city line along Fullerton Avenue.

Two days later, as the city lay in smoldering ash, the O'Leary home stood unscathed, marking the western limit of the fire that, owing to the direction of the wind and to pure luck, left much of the Near West Side intact. A monument shaped like a Pillar of Fire stands today in the courtyard of the Chicago Fire Academy at Jefferson and DeKoven Streets, where the O'Learys lived and the fire was believed to have started.

From the 1850s on, the Near West Side, broadly defined as the area just west of the Loop, was a study in social contrasts, the townhouses of wealthy merchants standing near the most wretched hovels of the immigrant families: at first, the Irish, Germans, and Bohemians; later, Jews, Greeks, and Italians; and still later, Mexicans and African Americans from the south.

Various urban-renewal schemes over the years and the construction of the University of Illinois Chicago campus transformed the once residential character of the neighborhood, but a number of important landmarks and vest-pocket neighborhoods have avoided the wrecker's ball, more by accident than design. Among them is Chicago's oldest church, St. Patrick's, at Des Plaines and Adams, dwarfed today by the Presidential Towers apartment complex.

Within the Jackson Boulevard Historic District, the 1500 block of Jackson (between Ashland and Laflin), some 31 Victorian-era middle-class homes were intentionally spared and restored to their spit-and-polish appearances through the sweat equity of some urban homesteaders in the early '70s.

Nothing stands to remind passersby today of the significance of the area around Des Plaines and Randolph Streets. The city's open-air market was once located here in a place called Haymarket Square, scene in 1886 of a political riot that in turn led to one of the great miscarriages of American justice. Workers staged a protest at the square on May 4 to denounce the killing of a fellow worker by the police at the nearby McCormick Reaper Works the day before. Mayor Carter Harrison personally surveyed the rally and concluded that there was no cause for alarm. Acting on his own authority, however, the commander of a reserve police force ordered the workers to disperse soon after the mayor left for home. Suddenly, in the moments preceding the dispersal, a bomb exploded, killing a policeman. The remaining police attacked the assemblage, leading to the deaths of six more policemen and four civilians, plus scores of injured among both groups.

Six of the eight labor and political leaders subsequently indicted and tried for conspiracy in the death of the murdered policeman had not even attended the rally. Of the eight, four were hanged, one took his own life in prison, and the remaining three were pardoned by Illinois Gov. John Peter Altgeld in 1893. Altgeld's gesture of personal honor was also an act of political suicide; the governor was himself pilloried in the press and thereafter shunned as a virtual renegade. But his heroic action came to be immortalized in Vachel Lindsay's widely known poem, "Sleep Softly, Eagle Forgotten." The bomb thrower himself was never found. (Some years ago I read a wire story in the *New York Daily News* reporting on the outcome of a scholarly investigation whose authors had uncovered a plausible suspect, a deranged German immigrant who, they claim, acted completely alone.)

A monument called the "Haymarket Statue" once stood in this square to commemorate the seven police officers who fell that day. But the monument was "repeatedly blown up in the 1960s" and so it now stands in the atrium of the Police Training Academy, 1300 W. Jackson Blvd.

## THE PRAIRIE AVENUE HISTORICAL DISTRICT

The two public attractions of the Prairie Avenue Historical District are the Glessner House, where the Architecture Foundation has its headquarters, and the Clarke House, Chicago's oldest surviving structure. From downtown, on South Michigan Avenue, the no. 18 bus will take you there. Get off at 18th Street and walk the two blocks east to Prairie.

As far back as the Civil War, this geographic swath of the Near South Side was a desirable residential neighborhood for the wealthy. On Prairie Avenue alone were the houses of such giants of industry and commerce as George Pullman, George Armour, Marshall Field, Joseph Sears, Charles P. Kellogg, William Kimball, and John Jacob Glessner, of which only the homes of Glessner and Kimball, a piano manufacturer, survive to this day. Since the Near South Side, though very close to downtown, was not destroyed by the Great Fire, the popularity of the area as the site for the mansions and townhouses of the city's "best families" increased proportionately after 1871.

But the area's desirability lasted for less than two more decades. The decline came with the encroachment on its periphery of "houses of vice," pushed south by the commercial development of downtown State Street. The final blow was the arrival of the railroad. Tracks were laid nearby, and warehouses sprang up where most local residents had assumed fine houses would someday stand. Some citizens who were farsighted in their day fought the plan to construct tracks so close to the lakefront, but they were defeated.

Today the rail lines that once traveled these tracks are mostly idle. But the scar of land occupied by the tracks—running on the surface all the way to Grant Park, just opposite the Loop—remains an incongruous strip of ugliness along what is otherwise one of the most beautiful urban stretches in the country. Practically speaking, this system of tracks occupies a forlorn no-man's-land that separates a long stretch of residential Chicago from the lakefront's beautiful parklands. Here in the Prairie Avenue Historical District, for example, Burnham Park can be reached only by crossing a long footbridge over the tracks. Only 23rd Street, several blocks to the south, goes across the tracks en route to the McCormick Place Convention Center, which sits on land within the park. (For the downtown pedestrian, the tracks also stand as an obstacle to negotiate between the Loop and several of Chicago's most important cultural institutions—the Field Museum, the Shedd Aquarium, and the Adler Planetarium.)

A shadow of the past, Glessner House (1886), at 1800 S. Prairie, stands practically alone on a block once lined with old mansions and guards a corner of historic Prairie Avenue at the intersection of 18th Street. The carriage house of the dramatic Romanesque stone building houses the Architecture Foundation's information desk, as well as a small gift shop with a wide selection of books on Chicago architecture, and some wonderful prints and postcards. In the main house, most of the common spaces and bedrooms are open to the public on an escorted tour. (The foundation's administrative offices are sequestered under the eaves upstairs, formerly the servants quarters.)

Glessner House was designed by the Boston architect H. H. Richardson— Louisiana-born, Paris-educated, and a great-grandson of Joseph Priestley, the famous English clergyman and chemist. Commercial and residential architects of that day widely imitated Richardson's Romanesque designs, until their vogue lapsed in favor of the simpler lines—vertical with skyscrapers, horizontal with dwellings—that reflected the rise of steel and the emergence of the "Chicago School" of architecture. Richardson's work, unlike that of his many imitators, was infused with intellectual and artistic notions that had emerged among thinkers and artists in Victorian England. He designed Glessner House after a stone abbey he'd seen in the English country town of Abingdon; he created the warm interior in the spirit of the arts and crafts movement that spurned mass production in favor of artisanship.

Glessner—then vice president of International Harvester—believed, as did most Americans, that, tragically, wilderness was shrinking rapidly, a victim of progress. Urban Americans dreamed of the rural life. That's not to say they didn't appreciate the necessity of a townhouse for work and society, but life in cities like Chicago turned inward, away from the harsh urban realities. Richardson's fortresslike designs expressed more forthrightly than most of his contemporaries this widely perceived contrast between the tranquility within and the barbarism without.

Even today the uninhabited rooms of the Glessner House radiate with a warmth that reflects not prosperity alone but a sensibility that can only be described as secure and "homelike." The 35-room house was filled with wallpaper and fabric designed by William Morris. It contains many of the family's original furnishings designed by Frances Bacon and by the Glessner family friend Isaac Scott, who also personally hand-carved many of the picture frames that decorate the walls. This appreciation and practice of manual crafts, like woodworking, was typical of those influenced by the arts and crafts movement. (Many Chicago architects in those days—Wright included—could work as well with their hands as with their minds.)

The Glessner House is the only surviving example of H. H. Richardson's work in Chicago—the others were demolished for one reason or another—and a visit here is worthwhile.

But that's more than I can say about Clarke House, at 16th Street and South Michigan Avenue. The restoration of the city's oldest home and building (1836) is as discordant as the Glessner House is harmonious and internally consistent. Much effort was made to preserve Clarke House, which had fallen into ruin in the service of many tenants, domestic and institutional, over the years. Documenting this restoration is an interesting display in Clarke House of black-and-white photographs that at least show the old homestead as was, however decayed: a wreck of a timber-frame house. Now it looks like an idealization of something that never existed.

Rooms are done up in different periods to accommodate imaginary former residents. The materials and finishing techniques used in the restoration have made Clarke House lose its 19th-century frontier feeling, and given it a much too contemporary aspect. The boards aren't old or worn, the bannister looks as if it's fresh from the lumberyard, the wallpaper sparkles, and the paint job is just too crisp. If the original Clarke family could see their frontier home today—built when most of their neighbors were still in log cabins—they'd probably think it belonged to the governor. The most authentic thing about Clarke House is outside on the well-cropped grounds; that's not a lawn you're walking on—it's prairie grass, Chicago au naturel.

The combined tour of these two houses costs $8 ($5 for just one house) and is led by one of the Architecture Foundation's 250 volunteer docents, who receive formal training in their areas, and often have a deeper knowledge of their subject as a result of individual research and study.

# PILSEN

Most of Pilsen remains an immigrant neighborhood, a narrow, rectangular box of streets stretching as far west as Damen Avenue, and shaped north and south by the old railyards and the remaining industrial infrastructure of the 19th century. The area is named for the second-largest city in what was then Bohemia, a part of the former Czechoslovakia. English is still the second language of Pilsen, but the first is no longer Czech—it's Mexican Spanish. The Bohemians left their mark on the physical appearance of the neighborhood, however, with the colorful brick- and stonework that decorates the facades of many houses.

Every September, before summer officially draws to a close, many artists and artisans of Pilsen throw open their studio doors and invite the public to view the work they've produced over the preceding year. The epicenter of the Pilsen art scene is located in the eastern corner of the neighborhood at Halsted and 18th Streets. Most of the studios occupy spaces in what are some of the oldest and most charming houses and commercial buildings in Chicago remaining within a single, unified residential zone. Behind the block-long row of buildings along the 1800 block of Halsted (between 18th and 19th Streets), a large courtyard lies hidden from public view. On summer days, artists and their patrons fill the courtyard, sipping white wine from plastic glasses.

Even if your stay in Chicago does not coincide with the Pilsen Artists' Open House, you can spend an interesting afternoon exploring this neighborhood. I would not recommend, however, that you stay beyond the daylight hours; the neighborhood has had something of a crime problem, and I don't think the typical visitor would feel nearly as safe here in the evening as, say, in River North or Lincoln Park. To reach Pilsen, I suggest catching the Halsted Street bus, if you are coming from the general vicinity of the Loop. Just walk west to Greek Town, crossing the south branch of the Chicago River until you get to Halsted, and take the bus heading south. Get off at 18th Street.

First wander among the side streets that encircle the intersection of Halsted and 18th, simple residential settings. Heading in a westerly direction, and zigzagging the streets between 18th and Cermak, see how many of the murals you can find of the 30 or more that have been painted on building exteriors by artists and their friends in the community. Many draw heavily from pre-Columbian myths and customs and combine them with a vision of social realism in the manner of Diego Rivera and other great muralists of Central America.

One of Chicago's most controversial experimental theaters, the Blue Rider, is in Pilsen (see Chapter 10). See Chapter 6 for some restaurant ideas in this area.

# CHINATOWN

Chicago's original Chinatown had its center on Clark and Van Buren Streets, but the ethnic Chinese later settled around Cermak Road and Wentworth Avenue on the Near South Side. Chicago's Chinatown is not nearly as big as those in several other major cities, such as New York or San Francisco. But it does have several good restaurants (see Chapter 6 for some suggestions) and a few interesting shops.

# Shopping 9

Don't be embarrassed. You're not alone. The vast majority of travelers love to shop. I'm told that one market research study indicated the average tourist spends a couple of hours in a museum and the rest of the time shopping. We could chalk up this trend to the consumer society in which we live, but I think a more accurate explanation would take into account the cultural clues gleaned from a shopping trip. What kind of clothes do people here wear? How do they furnish their homes? How do they entertain their guests? What do they eat? Okay, fine, maybe I am just defending one of my own favorite hobbies.

In any case, Chicago just happens to be one of the best cities in the world to shop. Although I moved to New York a couple of years ago, I still prefer shopping in Chicago. The quality of the stores is top-notch, and, since so many of the best are concentrated on North Michigan Avenue, the convenience is unmatched.

It should come as no surprise that shopping in the Windy City is first-rate. The art of merchandising has a rich history here. From the time when this city was little more than a frontier town up until just a few years ago, few homes lacked a catalog from Sears or Montgomery Ward, both of which grew up in Chicago.

By the nature of its Great Lakes port, its Chicago River system, and its domination of the railroads, the city was in a good position to build an empire of merchants. East to west, or back the other way, whether it was livestock, overalls, or the newest books, just about everything passed through Chicago. Trade was so predominant that, in 1877, the president of the Historical Society warned the city leaders, "We have boasted long enough of our grain elevators, our railroads, our trade. . . . Let us now have libraries, galleries of art, scientific museums, noble architecture, and public parks. . . . Otherwise there is the danger that Chicago will become a place where ambitious young men will come to make money . . . and then go elsewhere to enjoy it."

Clearly, the powers-that-be heeded that practical scholar's warning. Nonetheless, the 19th-century merchants' legacy is a lasting one, from the grand Merchandise Mart (still owned by the Kennedy family), which houses showroom after showroom of fine furniture, to the chic designer boutiques lining Oak Street.

This section concentrates on the Magnificent Mile, State Street, and a couple of trendy neighborhoods. It also provides a sampling, by merchandise category, of where you might find specific items.

# 1 The Shopping Scene

As a general rule, **shop hours** are Monday through Saturday from 10am to 6 or 7pm and on Sunday from noon to 5pm. Department stores outside of the Loop tend to keep later hours, remaining open until 8pm on Monday through Saturday, and until 6pm on Sunday. Many stores are open later on Thursday, and almost all have extended hours during the holiday season.

Almost all the stores in the Loop are open for daytime shopping only, generally from 9 or 10am to no later than 6pm Monday through Saturday. (The big department stores do have some selected evening hours; see below.) Many Loop stores not on State Street are closed Saturday, and on Sunday the Loop—except for a few restaurants, movie theaters, and cultural attractions—is shut down tight.

## THE MAGNIFICENT MILE

The nickname—hyperbole to some, an understatement to others—refers to the roughly mile-long stretch of North Michigan Avenue between the Chicago River and Oak Street. The density of first-rate shopping is, quite simply, unmatched anywhere. Taking into account that Oak Street is just around a corner, the overall area is a little like New York's Fifth Avenue and Beverly Hills' Rodeo Drive rolled into one.

Whether your passion is Tiffany diamonds, Chanel suits, or Gap jeans, you'll find it on this stretch of concrete. Window-shoppers, people-watchers, and others who prefer keeping their plastic pristine also will find plenty to amuse them.

### MICHIGAN AVENUE

For the ultimate shopping adventure, start at one end of North Michigan Avenue and try to work your way to the other. In this section are listed some of the best-known shops on the avenue and on nearby side streets. Unlike the following sections, which are organized alphabetically, here I've listed the stores as they come, beginning at the river and heading north. Note that each of Michigan Avenue's three vertical malls—each a major shopping destination in its own right—occupies its own section in this chapter.

**Hammacher Schlemmer**
445 N. Michigan Ave. (in the Tribune Tower). ☎ **312/527-9100.**

Be sure to stop at this favorite gadget shop—the choice when looking to buy a gift for "the person who has everything."

**Great Lakes Hot Tubs, Inc.**
15 W. Hubbard. ☎ **312/527-1311.**

Not for everyone, but a curiosity nonetheless, is Great Lakes Hot Tubs, where you can actually relax in a working hot tub in one of the store's separate rooms (by reservation) if you want to test-soak before buying.

**Avenue Five-Forty**
540 N. Michigan Ave. ☎ **312/321-9540.**

Artsy clothing and accessories.

**Timberland Company**
543 N. Michigan Ave. ☎ **312/494-0171.**

Outfitters for the great outdoors—urban, rural, whatever.

# The Magnificent Mile

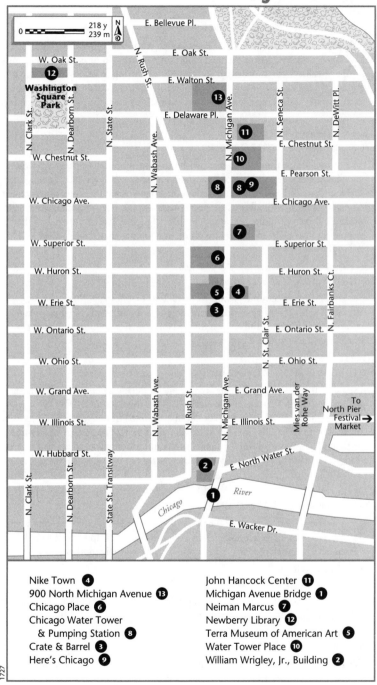

Nike Town ④
900 North Michigan Avenue ⑬
Chicago Place ⑥
Chicago Water Tower
& Pumping Station ⑧
Crate & Barrel ③
Here's Chicago ⑨

John Hancock Center ⑪
Michigan Avenue Bridge ①
Neiman Marcus ⑦
Newberry Library ⑫
Terra Museum of American Art ⑤
Water Tower Place ⑩
William Wrigley, Jr., Building ②

## Burberry's Limited
633 N. Michigan Ave. ☎ **312/787-2500.**

Where else would you go for the classic trench with that conservative chic plaid lining? Burberry's style hasn't changed much since creator Thomas Burberry furnished "impermeables" for the British quartermaster during World War I. But today Burberry's can also furnish your wardrobe with sports coats and other casual wear, such as cashmere sweaters for men and women or even flippy little skirts in the famous plaid.

## Crate & Barrel
646 N. Michigan Ave. ☎ **312/787-5900.**

Just try walking through this store without wanting to buy *something*. Countless varieties of glassware, dishes, cookware, and kitchen gadgets for everyday use line the shelves. Crate & Barrel is also a master at making you want to entertain—the light, airy store is filled with all sorts of special items—fondue sets, unusual vases, serving pieces, and even furniture. No wonder its bridal registry has become one of the most popular in town. The chain also has a store in the Loop at 101 N. Wabash ( ☎ 312/372-0100).

## Sony Gallery of Consumer Electronics
663 N. Michigan Ave. ☎ **312/943-3334.**

See the latest in electronic gizmos in this hands-on showcase that includes a video "shooting gallery" for live camcorder demos, a 10-foot diorama of Chicago complete with working El-train, and an area for portables to check out boom boxes, tape and disc players, telephones, etc.

## NIKETOWN
669 N. Michigan Ave. ☎ **312/642-6363.**

I've heard that NIKETOWN has become one of the most popular tourist attractions in Chicago. Well, Chicago is the ultimate sports town, and NIKETOWN is a virtual shrine to Michael Jordan (it also has memorabilia from a few other lesser superstars). The multilevel complex is a feast for the senses. The sounds of a tennis ball being hit back and forth fill the tennis pavilion, for example, and a putting green is ready for use in the golf department. You can try out your new sneaks right on the basketball court.

## The Gap
679 N. Michigan Ave. ☎ **312/335-1892.**

Does anybody not know what The Gap is? Does anybody not have one within a 15-mile radius of his or her home? This Gap also houses a Gap Kids and a Baby Gap. Chicago has a bunch of Gaps, at least one in every key neighborhood.

## Write Impressions
211 W. Huron. ☎ **312/943-3306.**

One of those magical stationery stores that stocks all the desktop goodies you could need, from the mundane to the whimsical.

## Tiffany & Company
715 N. Michigan Ave. ☎ **312/944-7500.**

What could be a better souvenir than a bauble in that famous Tiffany blue box tied just so with a white ribbon? For the finest jewels and tabletop accessories, head upstairs. For more affordable jewelry, including Elsa Peretti's "Diamonds by the Yard" and some sterling silver pieces for less than $100, stay downstairs.

## Manifesto
200 W. Superior. ☎ **312/664-0733.**

A serendipitous furniture store selling high-quality reproductions of architect-designed furniture by such superstars as Frank Lloyd Wright and Mies van der Rohe.

## Joan & David
717 N. Michigan Ave. ☎ **312/482-8585.**

Stylish shoes of fine leather for men and women.

## Neiman Marcus
737 N. Michigan Ave. ☎ **312/642-5900.**

My mouth waters at the thought of the Chanels, the Karl Lagerfelds, the Donna Karans, and the Calvin Kleins, all so skillfully merchandised on Neiman Marcus's selling floors. Yes, you'll pay top dollar for such designer names here—the store does, after all, need to live up to its Needless Mark-up moniker—but Neiman's has a broader price range than many of its critics care to admit. It also has some mighty good sales; among my many recent great finds here, I picked up a stunning long black velvet dress for less than $100. The four-story store, a beautiful environment in its own right, also sells cosmetics, shoes, furs, fine and fashion jewelry, and men's and children's wear. On the top floor is a fun gourmet food department as well as a pretty home accessories area, and Neiman's has two restaurants, one relaxed, the other a little more formal.

## Banana Republic
744 N. Michigan Ave. ☎ **312/664-5565.**

The clothes, for men and women, have that casually sophisticated flair. The store itself is quite attractive, with a two-way transparent staircase, wood floors, and leather sofas and chairs.

## Walgreens Drugstore
Michigan and Chicago Avenues. ☎ **312/664-8686.**

This full-line pharmacy is open 24 hours a day.

## F. A. O. Schwarz
840 N. Michigan Ave. ☎ **312/587-5000.**

The ultimate fantasy toy store. All the good stuff is interactive, and kids of all ages seem to find plenty to amuse themselves with—some Chicago parents even bring the tots here when the harsh weather does not permit a trip to the park.

## Plaza Escada
840 N. Michigan Ave. ☎ **312/915-0500.**

An elegant four-story building houses the country's most comprehensive collection of apparel and accessories from Escada, the German designer firm. The signature line is a favorite with women of a certain age, but the company recently signed hip New York designer Todd Oldham to spice it up a bit. The fourth-floor café offers a small but excellent lunch and dessert menu with a terrific view over Michigan Avenue.

## Williams-Sonoma
17 E. Chestnut. ☎ **312/642-1593.**

Just like the San Francisco original, the ultimate upscale kitchen store. Come here for the latest in gadgetry, both the snazzy and the utilitarian high-tech varieties, available today. Williams-Sonoma has a second location in Chicago Place, 700 North Michigan Ave. (☎ 312/787-8991).

## Material Possessions
54 E. Chestnut. ☎ **312/280-4885.**

Unusual items, from serving spoons to placemats, that will make your table setting stand out.

## Bulgari
909 N. Michigan Ave. ☎ **312/255-1313.**

The famed Italian jeweler's first Chicago store, opened in May 1996.

## Bally of Switzerland
919 N. Michigan Ave. ☎ **312/787-8110.**

A place for high-quality leather goods, including shoes, attaché cases, handbags, and accessories.

## Chanel
940 N. Michigan Ave. ☎ **312/787-5500.**

All those wonderful little French jackets—not to mention the shoes, handbags, and jewelry—with those perfect double-c insignias.

## Polo Ralph Lauren
960 N. Michigan Ave. ☎ **312/280-1655.**

The women's and men's apparel and home merchandise from the American designer who has appropriated the style of the English country gentleman and lady for his own.

## Water Tower Place

Chicago's first—and still busiest—vertical mall is Water Tower Place, a block-size building at 835 N. Michigan Ave., between East Pearson and East Chestnut Streets. The mall's eight floors contain some 130 separate stores, which reportedly account for roughly half of all the retail trade transacted along the Magnificent Mile. The construction in the last several years of two more vertical malls on the avenue has not seemed to affect the traffic flow at Water Tower; leases here are still among the most coveted retail real estate in the country.

Most of the shops at Water Tower Place fall roughly into the following categories: apparel (men's and women's, some two-score shops in all), beauty services, cards and flowers, specialty foods, home furnishings, jewelry, leather goods, paintings and graphics, shoes, sporting goods, toys and games, and, of course, dining in one of a dozen different cafés and restaurants. For entertainment, Water Tower houses seven cinemas.

## Accent Chicago, Inc.
Water Tower Place. ☎ **312/944-1354.**

Great Chicago souvenirs from wrapping paper to photos, and other tasteful gifts.

## The Disney Store
Water Tower Place. ☎ **312/280-1199.**

It's like Disney World without the rides.

## Georgette Klinger
Water Tower Place. ☎ **312/787-4300.**

If you're looking for a day of pampering, try a deep-cleaning facial, a tension-relieving massage, or a soothing scalp treatment at this salon—and maybe top it off with a manicure or a pedicure.

### Gymboree
Water Tower Place. ☎ **312/649-9074.**

Adorable, cuddly clothes in charming prints for babies and toddlers.

### Lord & Taylor
Water Tower Place. ☎ **312/787-7400.**

Lord & Taylor, one of two large department stores in Water Tower (see Marshall Field's, below), carries about what you'd expect: women's, men's, and children's clothing, cosmetics, and accessories. Its star department is most definitely shoes; the selection is fairly broad, and something's usually on sale.

### Marshall Field's
Water Tower Place. ☎ **312/335-7700.**

Although it's now owned by a Minneapolis company, Marshall Field's is still the hometown store in the minds of most Chicagoans. The Water Tower store—the mall's primary anchor—is a scaled-down but respectable version of the State Street flagship (discussed in detail below). Its eight floors are actually much more manageable than the enormous flagship, and its merchandise selection is still vast. Although it tends to focus on the more expensive brands, shoppers at this location still can find outfits for less than $100 or more than $2,000. One classic Chicago item that fits most any budget is Field's Frango Mints, a succulent chocolate candy that comes in a rainbow of flavors. I recommend the original in the green box.

### Rizzoli International Bookstore
Water Tower Place. ☎ **312/642-3500.**

A beautiful bookstore with loads of those chi-chi coffee-table books and a large selection of international magazines and music.

### Speedo Authentic Fitness
Water Tower Place. ☎ **312/944-9910.**

Workout fiends will enjoy the athletic clothes at this store.

### Warner Bros. Studio Store
Water Tower Place. ☎ **312/664-9440.**

Bugs Bunny, the Tazmanian Devil, and friends on all manner of merchandise.

## Chicago Place

Inaugurated in 1991 at 700 N. Michigan Ave., Chicago Place is the city's newest—and least compelling—vertical shopping mall. Other than Saks Fifth Avenue and Ann Taylor, I haven't found much here to write about—or to bring me back. On the eighth floor, though, is a pretty atrium, complete with fountain, skylight, and greenery. If you don't care for the fast-food counters that surround it, you might try buying a sandwich at Bockwinkel's (☎ 312/482-9900), a grocery located in the mall's basement, and bringing it up.

### Ann Taylor
700 N. Michigan Ave. ☎ **312/335-0117.**

A multilevel women's apparel store that's a favorite of professional women. The casual weekend clothes are also fun, and Ann Taylor usually has a good selection of tasteful little dresses.

### Body Shop
700 N. Michigan Ave. ☎ **312/482-8301.**

The cosmetics, bath, and body store with an environmentally friendly credo. It's virtually impossible to walk in here and not find something tempting to try—whether it's a watermelon shower gel or a peppermint foot soother.

### Hello Chicago
700 N. Michigan Ave. ☎ **312/787-0838.**

A souvenir shop for Chicago-related paraphernalia, such as Bulls T-shirts and other Michael Jordan merchandise.

### Petite Sophisticate
700 N. Michigan Ave. ☎ **312/787-4923.**

A store specializing in clothing for shorter women, generally under 5'4".

### Room and Board
700 N. Michigan Ave. ☎ **312/266-0656.**

Two floors of contemporary furniture and accessories for comfortable, but chic, urban living.

### Saks Fifth Avenue
700 N. Michigan Ave. ☎ **312/944-6500.**

Saks Fifth Avenue may be best known for its designer collections—Valentino, Chloe, and Giorgio Armani, to name a few—but the store also does a swell job of buying more casual and less expensive merchandise. Check out, for example, Saks' own "Real Clothes" or "The Works" women's lines. Plus the store has a very good large-size women's apparel department, as well as jewelry, accessories, and men's and children's clothes. I recommend a visit to the cosmetics department, where Saks is known in particular for its varied selection of fragrances. Saks offers one-on-one personal shopping consultants and interpreters, and the store can also boast a reputable beauty salon.

## 900 North Michigan Avenue

The most upscale of the Magnificent Mile's three vertical malls, 900 North Michigan avoids the tumult of Water Tower Place while still generating a vitality essential to a satisfying shopping spree. In addition to about 85 stores are a few good restaurants and a nice movie theater.

### Bloomingdale's
900 N. Michigan Ave. ☎ **312/440-4460.**

The first Midwestern branch of the famed New York department store, Bloomingdale's is on a par in terms of size and selection with Marshall Field's Water Tower store. The hoopla that surrounded the 1988 store opening has subsided, but Bloomingdale's still has a certain cachet. Among its special sections is the one for its souveniresque Bloomingdale's logo merchandise.

### Cashmere Cashmere
900 N. Michigan Ave. ☎ **312/337-6558.**

Cashmere, cashmere, and more cashmere.

### The Coach Store
900 N. Michigan Ave. ☎ **312/440-1777.**

All that soft, nice leather in handbags, briefcases, wallets, gloves, you name it.

### Episode
900 N. Michigan Ave. ☎ **312/266-9760.**

A store catering to professional women who prefer to dress with a little flair.

### Fogal
900 N. Michigan Ave. ☎ **312/944-7866.**

High-priced legwear and bodysuits for the well-heeled.

### Galt Toys
900 N. Michigan Ave. ☎ **312/440-9550.**

Okay, F. A. O. Schwarz is just down the street, but Galt Toys carries a more rarefied selection of children's playthings.

### Gucci
900 N. Michigan Ave. ☎ **312/664-5504.**

The Italian leather goods company has had a resurgence of late, as the legendary Gucci loafer has found a new generation of fans. Thanks to designer Tom Ford, the clothing is about the hippest around, favored by celebrities from Madonna to Alicia Silverstone.

### Henri Bendel
900 N. Michigan Ave. ☎ **312/642-0140.**

Designed to feel like a Parisian mansion, this New York–imported specialty store bills itself as a "lady's paradise." If she likes clothes, chances are she'll agree. Bendel's carries trendy designers, such as Todd Oldham and Cynthia Rowley, but the store also has a strong private label program, offering, for example, knit tops in more colors than Benjamin Moore. Bendel's has helped muster demand for the trendy new makeup artist cosmetics lines, stocking MAC, Bobbie Brown, Trish McEvoy, and others. Two tips for the uninitiated: go a little late in the season to revel in the sales, and the pronunciation is downright American (Henry BEN-dle).

### H20 Plus
900 N. Michigan Ave. ☎ **312/440-0171.**

A Chicago-based chain stocked full of colorful, yummy-smelling gels and lotions for the bath, body, and face.

### J. Crew
900 N. Michigan Ave. ☎ **312/751-2739.**

Women's and men's clothes with an easy way about them.

### Museum Shop of the Art Institute of Chicago
900 N. Michigan Ave. ☎ **312/482-8275.**

One of several shops the Art Institute has opened throughout the city. Although smaller than the museum's own store, this branch has a good selection of prints, books, postcards, and the like.

### Niedermaier 900
900 N. Michigan Ave. ☎ **312/266-7077.**

A home store with a distinct Gold Coast glitz.

## OTHER SHOPPING AREAS
### Oak Street

At the northern tip of the Magnificent Mile, where Michigan Avenue ends and Lake Shore Drive begins, is Oak Street, a posh one-block stretch of exclusive shops. Most of the city's designer boutiques are along this row, and for that reason some shoppers find the street a tad snobbish. But not every store charges a fortune for its goods. Most of Oak Street is closed on Sunday, except during the holiday season.

## Alaska Shop
104 E. Oak St. ☎ **312/943-3393.**

Somewhat offbeat, given its company, is the Alaska Shop, a showcase for Alaskan, Canadian, and Siberian Inuit arts and crafts.

## Barneys New York
25 E. Oak St. ☎ **312/587-1700.**

The store may be mired in a bankruptcy battle, but the clothes are still chic in that black, understated way. The shoes are also excellent, and the home accessories, interesting.

## Gianni Versace
101 E. Oak St. ☎ **312/337-1111.**

The Italian designer's Chicago boutique offers finely tailored—and severely sexy—clothes for both sexes.

## Giorgio Armani
113 E. Oak St. ☎ **312/427-6264.**

The Italian designer's sometimes somber, always elegant, fashions for men and women.

## Hermès of Paris
110 E. Oak St. ☎ **312/787-8175.**

The company that began in Paris as a saddle maker is still tops when it comes to leather. Today Hermès ties are favorites of the well-dressed men I know, and the women's scarves are simply heavenly.

## Hino & Malee Boutique
50 E. Oak St. ☎ **312/664-7475.**

Women's clothes that are almost architectural in perspective, with no adornment or fuss, from a Chicago-based design team.

## Jil Sander, Chicago
48 E. Oak St. ☎ **312/335-0006.**

The German designer of women's high-fashion ready-to-wear accessories and fragrances in the first freestanding Jil Sander store in the world. Both the stores and the clothes are sleek and minimalist.

## Marilyn Miglin
112 E. Oak St. ☎ **312/943-1120.**

Chicago's own makeup and skin-care expert.

## Nicole Miller
61 E. Oak St. ☎ **312/664-3532.**

Women's clothes and men's ties in those wacky pop-art prints, plus scores of great little dresses.

## A Pea in the Pod
46 E. Oak St. ☎ **312/944-3080.**

Maternity clothes that won't make you feel silly when you're pregnant.

## Pratesi Linens Co.
67 E. Oak St. ☎ **312/943-8422.**

Now we're talking luxury. Bed, bath, and table linens priced for more than most people pay in rent.

### Sugar Magnolia
34 E. Oak St. ☎ **312/944-0885.**

One of the more affordable shops on the street, full of fun, youthful fashions.

### Sulka
55 E. Oak St. ☎ **312/951-9500.**

A very exclusive men's clothing and furnishings store.

### Ultimo
114 E. Oak St. ☎ **312/787-0906.**

Without a doubt, the top designer shop in Chicago, Ultimo carries such labels as Isaac Mizrahi and John Galliano. One drawback, though, is Ultimo's atmosphere, not exactly conducive to browsing.

## RIVER NORTH

Along with becoming Chicago's primary art gallery district, River North—the area west of the Magnificent Mile and north of the Chicago River—has attracted many interesting shops, concentrated on Wells Street from Kinzie Street to Chicago Avenue. The neighborhood even has a mall of its own—The Shops at the Mart— in the Merchandise Mart, anchored by Carson Pirie Scott & Co. It has the usual suspects—The Gap, The Limited, and a food court among them.

### Elements
738 N. Wells St. ☎ **312/642-6574.**

A colorful store of decorative pieces and jewelry made by artists.

### Mig & Tig
549 N. Wells St. ☎ **312/644-8277.**

Charming furniture and decorative accessories in River North.

### Table of Contents
448 N. Wells St. ☎ **312/644-9004.**

In the shadow of the Merchandise Mart, Table of Contents carries both everyday and special-occasion table settings and services, generally more stylized than, say, Crate & Barrel.

### Tuscany Studios
601 N. Wells St. ☎ **312/664-7680.**

If you're into gardening, Tuscany is a fun place to browse for statuary or birdbaths.

## NORTH PIER

North Pier, located at 435 E. Illinois St., attempts to transcend the genre of shopping mall to become a shopping-entertainment center. Below is a select listing of North Pier's many unusual shops.

### City of Chicago Store
North Pier. ☎ **312/467-1111.**

It's a wonder that no one thought of it sooner. A store that recycles "real" street signs, manhole-cover coffee tables, parking meters, pieces of the old Chicago Stadium, even voting machines—all retired from active city service—and sells them to the public. It's all here at the City of Chicago Store, created under the umbrella of the city's Department of Cultural Affairs, with proceeds to benefit cultural and promotional programs. But that's not all you'll find here. The store also stocks a full inventory of T-shirts from every museum in Chicago, plus craft items, jewelry, calendars, and more.

**The Kite Harbor**
North Pier. ☎ **312/321-5483.**

If you want to take advantage of that wind off the lake, stop in here first and pick up a colorful kite, either standard kid-size or one of those spectacular jumbo things. The shop stocks all sorts of flying objects, from boomerangs to whirligigs.

**Light Wave Galleries**
North Pier. ☎ **312/321-1123.**

A gallery specializing in holographic art created with lasers. Portraits and custom holograms are available.

**Turin Bikes**
North Pier. ☎ **312/923-0100.**

A professional bike shop for rentals and repairs, as well as top-of-the-line mountain bikes and accessories for sale.

**Virtual World**
North Pier. ☎ **312/836-5977.**

Formerly Battletech Center, Virtual World is the ultimate video arcade. Using the same kind of simulator technology as NASA, Virtual World engages you in a 24-minute action-packed, lifelike high-tech battle. The cost is $6 to $8, depending on the day. Open daily from 11am until as late as 1am on Saturday.

## STATE STREET

Before the Magnificent Mile grew into Chicago's first boulevard of fashion, State Street, "That Great Street," was the center of retailing in Chicago for more than 100 years, ever since Potter Palmer's decision to develop the street and to establish his dry goods business there in 1852. Palmer's original emporium evolved over time into Marshall Field's.

Field's and Carson Pirie Scott, the other Chicago hometown department store, which set up shop just a couple of blocks south, became rivals, building State Street into a prime shopping district in the process. Both buildings are city landmarks and attractions in themselves. The Louis Sullivan–designed Carson's is the more celebrated of the two; Field's, with its Tiffany-domed and skylit courts, is eminently worth touring.

By the early '70s the Magnificent Mile had begun to supplant State Street. The Loop disintegrated as North Michigan Avenue flowered. Many of the Loop's old department stores—Sears, Roebuck & Co., Montgomery Ward, Goldblatts, Wieboldt—closed their doors in favor of greener pastures in the suburbs. Marshall Field's and Carson Pirie Scott managed to hang on, keeping State Street alive— if barely—until the city took notice in the '80s and began to revive it.

In a controversial move, the city turned State Street into a modified pedestrian mall by closing the street to all traffic but CTA buses on the stretch between Wacker Drive and the Congress Expressway. In recent years, State Street has seen an influx of stores, particularly in the moderate price range, such as Filene's Basement, and in 1996 the city was busy converting it back into a regular street open to cars and cabs as well. Although State Street has not recaptured the glamor of decades past, it has managed to draw loyal customers from the Loop's office towers and from Chicagoans turned off by Michigan Avenue's snob factor. And the residential development taking place in nearby Printer's Row and Burnham Park—where Mayor Richard M. Daley moved—bodes well for the district. (*A reminder:* If the quick change from north to south confuses you here, keep in mind that in Chicago, point zero for the purposes of address numbering is the intersection of State and Madison.)

### Carson Pirie Scott & Company
1 S. State St. ☎ **312/641-7000.**

Carson's still appeals primarily to working- and middle-class shoppers. But this venerable Chicago institution that was almost wiped out by the Chicago Fire has made a recent bid to capture the corporate, if not the carriage, trade. Carson's has added a number of more upscale apparel lines, plus a trendy housewares department, to appeal to the moneyed crowd that works in the Loop. The store also has a team of interpreters who can communicate with practically anyone in any language.

### Marshall Field's
111 N. State St. ☎ **312/781-1000.**

Spread over 73 acres of floor space, with 450 departments, Marshall Field's flagship is second in size only to Macy's in New York City. Within this overwhelming space, shoppers will find areas unusual for today's homogeneous department stores, such as the Victorian antique jewelry department, an antiquarian bookshop, and a gallery of antique furniture. Store craftspeople are still on hand to fix antique clocks, repair jewelry, and restore old paintings. A basement marketplace offers gourmet goodies, including Field's renowned Frango mints.

Field's breadth is what makes the store impressive; shoppers can find a rainbow of turtlenecks for $12 or $15 each a floor or so away from the 28 Shop, Field's homage to designer fashion, from the exquisite luxury of Yves Saint Laurent to the masterful artistry of Issey Miyake.

If you're in Chicago between Thanksgiving and New Year's, a visit to Field's to see the holiday windows and to have lunch under the Great Tree in the Walnut Room is in keeping with local tradition. To aid foreign or non-English-speaking customers, interpreters are on hand who are conversant in more than 20 languages.

## ELSEWHERE IN THE LOOP

In recent years, retailing in the Loop has spread out some, with shops finding homes on LaSalle Street, Chicago's main financial thoroughfare, and on a number of side streets. They tend to cater to businessmen, but some smart retailers are discovering a steady clientele of businesswomen as well.

### Brooks Brothers
209 S. LaSalle St. ☎ **312/263-0100.**

Businessmen of a certain set would probably go naked were it not for the existence of Brooks Brothers, where conservative never goes out of style.

### Charrett Enterprises
23 S. Wabash Ave. ☎ **312/782-5737.**

A very popular art-supply house. Custom framing is also available.

### B. Collins Ltd.
318 S. Dearborn. ☎ **312/431-1888.**

Whether you love to write or you love the status of owning a fine writing instrument, you'll find a visit here, located in the Monadnock Building, in order. The store specializes in old-fashioned fountain pens and is purportedly the only "full-service" pen (and pencil) store in Chicago. It also carries stationery.

**Lane Bryant**
9 N. Wabash Ave. ☎ **312/621-8700.**

Moderately priced, large-size apparel for women.

**Mother's Work**
50 E. Washington, on the second floor. ☎ **312/332-0022.**

A maternity store that understands that some pregnant women work.

**Riddle-McIntyre, Inc.**
175 N. Franklin St. ☎ **312/782-3317.**

Every man should walk around at one time or another in a custom-made shirt, the only product sold by Riddle-McIntyre—but you must order a minimum of three shirts at a clip.

## HYDE PARK

Commercial Hyde Park is centered on 53rd Street close to the lakefront, although the other numbered streets also house shops and restaurants. Considering its status as home of the University of Chicago, it's no wonder that Hyde Park is chockful of well-stocked bookstores.

**Harper Court,** on Harper Avenue between 52nd and 53rd Streets, today is an arts-oriented mall with about 20 shops and two restaurants. At one time it housed artists, displaced when the ramshackle wood houses in which they were living (built originally as souvenir and popcorn stands for the Columbian Exposition) were torn down. Although Hyde Park's artist colony once harbored such luminaries as Carl Sandburg, Theodore Dreiser, Sherwood Anderson, Vachel Lindsay, and Edgar Lee Masters, today only a single artist-in-residence remains. But the Harper Court Foundation is expanding its cultural programs, and the old art colony is saluted each year at the popular 57th Street Art Fair (☎ 773/667-0508), a weekend outdoor art show scheduled in early June.

### Harper Court Sampler

**Dr. Wax Records**
Harper Court. ☎ **773/493-8696.**

New and used LPs, tapes, and CDs, with a first-rate selection of jazz and classical music.

**Windows to Africa**
5210 S. Harper. ☎ **773/955-7742.**

An eye-catching shop of masks, fabrics, wood carvings, baskets, drums, and other artifacts imported from Africa. The store also carries a line of contemporary urban wear and hosts occasional fashion shows featuring African designs and fabrics.

### Hyde Park Bookstores

**57th Street Books**
1301 E. 57th St. ☎ **773/684-1300.**

The largest used bookstore in Chicago, known especially for its children's books. The shop also has a small working fireplace, and it sells coffee, two amenities of particular importance to the professional book browser.

**O'Gara & Wilson, Ltd.**
1448 E. 57th St. ☎ **773/363-0993.**

O'Gara and Wilson, a rumpled storefront of a bookseller that might easily have migrated from a back street in London or Cardiff, has good used books and old titles by the hopperful.

As you might expect, Chicago has shops selling just about anything you could want or need, be it functional or ornamental, whimsical or exotic. The following list only scratches the surface, but it will give you an idea of the range of merchandise available. Of course, many of the categories, such as apparel and toys, have been covered in depth earlier in the chapter.

## ANTIQUES

The greatest concentration of antiques shops can be found west of Sheffield Avenue on Belmont, or along intersecting Halsted Street. In addition to the stores detailed below, you might try Chicago Antique Mall, 3050 N. Lincoln Ave. (☎ 312/929-0200), with more than 50 dealers under a single roof; and Jay Roberts Antique Warehouse, 149 W. Kinzie St. (☎ 312/222-0167).

### Chicago Riverfront Antique Market
2929 N. Western. ☎ **773/477-6700.**

Formerly the Antique Palace, the market boasts the neighborhood's most voluminous display of old furnishings and artifacts spread over 55,000 square feet of floor space on two levels.

### Penn-Dutchman Antiques
4912 N. Western. ☎ **773/271-2208.**

Only the name is German, but collectors of odd bric-a-brac and similar curios, such as old photos, will find the pickings interesting.

### Victorian House Antiques
806 W. Belmont. ☎ **773/472-0400.**

The old manse is a bona-fide Victorian-era sampler in every detail, from its ornate bay window and trim boards to the rickety wrought-iron fence and gate that make the place look like a set from "The Addams Family." The stuff inside is interesting to look at, too.

## ARTS & CRAFTS

I recommend a stroll around River North; just wander in and out of the horde of galleries. The Bucktown/Wicker Park neighborhood, the heart of which is at the intersection of Milwaukee, North, and Damen Avenues, has become something of an artists' colony. Below, though, I have tried to list some alternative galleries not in those two areas.

### Fabrile Gallery
224 S. Michigan Ave. ☎ **312/341-9431.**

This gallery specializes in modern glass and carries works from many major artists and studios. It also has a collection of designer jewelry.

### Fly-by-Nite Gallery
714 N. Wells St. ☎ **312/664-8136.**

A treasure house for art-deco and art-nouveau objets d'art from ceramics to jewelry.

### Okee Chee's Wild Horse Gallery
5337 N. Clark St. ☎ **773/271-5883.**

Illustrative of the Native American presence that has reappeared on the Far North Side of Chicago in recent years are a number of shops that showcase the work of Native American artists and craftspeople. Such is Okee Chee's Wild Horse Gallery, which features local artists, with an emphasis on art on fungus, skins, skulls, rocks, and canvas. The shop also has crafts such as dream catchers, jewelry, and beadwork. Open Tuesday through Friday from noon to 7pm, and Saturday from 10am to 6pm.

### Paint It! Art That Werks, Inc.

1422 Webster (at the corner of Clybourn). ☎ 773/905-5732. Open Saturday from noon to 5pm or by appointment.

Part showroom, part studio, this shop specializes in objects that have been marbleized or otherwise decoratively painted. Most of the shop's work is done off-site in the form of murals, custom decorating, and hand-painted wall coverings. But the shop sells samples of work produced in the attached studio, where weekly classes are given. By the way, "Werks" is how they spell it.

### Palette & Chisel Academy of Fine Arts

1012 N. Dearborn Pkwy. ☎ 312/642-4400. Call for hours.

The Palate & Chisel is a nonprofit cooperative of painters and sculptors, who, beginning in 1921, pooled their funds to purchase this ca. 1870s mansion, one of the first buildings erected after the Chicago Fire. About 240 professional artists now use the facilities to paint and to sculpt—and to exhibit work in their own galleries and private studio areas.

### Steve Starr Studios

2779 N. Lincoln Ave. ☎ 773/525-6530.

Some of the city's finest art-deco items. More than 700 art-deco photo frames line the walls.

### Tobai

320 N. Dearborn Ave., in the Nikko Hotel. ☎ 312/661-0394.

Contains an extensive collection of Japanese prints and also features classic Korean temple paintings and works by contemporary Chinese artists.

### To Life!

224 S. Michigan Ave. ☎ 312/362-0255.

A gallery of fine crafts, including marionettes and puppets, music boxes, handmade jewelry, ceramic sculptures, wood puzzles, toys, and games. Another branch is at 333 N. Michigan Ave. (☎ 312/541-1951).

## BOOKS

Although the nationwide mega-chains, such as Borders and B. Dalton's, have a strong presence in Chicago, they have yet to wipe out the entrepreneurial bookstores, the owners of which seem to think of them like gardens in need of careful tending.

### Aspidistra Bookshop

2630 N. Clark St. ☎ 773/549-3129.

One of the city's best used bookstores, stocking 20th-century literature.

### Barbara's Bookstore

1350 N. Wells St. ☎ 312/642-5044.

A haven for small, independent press titles, as well as extensive selections of everything current. In addition, it has a well-stocked children's section, with sitting areas for the tots to peruse the books. If you enjoy author readings, call the store to see if your visit coincides with one of your favorite writers. The other two branches are at 3130 N. Broadway (☎ 773/477-0411) and in Oak Park at 1100 Lake St. (☎ 708/848-9140).

### Bookseller's Row
2445 N. Lincoln Ave. ☎ **773/348-1170.**

Stocks some 40,000 used and rare books.

### The Children's Bookstore
2465 N. Lincoln Ave. ☎ **773/248-2665.**

Chicago's largest children's bookstore, with storytelling hours several days a week and free parking in the rear of the store.

### Earful of Books
565 W. Diversey Pkwy.☎ **773/388-3611.**

Stop in here to pick up some books on tape for your long drive back home.

### Grand Tour
3229 N. Clark St. ☎ **312/929-1836.**

Probably the city's best source for foreign-language and travel books.

### Illinois Labor History Society Bookstore
28 E. Jackson Blvd. ☎ **312/663-4107.**

Rare and half-forgotten titles on labor history.

### N. Fagin Books
1039 W. Grand Ave. ☎ **312/829-5252.**

Nirvana for the person who yearns for natural-science books—from dinosaurs to primitive art and anthropology, and from botany to zoology.

### Powell's Book Warehouse
828 S. Wabash Ave., 4th floor. ☎ **312/341-0748.**

Used textbooks, dog-eared paperbacks, hardcover classics, and former best-sellers fill the shelves.

### Rand McNally Map and Travel Store
444 N. Michigan Ave. ☎ **312/321-1751.**

Map lovers will be satiated. The store also stocks, among its 15,000-item inventory, travel guides, videotapes, globes, and travel-related gift items from around the world.

### Sandmeyer's Bookstore
714 S. Dearborn. ☎ **312/922-2104.**

A historic Printer's Row shop stocked with fine literature, children's books, and travel literature.

### Seminary Co-op Bookstore
5757 S. University Ave. ☎ **773/752-4381.**

A classic campus bookstore located near the University of Chicago, this shop has extensive philosophy and theology sections and is one of the premier academic bookstores in the country.

### The Stars Our Destination
1021 W. Belmont. ☎ **773/871-2722.**

Calling all sci-fi fanatics in search of new or used books.

### Unabridged Books
3251 N. Broadway. ☎ **773/883-9119.**

Unabridged has strong sections in travel, film, sci-fi, and gay and lesbian literature. Yellow signs throughout the store indicate staff favorites.

### Women and Children First

5233 N. Clark St. ☎ **773/769-9299.**

Women and Children First holds the best selection in the city of titles for, by, and about women. Co-owner Linda Bubon holds a children's storybook hour every Wednesday at 10:30am. The store also hosts frequent readings by the likes of Gloria Steinem, Amy Tan, Alice Walker, and others.

## BUTTONS

### Tender Buttons

946 N. Rush St. ☎ **312/337-7033.**

Never given much thought to buttons? After looking at some of the thousands of buttons this shop has to offer, you'll look at the functional objects in a whole new way.

## CERAMICS

### Lill Street Gallery

1021 W. Lill St. (in Lincoln Park). ☎ **773/477-6185.**

Located just three blocks north of Fullerton, at Sheffield, is the Midwest's largest ceramics center, housing private and group studios, a gallery, a retail store, and six classrooms. Among the wares for sale is a large selection of high-quality, handcrafted artwork for home or office.

## CLOCKS

### Water Tower Clock Shop

Water Tower Place. ☎ **312/482-9922.**

Collectors will enjoy the variety, which spans the traditional, the modern, and the kitschy and the grandfather, the wall, and the wrist.

## FASHIONS

The stores listed in this section are only a sampling of those not mentioned above in the main shopping districts.

### CHILDREN'S

Besides such well-known chains as Benetton and Gap Kids, Chicago is well supplied with shops offering children's wear.

### All Our Children

2217 N. Halsted St. ☎ **773/327-1868.**

All Our Children is a small and friendly boutique carrying darling clothes from newborn sizes to 6X–7.

### The Second Child

954 W. Armitage Ave. ☎ **773/883-0880.**

A resale boutique offering quality clothing for a fraction of the price. The store also carries maternity clothes, furniture, equipment, and toys.

### MEN'S

### Bigsby & Kruthers

744 N. Michigan Ave. ☎ **312/664-5565.**

The unquestioned leader in men's apparel for years, with five locations in Chicago. One branch is in Water Tower Place (☎ 312/944-6955).

**M. Hyman & Son**

100 E. Walton St. ☎ **312/266-0060** or toll free 800/735-5009.

Clothing for big and tall men. In addition to this store off the Magnificent Mile, M. Hyman has five branches in the suburbs.

## WOMEN'S

**Cynthia Rowley**

808 W. Armitage. ☎ **773/528-6160.**

The Chicago native and new star of the New York fashion world has a boutique filled with her cute little dresses and other designs.

**Fitigues**

2130 N. Halsted. ☎ **773/404-9696.**

Cute, comfortable clothes in waffle-knit cotton favored by Lincoln Park's young mothers. The store also carries denim and some men's and children's things.

**Victoria's Secret**

835 N. Michigan Ave. (Water Tower Place). ☎ **312/440-1169.**

Loads of lingerie.

## UNISEX

**Eddie Bauer**

123 N. Wabash Ave. ☎ **312/263-6005.**

Reasonably priced clothing with an outdoorsy feel.

**Jennings, Inc.**

1971 N. Halsted. ☎ **773/587-7866.**

Looking a little like a neighborhood pub and serving complimentary cappuccino and espresso, Jennings bills itself as an accessories "bar," selling belts, bags, jewelry, some clothing and vintage cowboy boots.

# FOOD
## BAKERIES

**Cheesecakes by J. R.**

2841 W. Howard St. ☎ **773/465-6733.**

Twenty varieties of cheesecake, all baked on the premises, and an exclusive line of specialty cakes.

**Dinkel's Bakery**

3329 N. Lincoln Ave. ☎ **773/281-7300.**

Dinkel's, celebrating its 75th anniversary in 1997, specializes in authentic old-world German treats. Decorated cakes are available for all occasions. Gourmet sandwiches and coffee are served daily.

**Let Them Eat Cake**

60 E. Chicago Ave. ☎ **708/863-4200.**

A Chicago chain that bakes all sorts of delectables, from fresh-fruit tarts to banana-walnut fudge cakes to traditional and contemporary wedding cakes.

**The Swedish Bakery**

5348 N. Clark St. ☎ **773/561-8919.**

For nearly 60 years, this bakery has set the standard in European and Swedish-style baked goods, specializing in marzipan and fruit-glazed cakes.

# MARKETS

When you're shopping in Chinatown, try the Chinese Trading Company, 2263 S. Wentworth (☎ 773/842-2820), and Sun Chong Lung, 2220 S. Wentworth (☎ 773/225-6050).

## Chicago Fish House
1250 W. Division St. ☎ **773/227-7000.**

An excellent seafood market with fresh fish flown in daily from Alaska, Hawaii, Florida, the Great Lakes, the Gulf of Mexico, even New Zealand.

## Gepperth's Meat Market
1970 N. Halsted St. ☎ **773/549-3883.**

Gepperth's has one of the best reputations in town for meats, and it also sells cheeses.

## L'Appetito
30 E. Huron St. ☎ **312/787-9881.**

You'll find everything Italian here, including the 10-inch subs that are a favorite of the lunch crowd. There's even an outdoor patio.

## Oriental Food Market & Cooking School
2801 W. Howard St. ☎ **773/274-2826.**

Cooking staples from the Philippines, Japan, Thailand, and China—as well as the freshest of vegetables. Call for a schedule of weekly cooking classes.

# FURNITURE

One of the best-known buildings in Chicago is the Merchandise Mart, but its floors of wholesale furniture showrooms are open only to holders of Mart passes—which can be obtained by architects, interior designers, and others in the trade—and their clients. If you can't count yourself among that group, you might want to try some of Chicago's retail furniture stores.

## Cradles of Distinction
1445 W. Webster. ☎ **773/472-1001.**

As the name suggests, darling cradles, cribs, and other baby furniture are here, some of it handpainted. The Lincoln Park shop also carries some clothing and other items for the tikes.

## Henry A. W. Mundt
4143 N. Lincoln Ave. ☎ **773/935-5115.**

Worth a peek for the old-world artisanship of the furniture.

# GALLERIES

## Landmark
5301 N. Clark St. ☎ **773/728-5301.**

A gallery of shops on three floors, all individually owned businesses with a broad range of products—lamps, weavings, quilts, paper supplies, toys, handcrafts, and women's clothes—and services, from cross-stitch classes to photo restoration.

# GIFTS

## Findables
907 W. Armitage. ☎ **773/348-0674.**

A good place to scout for unusual Christmas ornaments and other doodads.

## Fly Paper
3402 N. Southport. ☎ **773/296-4359.**

One of several cute shops to have opened in the last few years on this stretch of Southport, in the Wrigleyville neighborhood. Fly Paper is known for its candles—aromatherapy, and just plain pretty—but also carries other treats.

# RECORDS

### Jazz Record Mart
444 N. Wabash. ☎ **312/222-1467.**

You can uncover some super finds in recycled jazz records (also big band, bebop, Latin, and so on) at the Jazz Record Mart, which also stocks a full jazz and blues line of new CDs.

# SALONS

### Charles Ifergan
106 E. Oak St. ☎ **312/642-4484.** Closed Sun and Mon.

One of Chicago's top hair salons. Rates, which vary according to the seniority of the stylist, are relatively pricey. But if you're a little daring, you can get a cut for the price of the tip. On certain evenings (call the salon for a schedule) junior stylists do their thing gratis—under the watchful eye of Monsieur Ifergan.

### Urban Oasis
12 W. Maple St. ☎ **312/587-3500.** Closed Mon; call for exact scheduling.

After a long day of sightseeing, try a soothing massage in a subdued, Zen-like atmosphere. The ritual begins with a steam or rain shower in a private changing room, followed by the spa treatment you elect—various forms of massage, mud or herbal body wrap, aromatherapy, and so forth. Fruit, juices, or herbal teas are offered on completion. A one-hour massage is $65; an herbal wrap is $40.

# TOYS

### Saturday's Child
2146 N. Halsted St. ☎ **773/525-8697.**

The clever toys range from rubber snakes and frogs to sidewalk chalk, from kids' large-faced wristwatches to books.

# TRAVEL OUTFITTERS

### Ed and Fred: A Traveler's Store
1007 Webster (near corner of Sheffield). ☎ **773/477-6220.**

Little and big things to smooth the traveler's journey, such as electric-current converters and transformers, water purifiers, maps, backpacks, and first-aid kits, plus a full line of guides and travel literature. Ed and Fred's other favorite hobbies revolve around the great outdoors, so they also stock books on hiking, biking, and such.

### Savvy Traveller
310 S. Michigan Ave. ☎ **312/913-9800.**

Smart travelers can buy their Frommer's guides from Savvy's. The Loop store, in fact, carries just about everything a traveler might need, from rain gear to duffle bags.

# WINE & LIQUOR

## Sam's Wine & Liquors
1000 W. North Ave. ☎ **312/664-4394.**

> A reader writes, "This is the most extensively stocked wine and spirits merchant I've encountered; a gold mine for anyone interested in the finer appellation."

# 10

# Chicago After Dark

Hearing the world-class Chicago Symphony Orchestra, attending a performance of the critically acclaimed Lyric Opera of Chicago, and seeing the Tony Award–winning Steppenwolf and Goodman theater companies are a few of the best—but by no means the only—ways to spend your evenings in the city.

Chicago's vibrant and innovative off-Loop theaters are dispersed throughout a wide range of neighborhoods. Chicago also has a thriving music scene, with clubs devoted to everything from jazz and blues to alternative rock, country, and Latin beats. Music haunts are scattered throughout the city, but many are concentrated in several distinct quarters: Rush Street, Old Town, Lincoln Park, and New Town. Many of the larger hotels provide on their premises some form of nighttime entertainment—sometimes just a cozy piano bar, but in a few cases, full-blown nightclub acts. And if you're just looking to hang out, you only have to pick a neighborhood and wander. You won't have to go far to find a tavern filled with locals, and maybe a pool table or a dart board or two.

For up-to-date entertainment listings, check the local newspapers and magazines, particularly the "Weekend" and "What's Happening" sections of the two dailies, the *Chicago Tribune* and the *Chicago Sun-Times; The Reader* and *New City,* both free weekly tabloids; and the monthly *Chicago* magazine. **Hot Tix Hotline** (☎ 312/977-1755) offers a recorded message listing all performances for the evening on which you call, and on Friday the message lists the weekend theater schedule for the entire city.

## 1 The Performing Arts

### CLASSICAL MUSIC

#### ✪ The Chicago Symphony Orchestra

Orchestra Hall, 220 S. Michigan Ave. ☎ **312/435-6666.** Fax 312/435-9032. Call or fax for ticket prices and availability.

The Chicago Symphony Orchestra is being led into its second century by Music Director Daniel Barenboim and Music Director Laureate Sir Georg Solti, and it remains among the best in the world.

A CSO concert proves Chicagoans can be as passionate about their music as they are about their sports. Although they're high in demand, good seats often become available on concert day. Call the number above or stop at the box office for the latest information. Among the guests scheduled for 1997 are violinist Itzhak Perlman, flutist James Galway, soprano Leontyne Price, and trumpeter Wynton Marsalis. Orchestra Hall is undergoing a major renovation designed to turn it and surrounding buildings into the new Symphony Center in the fall of 1997.

Summertime visitors have an opportunity to hear a CSO performance at the delightful **Ravinia Festival** (☎ 312/RAVINIA) in suburban Highland Park, led by well-known guest conductors.

The **Civic Orchestra of Chicago,** the training orchestra of the Chicago Symphony since 1919, is also highly regarded and presents free programs at Orchestra Hall.

## ADDITIONAL OFFERINGS

The **Chicago Chamber Musicians** (☎ 312/558-1404) present chamber music concerts by groups from around the world, with performances held at various locales around the city, including the Museum of Science and Industry.

The resident **Vermeer Quartet** gives an annual series of concerts at the Chicago Historical Society. Ticket prices vary with the concerts; often they're free. For more information, you can write to them at 410 S. Michigan Ave., Suite 911, Chicago, IL 60605.

The **Chicago Chamber Orchestra** (☎ 312/922-5570), under the direction of Dieter Kober, performs frequently at venues all around the city, including major museums and the Chicago Public Library. The group's premier yearly concert, the Blair Memorial, takes place in May at the Cathedral of St. James, 61 E. Huron St.

A great Chicago event from late June through August is the series of free outdoor classical music concerts given by the **Grant Park Symphony and Chorus,** performing in Grant Park at the James C. Petrillo Music Shell. Call 312/294-2420 for information.

For current listings, you can call the **Chicago Musical Alliance** (☎ 312/987-1123) for information on classical music concerts and opera.

# OPERA

### ✪ Lyric Opera of Chicago

Civic Opera House, at Madison Street and Wacker Drive. ☎ **312/332-2244.**

A major American opera company, the Lyric attracts top-notch singers from all over the world; its general director is the innovative Ardis Krainik. Once or twice a season, the company performs new and sometimes avant-garde works by contemporary American composers. Opening night in September remains the quasi-official kickoff of the Chicago social season, but don't be scared off by the snooty factor. The Lyric offers English supertitles, and in any case, the opera is a great spectacle with outstanding musical performances and sumptuous sets. The season runs through February. Tickets are hard to get, but turnbacks are often available just before the performance.

The opera has an adjunct, the Lyric Opera Center for American Artists, which also gives performances.

# DANCE

Chicago's dance scene is a lively one, with both resident companies and local groups, often hosting performances by visiting companies such as the Kirov Ballet, the American Ballet Theatre, and the Dance Theater of Harlem. For complete information on what's scheduled, contact the **Chicago Dance Coalition** (☎ 312/419-8383).

Under artistic director Daniel Duell, **Ballet Chicago,** 222 S. Riverside Plaza (☎ 312/251-8838), is notable for its specialty, the ballets of Balanchine.

## Hubbard Street Dance Chicago
218 S. Wabash. ☎ **312/663-0853.**

Lou Conte is the artistic director of this major contemporary dance company. Sometimes whimsical, sometimes romantic, the group incorporates a range of dance traditions, from Twyla Tharp to Kevin O'Day. Of the 10 or so pieces I've seen, my favorite is a romp called "The Envelope."

## Joffrey Ballet
70 E. Lake St. ☎ **312/739-0120.**

This major classical company has recently relocated to Chicago from New York and completed its successful first season in the spring of 1996. It's artistic director is Gerald Arpino. The company's commitment is to the classic works of the 20th century. It's repertoire extends from the ballets of Arpino, Robert Joffery, Balanchine, and Jerome Robbins to the cutting-edge works of Alonzo King and Chicago choreographer Randy Duncan. John Cranko's full-length *Romeo and Juliet* is scheduled for the 1997 season. Ann Marie DeAngelo is associate director.

# MAJOR CONCERT HALLS & AUDITORIUMS

## Auditorium Theater
50 E. Congress Pkwy. ☎ **312/922-4046,** or 312/902-1500 for ticket reservations or box office information. For tour information, call 312/431-2354.

Designed and built in 1889 by Louis Sullivan and Dankmar Adler, the Auditorium Theater is today a national landmark. Most of the building is now occupied by Roosevelt University, but the theater—one of the premier concert halls in the country—was restored in 1967 and now hosts a season of fine dance and musical performances and plays, attracting such names as Twyla Tharp, Itzhak Perlman, Luciano Pavarotti, Alvin Ailey, and the Moscow Ballet.

## Civic Opera House
Madison Street and Wacker Drive. ☎ **312/332-2244.**

The 3,600-seat art-deco Civic Opera House, home of the Lyric Opera company, was built in 1929. It is the enduring monument of its founder, Samuel Insull, who was probably the most hated man in Chicago during the Great Depression. His speculative empire crumbled during the 1929 stock market crash, dragging down thousands of small investors in its wake, and he himself died penniless.

# THEATER

Chicago's theater community is a vibrant one, about as varied and interesting as regional theater gets—more interesting than the frequently bland revivals produced on Broadway these days. The Steppenwolf and Goodman companies have led the way in developing Chicago's reputation, but a host of other performers are creating their own special styles.

With more than 120 theaters, Chicago may have as many as 70 different productions playing on any given weekend. The venues may vary from a space seating 40 to an auditorium built for 4,000. So if you're looking for a big, splashy musical imported from Broadway, there will usually be one or two productions playing in Loop theaters. And if you're up for something a little more offbeat, you should be able to find it at one of dozens of off-Loop theaters.

The listings below represent only a fraction of the city's theater offerings, but will lead you to Chicago's most noted venues and companies. For a complete listing of current productions playing on a given evening, check the "Weekend" and "What's Happening" sections of the *Chicago Tribune* and the *Chicago Sun-Times* or *Chicago* magazine.

## GETTING TICKETS

To order tickets for many plays and events, call **TicketMaster Arts Line** (☎ 312/902-1500), a centralized phone-reservation system that allows you to charge full-price tickets for productions at more than 50 Chicago theaters with a major credit card.

For hard-to-get tickets, try the **Ticket Exchange** (☎ 312/902-1888 or 800/666-0779). For half-price tickets on the day of the show, drop by the **Hot Tix Ticket Center,** located in the Loop at 24 S. State St.; or call 312/831-2822 to order by phone, 312/977-1755 for information. Hot Tix also offers advance-purchase tickets at full price. It's open on Monday from noon to 6pm, Tuesday through Friday from 10am to 6pm, and Saturday from 10am to 5pm. You can also try calling the theater box offices directly.

## DOWNTOWN THEATERS

### Arie Crown Theater

McCormick Place, 23rd Street and Lake Shore Drive. ☎ **312/791-6000.**

The Arie Crown Theater is a showcase for Broadway-style traveling musicals and the annual holiday run of *The Nutcracker*. Despite casts that often feature big-name stars, the theater has a reputation for tinny acoustics because of its enormous size (it holds almost 3,400 seats). I recommend paying the extra money for seats near the stage or bringing a good pair of opera glasses.

### Chicago Theater

175 N. State St. ☎ **312/443-1130.**

The Chicago Theater is the 1921 baroque centerpiece of the old Balaban and Katz movie-house chain. By the end of the Vietnam War, the Chicago Theater had deteriorated badly and was about to fall victim to the wrecking ball when developers' plans were foiled by a group of preservationists who restored this ornate landmark and reopened it in 1986.

Today the Chicago Theater is used as a performing arts center by local companies and hosts dance companies, touring concerts, Broadway shows, and private industrial shows. On many occasions, it fills a role similar to that of Radio City Music Hall in New York, as a venue for star-studded nostalgia performances by such perennial draws as Frank Sinatra.

### Goodman Theatre

200 S. Columbus Dr. ☎ **312/443-3800.** Tickets $26–$39 main stage, $18–$26 studio.

The dean of legitimate theaters in Chicago is the Goodman. Under artistic director Robert Falls, the Goodman produces both original productions—such as Pulitzer Prize–winning playwright August Wilson's *Seven Guitars*—and familiar standards, including Shakespeare, in its 683-seat house. On tap for 1997: Horton Foote's *The Young Man from Atlanta,* Moss Hart's *Light Up the Sky,* Keith Reddin's *All the Rage,* and a revival of August Wilson's *Ma Rainey's Black Bottom.* The theater also supports a 135-seat auditorium for experimental stagings, called the Goodman Studio Theater. The Goodman occupies a wing of the Art Institute complex in Grant Park. Gourmet buffet meals are served prix-fixe on the premises in the Rehearsal Room, open after 6pm on Wednesday through Saturday.

## Mayfair Theater

636 S. Michigan. ☎ **312/786-9120.** Tickets $23 Sun–Thurs, $28 Fri–Sat.

At the Blackstone Hotel's Mayfair Theater, located along South Michigan Avenue, the popular audience-participation spoof *Shear Madness* has been running for years, and is likely to continue for some time to come.

## OFF-LOOP THEATERS

Chicago's off-Loop theaters have produced a number of legendary comic actors, including comic-turned-director Mike Nichols *(The Graduate, Working Girl)*, as well as fine dramatic actors, notably John Malkovich and Gary Sinise, both of whom hail from the Steppenwolf. They toiled at Steppenwolf back in the days when the company performed anywhere it could. Steppenwolf may have hit the big time when it moved into its new digs on North Halsted Street, but the little non-Equity house occupying a small strange space on some remote block remains Chicago theater's energizing force.

### The Annoyance Theatre

3747 N. Clark St. ☎ **773/929-6200.**

The Annoyance has its own special definition of the word *irreverent:* Recent productions include *Co-Ed Prison Sluts, The Idiotic Death of Two Fools,* and *Your Butt.*

### Bailiwick Arts Center

1229 W. Belmont. ☎ **773/883-1090.**

The Bailiwick is one of Chicago's young and exciting regional theaters, each year producing a main-stage series of classics, the Director's Festival of one-act plays, and the Pride Performance Series. One daring recent production was *Bitches,* in which the female roles were played by men in drag.

### Blue Rider

1822 S. Halsted. ☎ **312/733-4668.** Tickets $10–$15.

One of Chicago's most controversial experimental theaters, the Blue Rider is located on the artistic fringe of Pilsen, which is essentially a Mexican immigrant neighborhood. The group was founded by Donna Blue Lachman, who once played the streets of San Francisco as a "loud mime" she called Blue the Clown. But the deeper inspiration for the name, she says, comes from the title of the Kandinsky painting *The Blue Rider.*

Now under the direction of Tim Fiori, Blue Rider produces only a single, original work each year, with a running time of three to four months. Last season it was *G-Man! A Day in the Life of J. Edgar Hoover.* The remainder of the year is devoted to writing and polishing upcoming productions.

### Briar Street Theater

3133 N. Halsted. ☎ **773/348-4000.**

The Briar Street Theater seats approximately 400 and has premiered the work of Chicago native David Mamet, as well as featuring the work of such other well-known playwrights as Tom Stoppard.

### ✪ Steppenwolf Theater

1650 N. Halsted. ☎ **312/335-1650.**

One of the great Chicago success stories of recent years is the brilliant repertory company Steppenwolf Theater. Steppenwolf has garnered many awards, including five Tonys—one for regional theater excellence. It has also launched the careers of several highly respected actors, including John Malkovich *(In the Line of Fire,*

*Dangerous Liaisons),* Gary Sinise *(Forest Gump, Apollo 13),* and Ted Levine (you know, the other psycho in *The Silence of the Lambs*), who frequently return to Steppenwolf to perform or direct. The works featured are almost always thoughtful, though occasionally a bit heavy-handed.

Steppenwolf's breakthrough, following the usual years of artistic struggle, now provides inspiration for other small theater companies. Many of those kindred workshops and theaters can be found in Lincoln Park and other North Side neighborhoods.

### Victory Gardens Theater
2257 N. Lincoln. ☎ **773/871-3000.**

Victory Gardens, a nonprofit group devoted to the development of the playwright, sponsors free weekly readings of new works.

## 2 The Club & Music Scene

### COMEDY CLUBS

In the mid-1970s, "Saturday Night Live" brought Chicago's unique brand of comedy to national attention. But even back then John Belushi and Bill Murray were just the latest brood to hatch from the number-one incubator of Chicago-style humor, Second City. From Nichols and May, Robin Williams, and Robert Klein to Joan Rivers, John Candy, and David Steinberg, two generations of American comics have honed their skills in Chicago before making their fortunes as film and TV stars. Chicago continues to nurture young comics at Second City as well as at numerous other comedy clubs.

Most clubs have a cover charge, which tends to be lower on weekdays; rarely will charges at these clubs exceed $15, even on Friday and Saturday nights.

### Improvisation Institute
2319 W. Belmont. ☎ **773/929-2323.**

Talk about high pressure. The Improv Institute Players perform totally improvised comedy shows in an intensely audience-interactive atmosphere. On Wednesday, the company also hosts Fun Nite, an open stage for aspiring improvisers.

### ✪ Second City
1616 N. Wells. ☎ **312/337-3992.** Tickets $5.50–$15.50.

Having celebrated its 35th anniversary, Second City remains the top comedy club in Chicago. A couple of the more recent alumni are Chris Farley and George Wendt. After the show, which is a series of sketches, the troupe sticks around—and so should you—for the "schtick," an improvisational session; no ticket is necessary if you skip the show. There's a special kids' show on Sunday.

### Zanies Comedy Club
1548 N. Wells. ☎ **312/337-4027.** Tickets $12.

Just down the street from Second City in Old Town is Zanies, which often draws its headliners straight off "The Late Show with David Letterman" and "The Tonight Show." Satirical skits and stand-up routines are the usual fare, played to packed, appreciative houses.

### JAZZ

Born in the Storyville section of New Orleans, jazz moved upriver to Chicago some 75 years ago, and it still has a home here.

Most (but not all) of the clubs listed below have cover charges; most are well under $10 unless a big-name performer is booked.

## ✪ Andy's
11 E. Hubbard. ☎ **312/642-6805.**

Andy's, a full restaurant and bar, is popular with both the hard-core and the neophyte jazz enthusiast. To hear the likes of Dr. Bop and the Headliners Rock and Roll Revival, take in a set Monday through Friday from noon to 2:30pm or 5 to 8:30pm, Saturday at 9pm, or Sunday from 6 to 11pm. There are usually three bands on weekdays, two on Saturday, and one on Sunday.

## Gold Star Sardine Bar
680 N. Lake Shore Dr. ☎ **312/664-4215.**

The Gold Star Sardine Bar, near the lake, is true to its name. It is lilliputian in size, with barely enough room for 50 patrons, but nonetheless remains a nightclub showcase for such big fish as Liza Minnelli. There's live jazz Monday through Saturday.

## Green Mill
4802 N. Broadway. ☎ **773/878-5552.**

On the fringes of Uptown, the Green Mill is "Old Chicago" to the rafters. A popular watering hole during the '20s and '30s, when Al Capone was a regular and the headliners included Sophie Tucker—the Red Hot Mama—and Al Jolson, it still retains its speakeasy atmosphere and flavor. On Sunday night the Green Mill hosts the Uptown Poetry Slam, when poets vie for the open mike to roast and ridicule each other's work. Most nights, however, jazz is on the menu, beginning around 9pm and winding down just before closing at 4am.

## ✪ Jazz Bulls
1916 N. Lincoln Park West. ☎ **773/337-3000.**

One of the liveliest spots in all Chicago, Jazz Bulls offers live musical entertainment 365 nights a year. One hot act that plays the Jazz Bulls is Insight, a young quartet—bass, keyboard, drums, and lead guitar/vocalist—performing a highly polished brand of new-age jazz. The drinks aren't cheap, and the café-style fare of burgers, fries, and pizza is mediocre. But the music is sustenance enough, and the neighborhood has plenty of great places to chow. The kitchen is open every night except Tuesday.

    Discount parking is available nearby at 2036 N. Clark, or on the fringes of the park, located only a block to the east.

## Joe Segal's Jazz Showcase
59 W. Grant St. at Clark. ☎ **312/670-2473.** Cover $15.

For jazz, Joe Segal's Jazz Showcase is a must. Over the years Joe has hosted the best, and still does. Reservations are recommended when a big-name headliner is featured.

## Oz
2917 N. Sheffield. ☎ **773/975-8100.**

With no stage, the musicians at Oz crowd into a corner of the room and play their sets Tuesday through Friday after 10pm. The bar is built of glass bricks, and an outdoor patio is open during the summer.

## Pops for Champagne
2934 N. Sheffield. ☎ **773/472-1000.**

A very civilized, elegant way to enjoy jazz, Pops has a champagne bar and live jazz seven nights a week. Pops also has a popular jazz brunch on Sunday, with three seatings at 10:30am, 12:15pm, and 2pm. Music runs from 8:30pm to 12:30am on Sunday through Thursday, from 9pm to 1am on Friday and Saturday. There's also an early set on Friday from 5:30 to 8:30pm.

## The Vu
2624 N. Lincoln. ☎ **773/871-0205.**

The eclectic offerings at the Vu encompass everything from jazz jams, country music, and big band sounds to live turtle races. The Vu begins to fill up by 10:30 or 11pm and remains open nightly until 4am.

# BLUES

With a few notable exceptions, Chicago's best and most popular blues showcases are located in entertainment districts of the Near North Side. As with the jazz venues listed above, most of the blues clubs have cover charges that are well below $10 unless a major act is performing.

## Blue Chicago
937 N. State St. (near Oak Street). ☎ **312/642-6261.**

Blue Chicago pays homage to the female blues singer by featuring women vocalists. Open Monday through Saturday, with music beginning at 9pm. A second location, open Tuesday through Saturday, is down the street at 536 N. Clark St.

## B.L.U.E.S.
2519 N. Halsted. ☎ **773/528-1012.**

On the Halsted strip, look for B.L.U.E.S.—the name says it all. It's open from 8pm to 2am on Sunday through Friday, until 3am on Saturday, with the show beginning after 9pm.

## B.L.U.E.S. Etcetera
1124 W. Belmont (at the corner of Clifton). ☎ **773/525-8989.** Opens nightly at 8pm and closes "when it's over"; the show begins around 9pm.

In New Town, B.L.U.E.S. Etcetera attracts the big names in blues, Chicago-style and otherwise, such as Junior Wells. It looks a bit like a cafeteria or a coffee shop, but then again, you don't go to a blues club for the decor.

## ✪ Kingston Mines
2548 N. Halsted. ☎ **773/477-4646.** The show begins at 9:30pm, seven nights a week, with two bands on two stages, and goes until 4am. Make that 5am on Sat.

One of Chicago's premier blues bars, celebrating its 25th anniversary, Kingston Mines is where musicians congregate after their own gigs to jam together and to socialize.

## Lilly's
2513 N. Lincoln. ☎ **773/525-2422.** Shows begin at 9pm and end in the wee hours, when the last customer has left.

In Lincoln Park, Lilly's still enshrines the old-time blues, featuring blues jams every Thursday night. The rest of the week Lilly's books jazz and blues combos.

## New Checkerboard Lounge
423 E. 43rd St. ☎ **773/624-3240.**

On the South Side, despite its location in a marginal neighborhood, the "in spot" is the New Checkerboard Lounge. The music is the real thing here, very close to its Mississippi roots.

## Rosa's Lounge
3420 W. Armitage (at Kimball). ☎ **773/342-0452.**

Rosa's is strictly a neighborhood hangout, but it has live blues every night of the year and all the atmosphere required to fuel its heartfelt lamentations. Most blues groups and music lovers feel right at home here. Rosa's also sponsors a Blues Cruise on Lake

Michigan every summer. The doors open at 8pm, and the show starts around 9:30pm and runs until 2am, 3am on Saturday. No cover on Monday.

# ROCK, FOLK & ETHNIC MUSIC

Lately Chicagoans—or at least some Chicagoans—have taken pride in the city's burgeoning alternative rock scene, which has produced such names as Liz Phair, Smashing Pumpkins, Urge Overkill, and Veruca Salt. The Bucktown/Wicker Park neighborhood is the center of the movement.

The major rock concert tours, on the other hand, generally play such huge places as the Rosemont Horizon, near O'Hare Airport, and tickets sell way in advance, generally through **TicketMaster** (☎ 312/902-1500).

The city also has a number of spots that cater to the tastes of those who like all the other musical forms, from mellow folk to suave salsa, spicy reggae, melancholy Irish, weepy country, and frenetic gypsy.

For who's playing where and when on a given night, check *The Reader, New City,* the *Trib,* or the *Sun-Times,* or call the clubs for their schedules. A few of these clubs don't have cover charges; the others usually keep their admission well below $10 (higher on weekends).

### Asi Es Columbia
3910 N. Lincoln. ☎ **773/348-7444.** Open Fri–Sun.

You can catch the latest in Latin jazz and samba at Asi Es Columbia.

### Biddy Mulligan's
7644 N. Sheridan. ☎ **773/761-6532.**

An Irish tavern that plays the blues, as well as R&B and soul. Tuesday is reggae night. The music and dancing last until 2am on Monday through Friday, until 3am on Saturday.

### Cubby Bear Lounge
1059 W. Addison. ☎ **773/327-1662.** Closed Sun, Mon, and Tues.

The Cubby Bear, across from Wrigley Field, is a showcase for new bands Friday and Saturday nights.

### Heartland Cafe
7000 N. Glenwood. ☎ **773/465-8005.**

On the weekends, you'll usually find something happening music-wise at the Heartland Cafe. The musical menu is eclectic—anything from funky rock to Irish tunes.

### Irish Eyes
2519 N. Lincoln. ☎ **773/348-9548.**

This place showcases Irish music on Friday and Saturday nights beginning after 9pm, and there's bluegrass music on tap about once a month.

### Irish Village
6215 W. Diversey. ☎ **773/237-7555.**

It's St. Patrick's Day every night of the week at the Irish Village.

### Lakeview Lounge
5110 N. Broadway. ☎ **773/769-0994.** Open 10pm–4am.

Uptown is country-music territory, and you'll find it live at the Lakeview Lounge. Open 10pm to 4am.

### Metro/Smart Bar
3730 N. Clark. ☎ **773/549-0203.**

The Metro has live alternative/rock music most nights, with three separate shows on Saturday night. The Smart Bar—at the same location—is a dance club open seven nights a week.

### No Exit Café
6970 N. Glenwood. ☎ 773/743-3355. Open Mon–Thurs 4pm–midnight, Fri until 1:30am, Sat noon–2am, Sunday noon–midnight.

The No Exit Café, which has been around for decades, is owned and run today by a woman named Suzanne who first came here as a waitress in 1968. The folk music featured here in the evening is among the tops in the city, and you can linger all day over a cup of coffee, hassle-free.

### Phyllis's Musical Inn
1800 W. Division. ☎ 773/486-9862.

A small, generally uncrowded club in Wicker Park with live new-wave music on Wednesday and Friday through Sunday nights.

### The Wild Hare
3530 N. Clark. ☎ 773/327-4273. Open daily at 7:45pm.

Number one on Chicago's reggae charts is the Wild Hare, in the shadow of Wrigley Field. Grab a Red Stripe and dance to the bands from Jamaica and elsewhere. The atmosphere inside the bar—dark and slightly dingy—might have been transported from a side street in Montego Bay, from the part of town tourists seldom wander through.

## DANCE CLUBS/DISCOS

The big, glitzy disco (though the term *dance club* is vastly preferred) still exists in Chicago, drawing an under-30 crowd. But plenty of other dancing takes place these days in clubs and bars that either specialize in one brand of music or that offer an ever-changing mix of rhythms and beats. A general note about dance clubs: Avoid wearing sneakers, baseball caps, and jeans, or risk the bouncer turning you away at the door.

### Baby Doll Polka Club
6102 S. Central. ☎ 773/582-9706.

No, I'm not kidding. The polka is alive and kicking in Chicago at the Baby Doll Polka Club. Relive those golden memories of Lawrence Welk and skip-step to the magic accordion of Ed Korosa. It's open daily, with live music on weekends only.

### Baja Beach Club
At North Pier, 401 E. Illinois St. ☎ 312/222-1992. Open daily, Sun–Thurs until 2am, Fri–Sat until 4am.

The conventioneers' special. A space of 18,000 square feet is frequented by people who want to hit on and want to be hit on.

### Bossa Nova
1960 N. Clybourn Ave. ☎ 773/248-4800.

A thoroughly modern version of the old-fashioned supper club, featuring world beat music and an extraordinary menu of appetizer-size dishes called tapas. There's live dance music after 8pm on Wednesday and Thursday, after 10pm on Friday and Saturday.

### Crobar
1543 N. Kingsbury. ☎ 312/587-1313.

An urban crowd comes to Crobar to dance to industrial music on weekends. Wednesday night features alternative music, and Thursday is SLAB (Super Loud Alternative Bands), with two local bands playing each week. On Sunday night, Crobar becomes the Glee Club, which stands for Gay Lesbian Everyone's Equal, and which counts Dennis Rodman among its regulars.

### Ka-Boom!

747 N. Green. ☎ **312/243-8600.** Open Thurs–Sat.

When it opened a few years back, Ka-Boom!, under the same ownership as Crobar, was amazingly trendy. Now the suburbanites have invaded, making it a little more tame. The place is huge, and the industrial motif is visually intriguing. Each night offers high-energy dance music in the main room, alternative rock in the rock room, and disco or '80s beats in the cabaret.

### Neo

2350 N. Clark. ☎ **773/528-2622.**

For new wave, it's Neo, a bit of a cavern at the end of a lighted alley, a holdover from the short-lived new-wave era of the late '70s and early '80s.

### 950 Club

950 W. Wrightwood. ☎ **773/929-8955.**

Alternative music à la Patti Smith is the hallmark at the 950 Club, which attracts a mixed crowd aged 21 to 50.

### Shelter

564 W. Fulton. ☎ **312/648-5500.**

Underground house and funk music attracts a young dance crowd at Shelter, a club that has outlived many rivals.

### Tania's

2659 N. Milwaukee. ☎ **773/235-7120.**

Offering the Latin beat and a primarily Hispanic scene is Tania's, located on the Northwest Side along the so-called Milwaukee Avenue corridor. Tania's serves Cuban and Mediterranean cuisine and has live music Wednesday through Sunday after 10:30pm.

## GAY/LESBIAN CLUBS & BARS

Pick up a copy of the Pink Pages, a free community telephone book published twice a year that lists, among other businesses, bars and clubs catering to gays and lesbians. If you'd like to order a copy in advance of your trip, send $5 to D.A.C. Marketing, 3023 N. Clark St., No. 779, Chicago, IL 60657. Another good resource is *Nightlines,* a weekly publication with an emphasis on entertainment.

### Berlin

954 W. Belmont. ☎ **773/348-4975.** Open daily from 4pm to 4am (until 5am on Sat).

Shades of the Weimar period are the intended vibes at Berlin, but the decadence is more style than real. Berlin describes the crowd as "pansexual," i.e., a blend of straights, gays, whatever. Continuous videos throb in the background, and male dancers perform some weekday nights.

### The Closet

3325 N. Broadway. ☎ **773/477-8533.**

The Closet is mostly gay, as the name might suggest, but also has a sports crowd.

### Glee Club

1543 N. Kingsbury. ☎ **312/587-1313.**

Most of the week this place is known as Crobar and features dancing to techno-pop and alternative music. But on Sunday night, Crobar is transformed into the Glee Club, a gay and lesbian dance party, with a $4 cover charge.

### Manhole

3458 N. Halsted. ☎ **773/975-9244.**

The Manhole attracts a youthful late-night clientele with recorded dance music.

### Sidetrack

3349 N. Halsted. ☎ **773/477-9189.**

Sidetrack is a video bar where the American musical is the sound of choice.

## 3  The Bar & Cafe Scene

For the atmosphere of a neighborhood tavern or a sports bar, it's best to venture beyond downtown into the surrounding neighborhoods. The Near North Side has a few entertainment zones that are saturated with bright, upscale neighborhood bars. And if you're feeling casual, the city also has its share of dives scattered around—the real no-frills "corner taps" are also well represented in the blue-collar neighborhoods of Chicago.

### AN OVERVIEW

Around Rush Street are what a bygone era called singles bars—attracting primarily a college-aged contingent. The bars are always crowded on the weekends, making for a frat party feel on the street, and some of the bars maintain the action on weeknights by allowing women free admittance.

Division Street, with its succession of singles bars, is still the place where, on any given night, pitchmen stand on the sidewalk before their respective establishments trying to attract customers. Most of the bars have special nights when the price of drinks for women is heavily discounted. The bars lining Division Street include the **Snuggery,** 15 W. Division (☎ 312/337-4349); **House of Beer,** 16 W. Division (☎ 312/642-2344); **Butch McGuire's,** 20 W. Division (☎ 312/337-9080); the **Lodge,** 21 W. Division (☎ 312/642-4406); and **Mother's,** 26 W. Division (☎ 312/642- 7251).

Old Town has Wells Street, with Second City and other comedy clubs, and a string of reliable restaurants and bars, many of which traditionally appeal to tourists. In Lincoln Park, concentrations of in-spots run along Armitage Avenue, Halsted Street, and Lincoln Avenue. The same is true for the middle-class-meets-gay atmosphere on the blocks surrounding Belmont Avenue.

As for hotel nightlife, virtually every hotel in Chicago has a cocktail lounge or piano bar, and in some cases, more than one distinct environment where you can take an apéritif before dinner or watch an evening of entertainment. The lobby bar at the Nikko Hotel and the piano bar at the Pump Room in the Omni Ambassador East Hotel are two standouts.

### BARS & PUBS

#### Burwood Tap

724 W. Wrightwood. ☎ **773/525-2593.**

Your basic neighborhood bar. Only this neighborhood is dominated by postcollege singles and young marrieds.

### Corner Pocket
2610 N. Halsted St. ☎ **773/281-0050.**

Started by a few Ivy League types who'd rather shoot pool than crunch numbers, the Corner Pocket has become a hangout for the same.

### Gamekeepers
345 W. Armitage St. ☎ **773/549-0400.**

Lincoln Park's most popular sports bar.

### ✪ Glascott's Groggery
2158 N. Halsted St. ☎ **773/281-1205.**

At the top of any self-respecting Lincoln Park yuppie's list of meeting places is Glascott's. You'll see the guys after their weekly basketball game, couples coming in after dinner to catch up with their friends, and singles hoping to hook up with old college buddies—and meet new ones.

### Jay's
930 N. Rush. ☎ **312/664-4333.**

One of the few "institutions" remaining on Rush Street is Jay's, catering to construction worker types by day and businesspeople and such by night. The TVs on both ends of the bar are usually tuned to some sporting event or movie, and the Italian beef sandwich with hot peppers is a treat to be accompanied by a bottle of Old Style beer. A dartboard completes the picture.

### John Barleycorn Memorial Pub
658 W. Belden. ☎ **773/348-8899.**

"Se habla Beethoven" announces the legend beneath the sign of the landmark John Barleycorn Memorial Pub, where the western point of this cross street intersects with Lincoln Avenue. This is a tavern for highbrows, who are treated to a background of classical music and a continuous slide show of art masterpieces. Patrons can order a meal from the menu, too.

### Old Town Ale House
219 W. North. ☎ **312/944-7020.**

One of Old Town's legendary bars is the Old Town Ale House, a neighborhood hangout since the late '50s, featuring an outstanding jukebox with an eclectic selection. It's open daily from noon to 4am (until 5am on Saturday).

### Otis
2150 N. Halsted. ☎ **773/348-1900.**

The Otis is more than just a bar, offering live music from Southern rock to reggae and blues three nights a week. Wednesday night features nothing but acoustic music, and on Tuesday night, draft beer is only 25¢. The ambience is attractive, with a beautiful wood floor and unique wooden fixtures and decorations throughout the bar.

### River Shannon
425 W. Armitage. ☎ **312/944-5087.** Open Mon–Fri 2pm–2am, Sat 2pm–3am, Sun noon–2pm.

Another popular Lincoln Park bar is River Shannon, part singles hangout and part sports bar.

### Sheffield's
3258 N. Sheffield. ☎ **773/281-4989.**

A neighborhood gathering spot—especially for the theater crowd—is Sheffield's, one block north of Belmont, on the corner of School Street. Sheffield's has a working fireplace and a cabaret stage for live sketches and music. It's particularly popular in the summer, when its large outdoor beer garden, complete with pool table, is open. Sheffield's, which boasts a selection of more than 80 beers, is open until 2am every day, 3am on Saturday night. The bar opens at noon on Sunday when a Bears game is on the tube.

### Sterch's
2236 N. Lincoln. ☎ **773/281-2653.**

Sterch's is one of the many neighborhood bars that dot Chicago. Pictures of carrots on the bar's awnings and on the canvas flaps that flank the doorway apparently refer to a former practice of serving carrot sticks as munchies instead of chips and pretzels.

## CAFES

Chicago is full of coffee bars, most of them chains such as Starbucks and Brothers Gourmet Coffee Bar. But there are only a few true cafés. In addition to those I've listed below, you might want to try Urbus Orbis in Wicker Park (see Chapter 6).

### Java
4272 W. Irving Park. ☎ **773/545-6200.**

Java, a bright and modish coffeehouse, is a hangout for youngish artists. Proprietor Cheryl Blumenthal offers great-looking sandwiches and bakes her turkeys and hams on the premises. Scones and pastries are also available, as are many different brews of coffee, including the popular cappuccino grande, served in a large bowl with a chunk of milk chocolate on the side.

### Sage, Rosemary, and Time
2562 N. Clark St. ☎ **773/935-2233.**

Recently opened in Lincoln Park, Sage, Rosemary, and Time looks a little like a living room, with mismatched tables, chairs, and sofas. The menu incudes salads and sandwiches, plus other munchies, sweets, and a slew of gourmet coffees.

### ✪ The Third Coast
29 E. Delaware. ☎ **312/664-7225.**

A seriously hip cafe just a block west of North Michigan Avenue, The Third Coast attracts the city's beautiful people as well as those with a more artistic or intellectual bent. The sidewalk tables are pleasant in the summer; the people-watching and see-and-be-seen atmosphere are good year-round.

## 4 Movies

It's not widely known, but between 1910 and 1918 Chicago was the film capital of the nation. Such classics of the period as Wallace Beery's *Sweedie* and Charlie Chaplin's *His New Job* were shot at the Essanay Studios, then located in a Chicago neighborhood called Uptown. This explains in part why Chicago was blessed with so many fine film palaces, such as the Chicago Theater, mentioned above.

For conventional fare, check the local papers for neighborhood theater listings. Several good theaters are clustered around North Michigan Avenue, including Water Tower Place, 900 N. Michigan Ave. (the Bloomingdale's building), and the Esquire. The going rate for a first-run movie these days is $7.50; many theaters offer special senior citizen prices.

## Oprah Watch

She's almost definitely the most famous female Chicagoan, and, next to Michael Jordan, she's probably the most famous local resident of either gender. Oprah Winfrey has built her media empire in Chicago, and though she seems to have her hand in everything these days, her top-rated talk show is still Oprah's bread and butter. She's one of the original audience stackers (preinterviewing would-be audience members to ensure a rambunctious discussion), but some tickets are available for average, run-of-the-mill folks who want to see a TV show taping. Oprah tapes from September through May at Harpo Studios, 1058 W. Washington St. (☎ 312/591-9222). If you'd like tickets, call (don't write) one to two months in advance. If you don't get reservations, don't bother showing up; no standby tickets are available.

The **Chicago International Film Festival** takes place annually at theaters announced during late October and early November.

Listed below are some of the houses showing unusual, artsy, or foreign films. In addition, you might want to check out the **Fine Arts,** 418 S. Michigan (☎ 312/939-3700), which offers foreign films on a regular basis; the **Music Box Theatre,** 3733 N. Southport (☎ 773/871-6604), a refurbished 1930s movie hall showing double features of golden oldies; and **The 3 Penny Cinema,** 2424 N. Lincoln (☎ 773/935-5744), across the street from the Biograph, which offers the best in foreign, commercial, and specialized films.

### Biograph
2433 N. Lincoln. ☎ **773/348-4123.**

At the sleek deco-style Biograph, John L. Dillinger saw his last flick before being gunned down in the alleyway next to the theater, fingered by his moll, the Lady in Red. Some of those indentations in the telephone pole near the sidewalk end of the alley are said to be bullet holes.

### Chicago Filmmakers
1545 W. Division. ☎ **773/384-5533.**

Chicago Filmmakers is a nonprofit exhibitor, strictly for shorts and documentaries. Here you will see the work of the world's current crop of experimental filmmakers. The group also sponsors workshops in basic filmmaking and performance skills.

### Facets
1517 W. Fullerton. ☎ **773/281-4114.**

At Facets, another nonprofit, the program typically features at least one film classic. Facets also supports an experimental theater company and sponsors an annual festival of children's films in October. Facets has daily screenings that mix a broad selection of old favorites with the work of contemporary independents.

### The Film Center
School of the Art Institute of Chicago, Columbus Drive and Jackson Boulevard. ☎ **312/443-3737** for a recorded message.

The Film Center screens contemporary feature films that are unlikely to be exhibited by the city's commercial theaters, as well as the great films of the past.

# 11

# Easy Excursions from Chicago

Chicago may be a gold mine of attractions, but the area around it has a good deal to offer as well. Yes, it's true, the suburbs have more to offer than shopping malls. The streets of Oak Park, for example, are a virtual open-air museum of Frank Lloyd Wright's Prairie School of architecture, and Highland Park is home of the Ravinia music festival every summer. And beyond the Chicago metropolitan area—Chicagoland—are dozens of other places to explore, most notably historic Springfield, where the state's most revered citizen, Abraham Lincoln, is memorialized.

## 1 Oak Park

Architecture and literary buffs alike make pilgrimages to Oak Park, a near suburb on the western border of the city that is easily accessible by car or train. The reason fans of both disciplines flock to this same small town is that Ernest Hemingway was born and grew up here and Frank Lloyd Wright spent a great deal of his career designing the homes that line the well-maintained streets. I like to think it was more than just coincidence that one town fostered two artists who contributed to their fields new, thoroughly American visions that would reverberate for generations.

## ESSENTIALS

**GETTING THERE** Oak Park is 10 miles due west of downtown Chicago. If traveling **by car,** take the Eisenhower Expressway (I-290) to the exit north of Harlem Avenue (Ill. 43). Follow the brown-and-white signs to the historic district parking lot at Forest Avenue and Lake Street.

By **public transportation,** take the Lake Street/Dan Ryan El to the Harlem/Marion stop, roughly a 25-minute ride from downtown. Exit the station onto Harlem Avenue, then backtrack along North Boulevard one block until reaching Forest Avenue, where you turn left (north), walking another block to Lake Street. On this corner you will find the **Visitors Center,** 158 Forest Ave. (☎ 708/848-1500), open daily from 10am to 5pm. Stop here for orientation, maps, guidebooks, and tour tickets.

# Oak Park

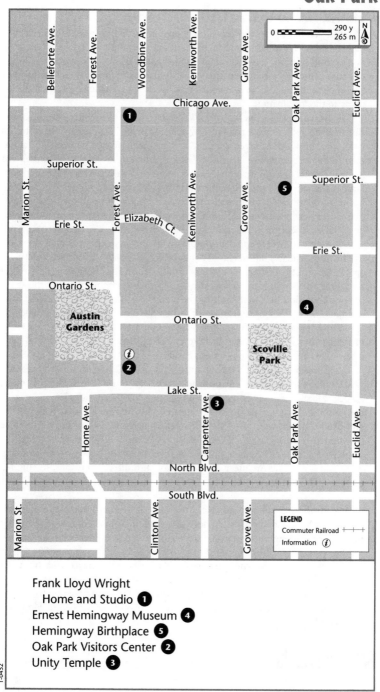

Frank Lloyd Wright
   Home and Studio ❶
Ernest Hemingway Museum ❹
Hemingway Birthplace ❺
Oak Park Visitors Center ❷
Unity Temple ❸

1-0452

## A FRANK LLOYD WRIGHT TOUR

Oak Park has the highest concentration of houses or buildings anywhere designed and built by Wright. People come here to marvel at the work of a man who saw his life as a twofold mission: to wage a singlehanded battle against the ornamental excesses of architecture, Victorian in particular, and to create in its place a new form that would be at the same time functional, appropriate to its natural setting, and stimulating to the imagination.

Not everyone who comes to Oak Park shares Wright's architectural philosophy. But scholars and enthusiasts admire Wright for being consistently true to his own vision, out of which emerged a unique and genuinely American architectural statement. The reason for Wright's success may stem from the fact that he himself was a living exemplar of a quintessential American type. In a deep sense, he embodied the ideal of the self-made and self-sufficient individual who had survived, even thrived, in the frontier society, qualities that he expressed in his almost puritanical insistence that each spatial or structural form in his buildings serve some useful purpose. But he was also an aesthete in Emersonian fashion, deriving his idea of beauty from natural environments, where apparent simplicity often belies a subtle complexity.

The three principal ingredients of a tour of Wright-designed structures in Oak Park are the **Frank Lloyd Wright Home and Studio Tour,** the **Unity Temple Tour,** and a **walking tour**—guided or self-guided—to view the exteriors of homes throughout the neighborhood that were built by the architect. Oak Park has, in all, 30 homes and buildings by Wright, constructed between the years 1899 and 1913, which constitute the core output of his Prairie School period. Tours of another 50 dwellings of architectural interest by Wright's contemporaries, scattered throughout this community and neighboring River Forest, are also worthwhile.

The **Chicago Architecture Foundation** (☎ 312/922-3432 for reservations and tickets) offers a combined tour that includes an informed visit to Unity Temple, a guided walk past homes designed by Wright and his contemporaries, and a visit to the Home and Studio, the latter tour presented by the **Frank Lloyd Wright Home and Studio Foundation** (☎ 708/848-1976), where tickets may also be purchased. The tour lasts approximately 2½ hours, costs $9, and is conducted on Sunday from March to October at 10:30am, noon, and 2pm, and from November to February at noon and 2pm. The Architecture Foundation also offers a bus tour, leaving from downtown Chicago, at a cost of $25. Reservations are required; call 312/922-3432, ext. 140.

Apart from the walking tour that joins the visit to Unity Temple to that of the Home and Studio, and only scratches the surface of Wright's domestic architecture in Oak Park, several other options are available. A more extensive tour leaves the **Ginko Tree Book Shop,** installed next to the Home and Studio, at 951 Chicago Ave., weekdays at 11am, 1pm, and 3pm, and continuously on weekends from 11am to 4pm. This tour lasts an hour, whether guided or on cassette, and tickets cost $6 for adults, $4 for youths ages 10 to 18 and seniors, free for children under 10.

A final worthwhile option is to purchase an **"Architecture Guide Map"** from the bookshop of the Visitors Center and fashion a walking tour to fit your own

*Chicago! Immense gridiron of dirty, noisy streets. . . . Heavy traffic crossing both ways at once, managing somehow; torrential noise.*

—Frank Lloyd Wright, *An Autobiography*

schedule. This map places each subject house schematically on the street plan and includes photos of all 80 sites of interest. In addition to Wright's work, you will see that of his several disciples, as well as some very charming examples of the Victorian styling that he so disdained.

## Unity Temple

875 Lake St. ☎ **708/383-8873.** The Unity Temple portion of the tour can be purchased alone for $3 a ticket, $2 for students and seniors on Mon–Fri; $5 a ticket, $3 for students and seniors on weekends.

Closest to the Visitors Center, and starting point for the tour described above, is Unity Temple. In 1871 a community of Unitarian/Universalists settled near here and built a Wren-style church, a timber-framed house of worship typical of their native New England. Fire destroyed the church around the turn of the century. The congregation asked Wright, who was a member, to design an affordable replacement. Using poured concrete with metal reinforcements—a necessity owing to the small budget of $40,000 allocated for the project—Wright created a building that on the outside seems as forbidding as a mausoleum, but that inside contains in its detailing the entire architectural alphabet of the Prairie School that has since made Wright's name immortal.

Following the example of H. H. Richardson (Glessner House), Wright placed the building's main entrance on the side, behind an enclosure—a feature often employed in his houses as well—to create a sense of privacy and intimacy. Front entrances were too anonymous for these two architects. And Wright complained, furthermore, that other architectural conventions of the church idiom, such as the nave in the Gothic-style cathedral across from the future site of Unity Temple, were overpowering. Of that particular church, he commented that he didn't feel a part of it.

Yet his own vision in this regard was somewhat confused and contradictory. He wanted Unity Temple to be "democratic." But perhaps Wright was unable to subdue his own personal hubris and hauteur in the creative process, for the ultimate effect of his chapel, and much of the building's interior, is very grand and imperial. Unity Temple is no simple meetinghouse in the tradition of Calvinist iconoclasm. Rather, its principal chapel looks like the chamber of the Roman Senate. Even so, the interior, with its unpredictable geometric arrangements and its decor reminiscent of Native American art, is no less beautiful.

Wright used color sparingly within Unity Temple, but the pale, natural effects he achieved are owed in part to his decision to add pigment to the plaster, rather than use paint. Wright's use of wood for trim and other decorative touches is still exciting to behold; his sensitivity to grain and tone and placement was akin to that of an exceptionally gifted woodworker. Wright was a true hands-on, can-do person; he knew the materials he chose to use as intimately as the artisans who carried out his plans. And his stunning, almost minimalist use of form is what still sets him apart as a relevant and brilliant artist. Other details to which the docent guide will call your attention, as you complete a circuit of the temple, are the great fireplace, the pulpit, the skylights, and the clerestory (gallery) windows. Suffice it to say, Unity Temple— only one of Wright's masterpieces—is counted among the 10 greatest American architectural achievements.

## Frank Lloyd Wright Home & Studio

951 Chicago Ave. ☎ **708/848-1976.** General admission $6, $4 for children up to age 18 and seniors. Guided tours, Mon–Fri 11am and 1 and 3pm, Sat–Sun every 15 minutes 11am–4pm. Additional hours are added in the summertime. Facilities for the handicapped are limited; please call in advance.

Known locally as *the* Home and Studio, it is first and foremost the sanctuary from which Wright was to design and execute more than 130 of an extraordinary output of 430 completed buildings. The home began as a simple shingled cottage that Wright built for his bride in 1889 at the age of 22, but it became a work in progress, as Wright remodeled it constantly until 1911. During this highly fertile period, the house was Wright's showcase and laboratory, but it also embraces many idiosyncratic features molded to his own needs, rather than those of a client. With many add-ons—including a barrel-vaulted children's playroom, and a studio with an octagonal balcony suspended by chains—the place has a certain whimsy that others may have found less livable. This, however, was not an architect's masterpiece, but the master's home, and every room in it can be savored for the view it reflects of the workings of a remarkable mind.

## ON THE TRAIL OF HEMINGWAY

Frank Lloyd Wright may be Oak Park's favorite son, but the town's most famous native son was Ernest Hemingway. Maybe because Hemingway left when he had the chance and didn't write much about the town of his boyhood, Oak Park only recently has begun to rally around the memory of the Nobel– and Pulitzer Prize–winning writer with the opening of a **Hemingway Museum,** 200 N. Oak Park Ave. (☎ 708/848-2222). A portion of the ground floor of this former church, now the Oak Park Arts Center, is given over to a small but interesting display of Hemingway memorabilia. A six-minute video presentation sheds considerable light on Hemingway's time in Oak Park, where he spent the first 18 years of his life, and is particularly good on his high school experiences. The museum's hours are limited; it's open Wednesday and Sunday from 1 to 5pm, and Saturday from 10am to 5pm. There is an admission fee of $2.

To see where Hemingway was born, continue up the block to 339 N. Oak Park Ave. Here, in the home of his maternal grandparents, on July 21, 1899, the author who redefined fiction writing for his time first saw the light. A local foundation recently purchased the home to serve as a museum and has restored it to reflect its appearance during Hemingway's boyhood. Hemingway's actual boyhood home, still privately owned, is located several blocks from here, not far from the Wright Home and Studio, at 600 N. Kenilworth Ave. The hours at the Hemingway Birthplace museum are the same as the Hemingway Museum above. A special $5 admission price covers both museums.

## 2  The Pullman Historic District

Although technically part of Chicago, the Pullman Historic District is so far to the southwest of the downtown area where most visitors stay that I am including it as a day excursion. Pullman is a monument to industrial paternalism in America. George Pullman, inventor of the Pullman railway sleeping car, was not content to compensate for poor wages with symbolic gestures. Rather than follow the more usual Dickensian example of his 19th-century industrialist peers who distributed turkeys at Yuletide, Pullman provided his workers with all the comforts of home—and made a profit on the experiment to boot. Much of the utopian village that Pullman built from 1880 to 1884 still stands near the Calumet Expressway between 111th and 115th Streets, and continues today as an active residential community.

Many workers, at least initially, must have counted themselves lucky that their employer had created such a comfortable nest for them. The rents they paid brought them both quality housing and many conveniences. But Pullman was more than a landlord; he was a social engineer, reinforcing a strict caste system in the community whereby each level of worker was permitted a particular type of housing deemed appropriate for his "station." (Pullman himself lived in a mansion on Chicago's elite Prairie Avenue.) The residents of Pullman's town quickly rebelled against his rule over their domestic life. When he began to turn the screw in response to their complaints by holding rents and utilities high during a serious economic depression, they warred against him in his factory as well. The Pullman Strike of 1894, which crippled the nation's rail traffic, was one of the great triumphs and tragedies of the labor movement, and a fascinating episode in American history in its own right. Government troops broke up the strike, an official failure that saw the jailing of its leader, Eugene V. Debs, and the weakening of its union, the American Railway Workers. But the public outrage that followed the strike ultimately helped the workers win many rights and reforms. And in the end, an embittered George Pullman finally bowed to a court order to divest his company of its nonindustrial property. Time has not been kind to Pullman's reputation in Chicago, where after nearly a century, his name is still mud.

## ESSENTIALS

**GETTING THERE     By car,** take the Calumet/Dan Ryan Expressway to the 111th Street exit, and proceed west. The most direct route to the historic district for travelers without cars is via the **Metra suburban train system,** with stations throughout the Loop, and which stops directly at 111th Street in Pullman. (For Metra information, call 312/322-6777.) The ride from the Loop takes approximately 30 minutes.

### EXPLORING THE PULLMAN HISTORIC DISTRICT

**TOURS & SIGHTS**     Guided tours of this fascinating community are conducted on the first Sunday of the month from May through October by the Historic Pullman Foundation. Tours begin at 12:30 and 1:30pm from the foundation's **Visitor Center,** 11141 S. Cottage Grove (☎ 773/785-8181), where you first view a 22-minute introductory video and then proceed with a guided walking trip through the neighborhood. The cost is $4 for adults, $3 for seniors, and $2.50 for students. Group tours can be arranged in advance on other days. On the second weekend in October, Pullman hosts an annual house tour in which at least seven private homes open their doors for public view.

At all other times, regardless of the season, you may guide yourself through the same itinerary, after first picking up a walking-tour map at the foundation's headquarters in the Hotel Florence, 11111 S. Forrestville Ave. (☎ 773/785-8181).

The Hotel Florence, built in 1881 in the Queen Anne style for about $100,000, was the showcase of the Pullman community. Here the owner maintained an elegant suite of rooms, housed his guests and clients, and entertained them amid the grandeur of the hotel's public spaces. Ultramodern in its day as well as fashionable, the Florence had indoor plumbing, central heat, and a built-in system of bells and alarms to summon servants or to raise the alert in the event of fire. The hotel closed in 1973, after which it was purchased by the foundation, and is now undergoing restoration. The hotel restaurant (☎ 773/785-8900) continues to function, serving meals on Monday through Friday from 11am to 2pm, Saturday from 9am to 1pm, and Sunday from 10am to 3pm (brunch). Guided tours of the hotel, which includes a museum, are offered daily during the restaurant's business hours.

What you will see on the neighborhood tour is a well-planned, hierarchical arrangement of row houses, from well appointed to plain, that once housed Pullman's

---

### The Last Pullman Car

The actual Pullman Palace Car Company plant, which manufactured railway sleeping cars for 114 years, finally closed its doors in 1979. A group of Chicago filmmakers documented the plant's final months of existence, as the local union desperately fought to keep the plant running and to save jobs. Of course, George Pullman himself probably would have agreed with the decision to close the plant. For information on *The Last Pullman Car,* contact Kartemquin Films, 1901 W. Wellington, Chicago, IL 60657 (☎ 773/472-4366).

---

executives and skilled workers, and a few remaining tenements that were reserved for the laborers and single men. Also extant within this parklike environment is the original Greenstone Church that Pullman had built as a nondenominational house of worship, and the Market Hall, a fire-plagued ensemble of buildings setting off a square where community members shopped for foodstuffs and dry goods.

## 3 Chicago's Suburbs

## THE NORTHERN SUBURBS

Between Chicago and the state border of Wisconsin to the north is the affluent section of suburbia known as the North Shore. Following are some of the most popular attractions here.

### EVANSTON

Despite being Chicago's nearest neighbor to the north—and a place much frequented by Chicagoans themselves—Evanston retains an identity all its own. **Northwestern University** makes its home here on a beautiful lakefront campus. Evanston was also the home of Frances Willard, founder of the Women's Christian Temperance Union. **Willard House,** 1730 Chicago Ave. (☎ 847/864-1397), is still the headquarters of the Temperance Union and is open to visitors. Nine of the 17 rooms in this old Victorian "cottage" have been converted into a museum of period furnishings and temperance memorabilia. Evanston is also known for its examples of fine domestic architecture, which you may view with the aid of a publication entitled *Evanston Architecture: A Sampler of Self-Guided Tours,* available in bookstores and at newsstands.

Neither cultural nor recreational facilities are lacking in Evanston. The unusual and informative **Mitchell Indian Museum** is located at Kendall College, 2408 Orrington Ave. (☎ 847/866-1395), with a collection ranging from precontact stoneware tools and weapons to the work of contemporary Native American artists. Open Tuesday through Friday from 9am to 4:30pm; Saturday and Sunday from 1 to 4pm; closed on holidays and the month of August. A donation of $1 is requested.

For an ecological experience, visit the **Ladd Arboretum,** 2024 McCormick Blvd. (☎ 847/864-5181), a public park where you will also find the **Evanston Ecology Center,** which houses nature exhibits.

### Where to Dine

**Café Provençal**

1625 Hinman Ave. ☎ **847/475-2233.** Reservations required. Main courses $16–$28. AE, DC, MC, V. Tues–Sun 7–11pm. FRENCH.

# Road Trips from Chicago

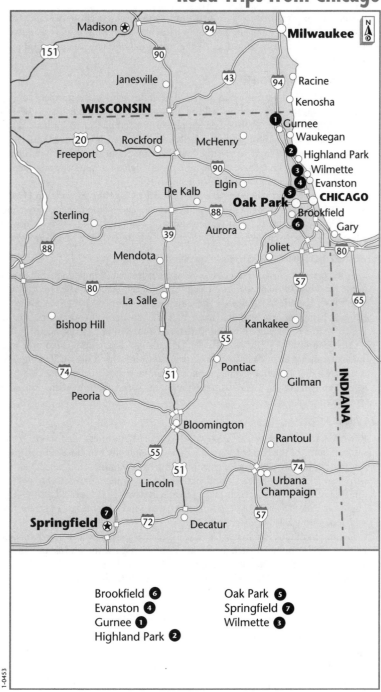

Brookfield **6**    Oak Park **5**
Evanston **4**    Springfield **7**
Gurnee **1**    Wilmette **3**
Highland Park **2**

Eating in Evanston requires no privation from the high culinary standards of Chicago's better restaurants. One spot in particular, Café Provençal, is a super-chic and pricey French restaurant that has the reputation of going sauce-for-sauce with any rival in town.

## BAHA'I HOUSE OF WORSHIP

Up the road in Wilmette is the most visited of all the sights in the northern suburbs, the Baha'i House of Worship, at Linden Avenue and Sheridan Road (☎ 847/ 853-2300), a very non–Prairie-style temple surrounded by formal gardens. With a lacelike facade and a 135-foot dome, designed by the French Canadian Louis Bourgeois, the temple strongly reveals the Eastern influence of the Baha'i faith's native Iran. Visiting hours are May to September from 10am to 10pm daily and October to April from 10am to 5pm daily. Admission is free.

To get there from Chicago, take the Howard Line of the El north to Howard Street. Change trains for Wilmette and go to the end of the line, 4th Street and Linden Avenue. Turn right on Linden and walk two blocks east. If you're driving, take the Outer Drive (Lake Shore Drive) north, which feeds into Sheridan Road.

## CHICAGO BOTANIC GARDEN

Despite its name, the Chicago Botanic Garden is located 25 miles north of the city in the suburb of Glencoe, on Lake-Cook Road just east of Edens Highway (☎ 847/ 835-5440). Experience intimately the variations of nature over four seasons in this 300-acre living preserve, with its variety of distinct botanical environments, from the Illinois prairie to an English walled garden and a three-island Japanese garden. Also on the grounds are a café, a library, a garden shop, and a designated bike path. The grounds are open daily (except Christmas) from 8am to sunset. Parking is $4, which includes admission to the grounds. Tram tours, for an additional $3.50, are offered every half hour from 10am to 3:30pm on weekdays, from 10am to 5pm on weekends.

## RAVINIA FESTIVAL

Ravinia is to Chicago what Tanglewood is to the Berkshires—and more. It's the summer home of the highly regarded Chicago Symphony, which has an eight-week season here. It's also a setting for chamber music, a new music series called New Perspectives, jazz and pop concerts, dance, and music study. Zarin Mehta is music director of the festival, which takes place at Ravinia Park, located in suburban Highland Park (☎ 312/RAVINIA from May to September). The series runs from mid-June through Labor Day.

Getting to the Ravinia Festival is easy. To reserve a place on a chartered bus, dial 312/RAVINIA, and then catch the bus at one of seven stops: the Art Institute (Adams and Michigan); the corner of Randolph and Michigan; the Drake hotel (Walton and Michigan); Harbor House (3200 N. Lake Shore Dr.); Sheridan and Hollywood; Sheridan and Devon; or at the Davis Street Station in Evanston. One-way fare is $6; round-trip, $12. Many of the major hotels also charter buses during the season, or you may ride the commuter train from the Northwestern station near the Loop at Madison and Canal, which stops in Highland Park directly at the festival.

### Where to Dine

Indoor dining, both formal and informal, is available at Rivinia. There's the **Rondo,** featuring a $13 buffet, and the **Cadenza,** serving main courses in the $9 to $16 range. Both are open from 5:30 to around 8pm, when the concerts begin. Lawn catering is also available for parties of six or more. But what most cognoscenti do is pack a picnic of delectables and eat on the great lawn; some go all-out with candles, flowers, the whole bit.

## SIX FLAGS GREAT AMERICA

This is the Midwest's biggest theme/amusement park. It is located midway between Chicago and Milwaukee on I-94 in Gurnee, Illinois (☎ 847/249-1776). The park has more than 100 rides, including the brand-new "Shock Wave," billed as the tallest and fastest steel roller coaster in the country. Six Flags also has shows, restaurants, and theme areas. Admission—$28 for adults, $18 for seniors, $26 for children ages 4 to 10, and free for children 3 and under (not including tax)—entitles you to unlimited use of rides, shows, and attractions. Open seasonally, usually beginning around the first of May and closing by the first week in October.

# THE WESTERN SUBURBS

So many corporations have taken to locating their offices beyond the city limits that today more people work in the suburbs than commute into Chicago. At the hub of this development is O'Hare International, and all around the airport are the kinds of shops, restaurants, and bistros that once only the city could boast of. Those people visiting the Chicago area who are quartered in and around O'Hare also have easy access to a variety of very special museums and nature-oriented facilities.

## WHAT TO SEE & DO

### Brookfield Zoo

First Avenue and 31st St., in Brookfield. ☎ **708/485-0263.** Admission $4 adults, $1.50 seniors and children 3–11. Free on Tues. Memorial Day–Labor Day, daily 10am–6pm. Labor Day–Memorial Day, daily 10am–5pm. Directions: The zoo is located about 14 miles west of the Loop and is accessible via the Stevenson (I-55) and Eisenhower (I-290) Expressways. Bus: RTA no. 304 or 331.

The Chicago area's largest zoo, Brookfield has an incredibly varied cast of residents from all branches of the animal kingdom. Have you ever noticed just how big a Kodiak bear is up close, or how squidlike a walrus's face appears when seen from a very short distance? How do those polar bears stay so white with all the grimy urban pollution in the air, and are those great apes really as angry as they look? These and a hundred other questions will pop into your head as you make the rounds from one habitat to another in this make-believe jungle.

### Lizzadro Museum of Lapidary Art

220 Cottage Hill, Elmhurst. ☎ **630/833-1616.** Admission $2.50 adults, $1.50 seniors, $1 students and teenagers ages 13–18, free for children under 13. Free admission on Fri. Tues–Sat 10am–5pm, Sun 1–5pm. Closed holidays.

Not far from the zoo, off I-90 in nearby Elmhurst, you will find the Lizzadro Museum. The museum's jade collection is internationally renowned, a fact that is punctuated by the presence of a chunk of jade weighing over half a ton that greets you at the entrance. The word *lapidary*, of course, refers to the art of stone cutting, and this repository of that art displays hard-stone carvings, gemstones, mineral specimens, and such oddities as an ivory carving of the Last Supper.

### Morton Arboretum

In Lisle. ☎ **630/968-0074.** Admission $6 per car, $3 per car on Wed. Daily mid-April to mid-October 7am–7pm, mid-October to mid-April 7am–5pm.

South and west of the Brookfield Zoo, in Lisle, is this 1,500-acre arboretum off Ill. 53, just north of the East–West Tollway. Not only is this park a nature showcase of flora from around the world, organized into both formal and natural settings, but it is also a wildlife refuge for many forest critters such as foxes and beavers, and of course, birds. There are 40,000 different tree specimens, classified into 4,000 species. Nine miles of roadways allow you to drive through the grounds, but a walk along the more than 25 miles of pathways will give you a more satisfying and intimate view of the plant and woods life.

### Lynfred Winery

15 S. Roselle Rd., in Roselle. ☎ **630/529-9463.** Free admission. Daily 11am–7pm. Tours Sat–Sun at 2 and 4pm.

Also off I-90, but closer to the airport, is the Lynfred Winery. This suburban winery purchases grapes from around the country and ferments them here in oak casks. You may sample up to seven of the company's fruit and grape wines for $2. The operation is planning to open a bed and breakfast in 1997.

### Fermi National Laboratory (Fermilab)

In Batavia. ☎ **630/840-3000.** Free admission. Guided tours, Mon–Fri 9:30am–1:30pm. Self-guided tours, daily 8:30am–5pm.

Named for the Nobel Prize–winning physicist, Fermilab houses the world's highest energy particle accelerator, the Tevatron. Here scientists probe the fundamental structure of the universe.

The main entrance to the laboratory is on Kirk Road, a north–south highway that exits from the East–West Tollway (Ill. 5). Kirk Road intersects with Butterfield Road (Ill. 56) and Roosevelt Road (Ill. 38), which originates in downtown Chicago near the Field Museum. The laboratory entrance is opposite Pine Street in Batavia, between Butterfield and Wilson Roads.

Free guided tours are available, by appointment, for groups of 10 or more people, consisting of an orientation talk and slide presentation, a visit to various laboratory environments, and an opportunity to take in a panoramic view of the accelerator from the 15th floor of the lab's main building. The tour lasts about two hours, after which you are welcome to drive around the 6,800-acre site, to look at the distinctive architecture of the Fermilab buildings, and to see the buffalo and waterfowl that also occupy these lands.

## WHERE TO DINE

### Carlucci Rosemont

111 N. River Rd., in the Riverway Complex. ☎ **847/518-0990.** Reservations accepted. Main courses $14.95–$19.95. AE, DC, DISC, MC, V. Mon–Thurs 5:30–10:30pm, Fri–Sat 5:30–11:30pm, Sun 5–10pm. ITALIAN.

Only five minutes by car from the airport is a restaurant that will make you forget that your flight was cancelled and you have to spend the night in an airport hotel. While not exactly offering the same menu as its cousin on Halsted Street in Lincoln Park, Carlucci Rosemont boasts the same superior standards of quality.

Console yourself here with a wonderful meal, beginning with the zuppa—something hearty, say, the lamb-and-bean vegetable soup ($3.95). The appetizers are all superb, including the giant portobello mushrooms with rosemary, roasted in a wood-burning oven, or the miniature sweet red peppers stuffed with herb ricotta and sautéed spinach. For your entrée, you could not choose better than the roasted quail stuffed with sausage and risotto, a true delicacy. The wines are sinfully potable; try a Tuscan vintage, the 1990 Mastrojanni. For a strong finish, the tiramisù is a must, creamy mascarpone with marsala and espresso-soaked ladyfingers.

### Le Français

269 S. Milwaukee, in Wheeling. ☎ **847/541-7470.** Reservations required. Main courses $28.50–$32. AE, CB, DC, DISC, MC, V. Mon 5:30–10pm, Tues–Fri 11:30am–2pm and 5:30–10pm, Sat 5:30–10pm. FRENCH.

One of the finest French restaurants anywhere, Le Français is located in Wheeling, northwest of O'Hare. The restaurant has two dinner seatings, and the average check is about $85 per person.

## AFTER DARK

### Studebaker

1251 E. Golf Rd., in Schaumburg. ☎ **847/619-3434.**

Former Bears running back and legend Walter Payton owns a raucous nightclub, also near O'Hare, called Studebaker, where patrons have been known to dance on the tabletops to their favorite Motown sounds.

### Rosemont Horizon

Mannheim Street between Higgins and Touhy Streets, Des Plaines. ☎ **847/635-6600.**

On the periphery of the airport is the 18,000-seat Rosemont Horizon, which holds big events such as rock concerts, the circus, and important college basketball games. Take the subway/El to O'Hare, then bus no. 220.

### Prairie Center for the Performing Arts

201 Schaumburg Court, in Schaumburg. ☎ **847/894-3600.**

The Prairie Center for the Arts holds symphony and jazz concerts, as well as theater, dance, and children's shows.

### World Music Theater

19100 S. Ridgeland Ave. ☎ **708/614-1616.**

The new venue for megaconcerts, just south of Chicago in suburban Tinley Park, is the World Music Theater.

## 4 Springfield

Outside Chicago, the state capital of **Springfield** is by far the most visited destination in Illinois. Springfield was first settled in 1821 but did not become the state capital until a young politician named Abraham Lincoln skillfully maneuvered the appropriate legislation through the Illinois legislature in 1837. Later that same year, Lincoln himself moved to Springfield.

For the next 25 years Springfield was to be the center of Lincoln's law practice, though he spent much of his time riding the circuit and arguing cases in county courthouses all around central Illinois. He was also busy politicking—running for one office or another—throughout the state. As a result, one may follow in Lincoln's footsteps over these years and visit dozens of locales in Illinois where his visits and speeches are commemorated in one form or another. The tourism bureau will be happy to help you fashion such an itinerary.

In Springfield itself, the principal Lincoln-related sights are the **Lincoln Home National Historic Site,** at 8th and Jackson (☎ 217/492-4150), open daily (except major holidays) from 8:30am to 6pm, admission free; the **Lincoln–Herndon Law Offices,** at 6th and Adams (☎ 217/785-7289), open from 9am to 5pm daily, donation suggested; and the **Lincoln Depot,** on Monroe between 9th and 10th (☎ 217/544-8695), where on February 11, 1861, Lincoln bade farewell to his

Springfield friends and neighbors en route to his inauguration in Washington, D.C., as the United States's 16th president. In the depot you will see a restored waiting room, various exhibits, and a multimedia presentation; it's open free of charge daily from 10am to 4pm from April through August.

On the outskirts of town is the **Lincoln Tomb,** Oak Ridge Cemetery, 1500 N. Monument Ave. (☎ 217/782-2717), open daily free of charge March through October from 9am to 5pm, November through February from 9am to 4pm. The tomb is the final resting place of Lincoln and his family. On Tuesday evenings from June through August, the cemetery has a flag-lowering ceremony from 7 to 8pm.

One other Springfield sight worth visiting is the **Old State Capitol,** on the Downtown Mall (☎ 217/785-7961), open daily from 9am to 4:30pm, except major holidays, donation suggested. Here Lincoln delivered his famous "House Divided" speech.

About 20 miles northwest of Springfield on Rt. 97 is **Lincoln's New Salem,** a reconstructed pioneer village complete with costumed interpreters, sort of Illinois's version of Williamsburg. Lincoln lived here for six years before moving to Springfield in 1837. He began to study the law here and was also elected to his first political office, as state legislator.

Lincoln was by far the state of Illinois's most illustrious citizen, but by no means the only one. In Springfield you may also visit the home of **Vachel Lindsay,** the "Prairie Troubadour," at 603 S. 5th St. The national landmark has been undergoing a restoration, so call to check for hours before going (☎ 217/785-7960).

Illinois has many other historic sights, and it is a state well endowed with parks and other areas of great natural beauty. For those who are interested in touring Illinois beyond Chicago, I suggest that you contact the **Illinois Bureau of Tourism,** 620 E. Adams, Springfield, IL 62701 (☎ 800/223-0121 or TDD 800/526-0844), or 100 W. Randolph, Chicago, IL 60601.

# Appendix

## HOTEL CHAINS

**Best Western International, Inc.**
800/528-1234 North America
800/528-2222 TDD

**Budgetel Inns**
800/4-BUDGET Continental USA and Canada

**Budget Host**
800/BUD-HOST Continental USA

**Clarion Hotels**
800/CLARION Continental USA and Canada
800/228-3323 TDD
http://www.hotelchoice.com/cgi-bin/res/webres?clarion.html

**Comfort Inns**
800/228-5150 Continental USA and Canada
800/228-3323 TDD
http://www.hotelchoice.com/cgi-bin/res/webres?comfort.html

**Courtyard by Marriott**
800/321-2211 Continental USA and Canada
800/228-7014 TDD
http://www.marriott.com/lodging/courtyar.htm

**Days Inn**
800/325-2525 Continental USA and Canada
800/325-3297 TDD
http://www.daysinn.com/daysinn.html

**Doubletree Hotels**
800/222-TREE Continental USA and Canada
800/528-9898 TDD

**Drury Inn**
800/325-8300 Continental USA and Canada
800/325-0583 TDD

**Econo Lodges**
800/55-ECONO Continental USA and Canada
800/228-3323 TDD
http://www.hotelchoice.com/cgi-bin/res/webres?econo.html

**Embassy Suites**
800/362-2779 Continental USA and Canada
800/458-4708 TDD
http://www.embassy-suites.com/

**Exel Inns of America**
800/356-8013 Continental USA and Canada

**Fairfield Inn by Marriott**
800/228-2800 Continental USA and Canada
800/228-7014 TDD
http://www.marriott.com/lodging/fairf.htm

**Fairmont Hotels**
800/527-4727 Continental USA

**Forte Hotels**
800/225-5843 Continental USA and Canada

**Four Seasons Hotels**
800/332-3442 Continental USA
800/268-6282 Canada

**Friendship Inns**
800/453-4511 Continental USA
800/228-3323 TDD
http://www.hotelchoice.com/cgi-bin/res/webres?friendship.html

**Guest Quarters Suites**
800/424-2900

**Hampton Inn**
800/HAMPTON Continental USA and Canada
800/451-HTDD TDD
http://www.hampton-inn.com/

**Hilton Hotels Corporation**
800/HILTONS Continental USA and Canada
800/368-1133 TDD
http://www.hilton.com

**Holiday Inn**
800/HOLIDAY Continental USA and Canada
800/238-5544 TDD
http://www.holiday-inn.com/

**Howard Johnson**
800/654-2000 Continental USA and Canada
800/654-8442 TDD
http://www.hojo.com/hojo.html

**Hyatt Hotels and Resorts**
800/228-9000 Continental USA and Canada
800/228-9548 TDD
http://www.hyatt.com

**Inns of America**
800/826-0778 Continental USA and Canada

**InterContinental Hotels**
800/327-0200 Continental USA and Canada

**ITT Sheraton**
800/325-3535 Continental USA and Canada
800/325-1717 TDD

**La Quinta Motor Inns, Inc.**
800/531-5900 Continental USA and Canada
800/426-3101 TDD

**Loews Hotels**
800/223-0888 Continental USA and Canada
http://www.loewshotels.com

**Marriott Hotels**
800/228-9290 Continental USA and Canada
800/228-7014 TDD
http://www.marriott.com/MainPage.html

**Master Hosts Inns**
800/251-1962 Continental USA and Canada

**Meridien**
800/543-4300 Continental USA and Canada

**Omni Hotels**
800/843-6664 Continental USA and Canada

**Park Inns International**
800/437-PARK Continental USA and Canada
http://www.p-inns.com/parkinn.html

**Quality Inns**
800/228-5151 Continental USA and Canada
800/228-3323 TDD
http://www.hotelchoice.com/cgi-bin/res/webres?quality.html

**Radisson Hotels International**
800/333-3333 Continental USA and Canada

**Ramada**
800/2-RAMADA Continental USA and Canada
http://www.ramada.com/ramada.html

**Red Carpet Inns**
800/251-1962 Continental USA and Canada

**Red Lion Hotels and Inns**
800/547-8010 Continental USA and Canada

**Red Roof Inns**
800/843-7663 Continental USA and Canada
800/843-9999 TDD
http://www.redroof.com

**Renaissance Hotels International**
800/HOTELS-1 Continental USA and Canada
800/833-4747 TDD

**Residence Inn by Marriott**
800/331-3131 Continental USA and Canada
800/228-7014 TDD
http://www.marriott.com/lodging/resinn.htm

**Rodeway Inns**
800/228-2000 Continental USA and Canada
800/228-3323 TDD
http://www.hotelchoice.com/cgi-bin/res/webres?rodeway.html

**Scottish Inns**
800/251-1962 Continental USA and Canada

**Shilo Inns**
800/222-2244 Continental USA and Canada

**Signature Inns**
800/822-5252 Continental USA and Canada

**Super 8 Motels**
800/800-8000 Continental USA and Canada
800/533-6634 TDD
http://www.super8motels.com/super8.html

**Susse Chalet Motor Lodges & Inns**
800/258-1980 Continental USA and Canada

**Travelodge**
800/255-3050 Continental USA and Canada

**Vagabond Hotels Inc.**
800/522-1555 Continental USA and Canada

**Westin Hotels and Resorts**
800/228-3000 Continental USA and Canada
800/254-5440 TDD
http://www.westin.com/

**Wyndham Hotels and Resorts**
800/822-4200 Continental USA and Canada

## CAR RENTAL AGENCIES

**Advantage Rent-A-Car**
800/777-5500 Continental USA and Canada

**Airways Rent A Car**
800/952-9200 Continental USA

**Alamo Rent A Car**
800/327-9633 Continental USA and Canada
http://www.goalamo.com/

**Avis**
800/331-1212 Continental USA
800/TRY-AVIS Canada
800/331-2323 TDD
http://www.avis/com/

**Budget Rent A Car**
800/527-0700 Continental USA and Canada
800/826-5510 TDD

**Dollar Rent A Car**
800/800-4000 Continental USA and Canada

**Enterprise Rent-A-Car**
800/325-8007 Continental USA and Canada

**Hertz**
800/654-3131 Continental USA and Canada
800/654-2280 TDD

**National Car Rental**
800/CAR-RENT Continental USA and Canada

800/328-6323 TDD
http://www.nationalcar.com/index.html

**Payless Car Rental**
800/PAYLESS Continental USA and Canada

**Rent-A-Wreck**
800/535-1391 Continental USA

**Sears Rent A Car**
800/527-0770 Continental USA and Canada

**Thrifty Rent-A-Car**
800/367-2277 Continental USA and Canada
800/358-5856 TDD

**U-Save Auto Rental of America**
800/272-USAV Continental USA and Canada

**Value Rent-A-Car**
800/327-2501 Continental USA and Canada
http://www.go-value.com/

## AIRLINES

**American Airlines**
800/433-7300 Continental USA and Western Canada
800/543-1586 TDD
http://www.americanair.com/aa_home/aa_home.htm

**Canadian Airlines International**
800/426-7000 Continental USA and Canada
http://www.cdair.ca/

**Continental Airlines**
800/525-0280 Continental USA
800/343-9195 TDD
http://www.flycontinental.com:80/index.html

**Delta Air Lines**
800/221-1212 Continental USA
http://www.delta-air.com/index.html

**Northwest Airlines**
800/225-2525 Continental USA and Canada
http://www.nwa.com/

**Southwest Airlines**
800/435-9792 Continental USA and Canada
http://www.iflyswa.com

**Trans World Airlines**
800/221-2000 Continental USA
http://www2.twa.com/TWA/Airlines/home/home.htm

**United Airlines**
800/241-6522 Continental USA and Canada
http://www.ual.com/

**USAir**
800/428-4322 Continental USA and Canada
http://www.usair.com/

# Index

## FROMMER'S COMPLETE TRAVEL GUIDES

*(Comprehensive guides to destinations around the world, with selections in all price ranges—from deluxe to budget)*

## FROMMER'S FRUGAL TRAVELER'S GUIDES
*(The grown-up guides to budget travel, offering dream vacations
at down-to-earth prices)*

Australia from $45 a Day

Berlin from $50 a Day

California from $60 a Day

Caribbean from $60 a Day

Costa Rica & Belize from $35 a Day

Eastern Europe from $30 a Day

England from $50 a Day

Europe from $50 a Day

Florida from $50 a Day

Greece from $45 a Day

Hawaii from $60 a Day

India from $40 a Day

Ireland from $45 a Day

Italy from $50 a Day

Israel from $45 a Day

London from $60 a Day

Mexico from $35 a Day

New York from $70 a Day

New Zealand from $45 a Day

Paris from $65 a Day

Washington, D.C. from $50 a Day

## FROMMER'S PORTABLE GUIDES
*(Pocket-size guides for travelers who want everything in a nutshell)*

Charleston & Savannah

Las Vegas

New Orleans

San Francisco

## FROMMER'S IRREVERENT GUIDES
*(Wickedly honest guides for sophisticated travelers)*

Amsterdam

Chicago

London

Manhattan

Miami

New Orleans

Paris

San Francisco

Santa Fe

U.S. Virgin Islands

Walt Disney World

Washington, D.C.

## FROMMER'S AMERICA ON WHEELS
*(Everything you need for a successful road trip, including full-color
road maps and ratings for every hotel)*

California & Nevada

Florida

Mid-Atlantic

Midwest & the Great Lakes

New England & New York

Northwest & Great Plains

South Central & Texas

Southeast

Southwest

## FROMMER'S BY NIGHT GUIDES
*(The series for those who know that life begins after dark)*

Amsterdam

Chicago

Las Vegas

London

Los Angeles

Miami

New Orleans

New York

Paris

San Francisco

# WHEREVER YOU TRAVEL, *H*ELP IS NEVER FAR AWAY.

From planning your trip to providing travel assistance along the way, American Express® Travel Service Offices are always there to help.

---

## *Chicago*

---

American Express Travel Service
2338 N. Clark Street
Chicago
312/477-4000

American Express Travel Service
625 N. Michigan Avenue
Chicago
312/435-2570

American Express Travel Service
122 S. Michigan Avenue
Chicago
312/435-2595

**Travel**

http://www.americanexpress.com/travel

**American Express Travel Service Offices are located throughout Illinois.
For the office nearest you, call 1-800-AXP-3429.**